INTERNATIONAL LAW
AND THE PUBLIC

INTERNATIONAL LAW AND THE PUBLIC

How Ordinary People Shape
the Global Legal Order

Geoffrey P. R. Wallace

CORNELL UNIVERSITY PRESS   **ITHACA AND LONDON**

First published 2024 by Cornell University Press

Library of Congress Cataloging-in-Publication Data

Names: Wallace, Geoffrey P. R., 1978– author.
Title: International law and the public : how ordinary people shape the global legal order / Geoffrey P. R. Wallace.
Description: Ithaca : Cornell University Press, 2024. | Includes bibliographical references and index.
Identifiers: LCCN 2023052758 (print) | LCCN 2023052759 (ebook) | ISBN 9781501776526 (hardcover) | ISBN 9781501776533 (paperback) | ISBN 9781501776540 (ebook) | ISBN 9781501776557 (pdf)
Subjects: LCSH: International law—United States—Public opinion. | International law—United States—Psychological aspects. | International law—Social aspects—United States. | Effectiveness and validity of law.
Classification: LCC KZ1249 .W35 2024 (print) | LCC KZ1249 (ebook) | DDC 341.0973—dc23/eng/20231128
LC record available at https://lccn.loc.gov/2023052758
LC ebook record available at https://lccn.loc.gov/2023052759

For Fia

Contents

Figures

Tables

Acknowledgments

This book has been a long time in the making, taking a few admittedly unexpected turns along the way. All throughout I benefited from listening to a large number of voices—some closer to the main subject matter, others a great deal farther away—but all contributing to a final book very different from what I originally envisioned (and, I believe, for much the better). I am truly thankful for the tremendous support I received from many people, both professionally and personally, during the journey of completing this book.

The earliest kernels of the ideas and approach behind this book came about over a dinner many, many years ago with Walter Mebane at Maxie's in Ithaca, New York. Walter, a scholar of American politics, pointed out the notion that the public matters for international law may not be all that far-fetched, and that incorporating experiments could be a promising way to study the public, both of which proved central to the path I eventually took. Indeed, owing insights to friends and colleagues across a variety of fields of expertise became a defining theme in the evolution of this book. During the rest of my graduate studies at Cornell, I turned to other endeavors, but musings about the role of ordinary people in international politics remained in the not-too-distant background. My dissertation committee composed of Peter Katzenstein, Christopher Way, Matthew Evangelista, and Jonathan Kirshner encouraged theoretical and empirical rigor, but in particular an openness to new ways of thinking. Little did I know that the dissertation that became my first book would serve as inspiration for this present book as well. *Life and Death in Captivity* offered a general study into the treatment of prisoners of war, but what struck me most was the role played by publics in captor states in sometimes restraining, and other times enabling, abuse against captured enemy combatants that was contrary to prevailing international rules. What followed was my desire to investigate more generally the place of publics in the operation of the international legal order.

My efforts in the ensuing years to answer this question were aided by a wide range of colleagues at several institutions. During my time as an assistant professor at Rutgers University, I was fortunate to be part of a fantastic international relations (IR) group who helped me think about specific questions in a broader context. Paul Poast would always come up with friendly, yet insightful, questions and our collaboration on studying the public and foreign policy confirmed to me the importance of looking at ordinary actors in the international legal sphere. Jack Levy is a true force who anchored our IR discussions; his penchant for reading deeply and widely encouraged me to get outside of my comfort zone, and he proved particularly helpful for thinking about how to combine historical context with experimental methods in ways that informed my subsequent work. While at Rutgers, I benefited from the time and intellectual environment of a postdoctoral fellowship in the Niehaus Center for Globalization and Governance at Princeton University. I thank Helen Milner as the center's director for giving me the opportunity to engage with the Princeton community and for bringing together a fantastic cohort of Niehaus scholars. Sometimes what we most need is space to think, and it was during my time at the Niehaus Center that I became convinced of the need to write this manuscript, even if its exact shape was still to be determined. Co-organizing a workshop the following year with Bob Keohane and fellow cohort member Giovanni Mantilla on multidisciplinary approaches to the study of the laws of war reinforced the importance of bringing a similar approach to my own work.

My good fortune continued after moving as an associate professor to the University of Washington in Seattle. Jim Caporaso, Beth Kier, Karen Litfin, Jon Mercer, and Aseem Prakash offered a great setting for thinking about how common processes may operate across seemingly disparate areas of international politics. Several conversations about international reputation with Jon proved essential in keeping me on the right track (or at least not straying too far off). The public law group of Rachel Cichowski, Megan Ming Francis, George Lovell, Jamie Mayerfeld, and Michael McCann emphasized that the study of law takes place from a variety of perspectives, but that all too often those voices are not speaking or listening to each other. George was pivotal in introducing me to writings on popular constitutionalism, which formed the basis for my own thinking about the idea of popular international law at the center of this book. Chris Parker showed me that attention to public opinion and history are not incompatible, but rather that both are better served when informed by the other. I see this book as adding to the sort of conversations around law and politics that several of my UW colleagues have been tackling throughout their careers.

Outside colleagues also provided extremely helpful feedback at various stages of the project. My deep-felt thanks go to Yonatan Lupu for his support and teamwork on a separate National Science Foundation (NSF) grant and several coauthored articles that helped me better put into context the argument and findings in this book. I am grateful for a number of conversations and collaborations with Sarah Kreps on drones and international law, some of which with her gracious permission come directly into the pages that follow. I am indebted to Emily Hencken Ritter who read the entire manuscript, providing thoughtful comments on each and every chapter. I would like to further thank many others who took the time to offer their thoughts verbally or in writing: Burcu Bayram, Ryan Brutger, Sarah Bush, Kristine Eck, Tanisha Fazal, Christopher Gelpi, Emilie Hafner-Burton, Geoffrey Harris, Isabel Hull, Hyeran Jo, Jesse Johnson, Stephen Krasner, Ashley Leeds, Keir Lieber, Jay Lyall, Sara McLaughlin Mitchell, Andrew Moravcsik, James Morrow, Jens Ohlin, Krzysztof Pelc, Lauren Prather, Elizabeth Saunders, Ken Schultz, Shirley Scott, Beth Simmons, Lucie Spanihelova, and Michael Woldemariam. I also appreciate the feedback I received on various elements of the research, including comments from participants in seminars and workshops at Carleton University, Chicago, Cornell, Princeton, Rice, and Yale. Al Tillery was very encouraging both personally and professionally early in my career to view a book-length study as not only of value intellectually but also a process that could even be enjoyable, which together made me excited to try do it again with this book. My thanks go to Mahinder Kingra at Cornell University Press for his early interest and enthusiasm in the project, as well as Jim Lance for identifying an invaluable set of reviewers and shepherding the work to its final publication. My sincere gratitude to other members of the Cornell University Press team, including Alfredo Gutierrez Rios, Ellen Labbate, and Karen Laun, for their tireless work throughout the production process for this book.

The research behind this book would not have been possible without generous financial support. I was fortunate to receive a number of grants from the Time-sharing Experiments for the Social Sciences (TESS) initiative, which is funded through the NSF. TESS is a huge collective good providing opportunities to conduct the sort of high-quality nationally representative survey experiments that are simply beyond the means of many scholars. The TESS PIs first took a chance on me as a graduate student, and continued to see the promise of a young assistant professor (and later a less young associate professor). My experience with TESS is a prime example of the value of cumulative social science. Each survey I conducted raised a new set of questions, and the PIs were open to discovering how the answers would continue to unfold with this book as the end result. I am grateful to all of the TESS PIs with whom I had the pleasure to work: Jeremy Freese, Arthur Lupia, Diana Mutz, and Penny Visser. Jamie Druckman, in particular, provided essential advice and support on several of the studies, and was encouraging throughout on tying together various surveys and pieces of evidence to tell a larger story.

Portions of this book are derived from the following publications, though with significant changes and additions: "International Law and Public Attitudes toward Torture: An Experimental Study," *International Organization* 67 (1) (2013); "Martial Law? Military Experience, International Law, and Support for Torture," *International Studies Quarterly* 58 (3) (2014); and, with Sarah Kreps, "International Law, Military Effectiveness, and Public Support for Drone Strikes,"

Journal of Peace Research 53 (6) (2016). I thank the journals and publishers for permission to adapt some of the materials for the book.

To make it through the book writing process happily and healthily requires the closeness and understanding of family, friends, and colleagues. I thank my parents, Paul and Gisèle Wallace, for their love and support. I am especially grateful to my great aunt Bern, who lived through many of the events described in this book—from the First World War through the War on Terror. It has been a while since she left us, but she instilled in me an innate curiosity and what we liked to call an ambitious humility, and for that I will always be bound to her. Friends from home in Toronto helped me find much needed levity. The pandemic and travel restrictions meant that some of the main writing of this book coincided with the longest period I had ever been away from Canada. Being finally able to go back brought immense joy and gratitude, which helped me push through to complete the final parts of the book.

And finally, I thank the three loves of my life: Sophia, Liam, and Dahlia. Liam and Dahlia grew up alongside this book, and somewhat (un)fortunately have gotten to know a lot about international law from a young age. They showed me the importance of looking for balance, and the merits of bringing some flexibility to rules at home and in life. And more than anyone, I am grateful to my wife and partner Sophia. You offered never-ending support, and always believed in this project during uncertain times. You read and talked through every single element, and without you these chapters would not have come together. This book is for you.

INTERNATIONAL LAW
AND THE PUBLIC

> **We the People of the United States, in Order to form a more perfect Union, establish Justice . . . do ordain and establish this Constitution for the United States of America.**
>
> —Preamble to the US Constitution (1789)

> **We the Peoples of the United Nations determined . . . to establish conditions under which justice and respect for the obligations arising from treaties and other sources of international law can be maintained . . . do hereby establish an international organization to be known as the United Nations.**
>
> —Preamble to the Charter of the United Nations (1945)

The opening passages to these two founding documents are remarkably similar in both content and form. The first is among the oldest continually operating national constitutions, laying down the fundamental legal principles governing US society, and serving as a template for many others.[1] The second probably represents the closest instrument that exists to a global quasi-constitution, outlining basic legal principles governing the collective international society.[2]

Yet looks can be deceiving, as the two could not seem more different in their reception and impact. Lauded as the "American crown jewels,"[3] the US Constitution is held up as the "supreme Law of the Land," to which almost all decisions public and private in the United States are subject. By contrast, the United Nations (UN) suffers a more checkered history with international laws at its charter's core often derided as far from supreme over any land. Variously described as a "masque" obscuring the real workings of power politics, international "legal restraint is illusory," or dismissed more poetically as a "fairy ship upon a fairy sea: a beautiful construct of the legal imagination floating upon a sea of false assumptions."[4] This imaginative language is apt since many critics doubt whether international law should even be considered law properly speaking, or mentioned in the same breath as "real law" like national constitutions operating within countries.[5]

But we should not be so quick to presume that international laws are entirely different from their constitutional siblings. The two bodies of law actually share a number of similarities. Each borrows from the other extensively. Many basic rights first espoused in national constitutions have found their way into international legal agreements, while international laws are frequently incorporated into constitutions.[6] Perhaps most importantly, neither possesses an overarching sovereign to enforce the rules. Just as there is no higher authority above states to ensure compliance with international laws, no higher power occupies a place above the US president, or other national leaders, to keep them in line with constitutional laws. This legal kinship is starkest in the high-stakes matter of the resort to military force. Treaties like the 1928 Kellogg-Briand Pact prohibiting war seemingly did little to prevent a Second World War just over a decade later. By the same token, the US Constitution on its own could not halt secession and the outbreak of the American Civil War, which remains the deadliest conflict in the country's history. Turning to more normal times, it is often taken for granted that rulings by high courts like the US Supreme Court or Germany's Federal Constitutional Court are final, but in structural terms these courts more closely resemble international judicial bodies like the International Court of Justice (ICJ) or International Criminal Court (ICC) criticized so much as weak and ineffectual.[7] Rather than entirely different legal species, similar questions can be asked about how each body of law operates, with important stakes for both.[8]

Belying its "supreme" position, in recent years the force of constitutional law has increasingly been called into question as well. Accelerating trends present in many respects since the founding of the US republic, a range of voices inside and outside of government have questioned whether constitutional law can, or should, in any way constrain government executives.[9] Whether it concerns the use of force abroad, the treatment of enemy combatants, or surveillance on one's own citizens, over the past few decades the US Constitution has seemingly done little to restrain what presidents could, or should, do. Similar criticisms and questions have plagued high courts in many other countries as well.[10]

Somewhat fittingly, the basic argument propounding the irrelevance of constitutional law almost exactly mirrors the rationale behind claims regarding the insignificance of international law—some of the same thinkers have even staked both positions.[11] International law appears unable to bind states who are instead guided by their external power and interests. Likewise, constitutional law seems unable to bind leaders who are similarly guided by their internal power and interests. Far from all-powerful national laws and powerless international legal rules, the more sobering conclusion appears to be one where law writ large plays little meaningful role.

Against this view, the opening preambles above point to a different source for the more effective operation of legal orders—"the People(s)." Not "the People" in some fanciful abstract communal will to be marshalled and given voice by sage and prudent leaders. Rather, "the people" as actual members of a community possessing their own beliefs and understandings, and who can play an active role in the operation of legal principles. The intricacies of laws both domestic and international are often thought to be beyond the concern or comprehension of ordinary folks. Yet at a time where the attachment of many leaders and government officials to legal rules appears increasingly tenuous, it seems essential to examine what role the ordinary public has played and can continue to play, especially when it comes to the rules of the international community.

What We Know about (International) Law

According to much of the existing literature, the short answer to the question of what is the role of the public in the operation of international law is, simply put, not much at all. The public is a largely forgotten actor when it comes to matters like international treaties, customary laws, or softer types of rules. This trend is perhaps most evident by how little space is devoted to discussing the mass public and their beliefs. Prominent studies might differ dramatically on the role of international law and whether it matters. Irrespective of a more favorable or skeptical orientation, a common pattern is one where the public and their sentiments on these questions are hardly mentioned, if at all, compared to the usual players of states, governments, and their official agents.[12]

The lack of attention to the public is not wholly surprising, since standard definitions of international law focus in quite literal terms on its inter*national* character, where the key (in some ways sole) actors are states. As the international legal scholar Hans Kelsen remarked, "international law obligates and authorizes states and *only states*" (emphasis added).[13] Scholars may disagree over whether and how international law binds, but share the belief that legal rules largely begin and end with states. Also sometimes referred to as "public international law," these rules govern the relations between "public" actors like states, and sometimes the international organizations they create, rather than to mass publics themselves. To the extent that ordinary people enter the conversation, it is as *objects* of international law, such as protections guaranteed (in theory) to individuals through human rights agreements. But such rights are granted and enforced (or not) by states, with their citizens seen as passive bystanders. According to conventional accounts, there is thus not much place for the actual public as *subjects* who are able to contribute as genuine agents to the operation of public international law.

Much of the debate is correspondingly situated at the level of understanding how international legal commitments affect interactions among states. The enforcement of international law in the absence of a higher sovereign authority is commonly described, and explicitly modeled, as a game taking place among state actors.[14] For instance, there may be greater or lesser reputational costs for a state failing to uphold its commitments, which could affect prospects for future cooperative opportunities with other states. Likewise, violators may face retaliation by the international community of states.

Russia's breaches of international laws of noninterference and territorial integrity when it annexed the Crimean Peninsula from Ukraine in 2014, as well as supporting separatists in the eastern Donbass region, were met with condemnation and concerted economic sanctions by many other countries. Yet these consequences seemed for many too light compared to the value to Russia of the territory obtained and the example set; in many other instances violators face few, if any, repercussions. Several years later, Russia followed up these more limited forays with a full-scale invasion beginning in 2022, seeking to conquer its neighbor, which included widespread reports of war crimes by Russian forces. This time the response by the United States, many European countries, and other members of the international community was far more assertive, providing military and economic aid that helped Ukraine push back and prevent its complete takeover.[15] These episodes illustrate how the relative effectiveness of the enforcement function of international law—whether legalizing a commitment sufficiently raises the costs of subsequent nonadherence—remains highly contested. Less disputed is *who* are the relevant actors involved, which almost invariably comes back to states and elites, sometimes including those from intergovernmental organizations.

Although there can be a tendency to fixate on enforcement, "Law, however, can and does perform many functions other than constraint."[16] This multitude of functions can include serving as a legitimation device, a process for reaching decisions, or as a particular form of language and communication, among others.[17] Another key function I focus on in this book is whether international law can shape underlying policy preferences and the desire to *want* to follow a particular course of action rather than simply out of cost-benefit calculations. As with enforcement, many accounts of preference formation and change emphasize interactions between states, perhaps allowing a role for international bureaucracies or nongovernmental organizations in influencing state interests.[18] While the particular function may differ, what is shared is an emphasis on these more "horizontal," or external, state-to-state mechanisms.

A great deal has been learned from these approaches for how international law can facilitate, even under significant limits, cooperative relations between states in the absence of higher authority. Another strand has sought to go *within* states to unpack how other actors and processes may affect the operation of international legal commitments. A "domestic turn," or a more a "Liberal" approach, to the study of international law shifts attention to the subnational for answering puzzles that have eluded more traditional state-centric approaches.[19] The shift is most evident for human rights agreements where traditional interstate compliance mechanisms appear fairly weak, but emphases on domestic processes extends to other issue areas as well.[20] As promising as these domestic approaches may be, much of the work in this vein makes several analytical choices that limit its scope for our purposes. First, internal and external mechanisms are frequently conceptualized as wholly distinct from one another, even though important domestic forces may be at play in the horizontal operation of international law. Second, a variety of domestic actors can be imagined to influence international law, but in practice these personalities are almost invariably drawn from more elite echelons of society. Leaders, legislators, judges, lawyers, and other sorts of experts are considered the appropriate domestic subjects outside of states themselves. By contrast, ordinary members of the public are usually presumed to have neither the capabilities nor competencies to grapple with questions of international law.

Skepticism toward the public is a staple of a long line of work on both foreign and domestic policymaking.[21] This parallels similar debates over who are the relevant actors in domestic legal and political systems. There may be disagreements over which actors are most important for the proper operation of constitutional law—executive, legislative, judicial, or some combination—but more often than not hopes reside with elites rather than the masses.[22] Just as international law was described earlier in fantastical terms by skeptics, the domestic "folk theory" celebrating "the wisdom of popular judgments by informed and engaged citizens" is similarly rejected as "amount[ing] to fairy tales."[23]

And yet, drawing on both theory and the historical record, a growing number of legal scholars have begun to question the supposed primacy of elite over ordinary actors on questions of constitutional law. Commonly grouped together under the handle of *popular constitutionalism*, the vision is one where "the people themselves" can play a significant and active role in fulfilling the main functions of national constitutions.[24] Through their thoughts, actions, and reactions, ordinary people help ensure constitutional principles are enforced, and it is with ordinary people where the beliefs and preferences enshrined in the Constitution ultimately reside and are given meaning. While popular constitutionalist theories have been most developed in the US context, accounts emphasizing a more active role for the public in domestic legal orders are evident in regions ranging from Europe to Latin America.[25] The people are not the only actors involved in the highest of domestic legal questions, but they are important ones. The public is better conceived as occupying a central place engaging in "constitutional dialogues" with state actors and other elites.[26]

The question is whether a similar series of "international constitutional dialogues" can exist between ordinary individuals and state and elite actors in the operation of international legal commitments. Some of the greatest advances to our understanding of international law have come from incorporating knowledge from other fields. As one review of the literature remarks, "Theorists of law compliance have been borrowing from one another's conceptual toolkits for years."[27] Much of this refinement has come from integrating the study of international law with theories from international relations.[28] The question posed here is what may be gained when we expand our toolkit still farther to investigate how research from constitutional legal theory might help us better comprehend the operation of international law as well.[29]

Argument of the Book

Throughout this book, I seek to take core insights from popular constitutionalism, combined with implications drawn from existing work on international relations and international law, to develop a theoretical framework of *popular international law*—where ordinary people can play an important role in the operation of core functions of international legal commitments.

I take a similar starting point to many other approaches to international law. The absence of a higher sovereign authority remains one of the defining (though not unique) characteristics of the international legal system. The ramifications for how international law operates in such an environment, however, are not necessarily so clear cut. As noted in the prior section, some approaches look at relations horizontally between states to see how they use international law to manage their interactions under anarchy, constraining one another's behavior or trying to influence each other's interests. Others instead look inside states to domestic processes emanating vertically from below to examine how functions like the enforcement of international agreements take place, or how preferences are formed.

There can certainly be some analytical value is emphasizing more external versus more internal processes of international law at one time or another. Yet the strict partitioning of horizontal from domestic mechanisms can obscure important areas of interplay. The beliefs, preferences, and actions of domestic actors do not stop neatly at the boundaries of their respective countries. Likewise, interactions among states in the context of international law play out in their own internal politics with domestic actors active in the background.

Rather than wholly separate, my contention is that there are important *domestic* sources that influence the more traditional *horizontal* mechanisms serving some of the main functions of international law. A country's reputation may form and change in response to noncompliance with prior legal commitments, but the beliefs underlying this reputational capital may have roots among foreign publics, not just their leaders. Preferences are not given and similarly do not exist in an interstate vacuum, but instead can be informed in part by domestic actors' understandings of, and responses to, international legal commitments.

Centering domestic actors shares much in common with Liberal second image–type theorizing concerning who are the most relevant agents in international law.[30] But the framework developed here is not a purely bottom-up account residing mostly inside domestic societies. External forces, particularly international legal ones, play an important independent role in shaping those domestic actors' preferences, beliefs, and actions. International laws differ from other sorts of rules in that they are embedded within a broader system of norms and expectations.[31] One of the most foundational is the principle of pacta sunt servanda, that "promises must be kept," bestowing an obligatory character on international laws that yields a number of implications. International law can be informative to domestic actors about prevailing commitments and the consequences involved. In particular, international laws can generate a form of *principled information* that creates news types of understandings for those domestic actors, changing their preferences, beliefs, and actions. However, this is also not simply a top-down second image reversed–type process of external factors having a singular unidirectional effect on domestic actors.[32] Changes to the preferences, beliefs, and actions taken by domestic actors can, in turn, scale back up to influence the operation of the international legal order.[33] Lack of public support for future cooperation with violators can facilitate the reputational sanctions that are one of the main theorized avenues for the enforcement of international law. Likewise, policy preferences espoused in certain international agreements can be reinforced through changes in attitudes at the domestic level. As a middle ground, I propose a *horizontally informed Liberal* account of international law, which links international law down to domestic politics, with those domestic actors in turn playing a role in shaping how these same laws operate in the international realm.[34]

What makes this approach to international law "popular" (and not to be confused with more reactionary "populist" impulses)[35] is that the mass public is seen as playing an important role in the interplay between international legal commitments and domestic politics. The public has long been maligned in foreign policymaking in general, and international law in particular. I instead contend that the public has both the cognitive and material capacity to play a constructive role in international law—even if this ability is neither absolute in general, nor necessarily at all times or across all places. Publics have a series of direct and indirect tools at their disposal for influencing the policies and preferences of their own governments and others across a range of circumstances. Far from common depictions as moody or incoherent, members of the public may even possess certain advantages over elites in their collective abilities to process and act upon complicated matters, including international law.

To further bolster the case for popular international law, my argument draws on theories of constitutional law through a four-point series of propositions. First as noted previously, the structure of international and constitutional law is remarkably similar. The absence of a higher authority means that the main functions of the two legal orders bear a close resemblance, with both depending to a large extent on how law shapes expectations, reputational calculations, and underlying preferences.[36] Second, the content of international treaties and constitutions are not disconnected, but overlap and inform each other in significant ways. Third, popular constitutionalism contends that the public plays an important role in shaping the functions of constitutional laws. The fourth and final point follows from the first three propositions—if the structure and content of international and constitutional law are similar, and the public can play an important role in constitutional order, then under popular international law the public correspondingly has the potential to play an important role in the international legal order as well. The approach put forward in this book offers an alternative interpretation of inter*national* law—not just as law between states and their leaders alongside other elites, but also among their larger national populations. Long seen as one of the main precursors to the modern international legal system, the ancient Roman notion of jus gentium ("law of peoples") is evocative in this regard, pointing to a purpose and role for the people in the exercising of law not only at home but also abroad.[37]

Why the Public, and Why It Matters

Although popular international law sees an important place for the public in international legal commitments, it is important to note some key qualifications and limits to my argument. First, I am not claiming that the public is the sole actor that matters in international law. That the public has frequently been overlooked is not the same as insisting they are now the only actor we should be looking at. Leaders and other elites continue to be a potent presence, especially on international legal issues. The state in particular remains central to the operation of the international legal order, not least because for the most part it is only states who can join and ratify international treaties, though even this is changing with the spread of softer forms of commitments that incorporate a multitude of other legal personalities.[38] The ways in which publics can be felt on international law is often not directly, but rather mediated through state institutions and channels. The public does not act alone, but operates in concert (and sometimes conflict) with other actors on questions of international law.

A parallel caveat is apparent on the relative place under popular constitutionalism of the public vis-à-vis other actors in domestic legal systems. Rather than asserting the predominance of the people, popular constitutionalism is in many ways rooted in an antisupremacy ethos rejecting the view that any actor (whether the Supreme Court, the president, or the masses) should be able to exert complete authority over constitutional questions.[39] The state also figures prominently in popular constitutionalist accounts, as domestic political institutions are the primary conduits through which ordinary people are able to exert constitutional influence.[40] Shifting back to external commitments, the point is that the public is a relevant (even if not the most powerful) actor, and should be part of the conversation over how international law operates. When one side has been largely discounted, however, it is incumbent on us to listen more carefully to their voices, which is why throughout the book I focus for the most part on examining the public's understanding of international law.

Second, just as the public is not the only relevant actor, international law is not the only factor that matters to them. Most foreign policy issues involve some legal implications, but touch upon a range of dimensions. Territorial disputes may engage rules over the sanctity of borders or the nonuse of force, yet can also have important military dynamics or rouse nationalist passions. The interrogation of enemy combatants falls under the laws of war and human rights law, but these rules exist in the context of threats to national security and where desires for revenge may be hard to resist. Other pressures may buttress, but at times undermine, the influence of international legal appeals. Some of the strongest critics acknowledge that international law can play a role in some circumstances, just not those areas where incentives for violations are at their greatest.[41] This is one of the reasons why in much of the empirics for the book, I examine harder cases with strong counteracting influences against the operation of international law. Yet it is important to keep in mind that legal obligation and self-interest are not mutually exclusive.[42] Laws can inform and shape actors' conceptions of their preferences and evaluations of their situations, one of the main functions of international law examined in later chapters.

Third, international law may not matter in the same way to all members of the public, or even to the public as a whole at all times in all circumstances in all countries. While "the people" is often used as a shorthand to conjure up an undifferentiated monolith, in reality the public is composed of various groups who may have very different understandings of, and reactions to, international legal commitments. Public support for international law, and active participation in conversations around international legal commitments, is neither automatic nor inevitable. Beyond differences in legal predispositions, the actual ability of national publics to influence their governments' foreign commitments can depend on the particular configuration of domestic institutional structures.[43]

In equal measure, a sense of worry pervades the relationship between the public and constitutional law under popular constitutionalism. Part of US popular constitutionalists' original motivation was lamenting that in recent decades US citizens had seemingly surrendered their role on constitutional matters to the Supreme Court and other elites.[44] A similar pattern can be seen with international law, where the US and many other national publics have sometimes deferred to elites, or not fully engaged in certain legal debates, with the War on Terror being perhaps the most prominent example.

Despite these qualifications, one of the aims of popular international law is to highlight how different groups within and across national societies may think and act in ways that offer some succor (however modest) to the operation of international laws in ways that would be more difficult in their absence. Several pieces of empirical evidence presented in this book indicate that international law can have a marked impact on not only some of the hardest issues, but also among segments of the population who at first sight would presumably be the most resistant to legal appeals. International law may not be able to do everything for everyone or everywhere, but it can have discernable effects that alter the terms of debate for all sides around controversial policy issues.

In his study of the role of contending groups (the public included) in politics, E. E. Schattschneider began by declaring that "The first proposition is that the outcome of every conflict is determined by the *extent* to which the audience becomes involved in it" (emphasis in original).[45] For Schattschneider, the public could be more (or less) active and influential on questions of domestic law and politics. Scaling up to the international level, the public can likewise be more (or less) active and influential on questions of international law and politics. Greater attention to the public and international law presents an opportunity to make several broader contributions. In particular, it offers a chance to provide microfoundations for important puzzles in international relations.[46] For instance, a large literature finds that democratic governments are more likely to keep their promises across a range of issues.[47] Various arguments have been put forward to explain general patterns in democratic commitments, from domestic institutions to political culture. Examining individual opinions can offer evidence for mass publics contributing to the operation of international legal commitments. We should still be mindful of the limits of public-centered accounts both within and across different regime types. Even among democracies, there may be important differences in domestic structures that shape the responsiveness of leaders to their constituents.[48] And although publics in nondemocracies can sometimes play an important role,[49] extending popular international law to autocratic regimes is speculative and more challenging still. Nonetheless, investigating public attitudes on their own terms presents useful avenues for delineating the contours in the operation of international law across different national and institutional contexts.

Taking the public more seriously as an actor in its own right also contributes to calls for a "micro-politics" reflecting a "refocused attention on the non-elites (the "little people") as the central object of inquiry."[50] A shift toward more ordinary people has taken hold in other fields, such as the movement toward a "history from below,"[51] or what some German historians have called *Alltagsgeschichte* ("everyday history").[52] Rather than focusing on leaders and other esteemed persons, this more grassroots approach takes "the writing of history from the perspective of non-elite groups."[53] A similar dynamic of "law from below" is evident with popular constitutionalism, but also in other work that seeks to understand the consequences of domestic legal rules and policies more from the perspective of ordinary people.[54] Popular international law, in turn, points to the potential for an "international law from below," where ordinary people are considered relevant actors in the operation of international commitments—with flaws and limits to be sure, but with particular strengths and promise as well.

Why the United States?

A few additional comments are in order regarding the scope and approach of this book—what it does, and does not, purport to accomplish. I primarily consider and evaluate the role of the public in the context of the United States, although references and implications are made to other countries throughout. The United States offers an interesting and appropriate case for thinking about the operation of international law for a number of reasons. First, across several different dimensions the United States presents a tough test for any claims regarding the effectiveness of international law in general, and among the public in particular. From the Donald Trump administration's "America First" stance explicitly rejecting a host of international agreements, to the disregard for many international rules in the earlier presidency of George W. Bush, it is perhaps an understatement to say that "International law is under attack in the United States."[55] Going by various names at different times—neoconservatives, new sovereigntists, populists, among others—these attacks were neither accidental nor incidental. Rather, for significant stretches of US foreign policymaking, "Disdain for global rules underpins the whole enterprise."[56]

What might describe the present or recent past could apply with equal or even greater force to earlier periods. Throughout its history, the United States has had a fraught relationship with international law—at times welcoming, but frequently keeping international obligations at arm's length.[57] Defined by long streaks of isolationism, the country often sought to "shield itself from the world" not only politically but legally as well.[58] This insular penchant extends beyond the White House to other branches of government. In some of the most notable instances where presidents sought to promote new ideals or bring their country in line with existing rules—from Woodrow Wilson and the establishment of the League of Nations, to Barack Obama and the promise to close the detention facility in Guantanamo Bay—they were often frustrated by a Congress that did not want to take on new commitments or uphold existing obligations.

Efforts against international law have also seemingly found a welcome audience among the wider American public. Support for international institutions like the UN has consistently been lower among US citizens compared to many other advanced industrialized countries.[59] The US public has shown itself to be comfortable with realpolitik thinking where matters of power generally trump the law—even support for multilateralism may reflect more pragmatic reasons instead of any sense of legitimacy or moral duty.[60] When facing security threats, the US citizenry has seemingly shown little hesitation at times in endorsing policies of dubious legality, whether abuse against suspected terrorists up to and including the use of nuclear weapons.[61] The retired Air Force judge advocate and major general Charles Dunlap, Jr., described the US public as largely unconcerned with the "niceties of international law," going so far as to remark that "Unlike international law devotees, many Americans are exasperated with the law."[62] Robert Kagan's diagnosis of the sources for the transatlantic divide between European countries and the United States in the post-9/11 era remains prescient to this day:

> Europe is turning away from power, or to put it a little differently, it is moving beyond power into a self-contained world of laws and rules and transnational negotiation and cooperation. It is entering a post-historical paradise of peace and relative prosperity, the realization of Kant's "Perpetual Peace." The United States, meanwhile, remains mired in history, exercising power in the anarchic Hobbesian world where international laws and rules are unreliable.[63]

The United States thus represents a harsher climate for cultivating international law, suggesting that if international legal appeals can survive there then the prospects may be even brighter in other countries and circumstances.

Although US mass preferences toward international law may seem strained, the country is conventionally described as one of the more open societies politically speaking, where numerous channels exist for members of the public to have their voices heard.[64] Some groups may admittedly be more politically active with voices ringing more loudly than others,[65] but it is fair to wonder whether a study of the US public with its greater structural influences should necessarily hold many lessons for citizenries in other countries. The US political system may be fairly responsive to public preferences, but a range of studies have shown comparable levels of responsiveness in democracies possessing a wide range of institutional configurations (with the United States far from an outlier positively or negatively).[66] Even a notable study of foreign policy emphasizing domestic structural differences between the United States and several other liberal democracies concluded that "mass public opinion mattered in each of the . . . countries, albeit to very different degrees."[67] As such, findings from the United States can offer a useful window into other countries, even if we still need to be mindful of different national contexts. On the other hand, and as noted earlier in thinking about the role of the public in general, making any generalizations from the US case to publics and international law in nondemocracies should be seen as more tentative and preliminary at best.

Second, despite a tradition of skepticism toward international commitments, the United States has also at times embraced and played an influential role in promoting international rules. This dual tension is evident even in what are portrayed as classical statements of the country's wariness of global rules, such as George Washington's oft-quoted warning in his farewell address—"to steer clear of permanent alliances with any portion of the foreign world." Yet almost immediately afterward, the outgoing first president dismissed any notion "of patronizing infidelity to existing engagements," insisting that "honesty is always the best policy," and that any "engagements be observed in their genuine sense."[68]

Counterbalancing any mistrust has been an acute sensitivity to matters of international law since the founding of the republic.[69] After all, the joining of the original thirteen colonies resembled more an international organization than a fully fledged state with the Articles of Confederation taking on certain characteristics of a treaty.[70] Looking outward, the United States has played a crucial part in the development of the current international legal system. The Lieber Code written for Union armies during the American Civil War served as a template for many of the modern laws of war, while a century later the United States was one of the key architects of the UN system and the complex web of international agreements governing much of world affairs in the post-WWII era.[71] Competing with isolationist impulses has been a brand of liberal internationalism with its outward orientation and commitment to the rule of law, which has endured among large segments of US elites and the wider public.[72] Questions remain over how strong such commitments were in the past, or their durability going forward. But given the outsized role—both constructive and destructive—played by the United States, examining US understandings of international law is crucial for comprehending the current character and future prospects of the international legal order.

Third, the United States is a fitting place to examine the overall argument of this book, where the public is viewed as a relevant actor in the operation of international legal rules. The country has a rich and varied legal tradition. Thomas Paine once proclaimed that "in America the law is king,"[73] while during the early days of the republic Alexis de Tocqueville observed the ever-present "influence of legal habits" on almost every question.[74] The central presence of the Constitution in political life—as a competitor but also companion to international obligations—offers a valuable opportunity to assess the potential influence of a corresponding set of "external" legal habits. Moreover, the notion of popular constitutionalism that serves an important basis for the theoretical framework of this book is not unique to the United States, but has been most fully developed and articulated within the US legal system. It thus seems appropriate to at least start by evaluating the extension of popular international law that will be articulated throughout this book in this same national context. Taken together, the United States represents a difficult, substantively important, and theoretically relevant case for examining the operation of international law in general, and the role of the public in particular.

Why Experiments? Why Not *Just* Experiments?

Turning to the methodological approach adopted in this book, several of the empirical chapters rely primarily on experimental designs.[75] One of the most formidable obstacles to the empirical study of international law arises from the reality that countries are mostly free to decide for themselves whether or not to join an international agreement. The instrument in question may not be their ideal pick, but countries nonetheless usually weigh the relative costs and benefits of committing versus opting out in light of their particular circumstances. A sizable subliterature has emerged offering myriad explanations for why states make the choice to commit to some international agreements, while delaying, modifying, or refusing to join others. Voluntary consent of the parties rests at the core of domestic contract theory and international law alike. The underlying international legal principle of pacta sunt servanda is predicated upon the supposition that states have the independent ability to agree in the first place to make the commitments, which subsequently (and supposedly) bind them.

The presumption that actors take seriously their obligations makes a lot of sense intuitively. Indeed, it would be more than a little concerning if countries were haphazardly joining some agreements while arbitrarily rejecting others. But the fact that governments do not flip a coin, or throw darts at a board, when deciding whether to commit to a given agreement poses serious inferential hurdles for answering even basic questions about the operation of international law. For it becomes a daunting exercise to disentangle whether any changes in outcomes or behavior are due to the international agreement itself, or rather preexisting differences between the states who joined versus those who did not. Even apparently strong findings in favor of international law remain vulnerable to charges that patterns observed simply reflect what actors would have done anyway in the absence of any agreement.[76]

Dynamics of strategic selection in commitment to international legal agreements make it difficult for finding comparable groups who are similar to each other *except for* the presence of an international law. In other words, we are faced with the problem of identifying the relevant counterfactual, which by definition cannot be directly observed since only one state of the world exists— we cannot see a country *simultaneously* inside and outside of a given international agreement, or a system with or without that treaty.[77] Empirical studies of international law using observational data seek to approximate the appropriate counterfactual through a variety of methods, but these techniques often require strong statistical assumptions, yielding inconsistent and sometimes contradictory findings.[78]

For these reasons, there have been increasing calls for the use of experimental methods to investigate international law.[79] In line with international relations more generally,[80] and domestic legal studies,[81] a small but growing body of experimental work has taken on questions about the causes and consequences of international legal commitments.[82] One of the biggest strengths of experimental approaches is that they help to address problems of strategic selection that can be especially confounding in observational studies of international law, even when compared to other international phenomena. Randomization ensures in expectation that treatment and control groups are as similar to each other on average across all baseline factors.[83] The result is that researchers are in a position to be able to make more reliable causal claims. Random assignment means that we can conclude with greater confidence that any differences observed between experimental conditions are actually due to the treatments themselves, and not unrelated or competing factors.

Implementing experimental designs is easier said than done depending on the research question of interest. In the realm of international law, it would be neither advisable nor feasible for researchers to randomly assign certain countries to joining, or keeping out of, particular treaties. A common problem for experimental studies in international relations more generally is frequently a mismatch between the unit of analysis at which theories operate—often at the national or systemic levels—and the level where experimental manipulations are executed, which normally involve individuals or small groups.[84] Fortunately, this is less of a concern for our purposes, since individual members of the public represent the appropriate units of analysis for the implications of the theoretical framework put forward. While we cannot change whether someone lives in a country that is part of a particular international agreement, we can control different elements of the international legal environment presented to them to see if they react in ways that comport with the expectations of popular international law. For this book, I designed a series of original survey experiments that involve different sorts of treatments and scenarios—sometimes involving the presence or absence of international laws, other times varying an agreement's design—to better understand how ordinary people think about legal commitments and how they can contribute to the operation of international law.

Although experimental approaches are useful for examining questions like the public and international law, they are far from a panacea and have their own limits.[85] Often of foremost concern are questions of external validity, or how generalizable the finding from experiments are to real-world outcomes of interest.[86] Unlike the complex ever-moving dynamics of actual international laws and politics, experiments by design focus on a few key attributes often in fairly artificial situations. The randomization afforded through experiments can increase confidence that the treatment effect captured in the study exists, but could still leave us uncertain as to whether participants would think or behave in similar ways when confronting these events in their regular lives as members of the wider public. On the flipside, research subjects do not exist in isolation—outside events and beliefs have a habit of intervening (or contaminating) supposedly clean and controlled experimental settings.[87]

Worries over external validity are especially pronounced when it comes to international law since there so often seems to be a formidable gap between what is written down in treaties or debated among international lawyers, and what is observed in practice. The puncturing of the promise and ideals of international law by reality was perhaps expressed most frankly by the former US secretary of state Dean Acheson when he said "Principles, certainly legal principles, do not decide concrete cases."[88]

To help address some of these concerns, I supplement and augment the experimental data with a variety of more tangible pieces of evidence. Some of the experiments themselves differ in the amount of realism injected—in certain cases modeled directly off real-world policy debates—to see how people respond to legal appeals in different sorts of situations. A host of other types of data is further leveraged both to make better sense of the experimental results, as well as to see how these findings stand in practice. This includes historical case studies of how publics have reacted in real life to actual violations of international law. Content analysis from media coverage of controversial policies is also employed to better understand the ways in which individual expectations come to be and may shape any subsequent changes. And data from more standard surveys help us better comprehend how people's substantive knowledge of international law can affect their policy views outside of the laboratory. Ultimately, the overall empirical strategy adopted here heeds the warnings espoused even by many experimentalists that "an exclusively experimental political science is neither realistic nor desirable."[89] This book instead seeks to continue in the vein of mixed-methods work that combines experimental and nonexperimental evidence to develop a deeper understanding of important questions, in this instance the role of the public in the operation of international law.[90]

All this being said, most (though not all) of the evidence presented comes from public opinion, focusing on the beliefs and attitudes of ordinary people toward the international legal commitments of their own country and others. Precisely because of the inferential hurdles in the study of international law, caution must be taken in drawing conclusions that public attitudes in a given setting necessarily have a direct and determinative bearing on a government's behavior, national policies, or international outcomes. Nonetheless, uncovering the attitudinal effects of international law is important in its own right. Given that governments, especially democratic ones, are generally responsive (albeit imperfectly) to the wants and needs of their citizens, public opinion remains an essential building block for theories of domestic and international governance. Indeed, one of the most preeminent theorists of democracy goes so far as to say that a genuine "democratic idea" involves "the legitimacy—indeed the necessity—for representation."[91] The "chain of responsiveness" from citizens' interests to eventual policies may be a long one with many pitfalls along the way.[92] As such, delving more deeply into that first step of ordinary people's beliefs and attitudes still promises to tell us a lot about the operation of international law, providing a firmer basis for addressing those questions that will undoubtedly remain.

Plan of the Book

The rest of the book is organized around investigating different facets of the argument put forward regarding the relationship between the public and international law. Chapter 1 begins by presenting a conceptual overview of what international laws are, and some of the main functions they seek to fulfill. I propose a working definition of international law as *legalized rules that seek to regulate the behavior of internationalized actors who are conferred certain rights and responsibilities.* The definition is purposefully broad to encompass international rules beyond formal treaties, but more importantly to incorporate a variety of actors outside of the usual focus on states. After addressing the frequent charge among many critics that international law should not count as law proper, the remainder of the chapter turns to evaluating contending views on two key functions of international law—enforcement against violators on the one hand, and the shaping of policy preferences on the other. Although chapter 1 provides important foundations for the remainder of the book, readers already familiar with international legal scholarship could safely choose to skim or skip these pages.

In chapter 2, I develop a theoretical argument to explain *how* international law operates to fulfill these core functions. In putting forward the notion of popular international law, I contend that national publics are an overlooked but important actor for the ways in which the operation of international law plays out. Although far from acting alone, ordinary people have the collective capacity and potential to reinforce key functions of international law that are most commonly thought to solely take place at the level of states or among elites.

The remaining chapters turn to assessing some of the observable implications of popular international law. They are divided into separate pairs to offer different pieces of empirical evidence for the role of the public in the functions of enforcement and preference change respectively. Chapter 3 centers on reputation as one of the most widely touted, but also contested, mechanisms for the enforcement of international law. Using a series of survey experiments, I show how the legalization of commitments heightens reputational stakes and changes in significant ways the willingness of the US public to support future cooperation with foreign violators, which can serve as a significant constraint on the latter's current actions. The survey evidence further shows that these effects are bound up in the public's understanding of the normative underpinnings of international legal commitments, and how such agreements influence their perceptions of other countries and the costs they are willing to support imposing. Chapter 4 shifts course through an in-depth case study of the role of reputation in foreign publics' beliefs and actions toward the United States during the War on Terror. Contrary to common depictions of the War on Terror as indicative of the weakness of international law, I argue that existing legal commitments played an important part in international reactions to US counterterrorism policies, which could be seen especially in various reputational sanctions felt by the country. In a case where the US public itself served as less of a constraint on its government's own conduct, other national publics more than picked up the slack to exert meaningful enforcement costs against the United States. Combining historical records, traditional polling, and quantitative observational evidence, the chapter illustrates how various national publics served as an important conduit for the exercise of reputational repercussions in response to US violations of international law.

The next two chapters then examine a second function of international law of changing underlying policy preferences. Chapter 5 takes on the hard case of torture where the ideals of international law may be expected to be of little import for populations facing severe threats to national security. The experimental evidence shows that international law can shape individuals' attitudes, even under trying circumstances, and especially for those who may be most skeptical of legal appeals. Chapter 6 stays on the rougher terrain of national security to investigate how international law may influence policy preferences in more practical terms. The chapter begins with a pair of survey experiments conducted in the midst of a vibrant debate in the United States at the time over the use of drones in counterterrorism operations. Supplementing the experimental data with other polling and media coverage, I trace how the reality faced by the US public affected their understanding of international law and attitudes toward drone strikes. The remainder of the chapter then shifts to examining how people's actual knowledge of the laws of war conditions their stance toward a range of wartime violations. The collective evidence points to the potential, but admittedly also some of the limits, of public preferences in the context of international law.

In the conclusion, I consider policy implications and several questions that arose or were left unanswered from the preceding chapters. In particular, I examine the argument and findings in light of recent and growing backlash to international law and norms in the United States and globally, among both publics and elites. I contemplate not only the limitations, but also some of the potential downsides, of a system that prioritizes legal considerations over others. Returning to the opening thoughts of this book, I close by reassessing the relationship between international law and domestic law, and the proper place of the public in the larger operation of legal rules.

The philosopher Judith Shklar once quipped that "No modern work on legal theory is complete without a chapter on international law."[93] Indeed, some of the most famous legal works expound in minute detail on domestic law, while conjuring a few obligatory references to international law but where external legal questions are often relegated to an afterthought.[94] This book is instead mostly about international law, taking on international legal commitments throughout each and every chapter. But in the end by looking at the place of the public in the international legal order, the hope is that the pages that follow have something to say about legal theory more broadly and the place of ordinary people in the law.

WHAT IS INTERNATIONAL LAW AND WHAT DOES IT (SUPPOSEDLY) DO?

Definition and Functions

> **I don't know anything about the law of nations . . . I'm a good enough lawyer in a Western law court, I suppose, but we don't practice the law of nations up there.**
>
> —US president Abraham Lincoln

This humble reflection from one of the most revered US presidents was in reference to the complications, especially international legal ones, related to his decision to impose a naval blockade against the Confederacy during the American Civil War.[1] The blockade's legal and strategic merits were hotly debated at the time and well after, especially whether Lincoln made the most advisable decision.[2] The president may have been tactically making use of a penchant for self-deprecation to diffuse some of the blunter criticisms over his choices, of which he appeared very much aware.[3] But this episode highlights enduring questions over the nature of international law—what it is and what it does, or at least is supposed to do. If international law escapes the grasp of even well-trained world leaders, then what could these commitments possibly mean for more ordinary members of the international community and their respective national communities?

This chapter aims to provide the conceptual foundations guiding the remainder of the book. After distinguishing international legal commitments from related but separate phenomena, I put forward a definition of international law understood as *legalized rules that seek to regulate the behavior of internationalized actors who are conferred certain rights and responsibilities.*[4] This definitional foray is not meant to simply serve as some pedantic exercise but rather reflects distinct understandings of the meaning and role of international law. Alongside disagreements over what exactly international law "is," diverging viewpoints are plentiful over what it "does."[5] Despite an ever-lengthening list, I turn to two functions at the heart of international law, and most any legal system: 1) enforcement against violators; and 2) changing policy preferences. Each is then discussed through the lens of different schools of thought positing whether (or how well) international law actually serves these functions.

What Is International Law?

International laws are all around us. Some of the most formidable international organizations, including the United Nations (UN) and the International Monetary Fund (IMF), owe their origins to international agreements. Avoiding any confusion, one of the strongest and most enduring military alliances, the North Atlantic Treaty Organization (NATO), builds the word "treaty" directly into its name. Yet these examples are in the minority when surveying the panoply of instruments commonly referred to as international law. For every esteemed and established body like the UN,[6] there are countless looser or more minor agreements receiving little notice.[7] Also unlike the UN, most international laws are not, nor do they seek to become, universal in membership. Many limit themselves to more modest ambitions of regulating the behavior of handfuls of countries from the same region, evident with the proliferation of preferential trade agreements (PTAs). In fact, the modal type of international agreement is bilateral, involving only two states, such as the alliance between the United States and Japan, which has formally governed their military relations in one form or another since 1951.[8]

How are such disparate agreements in any way related? Distilling what these international laws are, and just as importantly what they are *not*, proves crucial before addressing broader questions about the role of international law motivating this book. It is difficult to consider whether international law matters or how it operates if we lack a clear sense of what it is. Definitional issues are not trivial. Some misunderstandings and disagreements over the relative import of international legal affairs are bound up in different conceptualizations of the nature of international law. When skeptics like John Bolton, who served as the US ambassador to the UN under George W. Bush and later national security adviser under Donald Trump, write, "there is no reason to consider treaties as 'legally' binding internationally, and certainly not as 'law' themselves," this reflects not only an ideological stance but also a particular notion of what counts as international law.[9] To more clearly understand the position of both skeptics and proponents requires a clearer understanding of the concept of international law—what should be included as well as excluded.

What International Law Is *Not*—Related Concepts

Part of the confusion over the contours of international law is because a number of terms are used, often interchangeably, to refer to related but distinct phenomena. In international legal conversations, some of the most notable include "institutions," "organizations," "regimes," and "norms." Complicating matters further, many of these concepts themselves exhibit multiple, sometimes conflicting meanings.

Perhaps the broadest of these is "institutions," which generally concern "recognized patterns of practice around which expectations converge."[10] This description is more expansive than how the term is often used colloquially to refer to international bodies like the UN or European Union (EU). A broad definition of institutions would still encompass the UN and EU given the extensive practices involved in their running. But a more circumscribed term describing these and similar bodies would be as examples of international "organizations"—institutions with minimum levels of centralization and independence, reflected in traits like a professional staff and secretariat possessing the authority to act autonomously.[11] Other institutions are more informal, lacking such organizational structures, but nonetheless still hold the potential to shape actors' expectations and conduct, as is evident by the Group of Seven (G7) forum.

Tweaked in a slightly more social direction, others see institutions as "a set of habits and practices shaped towards the realisation of common goals."[12] While similarly not reducing institutions to refer only to centralized bureaucracies of international organizations, this conceptualization goes further to encompass any habit or practice advancing common goals of international society. International laws are included, but also making the list are such all-embracing forces as the balance of power system, diplomacy, war, and even states themselves.[13]

In light of institutions' immense conceptual breadth, some scholarship relevant to international law has tended toward employing the term "regimes." In probably the most widely used definition, regimes are described as "sets of implicit or explicit principles, norms, rules, and decision-making procedures around which actors' expectations converge in a given area of international relations."[14] Understood this way, regimes are both narrower and broader than the notion of institutions already outlined, narrower in that regimes are delimited to particular issue areas rather than covering wide swathes of behavior.[15] Yet they are broader by including not only practices (or procedures), but also more general principles, norms, and rules that influence expectations. Beliefs can be just as important as behaviors, and in many ways precede practices. For instance, the human rights regime is concerned not only with how governments treat their citizens, but also in defining and promulgating beliefs over rights all individuals should enjoy.

Ultimately, we should not stress too much over trying to parse the exact distinctions between institutions and regimes, or vice versa. At times there is a strong, bordering on near complete, overlap between institutions and regimes with both often used interchangeably. Definitions for one frequently reference the other. The definition of institutions noted above begins by first describing regimes as "social *institutions*" (emphasis added).[16] Likewise, scholars labeled as "institutionalists," mention regimes as much (if not more) than institutions.[17]

The last relevant concept to discuss is one contained within the most commonly accepted definition of regimes—"norms." As with other terms, a variety of definitions exist, but one of the most generally agreed upon sees a norm as a "standard of appropriate behavior for actors with a given identity."[18] A norm can involve a single standard, such refraining from engaging in torture, but can be aggregated together with other norms to form a larger regime (or institution) governing an issue area, such as human rights.[19] Alongside regime studies, a huge literature has developed around the formation, evolution, and influence of norms across a range of issue areas.[20]

To sum up so far, institutions, organizations, regimes, and norms are often invoked in legal discussions, yet none fit neatly with the notion of international law. Absent from the preceding discussion was reference to any inherent *legal* character. Standards, principles, norms, procedures, and even rules were mentioned, but little about "law" per se. This was not by accident. For instance, regimes may contain international treaties, but can also reflect expressly nonlegal elements. The post–World War II international monetary regime involved treaty-based bodies like the IMF, alongside more diffuse principles like embedded liberalism.[21] This is why even after Richard Nixon suspended the US dollar's convertibility to gold in 1971, thereby renouncing the pegged foreign exchange rate system that was one of the raisons d'être of the IMF, a form (albeit altered) of the international monetary regime endured.[22] Likewise, ratifications of an international treaty offer a useful metric for assessing a norm's spread, but are not a prerequisite for the latter's emergence. Women's suffrage norms gradually established themselves in more informal ways before anything resembling international legal agreements eventually materialized.[23]

An overly inclusive approach to the definitional boundaries of norms, regimes, and their ilk comes at the cost of conceptual clarity. This is especially the case with regimes, where identifying the precise components of a given regime is a recurring challenge. What ultimately limits this line of inquiry for some critics is the "wooliness," or "imprecision," of the concept of regime, where "people mean different things when they use it."[24] Even regime scholars acknowledge the problems posed by this vagueness, reformulating definitional criteria with varying success.[25] Indeed, one of the motivations in recent decades for a renewed interest in international law was recognizing the need for a more limited, but coherent, approach to studying an important area of global governance.[26]

However, equating international law only with international organizations risks going in an opposite, overly restrictive direction. International organizations are important actors in their own right, often with distinct interests, structures, and activities, some even bordering on pathologies.[27] Many of the most prominent organizations may be formed through international legal agreements, such as the Rome Statute establishing the International Criminal Court (ICC), or the Marrakesh Agreement creating the World Trade Organization (WTO). Yet such founding agreements are the exception rather than the rule, representing a tiny fraction of the immense body of international laws. The vast majority of international laws operate absent the active management of an international organization. As the precursor to the WTO, the General Agreement on Tariffs and Trade (GATT) regulated a huge proportion of global trade for decades without a full-fledged organizational structure. Similarly, the 1949 Geneva Conventions and related instruments already represented an intricate legal network before the ICC's advent as a permanent tribunal to prosecute perpetrators of war crimes and other serious offenses.

International law, institutions, regimes, organizations, and norms are undoubtedly interrelated. Just as it is advisable not to isolate the study of more loosely defined regimes from formal international organizations,[28] any examination of international law needs to keep in mind these related concepts. Equally important, however, rejecting isolation does not mean embracing equivalency. To do so ignores the particular origins, values, and operation of international law compared to its non- (or less) legal counterparts. Such a choice would also discount what is distinctive about the increasing "legalization" of world affairs, and the particular role of international law in regimes, organizations, and norms. While recognizing areas of convergence, what then are the distinguishing features of international *law*?

Defining International Law

Just as with regimes or norms, a wide range of definitions for international law have been proposed.[29] For this book, I define international law as *legalized rules that seek to regulate the behavior of internationalized actors who are conferred certain rights and responsibilities*. This definition contains six elements that merit elaboration. For reasons that will become clear, I devote the most time to explicating the first two relating to the *legalized* nature of *rules* before turning more briefly to the remaining four.

First, international law—like any law—is composed of *rules*. This might seem like an obvious statement, but the existence of a rule or rules is a necessary (but not sufficient) ingredient for international law. As the English School theorist Hedley Bull notes, "without reference to a body of rules the idea of law is quite unintelligible."[30] Others have sought to conceptualize law in other terms, such as the Yale (or New Haven) School's focus on a specific type of process,[31] or the critical bent of New Stream scholarship that law reflects a particular discourse.[32] While laws may follow a certain process (both when formed and in subsequent decision-making), or invoke a certain vernacular, they can only do so in relation to some set of rules, even if the exact character of these rules is subject to contestation and change.

Rules, in turn, can be thought of as "specific prescriptions and proscriptions for action."[33] Bull goes slightly further by describing rules as "general imperative principles which require or authorise prescribed classes of persons or groups to behave in prescribed ways."[34] If rules seem to bear a resemblance to the description of norms earlier as "standards of appropriate behavior," it is because the two closely overlap, with perhaps the minor distinction that rules may be slightly more specific.[35]

In refining our understanding of rules, and ultimately how they relate to laws, a great deal of intellectual debt is owed to the legal theorist H. L. A. Hart in his work *The Concept of Law*. Hart identifies a basic differentiation among rules themselves as primary versus secondary. Primary rules refer to the actual regulations (pre- or proscriptions) proclaiming what can or cannot be done. For a trade agreement, this would cover the schedule for lowering tariffs on certain goods, or what types of barriers a country is allowed to keep or impose against imports. When people think of rules, primary rules are usually the first that come to mind. Yet equally important are secondary rules, which regulate how primary rules are created, interpreted, modified, or terminated. In other words, secondary rules are "rules about rules."[36] Continuing with trade agreements, secondary rules are involved when adjudicating whether a given country's trade policy counts as a prohibited barrier against trade. Secondary rules also figure prominently in negotiations over the substance of any new primary rules governing trade policies, or changes to existing ones.

Most international legal agreements contain both sets of rules—primary rules on the substantive obligations on the one hand, and secondary rules on how those promises should be interpreted, implemented, and evolve. Although sometimes overlooked, secondary rules are far from second-rate. If anything, secondary rules give meaning to primary rules, and are essential for the latter's proper functioning. As Hart points out, "Rules of the first type impose duties; rules of the second type confer powers . . ."[37]

Second, irrespective of their content (or substance), rules come in many different forms. There are rules for playing board games like Monopoly, rules of etiquette when eating at fancy restaurants, or rules for joining college campus Greek organizations. As essential as any of these rules may be for navigating their respective social spheres, none would properly count as "laws." Although Edmund Burke was wont to say that "Manners are of more importance than laws," the conservative philosopher still accepted the two were separate.[38] What distinguishes laws from other types of rules leads to the next main element of our definition for international law, which concerns the *legalized* nature of select rules.

Borrowing from the legalization literature,[39] when defining international law I prefer the term *legalized* rules to highlight the wider spectrum of "legalness" along which laws can be placed instead of more binary connotations of "legal" versus "nonlegal." Legalized rules differ from other sorts because they impose particular forms of *obligation* on actors to behave in certain ways. Actors may feel the need to follow the rules of a game, or rules of etiquette and other mores, out of a sense of decency or to avoid social stigma, but this is far from the same thing as feeling obligated to do so.[40]

Laws may not be reducible to a particular process or discourse, but when rules are legalized they do invoke certain principles, values, and even language not found to the same extent in other categories of rules. Possessing a unique "pedigree" of attributes like coherence, determinacy, generality, and nonretroactivity distinguishes laws from other forms of rules.[41] These characteristics can imbue a distinct form of obligation for those subjected to legalized rules.[42] Even those skeptical of the particular pedigree of legal principles acknowledge some of the distinct attributes of international law.[43]

The importance of the nature of obligation can be seen in the distinction between laws and the sorts of norms discussed earlier. Norms may involve "standards of behavior defined in terms of rights and obligations,"[44] but the sense of the obligation involved is not necessarily embedded in any legal system. If it were, then the norm (or the relevant rules making up all or part of that norm) would be considered law, a process where some norms do become institutionalized as such.[45] Take, for instance, the alleged taboo around the use of nuclear weapons.[46] The law/norm distinction is relevant if the use of one of these weapons would yield qualitatively different calculations and consequences for both the perpetrator and audiences involved if the rules exist as part of international law than if they did not.

Various markers can illuminate whether a rule has attained the status of law—legislative procedures, judicial rulings, lawyerly writings, among others. But law ultimately relies on deeper socio-cognitive foundations—rules are considered laws because actors believe them to possess the status of law.[47] This should not be construed as a descent into circular reasoning. Rather, it is to observe that laws can emerge from diverse pathways, and to accept the real impacts these laws can have once collectively viewed in this way.[48] This is especially the case with international law. As Bull notes, "the activity of those who are concerned with international law . . . is carried on in terms of the assumption that the rules with which they are dealing are rules of law."[49]

The social and cognitive bases for international law are perhaps best exemplified by customary international law. Merely identifying the prevalence of behavior consistent with a rule (the material component) is not sufficient. Crucial is an additional psychological element where actors follow the rule out of a sense they are legally obligated to do so because an *opinio juris* ("opinion of law") exists.[50] It is actors' collective beliefs that a practice constitutes a law that differentiates customary law from simple usage, or habit. As the famed *The Paquete Habana* (1900) case attests, establishing that states had previously refrained from capturing foreign fishing vessels as a prize of war out of legal obligation rather than common courtesy meant that subsequent contrary acts were treated as actual violations of international law.

Discussing customary international law raises deeper questions about the origins and sources of international legal rules. The modern international legal system usually takes as a starting point Article 38(1) of the Statute of the International Court of Justice (ICJ) when outlining the main sources of law, which include custom, treaties, general principles of law, as well as judicial decisions and writings by legal scholars with a few others sometimes added.[51] Thoughts on the relative hierarchy and merits of these and other possible sources dovetail with larger debates over naturalist versus positivist understandings of the very bases of international law. Briefly, naturalist approaches (whether more theological or humanistic) view international laws as universal rules handed down divinely, or emanating inherently from human reason. By contrast, positivist thinkers argue international law is ultimately founded upon the consent of authoritative political actors like states—in other words, law is what the relevant actors say it is.[52] Despite differences over provenance, both naturalist and positivist approaches share a common standpoint on the particular obligatory nature of international law.

Equally debated is whether the myriad of sources of a looser sort, often labeled "soft law," should be considered part of the international legal corpus. Soft law instruments include declarations and other work product of many international organizations, such as Agenda 21 from the 1992 Earth Summit advancing sustainable development goals.[53] Also covered are other sorts of nonbinding instruments and recommendations, such as the Helsinki Final Act promoting human rights standards among European countries, or another 1992 Earth Summit agreement, the Statement on Forest Principles.[54]

Part of the commotion lays in different uses of the term "soft law."[55] In the legalization literature, soft law refers to agreements that may score lower not necessarily just in terms of 1) the level of obligation to follow the rules (probably the most common usage), but also along two other dimensions; 2) the degree of precision in the language of provisions; and 3) whether authority is delegated to third parties like international courts to interpret and enforce the rules.[56]

When criticizing the status of soft law, detractors tend to focus on the first dimension of obligation as the crucial (dis)qualifying criterion. Formal treaties—like the Convention Against Torture (CAT), or the Convention on International Trade in Endangered Species of Wild Fauna and Flora (CITES)—may differ in how precise their terms may be, or how much enforcement power is appointed to higher authorities, but there is seemingly little doubt these "harder" agreements entail legal obligations. As the legal scholar and former director of the UN's General Legal Division, Paul Szasz, remarked, treaties (as well as customary laws) are law because "hard law is, by definition, binding;" by comparison, "soft law is not binding, though superficially it may appear to be so."[57] Extending this logic further, soft law sows confusion because it is "oxymoronic [in] nature," and "should not have law anywhere in its name."[58] For many, the inclusion of soft law next to harder ones is far from harmless, and risks "destabiliz[ing] the whole international normative system and turn it into an instrument that can no longer serve its purpose."[59]

The downside of these narrower perspectives is that they (perhaps fittingly) construct firm boundaries between hard and soft law in ways that disregard the operation of international legal *obligations*, irrespective of a commitment's technically *binding* nature. For some, international law is *only* made up of binding commitments.[60] A more inclusive approach instead recognizes that both binding (hard) and nonbinding (soft) laws involve legalized obligations in their own ways. If law contains an important psychological element, then what ultimately matters is what actors believe to be the obligatory nature of their commitments. This point was already established above concerning the status of "hard" customary law, but applies equally to soft law. What unites both harder and softer instruments under the international "law" family is that both are part of a "system of rules which conduces to a fairly high level of *perceived obligation* among members of a voluntarist community" (emphasis added).[61] The seeds of this quality can also be seen in the initial skeptical quote from Szasz—the seemingly "superficial" commitments of soft law may actually represent crucial components to a legal system that actors view themselves as obligated to follow.

There are no doubt important differences between harder and softer forms of international legal obligations. The theory and empirics laid forth in subsequent chapters take this diversity seriously. But these differences are a matter of degree not kind, and soft law remains an important part of international law.[62] Even when accepted as "law," softer agreements are still sometimes viewed as lesser forms of commitment—at best precursors, supplements, or compromises— compared to the more serious obligations of harder law.[63] It is true softer agreements can be an intermediate step toward more binding commitments—the largely hortatory 1985 Vienna Convention for the Protection of the Ozone Layer eventually led to the binding terms of the 1987 Montreal Protocol for phasing out certain ozone-depleting substances. But softer agreements should not immediately be considered second-best options. Soft instruments possess distinct advantages of their own, leading actors at times to purposefully select more flexible agreements.[64] Despite their differences, what "binds" soft and hard law is that both remain embedded within a broader framework of legal obligation that can transform actors' beliefs and expectations.[65] It is these principles and values contained in legal obligations of various kinds that will play a large role in some of the main functions of international law discussed below, and in the theory proposed in the next chapter for how international legal commitments operate.

Putting the first two elements of our definition together, international law (like any law) refers to a set of rules that entails legalized obligations. Below, I discuss more concisely the remaining elements that help distinguish *international* law.

The third component follows from one of the general purposes of these rules (first element) that are legalized (second element). Legalized rules in part *regulate the behavior* of actors. This regulative function of international law takes various forms, but in all circumstances seeks to shape actors' conduct. Rules can be proscriptive (or entail "negative" commitments) in the sense that actors promise not to resort to particular types of actions, such as refraining from engaging in torture under the CAT. Rules can also be prescriptive (or entail "positive" commitments), requiring actors take certain concrete steps, such as ensuring equal gender rights under the International Covenant on Economic, Social and Cultural Rights (ICESCR). The exact line between proscriptive/negative and prescriptive/positive commitments can be blurred and depends on what is viewed as the status quo—under many environmental agreements, the positive promise to take concrete steps to reduce emissions sits alongside an implicit more negative baseline of avoiding further pollution. Most agreements are made up of a combination of both positive and negative rules. Returning to the CAT, besides the negative promise not to engage in torture (Article 2), parties are required to take positive measures like making changes to domestic criminal statutes (Article 4), or submitting periodic progress reports (Article 19).

All these examples refer to the *regulative* function of international law involving the management of actors' behavior. What is regulated are not thoughts of potentially torturing a suspect, but actually committing acts of torture. Similarly, discriminatory thinking is not managed under many human rights agreements so much as discriminatory actions against protected groups.[66] While regulative rules are largely behavioral in content, they may nonetheless influence the underlying preferences of actors. Given the importance (though contested) of preferences for understanding actors' behavior,[67] preference formation and change point to one of the general functions of international law to be discussed further below.

The fourth component concerns *who* are the *internationalized actors* whose behavior these legalized rules regulate. I prefer the term "internationalized" actors because actors can think and affect international forces even if they are located within a single national boundary. Taken literally, the most traditional meaning of inter*national* law is that it relates only to states. Oddly enough, this circumscribed view shares the state-centric tenets at the heart of many realist accounts that are dismissive of international law's importance.[68] Generally seen as one of the most definitive statements in the modern study of international law, Lasso Oppenheim declared "international law is a law not above but between *states*" (emphasis added).[69] As is often remarked, states occupy a privileged place in the pyramid of actors under international law, such as the authority to ratify treaties, or immunity for many of their actions.[70]

But states are not the only relevant players. International laws, both hard and soft, increasingly regulate the behavior of a multitude of actors other than states, including international organizations, multinational firms, transnational activists, rebel groups, and even ordinary individuals. On the one hand, these nonstate actors represent the incorporation of newer *objects* of international law.[71] As objects, any benefits enjoyed by such actors are granted solely at the behest of states, and taken away just as easily. Parts of the early international human rights regime could be seen this way. Rights were no longer accorded solely to states, but rather certain protections extended to all individuals as human beings. Individuals largely remained objects, however, because states were the ones primarily responsible for providing and protecting those rights.

However, nonstate actors are increasingly considered *subjects* of international law, not simply as holders of certain protections but having their own agency to promote and protect their rights and those of others. This can be seen institutionally in instances where nonstate actors possess specific powers within an agreement. Under the 1949 Geneva Conventions, the International Committee of the

Red Cross (ICRC) acquired the "special position" of guardian of the conventions.[72] Returning to the human rights realm, under the European Convention on Human Rights (ECHR), citizens of member states have the ability to petition directly to the European Court of Human Rights (ECtHR) to bring cases against their governments.[73]

Nonstate actors should be considered subjects of international law, not just under such formal situations. These actors also play an important role at all stages of the creation and implementation of international agreements—sometimes alongside states, sometimes in opposition. Firms are active in bilateral investment treaties; environmental activists in pollution agreements; and rebel groups in the laws of war. The practices and beliefs of states down to ordinary individuals, which is at the core of customary law and beliefs over a rule's obligatory nature, demonstrates all these actors "are, in this sense, both creators and subjects of the law."[74]

A subject is more comprehensive, incorporating actors who can meaningfully shape the operation of international legal commitments. Relevant subjects thus extend well beyond states. Yet states still remain crucial, both as one of the main institutions through which interests and actions of nonstate actors are filtered, but also by defining the political boundaries across which international laws operate. One of those groups often overlooked—on their own and in interacting with states—will turn out to be central to the argument put forward in this book and developed more fully in chapter 2—the public.[75]

Fifth, attention to subjects points to another general purpose of international law, that these actors are *conferred certain rights and responsibilities*. While the regulative role is often most visible, also important is the law's *constitutive* purpose. Associated more closely with constructivist thinking, international law also serves to conceive of the very identity of actors and their legal personalities.[76] International law, like institutions more broadly, do not simply constrain actors' behavior, but defines who are relevant actors in the first place.[77] Indeed, to speak of an "actor" means to accept that they are accorded certain rights and responsibilities. As in the previous element, the quantity and quality of those rights and responsibilities varies. States enjoy the greatest number, which helps to explain why so many groups have sought to obtain recognition as states themselves.[78] Rights and responsibilities need not be evenly balanced, which returns to the question of the status of a given actor as an object versus subject under international law. Actors can also take steps that alter their constitutive status. For instance, the laws of war guarantee certain protections to prisoners of war (POWs), but to qualify as a POW means that combatants must fulfill several criteria, which includes behaving in certain legal ways.[79] As will be discussed in greater detail in chapter 4, debates over detainees in the War on Terror were just as much about this constitutive question of *who* should be granted POW status as they were about *how* they should be treated.

Irrespective of the specific content or relative balance, by conferring rights and responsibilities international law helps constitute actors. Admittedly, most of the discussion in this book focuses more on international law's regulative side. It is nonetheless important to keep in mind that international regulative rules presuppose and are guided by this deeper purpose of legal commitments to define who are the relevant actors.

Sixth and finally, international law *seeks* to regulate the behavior of internationalized actors. Two different treaties could be more or less successful in regulating actors' behavior, but both would still be considered international law for our definitional purposes. It is the intended objective of legal rules to regulate actions that matters most—rather than those goals actually being accomplished—when deciding whether this final criterion is met. Consequences are thus not central for defining international law.[80] Observing a violation does not automatically mean a law is nonexistent. By this standard, almost all laws—international and domestic—would not be considered law proper. More important is how perpetrators view their own actions, and how audiences respond.

Although consequences should not figure into the definition of international law, they are paramount both theoretically and empirically for understanding the relevance of international legal commitments. Probably the fundamental axis of debate between proponents and detractors revolves around questions concerning the effectiveness of international law in shaping a range of outcomes. In the remainder of this chapter, I sketch out the broad outlines of this debate before turning to two core functions of international law—enforcement and changing preferences—and situate some of the main claims for and against the effectiveness of legal commitments in fulfilling each in turn.

Does International Law "Matter"? A View of Two Functions from Two Sides

Perusing past history would seem to make answering the question of whether international law "matters" in the affirmative an uphill battle. The apparent failures of international law are legion. The German chancellor Theobold von Bethmann Hollweg famously depicted the 1839 Treaty of London guaranteeing Belgian's neutrality as a mere "scrap of paper" in the lead-up to the First World War.[81] Five years afterward, the Versailles Peace Treaty formally concluding this "war to end all wars" became widely disparaged, both by contemporaries like John Maynard Keynes in his damning critique *The Economic Consequences of the Peace,* and in later retrospectives.[82] In the ensuing years, the 1928 Kellogg-Briand Pact outlawing war came to be seen as hopelessly idealistic; for many, becoming synonymous with the irrelevance of international law as the pact was swept aside by a series of conflicts culminating in the Second World War. The seeming chasm between ambitions and actuality led the former US secretary of state Henry Kissinger to reject the ideals underlying the pact "as irresistible as it was meaningless."[83]

That this repudiation comes from Kissinger is apt. As chief diplomat of the United States, he also became known as one of the foremost practitioners of a realpolitik foreign policy giving legal matters little weight. Among international relations scholars of various realist stripes, international law is likewise largely immaterial compared to calculations of power and interest.[84] This skepticism is not limited to the field of international relations, but also has a devoted following among a number of legal scholars.[85] The gap between rhetoric and reality can appear insurmountable: "The received rules of international law neither describe accurately what nations do, nor predict reliably what they will do, nor prescribe intelligently what they should do."[86]

What can possibly be said in response to this multi-front onslaught by various skeptics? Some proponents start by noting that, apparent flaws notwithstanding, many international actors sure appear to act *as if* international agreements matter, such as with military alliances:

> One must ask why leaders continue to form alliances. If contracts do not affect behavior in any way, why do state leaders act as if they will? Why do they continue to negotiate agreements and invest great effort in designing precise treaty provisions? Should not the difficulty in enforcing agreements affect the willingness of leaders to form them?[87]

It would likewise seem strange for actors to take such care over treaty language, often quarrelling over minor differences in grammar or vocabulary to the point of threatening to walk away from the negotiating table, if consequences were so slight. Matters of wording can matter a great deal as attested by a prolonged dispute between a still-young US republic and the Ottoman Empire over conflicting translations of an 1830 commerce treaty.[88] Indeed, an entire body of secondary rules has developed to resolve disputes over wording, especially for instruments in multiple languages.[89]

Equally peculiar, when denouncing international law, many critics just as often criticize treaties not because of their weakness, but because of their apparent *strengths* in undermining national interests.[90] The ominous warnings by neoconservatives like Bolton about the menace posed by the ICC to US interests appears overblown if these are all toothless tribunals.[91]

Part of the difficulty in making sense of these various claims is that at times critics and defenders appear to be saying much the same thing. While generally denying the importance of legal commitments, Hans Morgenthau acknowledged that "during the four hundred years of its existence international law has in most instances been scrupulously observed."[92] These remarks by one of the founders of modern realism bear a striking resemblance to the oft-quoted maxim from one of international law's staunchest defenders, Louis Henkin, that "Almost all nations observe almost all principles of international law and almost all of their obligations almost all of the time."[93] It is the meaning behind these two statements, and the implications for understanding international law, that is vastly different. While Morgenthau saw few real constraints from legal commitments, for Henkin international law can fundamentally alter actors' decision-making and outcomes. Actors comply with their promises not because it is costless or convenient to do so, waiting to defect the moment it provides an advantage. Rather, they take seriously their obligations because these commitments are legalized, affecting both how they think about their promises and choose to act.

Proposing that actors approach their commitments earnestly neither signifies international law is the only thing that matters to them, nor that the international legal order will solve all the world's problems. Just as we should avoid overstating skeptics' complete disregard for international law, we should be equally wary of extreme promotions of international law as a panacea. To be sure, some have always tended toward the farther end of the idealist spectrum, whether the more optimistic elements of Woodrow Wilson's Fourteen Points to periodic calls for a quasi-world government grounded in universal law.[94]

Yet the utopian "legalist-moralist" label pinned by many skeptics on their more legal-minded counterparts is itself somewhat of a caricature.[95] The vast majority of proponents, from the interwar period to the present, generally offer a more cautious view of both the potential and limits of international law, especially in relation to matters of power.[96] The "legalist-moralist" hybrid is equally a misnomer, since the positivist turn in legal studies at the turn of the twentieth century—especially in the United States—explicitly sought to separate law from morality. In calling for a "scientific" study of international law, Oppenheim was attempting to divorce legal from moral matters: "But we must not confound the facts of life as they are with what they ought to be, and we must not mix up the rules of international law which are really in force with those rules which we would wish to be in force."[97] As will be discussed in later sections, however, Oppenheim and other legal positivists may have taken this logic too far. Rather, underlying moral values may be activated when international commitments are legalized. Proponents' posture is more nuanced and realistic (even if not "realist") about what international law can and cannot do than what is often portrayed by critics.

Henkin's repetition of "almost" in his observation about countries fulfilling their promises can also be read as acknowledging certain limitations to international law.[98] One hundred percent adherence to the rules was never the expectation, nor even necessarily the goal. As the legal scholar Richard Falk attests, "perfect compliance suggests the triviality of a rule . . . If there is no pressure on the rule, there would be no social function for it."[99] The Managerial School similarly accepts that breaches will take place, but views violations as a challenge to be handled at "acceptable" levels, not a vice always to be denounced.[100]

The operation of international law can be seen as much in its breach as its adherence. Even the many "failures" mentioned above can be seen in a very different light. Take Bethmann Hollweg's reference to the Treaty of London as a "scrap of paper"—a common refrain for the purported ineffectiveness of international agreements.[101] It turns out the chancellor was not using the words derisively but rather in despair after realizing Britain would enter the war in large part over Germany's violation, suggesting the agreement was no simple fragment.[102] Equally deserving of another look is the Kellogg-Briand Pact decried as naïve because of its inability to prevent the Second World War. Yet stopping a cataclysmic global conflict is perhaps too much to ask of any agreement, especially in the face of an economic depression and rising extremist ideologies. What the pact did accomplish was to embed in the international order principles delegitimating the aggressive use of force between states. A careful reappraisal of the forces the pact ushered in shows that conquests still took place, but were less frequent, less extensive in terms of territory conquered, and less likely to be recognized by the international community.[103] Similarly, peace agreements like the one ending the First World War face the daunting task of trying to stabilize relations among embittered adversaries. The Versailles Treaty contained flaws but also had to contend with formidable structural obstacles and the difficult personalities tasked with its implementation.[104] Strangely enough, criticisms of Versailles contain an implicit admission of the *relevance* of international law—if treaties did not matter, then the deficiencies identified by Keynes and others should have had little bearing on the rocky interwar period that followed.

Debates over these and other historical examples touch on a methodological point that is also of great theoretical importance. To assess the impact of international law, we must not simply look at whether it achieved desirable outcomes, or avoided bad ones. We instead need to keep in mind the *counterfactual*—what would have happened in the absence of the agreement, or if a country had not been a party? Even bad results like Versailles can be evidence of effectiveness if the situation would have been *even worse* without the treaty. The metric should not be that international law has failed if it does not get the international community to heaven. Keeping us farther away from the depths of hell has its utility too, even if significant room for improvement remains.

Other defenses have been put forward to buttress the role international law. Some of these approaches may even cede ground to skeptics' claims about international law's weaknesses, but instead emphasize other ways the law functions, some of which have already been mentioned. These include a focus on constitutive rather than regulatory effects,[105] as a mode of communication,[106] process of decision-making,[107] or underlying discourse,[108] especially one serving to deconstruct gendered roles and structures.[109]

These are significant conceptions in their own right, broadening the meaning and understanding of international law. But an equally important defense is to take skeptics on their own terms to assess whether international law "matters" even in some of its more traditional functions—such as enforcement and changing preferences. Before turning to each of these functions, however, a deeper charge first needs to be addressed—that international law is not deserving of its legal designation in any genuine sense.

But Wait—Is International Law Really "Law"? A Definitional Redux

One reason this chapter began by dwelling on definitional issues is that one of the sharpest volleys launched by skeptics questions whether international law really is "law." No one denies treaties and similar instruments exist, are formally deposited in collections administered in places like Geneva, and invoked by public officials or dissected by lawyers. From critics' standpoint, international law may possess the outward trappings of a legal order, but lacks the essence to truly qualify as law. Or, as the writer and journalist Stephen Budiansky bluntly put it, "International Law is to law as Professional Wrestling is to wrestling. Nobody above the age of 9 mistakes it for the real thing."[110] If international law is an oxymoron, then the very question "Does international law matter?" (along with evaluating its core functions) makes little sense—there is no way for a phenomenon that does not exist to matter one way or the other without entering into metaphysics.

On what basis do skeptics assert that international law fails to meet the status of law? Naysayers would not necessarily disagree with the definition I laid out above. International rules certainly purport to regulate the behavior of international actors, though those of a more realist persuasion would likely emphasize the activities of states as preeminent. Rather, detractors would add an additional, and in their view critical, criterion for something to count as law.

This fundamental characteristic concerns *who* is doing the regulating. While my definition is agnostic on the nature of the actor (or actors) who regulate the rules or serve other functions, those who deny the existence of international law have a very particular personality in mind—a sovereign who possesses absolute power and authority over the relevant legal system.

The "international-law-is-not-law" logic generally follows a four-step sequence. First, for laws to be present, there must be a sovereign who creates and, most importantly, enforces the rules. Law does not, and cannot, exist without force to punish violators and deter would-be wrongdoers, and this coercive power must reside in a superior authority. Written as disorder prevailed during the English Civil Wars of the seventeenth century, in *Leviathan* the philosopher Thomas Hobbes pronounced, "Where there is no common Power, there is no Law."[111] This view was later refined into the "command theory" of law espoused by the nineteenth-century legal scholar John Austin. For Austin, "Laws properly so called are a species of *commands*" (emphasis in original) that are imposed and enforced by a sovereign, and backed by the threat and use of force.[112] Sovereigns could take various forms, "But every positive law, or every law strictly so called, is a direct and circuitous command of a monarch or sovereign number in the character of political superior." Austin and his disciples were very clear that only under situations of complete superiority "is a law proper, or a law properly so called."[113] An alliterative recapitulation of this position was formulated by Inis Claude, explaining that for a rule to count as a law it had to meet the "Five Cs"—Congress, Code, Court, Cop, and Clink—all of which rest on a set of higher government institutions (legislative, judicial, executive, and especially penal).[114]

Second, a common assumption across most mainstream approaches to international relations is that the international system is anarchic, meaning there is no higher authority than states who are the main constituent political units.[115] A clear separation is purported to divide domestic and international politics with implications for security, economics, politics, and law, among other affairs. Domestically, each state is sovereign over its respective territory. There may be challenges from within, or from without through interdependence and other forces, but in traditional Weberian fashion each state has a monopoly over the legitimate use of violence within its borders.[116] Internationally among states, however, there is no higher authority, no world sovereign. The neorealist Kenneth Waltz contrasts the international from the domestic system in ways Hobbes and Austin would recognize, "None is entitled to command; none is required to obey."[117] The bifurcated presence/absence of sovereignty represents the *Grundnorm* (fundamental norm) of the international system, providing the core ordering principle allowing separate sovereign state entities to interact within a larger anarchical society.[118]

The third link follows directly from the first two. If law does not exist without a higher authority, and if the international system is characterized by the absence of such authority, then international law does not exist. States sometimes cooperate with each other, even concluding agreements and forming organizations, but these outcomes do not fundamentally alter the anarchic environment.[119] Agreements may even lead some states or other actors to develop strong feelings about what rules should count as appropriate conduct. But absent a superior authority, these rules lack the force of actual legal obligations. For Austin, international laws instead represent "rules of positive morality"—actors could certainly choose to follow them, but would suffer no legal sanction if they decided otherwise.[120] Similar Austinian sentiments could be seen centuries later in the remarks of the former US secretary of state (and trained lawyer) Dean Acheson when he said, "Much of what is called international law is a body of ethical distillation, and one must take care not to confuse this distillation with law."[121]

Fourth and conversely, although there is no law internationally, law lives on domestically as each state is the highest authority within its territorial boundaries. Law thus exists within states, but not among or above them. Critics explicitly point to this domestic analogy to differentiate the *real* law prevailing inside states from the international "law" pretending to operate externally.[122]

There are several problems with this domestic analogy, and using domestic law (often Anglo-American conceptualizations at that) as the reference point.[123] Part of this concerns evolving conceptualizations of law writ large, with the sole importance attached to sanctions in Austin's command theory falling out of favor among many later legal theorists. Laws can be imperative and rely on coercion, but this is not their only mode. They can also be facilitative, such as by allowing actors to create contracts governing mutual relations, leading to desires to follow the rules absent sanctions from on high.[124]

Highlighting contracts is instructive for thinking about the status of laws at different levels. The domestic analogy might not serve to negate international law but actually shows its connection to national law, particularly the striking parallels between treaties and domestic contracts.[125] In his introduction to the topic, the legal scholar Mark Janis declared, "However styled, they [treaties] are in the first place essentially contracts."[126] Actors may comply with obligations—contractual or otherwise—created by the law for reasons beyond simply fearing punishment.[127] If sanctions are not nearly so critical for conceptualizing the law, then the presence (absence) of a sovereign authority with the power to sanction may not be a qualifying (or disqualifying) trait.

Rigidly following the domestic analogy also leads to some peculiar interpretations of what counts as law. In the United States, municipal, state, or federal statutes would all be considered laws because there are higher municipal, state, or federal institutions with the authority to enforce them. But what about constitutional laws, which are supposed to bind the federal government? Many cases reaching the US Supreme Court involve the federal government as the defendant, and concern its fundamental powers, such as the ability to indefinitely detain enemy combatants,[128] or putting citizens to death.[129] Similar dynamics are evident in other countries, such as the position of the German Federal Constitutional Court vis-à-vis the chancellor in Germany.[130] While we largely take it for granted the US, German, and other democratic governments (and even some autocracies) will comply with high court rulings adverse to their interests, what is *compelling* them to do so? After all, no sovereign authority exists above these governments. Strictly speaking, according to the domestic analogy, constitutional law does not qualify as law. Returning to the case of the US Constitution, if international law is not law, then it seems neither should be the "the supreme Law of the Land."[131] Curiously, some of international law's most ardent detractors make their case on the basis of maintaining the centrality of the Constitution in a national society's legal life.[132]

Definitional broadsides may not hold up to scrutiny, but critics do raise an important point that international legal commitments are a stranger sort of legal species—a point actually shared by many who assert the actuality of international law.[133] Having a higher authority, or Claude's "Five Cs," may not be necessary for international law to exist, but does mean that such laws may operate differently from their domestic siblings. In contrast to the hierarchical surroundings inhabited by many (though not all) domestic laws, the anarchical environment in which international law resides makes for more decentralized workings. Like the international system more generally, international law can be seen as a self-help legal order, where states, along with other actors, have to rely on themselves to form, interpret, follow, and enforce the rules.[134]

The legal theorist Hans Kelsen argues this "entirely decentralized" system for enforcement means that international law is a "primitive law" more akin to what prevailed in earlier human societies before the advent of modern political institutions.[135] Even others generally approving of the merits of legal systems characterized by little diffuse enforcement employ similar language.[136] International relations scholar E. H. Carr likewise distinguished domestic from international law by referring to the latter as "undeveloped."[137] Hart places less emphasis on enforcement, but comes to similar conclusions that international law is not a "developed legal system."[138] The absence of domestic-like institutions means the secondary rules crucial for defining, interpreting (and enforcing) laws do not appear to exist at the international level. International law looks like domestic law on its surface but is a shallower version underneath, or for Hart, "the analogy is one of content not of form."[139]

This tagging of international law as "primitive" or "undeveloped" is unfortunate on many levels, and reflects a broader tendency at times to rely on troubling Eurocentric terminology and ideas when discussing international phenomena.[140] One can acknowledge that international law operates differently than domestic law without resorting to problematic labels or comparisons.

Irrespective of the particular language used, the implications of these differences between international and domestic legal orders are potentially profound. Even if international law is accepted as "law," skeptics assert these differences make international legal commitments inescapably weaker. As the realist (and trained lawyer) Morgenthau warns:

> To recognize that international law exists is, however, not tantamount to asserting that it is as effective a legal system as the national legal systems are and that, more particularly, it is effective in regulating and restraining the struggle for power on the international scene.[141]

Advocates counter that dissimilarity is not equivalent to inferiority. Acknowledging that international law operates in divergent ways does not mean it lacks particular strengths. The legal scholar Anthony D'Amato remarks that the operation of international law "is on the whole an effective process—as effective for the international legal system as . . . of most laws in domestic systems."[142] The sections that follow walk through two of the main functions of international law—enforcement and changing preferences—though accepting significant disagreement over their relative impact.

(Weak) Enforcement—The (Non)Imposition of Ex Post Sanctions

Enforcement is not law's only function, but is typically viewed as crucial for its effective operation in many circumstances. Actors may follow rules for a variety of reasons beyond fear of punishment, but the lack of sanctions against offenders can undermine a community's belief in law's legitimacy and long-term stability. The Austinian view may be misplaced in its insistence on a single higher authority, but adherents highlight the important function of sanctions. Even some critics of Austin acknowledge the role of the threat of punishments for a range of laws.[143] Along similar lines, D'Amato "concede[s] that physical coercion is not a necessary component of 'law,'" but is "reluctant to conclude that it is totally unnecessary."[144]

Setting aside the Austinian debate on whether or not anarchy is a disqualifier for a rule to be considered law proper, skeptics often contend that the absence of a higher authority means enforcement of international law is sorely lacking.

Compared to what a sovereign can provide domestically, punishment for violations take place in an international self-help system. Unfortunately, any sanctions
will be characteristically unreliable, inconsistent, acrimonious, and of too little
severity to adequately restrain current or would-be wrongdoers.[145] States and
other actors have their own interests that do not always align with maintaining
the integrity of the international legal order, especially given the costliness and
collective action problems associated with sanctioning violations. The uneven
application of the Responsibility to Protect (R2P) norm, with interventions in
some humanitarian crises like Libya, but frequent inaction in others like Syria or
Myanmar, reflects this mercurial pattern in gruesome detail.[146] As Stanley Hoffmann reckons, "The failure of the constraining function has always been at the
heart of the weakness of international law."[147]

Skeptics stress the absence of a reliable international enforcement apparatus as
a counterpoint to what they feel is an obliviousness to these deficiencies by cham-
pions of "legalistic-moralistic" ideals.[148] Utopian beliefs in the inherent "sanctity
of treaties" portends the danger that promoters—and policymakers who believe
them—ignore fundamental limits in the ability to enforce international law at
their own peril.[149]

As noted earlier, Morgenthau and others agree with many proponents that
treaties are usually closely followed.[150] Where they diverge is over whether this
general condition of rule-following is evidence for the effectiveness of international law. In particular, what happens when treaties and other legal commitments are breached, however rare this may be? The answer for most skeptics
is that violators suffer few material consequences beyond what the aggrieved
party can themselves inflict using their own capabilities. Whether it was Hitler's
Germany releasing itself from the shackles of the Treaty of Versailles through
deception and force, or the invasion of Abyssinia by Mussolini's Italy in contravention of the Covenant of the League of Nations, international law seemingly
put up little resistance. Utopianism reflects a naivety, or for the Dutch philosopher Baruch Spinoza, "folly,"[151] of placing one's faith in legal promises lacking any
outside recourse to enforcement if (or when) they are violated. A corollary can be
seen in Niccolo Machiavelli's advice in *The Prince* that a shrewd leader should put
little stock in the fealty of others to keep their word, and mercilessly break one's
own when it suits the ruler's interests.[152]

Some skeptics acknowledge that international law may be more impactful
in matters of "low" politics, such as the environment, many technological standards, or the like, where enforcement concerns are less salient.[153] By contrast,
when it comes to issues of "high" politics, where core national security interests are at stake, international law is given shorter shrift and may be unable
to substantially alter actors' decision-making or outcomes.[154] Even those more

optimistic about the ability of international law to facilitate cooperation admit that the glow for this promise may be dimmer in matters of national security.[155] A middle option might be located where international law can be relevant, at least for issues of lower politics. But this seemingly moderate position cedes much of the ground to skeptics. If proponents want to say that international law matters, then legal commitments should also (and especially) operate in the *hardest* of circumstances, not just easier ones. As a skeptical Raymond Aron points out, "One does not judge international law by peaceful periods and secondary problems."[156]

International law may be less developed in certain respects compared to national legal systems, but enforcement can still take place in the absence of higher authority. Anarchy is not synonymous with the lack of sanctions. Or, a self-help system does not mean help is hopeless for those wanting a functioning international legal order that counters violations. As D'Amato asserts, "the absence of these institutions does not mean that international law isn't really law; rather, *it simply means that international law is enforced in a different way*" (emphasis added).[157] Although Kelsen was one of those jurists apt to describe international law as "primitive," he still very much saw a central place for enforcement. In his sanction-delict model, international law puts forth prescriptions or prohibitions (edicts), which many actors follow but some may violate (conduct constituting a delict).[158] The key for Kelsen is that the international legal system punishes delicts through sanctions by a force "monopoly of the community."[159] The nature of the international community may differ from the domestic community for national laws, but this community possesses a comparable capacity to engage in enforcement, albeit of a more decentralized character.

Violators may experience costs for flouting international law, which can take various shapes. One common formulation consists of what can be called the "Three Rs" of enforcement—reciprocity, retaliation, and reputation.[160] Reciprocity involves responding in kind to the conduct of others in a "tit-to-tat" manner in order to hurt the interests of the violator. Many areas of international law are conditional (though not all),[161] meaning that actors are not only allowed but authorized to respond in the same vein to breaches committed against them.[162] Reciprocity is especially common in trade, where the benefits of raising barriers against foreign imports can be blunted if other states respond with similar protections of their own. Historically, the laws of war involved large doses of reciprocity, since belligerents are often concerned about how any violations may result in mutual punishment against their own soldiers or civilians.[163] Reciprocal dynamics are common in international politics, but legalizing commitments has been shown to smooth these processes, such as between belligerents who have both ratified the prevailing laws of war.[164]

Retaliation concerns other sorts of sanctions directly imposed against a violator. These could involve everything from naming-and-shaming to economic sanctions and even outright military force.[165] Because retaliation is materially costly, collective action problems may make it difficult for actors to coordinate in implementing punishments. There may also be political costs to engaging in retaliation if such enforcement is viewed by others as self-serving or cynically motivated.[166]

Barriers of this sort are often assumed by skeptics to be too high to allow for any real enforcement outside the parochial interests of the most powerful states.[167] Yet these collective sanctioning costs are often exaggerated, and benefits from enforcement undervalued.[168] The relationship between law and power can also be seen in a different light. Powerful states certainly have a greater ability to violate international laws at will, but also tend to gain disproportionately from the existing system, and thus hold a greater stake in its proper functioning.[169] Great powers have played an outsized role in the creation and maintenance of international legal regimes, whether the catalyzing role of Tsarist Russia in the first Hague Conventions governing armed conflict, to the United States as the principal architect of the post–World War II liberal order.[170] Reservoirs for retaliation may be much deeper than presumed.

The third "R" of enforcement are reputational consequences, a topic given much further treatment in chapters 3 and 4. Briefly, reputation in the context of international law refers to others' beliefs about an actor's trustworthiness to fulfill its promises.[171] Instead of direct retaliatory actions, consequences for a violator may be damage to its standing as a reliable partner in the eyes of others. As a result, reputational costs to offenders take the form of forgone opportunities for future cooperation, or agreements on much stricter terms. For instance, a state defaulting on its outstanding financial commitments may find itself locked out of sovereign lending, or only able to borrow at onerous rates.[172] Reputation remains one of the foundational ways in which international law is thought to be enforced, and in various ways feeds into the reciprocity and retaliation sources of punishment.[173]

The "Three Rs" point to some of the main sources of enforcement for international law. For violators, breaches can result in substantial costs felt in the short term, but also further down the road. As in national legal systems, the purpose of enforcement is twofold—1) a punitive element to sanction wrongdoers; as well as 2) a deterrent purpose to dissuade the violator from engaging in similar actions again, but also a warning to others to think twice themselves in the future. Although enforcement is primarily thought of in terms of ex post costs, it may also have implications for ex ante expectations that an actor will abide by its commitments. The prospect of punishment should an actor deviate can have the additional benefit of improving the present credibility of its commitments, some-thing that might be especially attractive to those having a hard time convincing others of their reliability.[174]

Whether or not enforcement of this decentralized kind is able to function effectively raises important implications for the interests of actors vis-à-vis the law. For many skeptics, international law is irrelevant to an actor's self-interest. States will follow international rules when it is in their interests to do so, but break them the moment their self-interest (explicitly defined as *separate* from the law) calls for it. Adopting a rational choice approach, some skeptics argue that when actors are weighing the costs and benefits of their decisions, international law is an afterthought.[175]

Yet there is nothing in rational choice theory that inevitably leads to the con-clusion that law plays no role in decision-making. Nonmaterial factors, among other dynamics, have been shown to be readily integrated into rational choice models.[176] Decentralized enforcement suggests it would be eminently reasonable for an actor to conclude that fulfilling its legal commitments is in its self-interest. Rational actors are generally assumed to compare the costs and benefits of differ-ent courses of action, choosing the one that yields the highest average expected utility. Enforcement entails direct costs to the violator. As the legal scholar Oscar Schachter remarks, "States facing a choice on whether to comply with an inter-national obligation that it finds inimical to its interest will hesitate to violate its obligations. Violations, in short, are rarely cost-free even to powerful States."[177]

The issue is not so much whether rational choice models necessarily lead to pro- or con- positions on international law, but rather whether there are mean-ingful costs associated with violations of legal commitments. It is this latter issue of costs, rather than the rationality assumption per se, where many skeptics and proponents diverge. Indeed, "self-interest and obligation are not mutually exclu-sive in international . . . law"[178] Other explanations drawing explicitly on ratio-nal choice thinking have been developed to instead demonstrate the *relevance* of international legal commitments.[179]

Rational choice models are useful, but in some respects may be too narrow to offer a comprehensive account for the operation of international law. Declaring that legal commitments entail costs is all well and good, but *why* are the costs presumed to be greater for violating these sorts of commitments? Costs and ben-efits of compliance versus violation are not given, but rather shaped in substantial ways by international law itself.[180]

Consistent with rationalist accounts, international law is informative in that it provides details about actors' promises and behavior, which can aid in enforce-ment as well as other functions.[181] For instance, a government's reneging on a legalized commitment may be more illuminating regarding its reputation for trustworthiness than if it engaged in the same behavior absent such a pledge. This information is not simply neutral or value-free, reporting on the technical behavior of an actor. A government could engage in similar sorts of actions, such as raising trade barriers, or abusing enemy prisoners, but the information provided may be qualitatively different if such conduct took place in the context of a legalized commitment. Drawing on constructivist insights, international law can be seen as embedded within a broader set of principles and expectations.[182] Being so situated, international law is informative in a particular way—it generates *principled* information. The information created through engagement with international law is thus going to be more meaningful, activating normative considerations, and helping to make enforcement more purposeful and ultimately effective.

Constructivist and rationalist approaches have often been portrayed as diametrically opposed.[183] Instead of mutual exclusivity, scholars from both camps have increasingly identified areas of complementarity and cross-fertilization.[184] The possibility for synthesis is especially ripe in the study of international law, where legal principles can provide the normative foundations for strategic (or rational) behavior.[185] Foremost among these is the foundational principle, or metanorm, of pacta sunt servanda, that "promises must be kept," which sets the binding nature of international obligations and ensuing consequences from violating legal commitments.[186] Returning to the "Three Rs" of enforcement, punishment creates various costs that a rational actor would weigh when deciding whether or not to violate an agreement. But the meaning of those costs, and the understanding of obligations by both the actor and audiences, are bound up in the normative underpinnings of international legal commitments. The operation of international law is thus predicated upon, and evokes, a deeper set of moral considerations.

There is a certain irony in claiming that law evokes particular moral values. Perhaps earlier skeptics had a point in their characterization of the "legalist-moralist" worldview, even if they went too far in dismissing it as hopelessly utopian. This also represents a departure, however, from the early positivist legal tradition that sought to separate law from morality.[187] Questioning the supposed disjuncture between law and morality in the international legal order rests on firm precedents from debates over the nature of law more generally. Later developments in legal theory take seriously the role of underlying moral principles for law's operation.[188] Similar sentiments can be seen in the moral underpinnings of international law.[189] Attention to normative considerations, and how these inform more rationalist accounts, continue further when examining one of the other main functions of international law—the ability to shape actual policy preferences.

(Unable to) Change Preferences—What Actors (Do Not) Care About

The first function (or for skeptics, limit) regarding the enforcement of international law primarily deals with behavior—the ability to punish an actor's violations after the fact. A second debated function is whether these rules hold the potential to change the underlying preferences of actors toward particular policies. Of course, preferences for achieving a given objective are not neatly separable from the choice to behave in a particular manner.[190] And an actor holding certain preferences may tend to behave in distinct ways from others not sharing those desires. But the mode through which international law may influence preferences differs from the prior enforcement function in significant respects. For instance, an actor may comply with trade rules, even if it would rather not, out of fear of sanctions that would follow any violation. However, a change in actor's preferences toward trade liberalization may mean it *wants* to comply—perhaps because it has reconceptualized its interests, or views this policy stance as now part of its identity—with material costs or benefits no longer the sole or foremost concern.

Skeptics generally reject the notion that international law can fundamentally shape preferences. Rather, it is states' interests, informed largely by considerations of power, that shape the law. In concluding their study, *The Limits of International Law*, Jack Goldsmith and Eric Posner argue that "the best explanation for when and why states comply with international law is not that states have internalized international law, or have a habit of complying with it, or are drawn by a moral pull, but simply that states act out of self-interest."[191] Their framework sets out a particular understanding of self-interest—actors' preferences are in no way informed by international legal principles.[192] International law is thus epiphenomenal to states' existing power and interests, exerting no independent effect of its own.[193] It is not simply that international laws depend on states' consent; even proponents acknowledge this point.[194] It is also that by strategically self-selecting what sorts of treaties to ratify or what commitments to make, the process of joining or participating in an agreement has no discernable effect on actors' behavior or interests in either the short or long term.[195] Ratifying a trade (or human rights) agreement is going to have no meaningful impact on a country's preferences for engaging in economic liberalization (or repression). A country's policy preferences may evolve, but are unlikely to be due to anything about the treaty itself, instead reflecting changes in the country's material circumstances, such as technological innovations, or the severity of economic and security challenges.

Even the initial choice to negotiate a treaty can be more a function of states changing international laws to suit their preexisting interests rather than vice versa. The push to prohibit submarine warfare during the interwar period was partly motivated by US–British desires to maintain their conventional naval superiority, instead of anything about the inherent immorality of this new weapon of war.[196] Treaties may put forth lofty goals for transforming the worldviews of participating countries, reflected in soaring language in their preambles or pronouncements at ornate signing ceremonies.[197] For skeptics, the idea of law trumping power comes crashing down when faced with actual facts on the ground, which are stubbornly determined by states' existing capabilities and interests. Aron offers a telling rejoinder: "International law can merely ratify the fate of arms and the arbitration of force."[198]

The contention that international law simply follows from existing power and interests can be taken a step further—law can actually be used to *advance* and *amplify* the desires of the powerful.[199] International law may not only serve as a mirror reflecting existing disparities, but becomes transformed into a cudgel the strong can wield for further self-aggrandizement. In place of a "rule of law" system in which the weak seek shelter from the vagaries of the powerful, the international system may more closely resemble the domestic legal regimes in certain authoritarian states characterized by "rule by law" brandished by the strong to serve their own narrow interests.[200] In his treatise *Power Politics* (the first edition of which appeared in 1941 as the Second World War was in full gear), the legal scholar Georg Schwarzenberger commented:

> In a society in which power is the overriding consideration, the primary function of law is to assist in maintaining the supremacy of force and the hierarchies established on the basis of power, and to give to this overriding system the respectability and sanctity law confers.[201]

There is a certain tension in the notion of law boosting the powerful when put next to other (or sometimes the same) skeptics' claims discussed earlier alleging the weakness of international law, or whether it even counts as law properly speaking. If law can be used by the powerful to better advance their interests, then law is "working" even if not in the egalitarian or progressive directions many proponents may favor.

Bringing all of this together, it is important to avoid the "straw man" attached to many realists and similar skeptics that international law does not matter at all.[202] Several scholars who would count themselves as skeptics, including Carr, Morgenthau, or Goldsmith and Posner, still acknowledge that international law is "law" and serves some purposes.[203] What should not be overlooked, however, is that the varieties of detractors share a common assumption on the fundamental limits of international law. To paraphrase from the Melian Dialogue in Thucydides's *The Peloponnesian Wars*, skeptics are closer to Athens's position that might makes right where "the strong do what they can and the weak suffer what they must," instead of the pleas by the more vulnerable Melos that international rules create obligations all actors are expected (and interested) in respecting.[204]

Although the Melians were proved wrong in their attempt to call upon higher principles against a more powerful Athens, in what ways might proponents more generally be vindicated regarding the potential for international law to shape actors' underlying preferences? In other words, how can international law influence not only how actors choose to behave, but also what they may actually *want*?

Compliance with an international agreement may depend on external costs and benefits, or clear signaling of intentions, but also depends on whether actors come to believe it is in their interests—even their very identity—to abide by legal obligations. We do not have to go so far as to say that compliance becomes an end in itself. Rather, obligations created by international law become intimately connected to an actor's conception of its preferences—fulfilling one's obligations comes to be viewed as furthering one's self-interests.[205] In contrast to many rational choice models' emphases on stable and externally determined interests, institutions like international law may be able to endogenously change actors' preferences.[206]

Law's distinctive normative foundations suggest a pathway through which international legal commitments may be well-situated to shape actors' preferences. The particular attributes differentiating legalized rules from other forms of social organization—including generality, constancy, and clarity—can engender a sense of "fidelity" to the law.[207] Legal rules possess a particular legitimacy encouraging a desire to obey, blunting reliance solely on material inducements or punishments.[208] Scaled up, international law is thought to exhibit a similar "compliance pull" based on the legitimacy created by its unique pedigree.[209]

The content of a treaty or similar legal agreements concerns what international actors are called upon to do, whether in matters of human rights, war, commerce, among other issues. Actors may vary in the extent to which they internalize these or other rules as a part of their interests, where for some following the rules eventually achieves a "taken-for-granted" status.[210] Internalization can take place across a variety of rules, from treaty law to more informal norms.[211] Yet the particular form of international law has deeper implications for the prospects that an actor will change its preferences in the direction of the rule's content. By invoking certain normative considerations, international law may have the potential to fundamentally shape what actors view as their preferences, rather than simply reflecting preexisting power and interests as skeptics generally presume.

A picture should now be more clearly emerging about what international law *is* and what it *does*, or at least is intended to do. Despite many calls to the contrary, international law very much meets the criteria for counting as "law," although it may look and operate differently in several respects. Like their domestic counterparts, international legal commitments also fulfill a number of important functions for guiding relations among actors—including enforcement and changing preferences—though there are a great many debates over the extent to which these ambitions are truly met.

Left untouched thus far is *how* international law goes about serving these functions. The next chapter lays out some of the main existing approaches to understanding the operation of international legal commitments before developing a theoretical framework that centers on the role of an often-overlooked set of actors, ordinary members of national publics.

THE OPERATION OF INTERNATIONAL LAW

From Top to Bottom . . . and Back Up Again

For hundreds of years, if not longer, political cartoons have represented a powerful medium for expressing opposing viewpoints across issues large and small, often courting controversy along the way.[1] Despite being composed of one or a handful of images containing few if any words, these cartoons display the qualities of a narrative, connecting viewers together in the telling of a larger story.[2] Like most any story, however, political cartoons are open to multiple interpretations, sometimes creating very different meanings.

With a common desire to needle those in positions of power and authority, political cartoons frequently take on subjects like the justice system or armed conflict. An image I came across several years ago by the Australian illustrator Bruce Petty delves into both themes, but its significance for me has changed drastically over time.[3] The story takes place in a courtroom with the esteemed judges of the International Criminal Court (ICC) declaring on high from the bench: "You are charged with evading world justice—how do you plead?" The apparent defendant in the proceedings is the United States; Petty drew this cartoon during the time of the War on Terror and numerous allegations of US violations of international law.[4] But in the scene, the United States look less a defendant than its own arbiter. Towering above the ICC judges, the US representative does not answer with the customary "guilty" or "not guilty," but rather with a terse "Bigger."

At first glance Petty's cartoon seems to confirm a core takeaway from many skeptics discussed in the previous chapter—that international law is helpless against the mighty. Questions of law and justice appear beside the point when dealing with great powers. Also depicted is a message of *who* are the relevant actors in international legal politics. Only a state and an international organization are named, and the sole actors speaking are representatives of those institutions. The impression left is a common one—that international law takes place among narrow elite circles detached from the larger society.

Yet upon closer inspection and reflection, a contrary message lurks behind this seemingly straightforward plotline. Surrounding the two speakers is a crowd of onlookers taking in the exchange. In particular, in the background is a gallery holding a cluster of faceless, seemingly ordinary individuals. These people are silent, but they may not be mere spectators. Indeed, they may be sitting not in a gallery but instead a jury box—important, even pivotal, actors in their own right.

Conveyed in a few sketches is what this chapter seeks to fill out by considering the question, "just who are the relevant actors in international law?" In the next section, I begin with an overview of existing approaches, which tend to prioritize states and various elites at different levels of analysis. Although diverging in several respects, the public is largely absent or incidental in all these accounts. I instead propose a theoretical framework that incorporates ordinary people into the operation of international law. The balance of the chapter then outlines the main components of an approach that takes seriously the "public" in public international law. Integrating insights from international relations, domestic politics, and constitutional law, I propose the notion of *popular international law*, where international legal commitments are closely connected to domestic arenas in which mass publics play an active and important role in the main functions of the international legal order.

Existing Approaches to the Operation of International Law: From Top to Bottom . . .

Having set out two of the main functions of international law in the previous chapter, how then does international law operate (or, for skeptics, fail) to fulfill them? Who are the actors facilitating the enforcement of agreements, or the shaping of preferences? Or, whose beliefs, expectations, and actions matter?

Proponents' common commitment to the importance of international law hides deeper divisions concerning the actual operation of legal commitments. A variety of arguments have been put forward for *how* international law operates, and especially *who* are the relevant actors. One of the most common ways to classify explanations for international phenomena is by different levels of analysis from the micro up to the macro.[5] Actors can correspondingly be arrayed along these different levels—for instance, from domestic actors, to states, to international organizations.

This is a necessarily stylized model. States vary greatly in their domestic institutions and cultures, but also in material capabilities, with stronger powers likely playing a more outsized role in the development and operation of international law. International organizations likewise differ in their design and resources.[6] Domestic actors cover a wide range of players from elites all the way down to mass publics. Each level is also not hermetically sealed off from the others, with level-specific actors and processes interacting in various ways.[7] Nevertheless, the following sections offer a general sense of the distinguishing features of existing general approaches to understanding the essential actors in the operation of international law.

Horizontal: From State . . . to State

In many respects, horizontal mechanisms connecting state-to-state interactions remain by far the most prominent in the study of international law, and cooperation more generally.[8] Although the definition for international law formulated in the prior chapter allows space for nonstate actors, much legal scholarship shares a similar assumption to many mainstream international relations approaches where legal agreements largely begin and end with states.[9] Other actors may periodically gain notice, but only states are seen as the true subjects of international law with the authority and wherewithal to manage international legal affairs.

Approaches of varying predispositions—whether more rational or sociological—frequently start from the same basis of states as the main units of analysis.[10] Whether referring to "decentralized enforcement" or "reciprocal-entitlement violation," sanctions are seen as enacted principally by states coordinating and responding to the (il)legal actions of other states.[11] Much international law scholarship thus shares with skeptics of legal commitments core state-centric building blocks.[12]

Many proponents view this commonality as a virtue, adopting the same premises as critics to instead demonstrate the promise of international institutions and cooperation.[13] For the enforcement of international agreements, the "Three Rs" of reciprocity, retaliation, and reputation are conceived as primarily taking place at the level of relations among states—updating their beliefs about the reputations of other states, or retaliating against other states' violations.[14] Other actors play at best a secondary role, with the real action around compliance and enforcement occurring among state actors.

Likewise, it is by joining a treaty or similar instrument, and interacting through more legalized channels, that states' preferences may alter over time.

Unlike their more rationalist counterparts, more constructivist-leaning scholars do not take preferences as given, but still tend to emphasize various processes of socialization through interstate pathways.[15] Although differing in their orientations, many rationalist and constructivist approaches overwhelmingly focus on interstate interactions, erecting a "black box" around the environment in which preferences form and compliance decisions are made.[16] Other actors may enter into horizontal accounts, such as by communicating the form and content of laws, but mainly through policymakers and other government representatives serving wider state interests.[17]

Vertical from Above (Sort of): International Organizations

If not between states and their agents, through which other actors may international law operate? Looking first vertically from above, another set of mechanisms locates the operation of international law and related norms primarily at the level of international organizations. The United Nations (UN) occupies a privileged position with the power to (de)legitimize the use of force by states in a way that "contradicts the 'anarchic' premise of much contemporary IR [international relations] scholarship."[18] Perhaps the clearest manifestation of enforcement from above can be seen with international courts. From the World Trade Organization (WTO) to various human rights bodies, through their investigations and rulings international courts are contributing to the "constitutionalization" or "judicialization" of international affairs.[19]

International organizations not only punish past infractions, but also work to shape expectations about appropriate behavior. They can even "teach" other actors to care about new issues, such as the World Bank bringing greater attention to poverty reduction in national development policies.[20] Although differing in structure from these intergovernmental agencies, nongovernmental organizations (NGOs) can play similar functions through transnational advocacy networks to coerce, but also persuade and teach, other actors to follow international rules.[21] International organizations are not always viewed as an unalloyed good. Power and autonomy can lead them to engage in behaviors—bordering on pathological—that harm global governance.[22]

Despite these pronouncements, limits remain in the ability of international organizations to serve as the main agents helping (or hurting) the international legal order, at least for the foreseeable future. Principal-agent problems may loom large in many organizations but should not be overstated.[23] International organizations are ultimately state creations, and states retain a great deal of power to rein them in.[24] Even for exemplars like the European Court of Justice (ECJ), there is a great deal of debate over the court's autonomy and ability to issue rulings at odds with powerful member states.[25] The seemingly unstoppable WTO is similarly subject to state power and interests, made most evident by its dependence on them to mete out any punishment called for in its rulings.[26] WTO limits are perhaps best highlighted by US intransigence under President Donald Trump against appointing new members to the body's appellate panel, hobbling the organization's supposedly formidable dispute resolution system.[27]

International courts are not alone in these weaknesses. Common tactics of enforcement through "outcasting," where material and social costs are imposed upon violators, may frequently be initiated by international organizations, but ultimately given teeth by states.[28] The European Union probably has some of the strongest enforcement tools at its disposal, but its authority is much weaker to nonexistent in areas like security, defense, and fiscal policy, where member governments still wield enormous control.

International organizations may possess many resources, but it is difficult to claim that they are somehow replacing or supplanting state sovereignty. In rare cases, groups of states may go beyond a traditional organization to form a federation or deeper union to enforce obligations or define interests among members.[29] But at this point authority would no longer be "*inter*national"—the newly constituted unit is better viewed as a state proper, whether the federation that became Australia, or the many Swiss cantons' eventual unification. The halting, conflictual experiences in these smaller cases do not bode well for scaling up the present international legal order anytime soon, despite pronouncements that a world state is "inevitable."[30] International organizations have never been the autonomous actors proclaimed by proponents (or decried by detractors), and limits on their abilities as managers of the international legal order are readily apparent.

The operation of international law thus seems firmly entrenched (for good or ill) between states, with international organizations playing a subsidiary role. Yet vertical mechanisms operate not only *above* states, but also potentially from *below*. Research on the coercive and legitimating role of international organizations like the UN have already pointed to an important role for domestic politics and potentially mass publics.[31] Public attitudes also prove important for the legitimacy of international courts.[32] In place of *external* mechanisms—whether vertically from above, or horizontally across states—come calls for greater attention *internally* to domestic politics for the operation of international law, though with many actors and avenues available.[33]

Vertical from Below: Domestic Actors

In diplomatic negotiations, a well-worn adage is that "Domestic politics and international relations are often somehow entangled."[34] Extended to the legal realm,

domestic politics and international law likewise seem intertwined in some fashion. Attention to the domestic is most apparent in what are usually referred to as
"Liberal" approaches to international relations. Capital "L" Liberalism should not
be confused with other "liberal" thinking, such as neoliberal institutionalism and
much of regime theory.[35] Small "l" liberal perspectives take similar starting points
to realist and other mainstream approaches regarding the centrality of states and
interstate interactions, even as they come to different conclusions regarding prospects for cooperation.[36]

Broadly speaking, a capital "L" Liberalism instead assumes: 1) the primacy
of domestic societal actors, both individuals and groups; 2) states and other
political institutions represent segments of these domestic actors (and not necessarily equally), which then reflect national preferences; and 3) the configuration of various states' preferences then determines their respective behavior
and outcomes.[37] Liberal tenets contrast with the "top-down" model of horizontal
interstate or vertical-from-above accounts.[38] Liberalism promotes a "bottom-up"
vision where state–society relations are paramount, opening up new questions
about the internal sources of foreign commitments.[39] No longer solely a "stately"
affair, a host of domestic actors—political, judicial, economic, among others—
are taken seriously as agents, rather than bystanders, in international law.

In the realm of international legal affairs, two tendencies characterize much
of this Liberal-inspired research. First, domestic mechanisms are conceived as
largely (if not entirely) *separate* from more traditional external mechanisms
already discussed. This is especially evident in human rights, where some of the
most innovative domestic-centered theorizing has taken place.[40] Unlike other
issue areas, reciprocity to induce violators to return to compliance with human
rights agreements does not make much sense,[41] while collective action problems
loom large for enforcement through reputation or retaliation. As Louis Henkin
cautions, "The forces that induce compliance with other law . . . do not pertain
equally to the law of human rights."[42]

Some scholars go further, arguing that mainstream scholars' devotion to the
usual story for how international law operates is "largely looking in the wrong
direction: *outward* at interstate relations rather than *inward* at state-society relations" (emphasis in original).[43] To explain compliance with human rights treaties requires departing from the usual "Three Rs" to embrace distinct domestic
enforcement mechanisms, such as agenda-setting on legislation, empowering
national courts, or mobilizing civil society. But a vertical-from-below "alternative mechanism of compliance" may go beyond human rights, and can be seen
in the active role played by domestic actors and processes in many other issues.[44]

Shifting to international law writ large, the distinctiveness of domestic mechanisms is made explicit in this "bottom-up" approach. Citing the importance

of domestic judicial actors, Anne-Marie Slaughter contends that "rule of law enforced by national judiciaries should lead to more 'vertical' enforcement through domestic courts. This mode of enforcement *contrasts with the traditional 'horizontal' mode* involving State responsibility, reciprocity, and countermeasures" (emphasis added).[45] Andrew Moravcsik underlines this separation: "*compliance with many international legal norms does not rely on "horizontal" interstate reciprocity and retaliation, but instead on "vertical" enforcement embedded in domestic politics*" (emphasis in original).[46] Domestic processes thus substitute for international mechanisms, serving in more modest formulations as an additional (yet separate) pathway, while in stronger versions completely supplanting traditional external accounts.

In addition to conceptualizing domestic mechanisms as largely separate, a second tendency is to mostly prioritize certain actors—especially elite voices and choices.[47] In the abstract, Liberalism allows for all sorts of domestic actors, but the resources, connections, and knowledge enjoyed by elites mean they occupy a privileged place in practice. Inis Claude's "Five Cs" of law (Congress, Code, Court, Cop, and Clink) discussed in the previous chapter all concern domestic institutions led by elites holding substantial power and authority compared to the ordinary masses. In H. L. A. Hart's general conception of law, core legal functions are undertaken by "officials," "legislators," "courts," and "experts"—"ordinary citizens" only enter "largely by acquiescence in the results of these official operations."[48]

Hart's views on elites extends to other scholars' treatment of who are the most relevant international legal actors. W. Michael Reisman sees international lawmaking as a complex multilevel process, but one revolving around "communication between elites and politically relevant groups," with ordinary people not party to the latter.[49] Thomas Franck adopts an even more expansive view of the international legal process, but likewise looks to elites as the main actors of interest.[50] Hedley Bull takes a similar tack emphasizing the centrality "of those who are concerned with international law, public and private"—cataloging a variety of elites, but leaving out the public among those "concerned" with legal matters.[51]

Within this overall consensus on the importance of elites, accounts can disagree on which groups to prioritize. Executives have a range of tools at their disposal—from constitutionally granted powers to a vast bureaucratic apparatus—to (refuse to) comply with international agreements.[52] Legislatures can also prove pivotal throughout the negotiation, ratification, and (non)implementation of treaties, where jockeying between constellations of political parties is more pertinent than the "random factor" of the ordinary voters electing them.[53] Turning to the third main branch of government, it is perhaps not surprising that judicial actors figure prominently in many accounts of international law.[54] Beyond any interpretive authority, the technical knowledge seen as necessary for grasping legal intricacies means that when judges are not at the forefront, lawyers (whether inside or outside of government) are not too far behind.[55] It is perhaps apt that the single person most associated with the modern laws of war is the law professor Francis Lieber, author of rules during the American Civil War that became commonly known as the "Lieber Code," and which inspired many later conventions.[56]

Farther afield from the usual channels of power, knowledge and expertise of various stripes are credited for the prominent role played by other nonstate actors. While a robust civil society is often seen as crucial for holding governments accountable to their international commitments, it is often less the grassroots at large than the outsized place of smaller circles of activist leaders.[57] Many accounts stress select "norm entrepreneurs" or "epistemic communities" rather than movements' wider membership.[58] The network of "international law activists," who over the course of the nineteenth century promoted rules prohibiting wartime plunder, was composed not of ordinary folks, but rather "lawyers, diplomats, and scholars" drawn from the upper echelons.[59] Indicatively, the closest competitor to Lieber for originator of the modern laws of war is probably the wealthy (at least initially), well-connected businessman Henri Dunant who helped found the International Committee of the Red Cross (ICRC) and advocated for the first Geneva Convention of 1864.[60] Accounts involving nonstate actors may differ in important ways from those concerning governments or organizations, but share a focus on elites and are often described in similar terms.

Summing up so far, domestic approaches have raised new questions about the operation of international law. Yet there is a tendency to: 1) conceptualize domestic mechanisms as entirely separate from their international counterparts; and 2) view elites as the only actors who really matter. In the remainder of the chapter, I question both assumptions and offer an account that places national publics firmly at the center of the mechanisms traditionally thought to govern some of the main functions of international law.

. . . And Back Up Again: Mass Publics and the Domestic Sources of International Law

In this section, I outline in two parts a theoretical framework that locates national publics in the external operation of international law. In the first part, I interrogate the relationship between domestic and international legal mechanisms. I propose that domestic actors not only influence the operation of legal commitment through distinct *internal* processes, but are also consequential for the effective operation of more traditional *external* mechanisms related to functions like enforcement or shaping preferences. Second, when it comes to *who* are the relevant domestic actors, I propose that mass publics play an overlooked, but important, role in the operation of these international mechanisms. While often dismissed as irrational or irrelevant, ordinary people collectively have the capacity to influence the actions of their own governments, and by extension other governments, in their relations toward international law.

A few important qualifications are in order before moving forward. My argument does not deny that more distinct domestic mechanisms for enforcement or other functions of international law exist. Rather, I advance that in addition to these internally oriented processes, domestic politics and domestic actors also infuse the operation of more conventional horizontal mechanisms. Likewise, I fully acknowledge that leaders, judges, and other elites are powerful actors in international legal politics. What I seek to highlight, however, is the often-neglected place of ordinary people in the operation of international law in the past, present, and likely future. It is in making a theoretical case for the importance of the actual "public" in public international law that the next sections now turn.

The Second Image Re-Reversed: Relationships between Domestic Politics and International Law

There are two general approaches for understanding the relationship between international and domestic politics when it comes to subjects like international law. On the one hand are "second image reversed" perspectives, emphasizing international factors as causes of domestic structures and processes rather than being consequences of the latter.[61] Commonly cited international forces include the distribution of military power across states, or deepening economic integration leading to the "'internationalization' of political economies," which can alter the capabilities and preferences of different domestic groups.[62] Domestic factors may play an intermediating role, but external factors predominate—"over the long run a state's foreign policy cannot transcend the limits and opportunities thrown up by the international environment."[63]

Despite being primarily thought of in terms of security and commercial exchange, ideational factors can exert similar influences.[64] Resting on particular conceptualizations of social ordering, international law fits readily into second image reversed accounts. Part of this can be seen in extensions to new issues, such that "international law has penetrated the once exclusive zone of domestic affairs to regulate the relationship between governments and their own citizens."[65]

Beyond the activities regulated, international laws can reconfigure domestic politics all the way down to the very actors themselves.[66]

On the other hand, "second image" perspectives flip the causal direction, concentrating instead on domestic actors and institutions as the drivers of international outcomes.[67] The "Liberal" approaches to international law discussed in the prior section fall firmly into this realm where everything is initiated at the domestic level.[68] Second image theories have a long pedigree in international relations, from the democratic peace to open economy politics models, with important implications for international legal commitments.[69] What unites second image theorizing is that the causal arrow runs from the bottom up—beginning with the domestic to then scale up to the international.[70]

Second image (reversed) approaches are ideal types—each acknowledges to some extent a role for the other.[71] Two-level games frameworks go further, dispensing with any contrast on the presumption that "it is fruitless to debate whether domestic politics really determine international relations, or the reverse."[72] As appealing as such a synthesis might be, theoretical and practical problems arise when simultaneously allowing for so many moving parts.[73] Even when recognizing a role for both the international and domestic, any approach ultimately must place some theoretical bet on the directional structure across levels—this is especially true for the relationship between international law and domestic politics.[74]

The approach developed here admittedly leans more heavily toward second image "bottom-up" approaches, where domestic actors play an important role in the operation of international legal politics. Yet international dynamics bookend this domestically centered framework in two important ways.

First, the preferences and beliefs of domestic players are not preordained or solely generated internally, but rather influenced to varying degrees by international laws.[75] Just as with military power or economic flows, as a set of ideas international law can shape the strategies and interests of domestic actors. International law provides new information to domestic actors, but a *principled* form that can transform actors' beliefs about right and wrong, what is expected, and what actions should be taken. Existing domestic structures, as well as the predispositions of different domestic actors, can serve as moderators that either amplify or dampen the effects of international law. For instance, more conservative individuals may express greater skepticism toward multilateralism and global rules.[76] Nevertheless, domestic actors are conceived as largely reacting to the presence of international law, where these rules are doing most of the work with domestic factors serving more as subsequent filters. Consistent with second image reversed thinking, international law can thus be seen as more of an "exogenous shock" to national politics, and taken as largely given by most domestic actors, at least in the near term.[77]

Treating an international treaty as exogenous is admittedly a strong assumption. Part of the difficulty in ascertaining the effect of international law is precisely because governments strategically choose which agreements to (refuse to) join.[78] But taking the presence (though not necessarily effectiveness) of an international law as given makes sense for several reasons. While ratification may be a national decision,[79] the negotiation and design of an agreement is often a collective process involving a plethora of actors.[80] Talks leading up to the 1998 Rome Statute establishing the ICC illustrate how the eventual product diverged sharply from the initial desires of powers large and small.[81]

Customary law exemplifies the lack of individual control over international rulemaking, depending heavily on the community of nations.[82] Even for key powerbrokers, circumstances under which a treaty impinges upon their actions may arise well after their country originally joined the agreement. As will be discussed in greater detail in chapter 4, the 1949 Geneva Conventions significantly shaped reactions to policies enacted by President George W. Bush during the War on Terror even though the conventions had been in place for decades before his administration took office.[83] For domestic actors, most will have never taken part in any meaningful way in negotiation or commitment decisions, meaning an agreement can be considered exogenous from their perspective. This assumption is especially plausible for more ordinary actors not drawn from elite circles, but whose subsequent beliefs and actions may significantly affect how those international laws operate.

The second way in which external dynamics enter into this framework is how domestic understandings of, and reactions to, international law percolate back up to the international level, giving force and meaning to these rules. The preferences and actions of domestic actors can have impacts—both direct and indirect—beyond their country's borders, influencing the main functions of international legal commitments.

Attention to domestic politics helps resolve some of the deeper criticisms of international law covered in the prior chapter. We should take seriously skeptics' charge that the absence of higher authority poses formidable challenges to the operation of international law.[84] To be effective, an international agreement should be "self-enforcing," meaning it is in the interests of parties to comply because they achieve greater net gains from following instead of violating its terms.[85] The anarchical system complicates self-enforcement and incentives for states to care about fulfilling their obligations—especially in trying times—hence why traditional horizontal state-to-state mechanisms can feel so feeble.[86]

The diagnosis makes sense, but many skeptics and proponents alike tend to look to fill this authority gap in the domain *above* states through world government or similar international institutional setups, even if they differ over their viability or attraction.[87] Yet, as discussed earlier, verticality flows in two directions—*above* states, as well as *below* them. If the absence of hierarchy internationally represents an impediment to the operation of international law, then the purportedly more hierarchical relations within states through domestic politics presents a potential salve. States may come to weigh more heavily the benefits of following international rules less due to the direct effects of horizontal interactions but rather because domestic actors make them care more about the compliance behavior of both themselves and other countries. States may give shorter shrift to the anarchical international society, but are concerned to differing degrees about reactions from their own domestic societies. The interwar scholar E. H. Carr was on the right track when he observed, "Behind all law there is . . . [a] necessary political background. The ultimate authority of law derives from politics."[88] While Carr assumed global power politics hampered the application of international legal principles, attention to *domestic* politics opens other possibilities.

Of course, the space available will depend in large part on the relative vulnerability of government leaders to domestic actors, where accountability is generally higher in democracies compared to autocracies.[89] And while internal constraints can still vary significantly among autocracies—even leading certain autocrats to behave similarly to democracies in foreign policymaking—their politically relevant domestic audiences are often drawn from much narrower and more elite segments of society.[90] As such, any account emphasizing domestic politics in the operation of international law will be most applicable to democracies, though elected leaders can themselves face more or less restrained internal environments.[91] Nonetheless, the point remains that national processes can matter across a range of domestic institutional contexts, even as the particular channels of influence or local actors involved may differ.

Because states generally listen more closely to their domestic constituents, they also need to be mindful of the attitudes toward international law held by those same actors. If domestic actors desire to observe compliance with international agreements, then their preferences may shape the views of their governments as well. Capital "L" Liberal approaches are partially correct when they declare, "As a practical matter, enforcement of nearly all international norms [and laws] *remains* at home" (emphasis added).[92] The operation of international law need not be limited to domestic actors' own backyards, but can scale up to shape dynamics internationally as well. Amending the previous statement suggests instead the following: "enforcement of nearly all international norms [and laws] *starts* at home." Some of the main functions of international law—enforcement or shaping preferences—may ultimately play out *horizontally* among states, but remain embedded in important *domestic* foundations.

Incorporating these two international bookends into a domestically centered theory means that international law can reach down to shape the preferences, beliefs, and actions of domestic actors, but these same actors in turn can reach back up to affect how international law is exercised externally. This account does not presuppose some global civil society full of cosmopolitan individuals untethered from national boundaries.[93] Domestic actors and forces may mostly be confined domestically, but their preferences, beliefs, and actions can nonetheless influence their own governments alongside other foreign actors. International law operates horizontally through functions like reputation or the spread of new ideas and values, but these dynamics are underpinned by domestic politics. The approach developed here is heavily "Liberal" in the sense of endowing agency to domestic actors. Yet by connecting domestic actors to international relations both in the formation of their own beliefs and preferences, and especially in how those beliefs then extend back up beyond their immediate country, this approach is better conceived as a *horizontally informed Liberal* theory of international law. Or what I propose as a *second image re-reversed* approach linking international legal forces to domestic politics (as in the second image reversed), which in turn shape how those same laws operate in the international realm (the re-reversal of the second image).

Where does the state—often seen as the primary personality of inter*national* law—fit into this horizontally informed Liberal account? Like other Liberal approaches, the state does not disappear, and continues to be central to the operation of international law. But the state is conceptualized less as an autonomous actor, and more a representative institution of segments of domestic society.[94] Many accounts of international law likewise view the state as "a dynamic aggregator of individual, group, and coalition preferences."[95] Even skeptics who skew toward more statist perspectives, acknowledge that in the end, "States are vehicles through which citizens pursue their goals."[96]

More pluralist understandings of the state lead to different conclusions about where "sovereignty" ultimately resides. States are usually considered the sole holders of sovereignty—the apex within their own domestic societies, while situated among like autonomous political units in the interstate system.[97] Described as "Janus-faced," the state sits at the nexus of these two political spheres—"In short, the state is the gatekeeper between intrasocietal and extrasocietal flows of action."[98]

But what is the nature of this state-as-gatekeeper? If "intrasocietal" flows are to be taken seriously, and greater agency accorded to domestic actors, then it is with those actors rather than the state where sovereignty really rests. This should not necessarily be a controversial claim. James Madison, a key architect of the US Constitution and often associated with countermajoritarian fears of the *demos* and the need for strong state institutions, wrote, "Public opinion sets bounds to every government, and is the real sovereign in every free one."[99] If domestic actors are truly sovereign with the state functioning more as a vessel for their beliefs and interests, then it is these same actors who represent a sort of "collective Janus," looking both within to their own national society and without to international society.

The prominence of domestic actors, relative to the corporate body of the state, can be seen in various ways in international law's operation. While leaning toward state-centric views of international society, Bull acknowledges the place of nonstate actors as legal *subjects*—"that is to say, that they are not merely affected by the rules of international law but have duties and rights conferred upon them by those rules."[100] These rights and duties are not minor, but go to the core functions of international law. When it comes to the enforcement of international rules, Hans Kelsen notes that it falls not to states so much as "the individual who carries out the sanction act[ing] as an organ of the community constituted by the legal order."[101]

In more contemporary times, President Barack Obama recognized that it was not just states who were necessary for the effective operation of international law. In the aftermath of Russia's annexation of the Crimean Peninsula from Ukraine in 2014, he remarked, "we also know those rules are not self-executing. They depend on people and nations of goodwill continually affirming them."[102] Similar sentiments were heard a decade later by President Joe Biden describing the collective resistance of many governments and their publics to Russia's full-scale invasion of Ukraine.[103] Domestic actors are relevant to the very process of defining what counts as an international law. Returning to customary law, alongside the material fact of consistent practice is the need for *opinio juris* ("opinion of law") to prevail where a sufficient number of governments believe they are legally obligated to follow the rule.[104] Yet if governments' beliefs are fundamentally shaped by the vox populi ("voice of the people"), then domestic actors hold considerable sway over custom as well.[105]

Instead of confined to states and their official agents, international law reveals certain underlying democratizing impulses—not in the sense of formal majoritarian voting, but rather opening international legal rules to a wider set of actors. As one reflection of this character, "International law might be seen, not as a mechanism for ensuring the cooperation of sovereigns, but the cooperation of political communities organised as sovereign states."[106] In this light, international law serves as an institution linking together national communities within a larger international society. Domestic actors can exert influence over their own governments through internal public authority, but also externally over other governments through a broader international public authority.[107] By way of continuing interactions between the domestic and international levels, the international legal order unlocks a route for the influence of domestic actors on the main functions of international law, which have conventionally been confined to horizontal state-to-state relations. International legal commitments instead provide "the standard instrument for giving foreigners a voice in national law-making" in other countries.[108]

Pulling all this together presents a picture of international law where states are still doing a lot of work, but are shaped by the preferences, beliefs, and actions of domestic actors who are themselves informed by international legal principles. It is less states who are sovereign, but rather various national groupings of domestic actors who then feed into a broader collective "quasi-sovereign" that we commonly refer to as the international community. Or in encapsulating the philosopher Jean-Jacques Rousseau's conception of this quasi-sovereign: "the general will of the *world's* peoples, mediated through the decision-making procedure of each state as it participates in the formation of international legal rules" (emphasis in original).[109]

According to this framework, domestic politics remain intimately connected to the international level, where domestic actors are influenced by external legal factors, but in turn exert influence over the external operation of international law. What is left open is *which* domestic actors are central to how these processes play out. Various references have been made above to "the people" in particular. In the following section, I contend it is those ordinary actors most often neglected in many international legal accounts—mass publics—who should be accorded greater attention.

Putting the "Public" in Public International Law

A second tendency in much existing theorizing on domestic actors and international law is to prioritize elite voices. When the public is mentioned, it is often an afterthought to the long list of those who really matter—government officials, legislators, parties, interest groups, and the like.[110] But the vox populi in my account is not some abstract collective will given meaning by elites, but rather embodies in a literal sense the beliefs and actions of ordinary people.[111]

Locating the people in the operation of international law is a controversial analytical choice, but one shared by other work that privileges the role of ordinary people in world politics.[112] Yet this contention must confront a long line of research that questions both the disposition and ability of mass publics to influence foreign policy. Limits may be especially stark for international law given its technicalities and the many steps interposed between public opinion and policymaking. Criticism generally falls into two main strands: 1) the nature of public opinion and whether the public holds structured and coherent attitudes about issues like international law; and 2) influence and whether the public has channels through which it can actually express its attitudes and affect policy. The strands are related in certain respects, but highlight two prerequisites for any actor to meaningfully impact policy—the ability to form reasoned opinions and interests in the first place, and the ability to pursue those interests in the second. Examining these two dimensions in reverse order, I make the case that publics have both the cognitive capacity to understand and think about international law, and the institutional ability to influence policy across many contexts.

INFLUENCE OF PUBLIC OPINION

Starting with the basic capacity to sway policy, the resources and avenues available to ordinary people might seem quite limited. This includes democracies where "power to the people" is a frequently invoked slogan, but one that for many does not seem to be exercised in practice. Executives like the US president have numerous tools at their disposal and can distance themselves from other domestic actors' reach, though their room for maneuver varies significantly by issue area and policy instrument.[113] Across democratic systems, legislators frequently enjoy significant incumbency and other institutional advantages that can lessen the need to follow constituents' interests, especially on international affairs. Politics is often said to "stop at the water's edge," with domestic factors like partisan control, electoral cycles, and public sentiment having little impact.[114]

Even where politics may flow beyond national borders, attention frequently focuses on domestic elites. Compared to the rich and well-connected, who readily access the revolving door between government and industry, the public's voice may be too fragmented or weak to be heard.[115] Domestic structures and coalition building among political elites across many democracies can weaken the ability of public opinion to shape foreign policy.[116] Whether due to low policy salience or institutional disadvantages, the public would seem to have little ability to hold leaders accountable. What this means is that politicians may "have great freedom in taking substantive positions on foreign policy issues" at odds with their constituents' wishes.[117]

Accounts of elite classes controlling the levers of power—lording it over a helpless and hapless public—may be intuitively compelling. Yet the masses are not nearly so powerless. There are four main reasons why we should not immediately discard the role of the public on foreign policy matters, including international law.

First, if the past is any guide, leaders and other elites often talk and act *as if* they take seriously the public's opinions.[118] In the pivotal 1860 US presidential election, then-candidate Abraham Lincoln declared during a debate that "with public sentiment on its side, everything succeeds; with public sentiment against it, nothing succeeds."[119] Napoleon Bonaparte, not exactly known for his democratic credentials, acknowledged that for all rulers "Power is founded upon opinion."[120]

It may be tempting to dismiss these or similar musings as paying lip service to what audiences wanted to hear, hiding the speaker's truer dismissive feelings. Various historical episodes nonetheless suggest leaders take seriously the reactions of publics in both word and deed. In the lead-up to the 1990–91 Persian Gulf War, the US president George H. W. Bush was especially concerned about public reactions at home and abroad when seeking to build a multilateral coalition through the United Nations Security Council to push the Iraqi dictator Saddam Hussein's forces out of neighboring Kuwait.[121]

The public's influence is further evident outside of dramatic events like war. A review of the growing literature on various democratic governments' responsiveness to their citizens concludes that on the whole public officials closely follow mass opinion, including on foreign policy.[122] Cross-national evidence confirms government officials are quite sensitive to the public's foreign policy priorities.[123] Publics need not actively express (dis)pleasure to have an impact; even a "silent" public can speak loudly, with leaders worried about "latent" opinion and calibrating their actions in anticipation of likely popular reactions.[124]

In the end, the impact of the public relative to other actors probably falls somewhere between all-powerful and irrelevant. Comparing the role of various domestic factors across a number of US foreign policy episodes, one prominent study reckoned public opinion was "an important factor in decision making, but by no means the most important single factor."[125] Proclaiming the public to be the *only* significant actor is unnecessary for our more modest position that the public remains *a* relevant actor even among more well-placed elites.

A second more direct indicator is the extremes to which leaders of various stripes have taken to find out about mass sentiment, most evident in the practice of polling. The US president Franklin Roosevelt was one of the first leaders to extensively use polls to inform his decisions.[126] George Gallup, an originator of modern polling methods, argued one of the main reasons for systematically measuring public opinion was so that leaders could (and would) respond to popular views.[127]

Attention to polling by executives is not necessarily indicative of a government beholden to the public. Rather, conducting and analyzing polls may simply provide leaders the means to more effectively manipulate mass sentiment for their own benefit.[128] As will be detailed further below on the nature of public opinion, however, mass attitudes as not always so pliable. Polls may allow politicians to figure out how to best "craft" their arguments for wider appeal, but elites still operate within boundaries set by mass preferences.[129] With their growing number and coverage, polls have also become a channel for citizens to obtain important information on domestic and foreign policies.[130] As such, leaders come to care a great deal about polling on various issues in ways that are significantly beyond their control.

Worries over polling can become internalized into government practices. The Weinberger Doctrine, named for Ronald Reagan's secretary of defense Caspar Weinberger, outlined one of his six criteria for using US military force abroad: "there must be some reasonable assurance we will have the support of the American people."[131] Later chairman of the Joint Chiefs of Staff, Colin Powell espoused a similarly surnamed doctrine including additional criteria, but agreed "we should have a purpose that our people understand and support."[132] Outside the United States, a 1958 British military manual on the laws of war shared this view, stressing "no State can afford to be wholly regardless of public and world opinion."[133] Public opinion appears to have some effect on government behavior, or at least leads officials to take steps to fit their behavior to mass sentiment.

Third, polls taking the nation's pulse are all well and good, but for many what really matters are actions holding leaders accountable, where elections or the risk of removal from office represent the ultimate test. A common caution against survey evidence on international law is that it is not always clear how public preferences scale up to electoral pressures.[134] Conventional wisdom holds that elections are driven primarily by domestic politics and the economy with little room for foreign issues like international law.[135] However, a study of four decades of US presidential campaigns found that candidates devoted significant time and energy to foreign policy; citizens likewise ranked these issues high for their vote choices.[136] The salience of foreign affairs was not just a Cold War phenomenon; more recent surveys show the public consistently ranks issues like terrorism and national security (each with important legal implications), equal to or higher than many domestic matters.[137] Cross-national experimental evidence confirms a more direct causal link, where voters' evaluations of candidates' foreign policy stances had effects on par or greater than economic platforms or personal attributes.[138]

The fact we do not always see voters punishing leaders for their foreign policy choices is not necessarily evidence for the absence of threats from the ballot box. Politicians may adjust their behavior in anticipation of potential wrath from voters in the next election.[139] Even nonevents, or less serious violations, can illustrate leaders taking into account public attitudes. One of the Reagan administration's most notable foreign adventures was supporting rebel "Contras" and mining harbors against the Sandinista regime in Nicaragua. Despite concerted appeals by the White House, support among the US public was not forthcoming. The episode also raised a number of international legal issues, with the International Court of Justice (ICJ) ruling US policies violated several laws of war.[140] On the one hand, circumstances surrounding the episode show that Reagan was willing to take controversial actions. On the other hand, the lack of public support arguably deterred him from engaging in even more egregious violations.[141] Electoral threats can thus influence both the actions, but also inactions, of leaders with respect to international law.

Fourth, the Nicaragua case shows that publics can constrain leaders throughout their tenure, not just electorally. Winning campaigns is a requisite, but ultimately leaders want to govern, and a large body of work suggests they need public support to do so. Formal constitutional powers are important, but an equal if not greater source of authority comes from their "prestige" (or "public standing") among the masses.[142] Prestige is an attractive yet hazy concept to rest leaders' influence upon. A more apt term, especially relevant to international law, concerns leaders' "credibility" in the eyes of the public, providing them the trust and discretion to rule effectively.[143]

Credibility depends heavily on the public, which in turn informs the prospects for a leader to gain legislative support for their programs and initiatives. A senior congressional aide from Clinton's time in office summed up the stakes— "It's an absolute rule up here: popular Presidents get what they want; unpopular ones don't."[144] Studies confirm that US presidential popularity is associated with increased influence over Congress in attaining leaders' preferred legislation.[145] V. O. Key's even earlier image of a government constantly linked to its public seems fitting.[146] Instead of caring about the public only when elections loom, governments appear regularly constrained in seeking "contemporary consent."[147] One review of decades of scholarship concludes that "a mounting body of evidence suggests that the foreign policies of American presidents—and democratic leaders more generally—have been influenced by their understanding of the public's foreign policy views."[148]

One important qualification on the public's powers discussed so far is that they may operate with the greatest force in democracies. And even among democratic polities, domestic structures and social forces mean that not all publics will be equally influential across all democracies at all times.[149] We should be doubly tentative about the role of publics in autocracies, where formal and informal channels between the masses and those in power are even more tenuous.

More speculative for the reach of the theoretical framework being proposed here, some initial thoughts can be offered on the potential place of publics in autocratic policymaking. Precise mechanisms of accountability may differ, but publics have proven influential in autocracies ranging from China to Eastern Europe to the Middle East.[150] Like their democratic counterparts, many autocratic leaders act *as if* they are beholden to their publics.[151] Significant resources are devoted to monitoring public sentiment (though not necessarily through traditional polling), while efforts to censor content are actually suggestive of how much autocratic regimes worry over public reactions.[152] Writing over two centuries ago, the philosopher David Hume contended one element uniting democratic and despotic regimes was that authority ultimately rests with the governed.[153] Even those drawing firmer distinctions between democracies and autocracies point out that accountability to domestic audiences is a mainstay for both.[154] Looking specifically at international law, the potential for treaties to spur mass mobilization may be *greatest* in those regimes with at least some autocratic characteristics.[155]

Our focus will still mostly center on democracies as the main locus for investigating mass politics and international legal affairs. Nevertheless, it is incumbent upon us to entertain the possibility that the public may be an influential actor in its own right across a variety of political environments and should be granted its due attention.

NATURE OF PUBLIC OPINION

A second strand critical of the public shifts focus from material resources or institutional capacities, and instead disputes the cognitive faculties of the masses. What has become widely known as the Almond-Lippmann consensus (so named after its two most prominent advocates) answers the question of whether public opinion can be considered consistent or coherent with a resounding "No." Public opinion is seen by its nature as volatile, prone to wild swings incommensurate with actual facts on the ground. Gabriel Almond charged that the public's foreign policy stances form less an opinion than "one of mood, and mood is essentially an unstable phenomenon."[156] A "moody" foreign policy would not bode well for international legal commitments, which are predicated upon stable expectations of compliance and consequences for violations. The foundational principle of pacta sunt servanda would be moot if faced with public vacillations; perhaps better rewritten with the caveat pacta sunt servanda *in potentia* ("promises must *potentially* be kept"), a shakier basis for an international legal system.

Beyond their changeability, a further critique by Walter Lippmann is the lack of any coherence in public sentiments.[157] For Almond as well, a symptom of the public's "mood" is that "foreign policy attitudes of most Americans lack intellectual structure and factual content"[158]—a tendency that could apply equally to citizens from a range of other countries. In a seminal study, Philip Converse found no underlying structure to explain patterns of public support across different issues or time periods, later going so far as to describe the public's views as "non-attitudes."[159]

Volatility and weak structure are thought to be made worse by low levels of political knowledge and the inability for nuanced understanding of the complexities of international affairs among "inattentive" publics.[160] Greater civic education might help at the margins, but the perceived fundamental flaw is that public opinion is driven by emotion rather than reason to its own and the country's detriment.

As an important aside, these discussions about the nature of opinion stand in some tension with the first stream of criticisms outlined in the prior section questioning the public's political impact. Scholars in this second strand worried about the weak structure of public opinion because they recognized the *power* of the masses. Lippmann generally feared the *over*responsiveness of governments to deficient citizens' wishes—"destructively wrong at the critical junctures" when a steady hand was needed most.[161] Hans Morgenthau's realist thinking counseled leaders to carefully shield themselves from their publics, since "the need to marshal popular emotions to the support of foreign policy cannot fail to impair the rationality of foreign policy itself."[162]

The focus on elites in many domestic theories of foreign policy and international law also appears more sensible in light of the public's alleged shortcomings. Worries that the masses are unfit, and consequently need "enlightened" members of the privileged classes to represent the true interests of "the people," goes at least as far back as Aristotle's call for aristocratic republics.[163] In the US tradition, writing under the pseudonym "Publius" in *Federalist* 49, Madison warned against vesting too much authority in the people, where "The PASSIONS, therefore, not the REASON, of the public would sit in judgment." Flavors of doubt toward the "folk theory" of an informed and engaged citizenry endure, evident in various contemporary proposals to limit the influence of the masses in domestic and international political spheres.[164]

What can possibly be the reply to such damning accusations against the thinking of ordinary people, especially when compared to erudite and tempered elites? Each claim on the deficiencies of public opinion can be countered in ways revealing the merits of the masses. First, a growing body of work suggests that mass publics are far less volatile in their beliefs, including on foreign policy. An examination of surveys from the same post–World War II period as Almond's pathbreaking study found "remarkable stability" in the US public's "moods," and strong internationalist support for an active role in foreign affairs.[165] Covering a longer time period and over 6,000 survey items, later work reached similar conclusions—a steadiness in foreign policy preferences such that "[t]he notion of a capricious public is a myth."[166] When opinion does change, it is due less to wild mood swings than sound reactions by a "pretty prudent" public to new circumstances.[167]

Second, alongside this general stability, the ordering of preferences is more coherent than previously thought. Studies using finer-grained and more sophisticated measures show a structured set of foreign policy preferences arrayed along distinct dimensions.[168] This is not to suggest all members of the public share the same beliefs; a large body of work seeks to uncover sources of variation in attitudes among different segments of society.[169] But what it does mean is that those who hold certain values—for instance, more or less internationalist—tend to react in systematic (not haphazard) ways toward different foreign policies.[170]

Third, more stable and structured attitudes do not necessarily presuppose the public always possesses high levels of political knowledge—one area of possible agreement with the Almond-Lippmann consensus, though with less clear-cut implications.[171] People can be thought of as "cognitive misers" who deal with their mental and intellectual limits in a complex world by relying on cues alongside other values and experience.[172] Employing cognitive shortcuts, or heuristics, individuals focus on key elements to simplify otherwise complicated situations to guide their choices.[173] Given the values imbued in international law, legalized commitments can be seen as potentially useful heuristics, signaling principled information and activating beliefs that lead citizens to respond in certain ways.[174]

Fourth, touching on heuristics raises the specter of what is often taken to be the most powerful information shortcut—cues from elites. Through their authority and privileged positions, frames spread by elites are commonly thought to play a crucial (even decisive) role in affecting public opinion, even supplanting actual facts on the ground.[175] Messaging from various elites has been argued to shape public perceptions of the legitimacy of international organizations.[176] The epitome is with the elite among elites—where political leaders can use the "bully pulpit" to mold the public to suit their own ends.[177] Instead of beholden to the public, "In reality, they [leaders] treat public opinion as a movable object, not as a fixed threat."[178]

The literature on opinion formation is vast, and settling debates over the role of elites is not possible here. Yet it is important to note that even some of its foremost proponents acknowledge limits in elites' influence over the public.[179] Bullying does not always readily come from the pulpit, as persuasive attempts by the White House (or likeminded heads of state in other countries) often fall on "deaf ears," with leaders just as often following as leading public sentiment.[180] This is equally the case in international law, where elites just as often take their cues *from* the public, while their attempts at counter-messaging can prove ineffective in moving mass opinion.[181]

Ordinary people have also shown a capacity to form judgments in ways *superior* to those of coteries of elites.[182] The biases, even irrationality, of individual

members of society do not necessarily prevent larger groups from reach rational decisions. This "wisdom of the crowds" is supported by a wealth of evidence, where collective rationality aggregates and overcomes personal biases to
reach better decisions than individuals or small groups acting alone, including
experts.[183] Earlier discussion of critics' portrayal of publics as "emotional" should
also not automatically be taken as a liability. Work from cognitive psychology
shows that emotions are actually a prerequisite for models of rational choice.[184]
The emotional and moral reasoning frequently drawn upon by ordinary people
often leads to better overall decisions compared to narrower specialized technical
knowledge employed by many elites, especially on legal matters.[185]

In sum, there are firm grounds to believe that publics possess both the capacity to form reasoned opinions, and the influence to have those opinions heard.
Nothing about a reasoned, influential public, however, should lead to presum-
ing that ordinary individuals inherently favor international law. Some or many
members of the public may, in fact, be quite comfortable with a "folk realism"
worldview when it comes to international law or similar matters.[186] A significant
gap is also thought to exist between publics and elites in the related area of international organizations.[187] The public may thus have an impact on the operation
of international law, just not a constructive one.

Proposing the public is important to the international legal order remains a
tall order. Up to this point, incorporating various insights from work in the fields
of international relations, domestic politics, and political behavior offers a rough
outline of the disposition and capabilities of ordinary people vis-à-vis international legal commitments. Greater confidence may be had by reflecting on the
relationship of citizens to related legal matters, which provide closer parallels to
the operation of international law. Such seeds of support might be gleaned from
the public's role in an equally important legal sphere where ordinary actors have
also been discounted for a long time—constitutional law. Looking at the operation of constitutional law, in turn, offers lessons for its international counterpart,
and the importance of the public in legal systems writ large.

Making a Constitutional Case Out of It: From Popular Constitutionalism to Popular International Law

What can constitutional law tell us about international law, particularly regarding
the role of the public? The answer I put forward rests on a series of four logically
connected propositions. First, that constitutional law is actually remarkably similar in structure to international law. Second, that the lines between the two bodies of

law are not neatly divided, but rather blur together with international laws incorporated into many national constitutions, and vice versa. Third, drawing from scholarship on *popular constitutionalism* and related work, the ordinary public matters for the operation of national constitutions. Rather than the supremacy of elites, it is "the people themselves" whose choices are crucial for understanding the power of constitutions in shaping the preferences, beliefs, and behavior of their governments and other domestic actors.[188] Fourth and finally, if the third proposition is true that the public matters for constitutional law, then it follows from the first two claims that national publics also likely matter for the operation of international law. The ways that ordinary people matter may differ in certain respects for constitutional versus international law. But the existence of an active and influential public points to a corresponding *popular international law* operating in the international legal sphere.

The popular international law proposed here is not the first attempt to link theories of constitutional and international law, and the ways in which each can inform our understanding of the other.[189] Indeed, some of the most vociferous *critics* of international law rely on similar reasoning when making the exact opposite case alleging the fundamental weakness of legal orders. There is a discernable overlap in the cast of characters proposing that just as international law does not constrain states,[190] constitutional law does not constrain executives.[191] The following passage from the legal scholar Jens Ohlin captures this symmetry:

> These two arguments are very similar. Indeed, the arguments are similar because at their heart, they have the *same* structure. The international law argument is *external* and concludes that state interactions are mostly governed by rational self-interest—not law. The bigger constraint is not law but power and diplomacy. The constitutional law argument is *internal* and concludes that disputes between Congress [or other branches] and the president are governed by rational self-interest; again the bigger constraint is not law but power politics [emphasis in original].[192]

I agree with these legal skeptics that certain underlying similarities exist between constitutional and international law. I arrive at starkly different conclusions, however, about the influence of each legal order and the role played by the public. Let us look at each proposition in turn.

Structural Similarities between Constitutional and International Law

At first sight, constitutions could not appear more different from international law. According to the domestic analogy discussed in chapter 1, national and other municipal laws are often viewed as wholly distinct and, for some, the only "real law."[193] A country's constitution sits at the apex of a domestic legal pyramid, the archetype of law properly defined. The Supremacy Clause (Article VI, Clause 2) declares the US Constitution "shall be the supreme Law of the Land."[194] Varying greatly across countries in their content, design, and longevity, one attribute generally shared is the primacy of constitutional provisions over other domestic laws.[195]

Upon closer inspection, however, the structure of constitutional law bears some uncanny resemblances to international law. Take the key criterion espoused by many jurists of the need for a higher sovereign authority to enforce the rules. In an anarchical system, international law does not meet this standard. But does constitutional law either? In the Supreme Court in the United States, the Federal Constitutional Court (FCC) in Germany, and high courts in other countries, these judicial bodies are the presumed guardians of their respective constitutions, yet their formal enforcement powers are actually quite limited.[196] This frailty is less obvious for cases concerning private litigants, or political subunits like US states or Canadian provinces, where the federal government has the coercive capacity to ensure parties adhere to court rulings. But some of the most controversial cases in the United States have involved the executive as the defendant, or with federal laws at stake: take the internment of Japanese Americans during the Second World War, abortion rights, presidents withholding evidence from criminal trials, or detainee treatment in the War on Terror.[197] When the US Supreme Court rules against the federal government or its officials (or the FCC against the German federal government), it is those same sovereign actors who are supposed to enforce the ruling—a daunting proposition for a legal order predicated upon sovereign enforcement.[198] Even court orders involving subnational actors depend on the executive to be carried out, which is far from automatic. In response to an early nineteenth century ruling that the state of Georgia must release several convicted missionaries, President Andrew Jackson reportedly retorted, "John Marshall [the US chief justice] has made his decision; now let him enforce it!"[199]

The "Law of the Land" thus appears to face the same enforcement problems decried by so many of international law's detractors. The legal scholar John Austin was at least consistent when he put constitutions into the same category as their international siblings—not law, but merely "positive morality" lacking any *legal* constraint upon sovereigns.[200] While still allowing a legal descriptor, constitutional and international law are sometimes classified together as "public laws," distinguished from "ordinary" or "private" laws governed by sovereign coercion.[201] As one legal scholar concludes, "the structural differences between domestic and international public law generally are differences of degree, not kind."[202]

It is precisely their structural similarity that leads some skeptics to question the relevance of both international *and* constitutional law.[203] To be sovereign for some means the state is unconstrained by law domestically, and likewise unfettered by legal obligations internationally.[204] Concerns over constitutional laws being "parchment barriers against the encroaching spirit of power" go at least as far back as Madison's warnings in *Federalist* 48. A number of empirical studies seem to confirm constitutional provisions alone are ineffective in constraining state behavior.[205]

Yet other work suggests constitutions play a greater role in shaping the conduct of governments and their citizens, though with some important qualifications.[206] Part of the answer for how constitutions can have these effects without sovereign authority mirrors our earlier discussion of how international law can operate in the absence of a world sovereign. A system of decentralized enforcement at the international level parallels in many ways the "checks and balances" by "distinct and separate departments" that Madison and other Federalists saw as crucial for giving force to the Constitution's parchment barriers.[207] Actors can also comply for reasons other than fear of punishment in ways that overlap in both domestic and international rules.[208] A sense of obligation to the law (constitutional or treaty) is not mutually exclusive from self-interest, shaping actors' expectations and preferences in substantial ways.[209] Recognizing structural commonalities between constitutional and international law does not mean accepting their inherent weakness, but rather allows us to be aware of a common set of functions through which *both* public legal orders operate, including enforcement and changing preferences.[210]

Substantive Ties between Constitutional and International Law

Besides structural kinship, the *content* of constitutional and international laws is intimately linked. As the constitutional scholar Mark Graber notes, "The Constitution shapes and is shaped by foreign affairs as well as by domestic politics."[211] At the most elementary level, for many countries international law is directly incorporated into their national constitutions. The Supremacy Clause in Article VI deems the US Constitution to be the "supreme Law of the Land," yet includes "all Treaties made, or which shall be made" as supreme as well. When judges, legislators, and the president are called upon to uphold the Constitution, international laws are by extension included in that list.[212]

The United States is not alone in incorporating international law into domestic legal doctrine. Article 25 of Germany's Basic Law states: "The general rules of international law shall be an integral part of federal law. They shall take precedence over the laws and directly create rights and duties for the inhabitants of the federal territory." Some constitutions lack explicit reference to international law (e.g., Switzerland, the Netherlands, and Belgium), yet jurisprudence points to international legal rules still taking effect. Written and unwritten traditions across a number of countries recognize international law as "part of the law of the land."[213] One prominent survey of domestic legal doctrines concludes that "it would be difficult to discover a municipal law system which did not utilise international law rules as the norms of decision."[214]

Returning to the US context, various cases seem to confirm the place of international law in the Constitution. When discussing the power of treaties to establish new constitutional obligations (even those not necessarily possible through purely domestic channels), Chief Justice Oliver Wendell Holmes in *Missouri v. Holland* (1920) affirmed that "acts of Congress are the supreme law of the land when made in pursuance of the Constitution, while treaties are declared to be so when made under the authority of the United States." Holmes's words evoked those of fellow Chief Justice Marshall from a century earlier, "Our constitution declares a treaty to be the law of the land."[215]

Although Article VI in the US Constitution only directly mentions treaties, customary laws are also often incorporated. Returning to *The Paquete Habana* (1900), the Supreme Court ruled the US seizure of Spanish fishing vessels in the run-up to the Spanish-American War violated customary international rules prohibiting the practice. By breaching customary rules, US ships had also violated US law even though no pertinent domestic statutes were on the books. In the decision, Justice Horace Gray declared more generally that "International law is part of our law."[216]

Some critics question the domestic status of international law relative to the Constitution.[217] Even those more amenable toward a place for international law domestically generally agree that the Constitution remains paramount, especially in instances of "dissonance" between the two sets of commitments.[218]

Albeit not always on par with the Constitution, treaties and customs can be important not just as a separate source of law, but for better understanding the very "domestic" obligations within constitutional legal orders. By design, constitutions conjure broad principles, offering a roadmap but leaving specifics to circumstances as they arise. Much of the debate among courts and political actors is less about how constitutional rules should be applied, but more over what those rules actually entail. It is on this point that international law and laws from other countries have played a growing interpretative role for understanding the meaning of particular constitutional rules.[219]

In practice, the lines between constitutional and international laws are fuzzy both in terms of the status of each body of law in a given country, but also their influence over one another. Provisions from national constitutions like the US

Bill of Rights have served to inspire parts of human rights treaties, such as the 1966 International Covenant on Civil and Political Rights. Rights espoused in this and other international agreements have likewise often percolated downward into national constitutions.[220] Constitutions no doubt continue to differ in their particular content and arrangements concerning the relative place of international laws within domestic legal systems.[221] Despite these distinctions, a fundamental connection remains in both structure and substance between constitutional and international law.

Popular Constitutionalism: The Public and the Operation of Constitutional Commitments

One of the most enduring and contentious questions in constitutional theory and practice concerns which actors are central to a constitution's operation. Or, as one review asks, "Who is authorized to say what the Constitution means?"[222] Such debates are not unique to the United States,[223] but have in many ways been fiercest and extended in the US context. Differing over which elite actor is paramount, a long tradition agrees the location of constitutional authority resides in one or more of the main government institutions—judicial, legislative, or executive.[224] Drawing on more recent legal theorizing as well as constitutional history, popular constitutionalism takes a contrarian stand, declaring the courts (and other branches) should "have no normative priority in the conversation" about the Constitution.[225] Although most space in the US founding document is taken up outlining the powers of the various branches of government, popular constitutionalists point to the opening words in the preamble—that "We the People" are key.

The phrase "We the People" has been invoked for all manner of purposes. For popular constitutionalism, it is not "the People" as some mythical abstraction of the popular will to be represented by leaders. Rather, "the people" is understood to refer to actual members of the populace, agents in the Constitution's operation.[226] Sometimes canonized (other times reviled) as the "Founding Father" of popular constitutionalism,[227] the legal scholar Larry Kramer offers not only a historical account of ordinary people's role in the development of the US Constitution, but also a normative case for public participation in constitutional affairs due to the "superior authority of 'the people themselves,' conceived as a collective body capable of independent expression and action."[228] The "wisdom of the crowds" referenced earlier may accordingly apply not only to political matters, but so too legal questions.

Rather than a single unified theory, popular constitutionalism comes in many flavors. But what ties these threads together is an emphasis on the role of ordinary people in constitutional affairs.[229] Kramer distills its essence: "basically it's the idea that final authority to control the interpretation and implementation of constitutional law resides at all times in the community in an active sense."[230] Attention shifts away from the sovereignty of the state as reflected in executive prerogatives or legislative and judicial checks, and instead toward popular sovereignty—simply put, "Bringing the people back [in]."[231]

The public's constitutional actions can be felt through channels both direct and indirect, and at different moments.[232] Irrespective of the particular actions taken or tools employed, the place of "the people" in constitutional orders shows many parallels to several of the core functions identified in the previous chapter for the operation of the international legal order. Enforcement presents a challenge for both international and constitutional law because of the absence of a higher sovereign. Yet for popular constitutionalism, one of the "the role[s] of the people . . . includes active and ongoing control over the interpretation and enforcement of constitutional law."[233] Punishment for violations of the Constitution by agents of the state ultimately relies less on checks by other branches of government than vertical enforcement from below by the people through (non)institutional means.[234]

Beyond ex post enforcement, the people serve an important interpretive function, setting expectations for constitutional rules and the behavior of all within this legal framework. A "deep" form of popular constitutionalism emphasizes the role of the masses in the fundamental "rule of recognition" which determines what rules qualify as "law" proper. Rather than authority held solely by elites in accounts from jurists like Hart, the public forms a core part of the "recognitional community" of what counts as law and the expectations that ensue.[235] Far from relegated to the sidelines, the public's involvement in the process of constitutional formation and evolution represents a form of "higher lawmaking."[236] Instead of the state being paramount, "In a world of popular constitutionalism, government officials are the regulated, not the regulators, and final interpretive authority rests with the people themselves" (emphasis in original).[237] More fundamentally, "It was the community at large" as a collective sovereign informed by legal reasoning, whose underlying preferences are shaped by constitutional principles, and whose actions, in turn, "controlled the meaning of the Constitution and was responsible for ensuring its proper implementation in the day-to-day process of governing."[238]

Popular constitutionalism is "nonideological" in the sense that it fits with both traditionally liberal and conservative concerns about government overreach contrary to the popular will.[239] Although developed mostly in the US context, the approach has been applied to other domestic legal orders, such as Britain's common law system.[240] Popular constitutionalist arguments have even been extended to authoritarian systems, such as China and Vietnam, where ordinary actors can be found to play sometimes surprising legal roles.[241] The general idea behind popular constitutionalism also overlaps with a variety US and comparative research into the role of the public in facilitating and giving force to the rulings of domestic high courts; even if much of this literature more narrowly focuses on public-judicial relations rather than affording a broader legal position to the masses.[242]

How it is possible to seriously consider ordinary people as active constitutional players in the United States or elsewhere? Part of the answer goes back to our earlier discussions of constitutions as a type of public law distinct from the "ordinary," or "private," laws making up most domestic statutes. It is not despite, but because of, the characteristic structure constitutions share with international law that ordinary people may matter. The Constitution is distinctive, described by Kramer as "political-legal," or what the legal scholar Mark Tushnet and others call "political law."[243] The Constitution is legal in the sense that it imposes obligations and invokes certain normative principles. But "constitutional law also purported to govern the sovereign itself," making it inherently political as well.[244] As political actors upon which the authority of the sovereign state ultimately rests, the public thereby becomes an important legal actor in the operation of the Constitution.

Other legal scholars acknowledge the public could inhibit state actions, but take pains to distinguish this political role from actual legal constraint. Dismissing constitutional (and international) law as "positive morality," Austin went on to say:

> [The government] would not and could not incur a legal pain or penalty, but it probably would incur censure, and might chance to meet with resistance, from the generality or bulk of the governed.[245]

What we now think of as public opinion, or what Austin called "opinions prevalent in the community," could pressure governments into complying with constitutional rules.[246] Almost two centuries later, the legal scholars Eric Posner and Adrian Vermeule channel Austin when claiming:

> the major constraints on the executive, especially in crises, do not arise from law or from the separation-of-powers framework defended by liberal legalists, but from politics and public opinion.[247]

The common assumption here is that the politics brought to bear by publics are orthogonal to questions of law. The public may be grudgingly granted some political sway, while constitutional rules can still be dismissed for having "a Potemkin quality: they stand about in the landscape, providing an impressive facade of legal constraint on the executive, but actually blocking very little."[248]

Yet what critics see as false fronts may mask stronger edifices constructed by the populace's underlying commitment to legal principles. Just as obligation and self-interest are intertwined, law and public opinion are not mutually exclusive—how publics evaluate government policies are informed in part by how that conduct comports with the law.[249] Speaking about the United States but in ways relevant cross-nationally, Richard Pildes declares "The key point is this: the world of public and political responses to presidential action is filtered through the law itself."[250] Popular constitutionalism, in turn, reconciles the political-legal nature of the Constitution, where ordinary people give meaning to constitutional law by performing legally motivated political actions.[251]

Not surprisingly, popular constitutionalism has its fair share of detractors. One line of attack derides its "sponginess," where a multitude of uses makes it "deeply ambiguous at best and deeply confused at worst."[252] Popular constitutionalism's bounds could certainly be better specified—a point openly acknowledged by proponents.[253] But if conceptual ambiguity was an exclusionary criterion, then mainstream alternatives should be similarly dismissed, such as the many versions of "departmentalism" putting forward the constitutional authority of various combinations of government institutions.[254] Doctrines for interpreting the Constitution common in conservative legal circles, such as "originalism" or "textualism," likewise offer little in the way of consistency or coherence.[255] A better yardstick is whether an approach tells us something useful about how the world works. Popular constitutionalism opens new avenues of inquiry by centering ordinary people in how they think about and act toward the Constitution, representing a significant shift away from elite-based approaches.[256]

A second related strand of criticism depicts popular constitutionalism not just as a dramatic departure, but a radical one at that. Using words that would prick up the ears of international relations scholars, some critics contend that allowing the public any meaningful constitutional role would invite "anarchy" and raise the "Hobbesian specter of social chaos."[257] An assumption—sometimes explicit, other times implicit—is that the public has neither the disposition nor capacity to be trusted with something as sacred as the Constitution with political, social, and legal stability suffering as a result.[258]

If these criticisms sound familiar, it is because they mirror the alleged deficiencies in the general coherence and stability of public policy attitudes described earlier. A long line of legal research questions whether publics are legitimate "legal participants," placing ordinary people in the "outer circles."[259] The subject matter may differ—foreign and domestic policy before, constitutional law now—but the reasoning is essentially identical. The problem with these broadsides is that if the public has the capacity to reason and act on often complex policy issues, then it is not a stretch to presume they possess comparable faculties when it comes to the foundational laws upon which their societies rest.

Equally telling, as a solution to the public's limits, naysayers similarly advise that constitutional order is best assured by taking power away from the masses, entrusting instead in some set of elite actors. This could take the form of departmentalism's sharing of constitutional authority, or variants favoring the supremacy of a particular branch. Indeed, popular constitutionalism was largely conceived as a reaction to judicial supremacy—"the notion that judges have the last word when it comes to constitutional interpretation and that their decisions determine the meaning of the Constitution for everyone."[260] An equally powerful alternative is executive supremacy, in certain respects the apogee of the imperial presidency—the "power of the executive 'to say what the law is.'"[261] Executive supremacy is especially relevant for our purposes as it provides a clear link between skeptics of both constitutional and international law, where leaders should be unconstrained by (or solely determinative of) *both* sets of rules.

Support for dispensing with the public in favor of some form of elite control over the Constitution is lacking on factual and normative grounds. Critics can readily point to historical instances of the public's poor constitutional performance, but the records for justices, leaders, and politicians are not exactly gleaming.[262] Across the United States and a range of other countries, members of the public actually exhibit impressive practical legal knowledge, and tend to hold deeper principles of fairness and justice compared to the more rigid reasoning of judges and lawyers.[263] And public opinion has been shown to have significant effects on the behavior of judges and other elites, questioning the autonomy and supremacy of the latter.[264] Ironically, those advocating an "executive unbound" provide an opening for popular constitutionalism by acknowledging public opinion serves as a constraint on leaders,[265] especially if that opinion is informed by law. Rather than negating popular constitutionalism, these criticisms help lay out the scope of an approach taking the people more seriously in domestic legal affairs.

At times stark in its rhetoric, a closer look shows that popular constitutionalism offers a more moderate position in two respects.[266] First, little desire exists for some version of "popular supremacy," where the people are the sole constitutional players. One of the drivers of popular constitutionalism has been to reject *any* one actor from holding constitutional supremacy.[267] The public nonetheless occupies a constructive role in what can be termed "constitutional dialogues" between elites and the ordinary masses.[268]

A second way in which popular constitutionalism is more moderate is that the public's preferences and actions are less direct, and mostly transmitted through institutional channels. Critics raise the alarm of constitutional rule via the "mob,"[269] yet many of the actions described by Kramer and others—voting, petitions, pamphlets, protests, and boycotts, among others—represent fairly conventional forms of political participation.[270] Tushnet likewise portrays popular action as institutionalized: "People *perform* constitutional law as political law through (some of) their mobilizations in politics" (emphasis in original).[271]

A more apt label may be "mediated popular constitutionalism," where interactions between the public and constitutional law take place through domestic institutions.[272] This applies not only to how the public influences the operation of the Constitution, but also how constitutional law shapes the public's reasoning. The public is not a blank slate—existing rules and principles inform how ordinary people think about legal obligations, and how those obligations should then be carried through.[273] At its core, popular constitutionalism centers the public as important legal and political actors in the operation of constitutional law, whose preferences, expectations, and actions are filtered through domestic institutions.

Getting to Popular International Law: The Public and the Operation of International Legal Commitments

The three prior subsections together provide a justification for what I call *popular international law*—an account where the public has the potential to play an important role in the core functions of international legal commitments. Popular international law represents an international corollary to popular constitutionalism. If the structure (Proposition #1) and content (Proposition #2) of constitutional and international laws are closely related, and the people play an important role in the operation of constitutional law (Proposition #3), then it stands to reason that ordinary people may also be relevant to the operation of international law. Importantly, this popular form of international law should not be confused with similarly termed but radically distinct populist movements, which generally stand in opposition to international legal rules and accord little comparable agency to ordinary people in legal orders.[274]

As noted at the outset to this section, there is precedent for claiming that explanations for constitutional and international law are interrelated. Those arguing that both international and constitutional legal rules do *not* matter often draw on similar tenets. Others positing that domestic legal systems can shape actions toward international law are likewise drawing connections between the internal and external legal spheres, though with a tendency to focus more on the beliefs and actions of elite actors.[275] Popular international law starts from similar premises regarding connections between domestic and international legal systems, but arrives at very different conclusions in two important ways: 1) that international law does matter; but also 2) that ordinary people can play an important role in international legal commitments.

Combining insights from constitutional law and international relations, popular international law represents in many respects a different theoretical route for arriving at the horizontally informed Liberal account outlined in the first half of this chapter regarding domestic actors and international commitments. Popular international law sees the public as significant interlocutors in the operation of international legal commitments, just as those same publics are important for upholding constitutional commitments. In a corresponding manner to popular constitutionalism, it is incumbent to affirm that popular international law is not nearly so radical, and is rather informed by more measured understandings of the role of the public in international law in two crucial respects.

First, greater attention to ordinary people does not negate the presence and influence of other actors. What is rejected is the notion that any particular actor is paramount in the operation of international law. Popular constitutionalism denies anyone's supremacy over the Constitution. Popular international law embraces a similar antisupremacy ethos, dismissing the view that any single type of actor reigns over international law. In particular, popular international law challenges traditional conceptions of the state as the sole, dominant international legal personality. International law is better seen as involving a series of "treaty (or customary) dialogues" among various members (both elite and ordinary) of the international community, akin to the "constitutional dialogues" observed in domestic legal communities.[276] Of course, the volume of public voices in these dialogues will also vary depending on domestic institutional structures, as well as considerations such as the relative salience of the legal issue at hand.

What makes popular international law distinctive is that ordinary people are not seen as bit players, instead occupying a central (even if not paramount) place in international legal relations. Recognizing this privileged position does not mean the public is always perfect in its reasoning. Ordinary people can have limited knowledge, hold biases, make errors—incidentally, attributes shared in equal or greater measure by their elite counterparts. Through their awareness and understanding of core legal principles and values, publics can nonetheless contribute to the international legal order, just as they do in domestic legal orders.

The second way in which popular international law is more modest is that preferences, beliefs, and actions of publics are not unfiltered, but rather mediated by institutions. The vision is not necessarily one of a global civil society free from traditional political boundaries, determining international legal outcomes on its own. States continue to matter a great deal, serving as the primary institutional link between domestic and international law and politics. This is evident from the simple fact that it is states—not individuals, or national populations—who have formal legal standing to ratify international treaties. But citizens still take part indirectly at various stages, especially in the subsequent operation of these agreements. The use by some legal scholars of the term "ratifies" to describe the public's "collective conception of the Constitution" is fitting given their analogous external role in international legal commitments.[277]

With the state as the main intermediary between ordinary people and the international legal order, attention rests on *national* publics and relationships with their respective states rather than a more diffuse "world opinion."[278] Yet through their opinions and behavior, national publics can influence outside actors and the broader operation of international law. Just as publics can be described as "perform[ing] constitutional law" through mobilizing and generally making their voices heard in the corridors of power at home,[279] those same national publics can also "perform international law" through similar forms of mobilization with implications abroad. A more modest form of popular international law thus resembles "mediated popular constitutionalism," where interactions between the public and legal rules (domestic or international) are largely enacted through domestic institutions.[280] Mass publics may not directly control the levers of international law, but through states they can have their preferences, beliefs, and actions felt externally.

To the query of "Who are the most relevant actors in the operation of international law?" this chapter has proposed that we take a closer look at mass publics. States and elite actors are commonly thought to be the key players in international legal politics. Extending insights from the domestic turn in the study of international relations and law, I have put forward a theoretical framework that takes seriously the role of ordinary people in international legal commitments. Mass publics collectively have the faculties, commitment, and ability to promote core functions underlying international law. The logic behind this argument is bolstered by drawing on theories of popular constitutionalism to make the case that the public matters for the operation of legal orders, domestic and international. The result is popular international law, the notion that international legal commitments are not separate from domestic politics, but actually depend on the sentiments and mobilization of national publics from below for their proper operation.

Questions about whether the public cares about, is influenced by, and influences international law are ultimately empirical ones. Subsequent chapters in this book leverage a variety of data with the aim to more systematically examine the relationship between the public and international law. These empirical chapters, in turn, are organized around assessing the role of the public in each of two of the main functions of the international legal order spelled out in the previous chapter—enforcement and changing preferences.

REPUTATION AND ENFORCEMENT I

Experimental Evidence That Image Is
Something (But Not Everything)

The First World War might seem like a strange place to look for the effectiveness of international law, much less the importance of the public. As alluded to
in chapter 1, "the war to end all wars" was bookended by two of the most widely
cited failures of international agreements—beginning with Germany's ripping
up the "scrap of paper" that was the Treaty of London guaranteeing Belgium's
neutrality, and ending with a Treaty of Versailles denounced for causing more
problems than it solved.

As damning as these two episodes may be, it is in the gruesome fighting of the
intervening years that an even stronger case has been made for the irrelevance
of legal constraints. With seemingly little concern for established rules, brutality directed toward civilians, the wounded, and prisoners alike, alongside newer
technologies like chemical weapons, led historians like Liddell Hart to conclude
the Great War ushered in a marked "decline of civilized behaviour," or what Omer
Bartov later deplored as the "emergence of industrial killing."[1] Reflecting a rupture from the past and foreshadowing a bleaker future, a direct line was drawn
from the brutal treatment of the conflict's millions of prisoners of war to later
Soviet gulags and Nazi extermination camps.[2] Taking a broader view, the US diplomat and historian George Kennan described the First World War as *the* great
seminal catastrophe of the century" (emphasis in original, described by German
historians as *Urkatastrophe*),[3] serving as the basis for the rise of extremist ideologies, and the even deadlier Second World War.

As compelling as the picture of the Great War as a legal no man's land may appear, it reflects an active process of forgetting and erasure by many belligerents in the years afterward belying much of what actually took place during the conflict.[4] Conditions for prisoners of war could be harsh, and abuses certainly occurred, but were far from a precursor to Soviet and Nazi forced labor and concentration camps. Many belligerents made good faith efforts to care of their captives; much of this motivation could be credited to multilateral treaties like the 1899 and 1907 Hague Conventions, supplemented by bilateral agreements.[5]

The reasons *why* international law mattered for prisoners and other issues also often depended on *who* was involved, including many neglected actors. Several well-known accounts see the beginning, middle, and end of the First World War purely through the eyes of countries' leaders, high-ranking diplomats, and generals.[6] Countering this elite-centric focus is growing attention to a "history from below" involving more ordinary actors, including for the Great War.[7] Archival evidence shows that Imperial Germany was acutely aware of how its actions were received by foreign publics, treating public opinion like "hard goods" as real as troops or weapons.[8] Germany had good reason to worry about how its actions were viewed not only in the halls of power but also on the streets of its main adversaries. German violation of the Treaty of London's "scrap of paper" served as a catalyst for mobilizing initially skeptical segments of the British public to support their country's entry into the war.[9] While nothing stopped Germany from ignoring the Treaty of London, it could not so easily dismiss the costs that followed from widespread international criticism and a more unified and determined adversary. Starting with this failed opening gambit and continuing throughout the conflict, belligerents on both sides expressed concern over how actions taken vis-à-vis international law could affect their country's image (or reputation) among foreign publics. The war was fought as much in ordinary people's minds as in the trenches, so much so that "The propaganda war during the conflict was almost as intense as that on the battlefield."[10]

This bottom-up view of legal rules in the First World War raises broader questions about the functions—international and domestic—underlying the operation of international law. In this chapter, I examine the popular foundations for the enforcement function of international law. I begin with enforcement because the ability to impose costs against violators is generally seen as vital for an effective legal system, and it is law's ability to constrain that skeptics see as especially weak.[11] International law has the potential (or lack thereof) to check violators through a variety of avenues with a common formulation discussed in chapter 1 being the "Three Rs" of enforcement—reciprocity, retaliation, and reputation. Of the three, I choose to focus mostly on reputation. Depending on more direct and immediate sanctions, reciprocity and retaliation are important but often considered less crucial mechanisms for enforcement compared to the more diffuse "collateral consequences" associated with reputation.[12] Reputation is also in many respects foundational for enforcement—reciprocity and retaliation (to the extent they exist) ultimately rely on underlying reputational dynamics for their workings.[13] Attention to reputational dynamics in international law also has wider implications, given the prominence of reputation in theories of foreign policymaking more broadly, and the role of public opinion in particular for its functioning.[14] A closer look at international legal commitments is warranted in what it may add to larger debates regarding the (un)importance of reputation.

One reflection on the state of the art several decades ago remarked, "Whatever one thinks about the importance of reputation should be based on sound theory, method, and evidence."[15] This sentiment remains pertinent in the present given ongoing disagreements over the place of reputation across a variety of international phenomena. I seek to offer a sounder assessment of reputation in international law on each of these scores. In the next section of this chapter, I provide an overview of reputation as a source of enforcement for international law. I connect this to a theoretical explanation for the role of national publics in the functioning of reputation, and lay out several expectations for when and under what conditions public support for reputational consequences should be more or less present. I then discuss some of the methodological challenges in assessing reputational mechanisms, and describe the main design strategy for this chapter, which relies on a series of survey experiments. The remainder is devoted to presenting the empirical results, demonstrating that ordinary members of the mass public are capable of understanding the meaning of international legal commitments, as well as willing to endorse actions that impose reputational costs on would-be violators across a range of circumstances. As such, the evidence points to the public as a potentially important conduit in the use of reputation as a mode of enforcement for international law.

Reputation and International Law: A Theoretical Overview

Reputational accounts (and their critics) are common across various areas of political science, as well as outside fields ranging from economics to sociology to criminology.[16] At its core, reputation concerns beliefs about an actor's "type."[17] "Type" can refer to a host of possible qualities, meaning actors could have distinct reputations for resolve, honesty, or even irrationality.[18] In the case of international law, the general focus involves an actor's reputation as a reliable, trustworthy partner who upholds and complies with its commitments.

Irrespective of the variant, an actor's reputation is not something solely under its control; it is rather a function of *others'* beliefs and how they expect the actor to behave in the future.[19] An actor's underlying type does relate to an actual attribute (or disposition) it possesses, such as being a reliable partner. Ultimately, however, this is hidden information that only the actor themselves know for sure, making it difficult for outsiders to definitively detect. This fundamentally private nature creates an inescapable level of uncertainty among audiences about an actor's attributes, in particular its trustworthiness.

To help alleviate this uncertainty, audiences can look to the actor's behavior to make inferences about its type and likely future conduct—it is these inferences that form the actor's reputation in the eyes of others. Reputations thus involve a temporal connection, where "judgments about an actor's past behavior [are] used to predict future behavior."[20] A state complying with past commitments is more likely to develop a reputation for trustworthiness, while one who reneges risks being branded a delinquent. Of course, past behavior is not a perfect predictor of future actions. How a state previously behaved may be indicative of a true disposition to abide by its promises, but could also be partially or fully a function of situational elements peculiar to the prior episode.[21] A level of uncertainty is always present, but to the extent that audiences make reasonable judgments about an actor's reliability based on prior behavior, then in an important sense "Reputation is information," helping actors better navigate an uncertain world.[22]

Uncertainty means that gaps can still exist between an actor's underlying disposition to comply with its commitments, versus its perceived reputation. A truly dependable "stalwart" may incorrectly be viewed as a "lemon" by others, while an unreliable "lemon" may somehow get away with being trusted as a "stalwart."[23] Yet a record of (non)compliance may help to reduce uncertainty and such gaps in image over time.

Whatever its underlying type, however, what matters from a practical standpoint for the state in question are those beliefs (i.e., reputation) held by others in the international community. This is one reason why thinkers who diverge on much nonetheless generally agree on the import of reputation, and why states often care a great deal about how they are viewed.[24] The legal scholar Louis Henkin places reputation front and center in decisions over compliance:

> Every nation's foreign policy depends substantially on its "credit"—on maintaining the expectation that it will live up to international mores and obligations. Considerations of "honor," "prestige," "leadership," "influence," "reputation," which figure prominently in governmental decisions, often weigh in favor of observing law. Nations generally desire a reputation for principled behavior, for propriety and respectability.[25]

Although skeptical of the overall enforcement capabilities of international law, Hans Morgenthau was acutely aware of the importance of maintaining a trustworthy reputation:

> A nation will likewise be reluctant to disregard its obligations . . ., since the benefits that it expects from the execution of the treaty by the other contracting parties are complementary to those anticipated by the latter. It may thus stand to lose more than it would gain by not fulfilling its part of the bargain. This is particularly so in the long run, since a nation that has the reputation of reneging on its . . . obligations will find it hard to conclude . . . treaties beneficial to itself.[26]

Morgenthau's warning points to one of the main reasons for countries to worry about their reputations. What remains unanswered for Morgenthau and many skeptics is the relative impact of international law on an actor's reputation, and how much such concerns shape their actions.

No world government exists with the coercive capabilities to inflict punishment, but states still appear to think about "reputational sanctions" for their transgressions, or "costs imposed on a state when its reputation is damaged."[27] Costs may differ from reciprocity's tit-for-tat violations in kind, or retaliation's resort to economic, diplomatic, or other direct penalties, but reputational sanctions can be equal to, or even greater than, other forms of enforcement.

Reputation's "collateral consequences" may take many forms, but are primarily felt in more indirect ways over the longer term.[28] States often find it beneficial to cooperate with other actors on a variety of matters, with reputation having some bearing. As Robert Keohane observes, "A good reputation makes it easier for a government to enter into advantageous international agreements; tarnishing that reputation imposes costs by making agreements more difficult to reach."[29] Since a reputation for trustworthiness is partly a function of past behavior, compliance with prior commitments influences the ability to engage in, and benefit from, future cooperative opportunities.

Military alliances nicely illustrate the compliance-cooperation nexus. An alliance can be appealing for large and small states alike by combining capabilities or offering access to specialized resources to bolster security. But these partnerships also come with downsides if an ally has to come to another's aid in time of war—potentially putting their own citizens and finances at risk—leading to perennial concerns over their reliability.[30] Those states who develop a reputation as a dependable ally find it easier to form new military partnerships, while those known to renege may eventually be left with few partners.[31] Should a later alliance be successfully concluded, a state's reputation can also affect the terms of negotiation.[32] The relative costs of a poor reputation are also apparent in the world of finance, where states who have previously defaulted on their debts (or engaged in other violations) can find themselves facing harsher sovereign risk ratings and more expensive premiums on subsequent borrowing.[33]

These and similar episodes are consistent with the view that harm to a country' reputation can impair its ability to reap the benefits of cooperative opportunities for some time to come. Concerns over *future* reputational consequences have, in turn, been shown—both more formally and through an array of empirical evidence—to serve as important motivators for actors to comply with *present* commitments.[34]

Reputational accounts do not need to assume that actors hold some innate preference to follow through on their commitments.[35] Rather than an end in itself, reputation is largely seen as instrumental, incentivizing states to uphold their commitments because the total benefits of doing so outweigh whatever short-term payoffs might accrue from reneging.[36] Reputation is portrayed by proponents and opponents alike in largely rationalist terms.[37] While differing about the existence and relative size of consequences arising from noncompliance, both sides generally concur that reputation works through a fairly straightforward cost-benefit calculus.

Yet this begs the question of *why* reputational costs from violating an international legal agreement may be so much greater compared to engaging in outwardly similar behavior in the absence of a prior commitment. For this is the key claim behind how international law can serve an enforcement function through reputational sanctions. In looking at why states are more willing to comply with Article VIII under the Articles of Agreement of the International Monetary Fund (IMF) prohibiting current account restrictions, Beth Simmons reasons "An international legal commitment is one way that governments seek to raise the reputational costs of reneging, with important consequences for state behavior."[38] More generally, Andrew Guzman asserts that, unlike less legalized promises, a "formal treaty represents the most serious form of commitment . . . because it is understood to be a maximal pledge of reputation."[39]

One reason reputational stakes may be a great deal higher is because these sorts of commitments are embedded within a deeper normative system of international legal principles, which shape actors' understandings of their and others' actions.[40] It is no coincidence that in decrying Britain's threat to repudiate prior agreements with the European Union during the later stages of Brexit negotiations, the European Commission president Ursula von der Leyen specifically invoked pacta sunt servanda ("promises must be kept")—the foundational metanorm of the international legal system.[41] Breaking legalized commitments sends a particularly strong signal to others about an actor's "type." In an uncertain world, reputation may be information, but legal breaches generate a particular *principled* form of information about the violator's trustworthiness. The actual actions taken (or not taken) may ostensibly appear similar, such as raising tariffs, or refusing to help another state militarily. It is the *meaning* of those actions that can differ dramatically—violating a trade treaty, or abandoning an ally. Although the reputational costs and benefits of international law may be measured in instrumental terms, they function in the context of important normative underpinnings.[42]

Similar understandings of the sources and workings of reputation are evident in the operation of legal systems broadly construed, including constitutional law—a body of legal rules which the prior chapter showed to be remarkably similar in structure and function to international law. Like its international sibling, constitutional law lacks a higher sovereign authority to enforce the rules. If the US president violates the Constitution there is no superior actor to punish them. The Supreme Court could declare a violation took place, but why would the White House listen? This question gets to the heart of constitutional legal theory, and why and how a constitution is thought to be obligatory, enforcing rules among the community's members.

Answers to questions about how constitutional law is enforced point to comparable mechanisms shared by international legal commitments.[43] This is especially the case with reputation, which plays an important role in accounts for why even some of the strongest of actors are motivated to comply with constitutional rules.[44] To govern effectively, leaders depend to a large extent on the trust of other domestic actors.[45] After all, pure coercion is expensive, inefficient, and infeasible in the long run, meaning that democratic (and to a certain extent even some autocratic) governments have good reasons to place certain constraints upon their own freedom of action to achieve broader aims.[46]

Reputations can be built in assorted ways, but demonstrating a commitment to constitutional principles can prove particularly rewarding (and breaking those rules unattractive). The rationale for how constitutions constrain has parallels to the discussion above regarding the ways in which the reputational stakes of international law are rooted in specific normative understandings. Richard Pildes highlights the not purely instrumental pull of constitutional principles in language familiar to international relations scholars:

> Even in a *realpolitik* world in which presidents feel no normative obligation to comply with the law, but instead engage in cost-benefit calculations regarding compliance in individual contexts, presidents are likely nonetheless to end up complying with the law a great deal of the time to maintain their credibility and elicit support and cooperation from others [emphasis in original].[47]

Like international law, compliance with constitutional principles is not necessarily for its own sake, but rather a means of bolstering one's reputation to help secure other actors' cooperation. And as with states dealing with international legal commitments, the costs and benefits for leaders of following constitutional commitments are given meaning through a deeper conceptualization of legal rules.

In the context of constitutional law, it is also instructive to consider *who* are the "others" whose support and cooperation is sought. While attention often centers on other elites, ordinary people may also be at the forefront of leaders' minds. The need for cooperation often expands to a wider swathe of the citizenry. As Robert Axelrod cautions: "Even the most powerful government cannot enforce any rule it chooses. To be effective, a government must elicit compliance from the majority of the governed."[48] To more assuredly achieve that compliance, in turn, requires governments to be mindful of their own reputations in the public's eyes.

Obtaining cooperation of the public is far from guaranteed, even in times of great danger to the nation like war. Returning to the First World War, those countries who introduced mass conscription varied a great deal in the level of citizen support with some encountering stiff resistance.[49] Differences in military recruitment had a direct bearing on the ability of belligerents to field sufficient numbers of troops, while simultaneously needing to deal with potential unrest at home. Cooperation from the population is necessary for governments to govern effectively, but is conditional on the government's own status and actions, and citizens' resulting perceptions of their government's "type." This "contingent consent" depends in significant part on citizens' beliefs that their government is trustworthy by making "credible commitments," following "standards of fairness," and avoiding "immoral policies."[50] Citizens evaluate their government's trustworthiness on a regular basis, but the offering or withdrawal of "[c]ontingent consent is reducible to neither material self-interest nor normative and moral considerations."[51] Evaluations of the costs and benefits for a given course of action are thus inseparable from normative principles.

Ethical standards themselves are subject to change, and what may count as "fair" or "moral" in one context may differ in another. Perceptions of fairness may be a function of the government acting legally, but could involve other considerations. Connecting contingent consent to matters of constitutional law, popular constitutionalism affirms the role of the ordinary masses and highlights the importance for a government's reputation that its behavior is interpreted by the people as consistent with constitutional principles. According to popular constitutionalists, members of the public weigh heavily the concordance between their government's actions and the Constitution for reputational calculations. For instance, the US Supreme Court's *Dred Scott* decision refusing to grant citizenship rights to African Americans has gone down in history as one of the country's worst judicial rulings. Being so at odds with constitutional understandings among wide segments of the citizenry even at the time, the decision had immediate ramifications, where "The wounds inflicted on the Supreme Court's *reputation* as a result of this assault took nearly a generation to heal" (emphasis added).[52]

According to popular constitutionalism, the public does not think solely in legal terms, but evaluations of policies and politicians are still very much filtered through legal understandings. When navigating such a rich socio-legal environment, leaders may have strong instrumental motivations for following constitutional principles. As Mark Tushnet observes, leaders have "a *political* incentive to be serious about the Constitution . . . when the people themselves care deeply about constitutional rights" (emphasis in original).[53] In the domestic legal context, the public can play an important role in the operation of constitutional laws where reputational stakes for leaders' compliance decisions serve an important enforcement function.

As the external corollary to popular constitutionalism, popular international law sees ordinary people as playing a similarly important role in facilitating the enforcement of international commitments by raising the reputational stakes for states' compliance decisions. Just as the public is often a neglected actor in international law, the same holds true for reputational accounts more generally. When discussing different actors, the most common question has been whose reputation matters, or "*To whom* do reputations adhere?" This debate is far from settled, but different answers put forward generally refer to reputational consequences for the state as a whole versus specific domestic elites including leaders.[54]

Popular international law is less concerned with the issue of who holds a given reputation, but rather asks a corresponding question of whose beliefs matter in shaping that reputation, or "With *whom* do reputations reside?" Because an actor's reputation (whether state or leader) is based on the beliefs of others, it is critical to appreciate who exactly are the relevant "others." When it comes to traditional understandings of either the potential or limits of reputation in international law, the discussion largely mirrors the initial question of whose reputation matters—it remains states, leaders, or perhaps other elites.[55] Some may recognize that "reputational analysis is highly contingent on domestic politics,"[56] but this mostly pertains to institutional structures or coalition politics of the country whose reputation is in question.

Yet domestic politics also weighs heavily in those other countries who are forming reputational beliefs. Looking back to the opening example of the First World War, the main belligerents were concerned with how their behavior toward international commitments would be received not just by the leaders of allies and adversaries, but also foreign citizenries. More generally, leaders have been shown to be reluctant to cooperate with counterparts who have developed an untrustworthy reputation by reneging on prior commitments.[57] To the extent that leaders are accountable to their populations, then an important source for the beliefs underlying the reputations of foreign countries will be located in national publics. Reputation is commonly portrayed as a *horizontal* state-to-state enforcement mechanism, but may also involve discernable *domestic* processes in its actual operation. We should thus be looking more closely at how publics think about the commitments and compliance of foreign countries in determining whether and how reputational consequences function.

In this section I have laid out a theoretical rationale for why reputation matters for the enforcement of international law, and the particular role played by national publics in its functioning. Reputational accounts are not without their detractors who doubt the role of reputation in general and for international law in particular. A number of critics dispute the purported link between past actions and subsequent expectations, questioning whether audiences readily use an actor's prior behavior to assess the credibility of its commitments.[58] Audiences may sometimes refer to an actor's past actions, but only to reinforce their pre-existing beliefs rather than as a means for drawing more objective inferences.[59] If reputation is information, then for these critics it may not very informative, especially in an international arena teeming with a multitude of states with differing interests and commitments.[60] The practical result is that the risk and size of reputational sanctions may be modest, bordering on nonexistent.[61] Prior violations are readily explained away by extenuating circumstances, or obfuscating what actions are actually required.

States may also cultivate reputations covering other types of attributes as noted earlier, such as for resolve, unpredictability, or even irrationality. A reputation as a trustworthy partner may not be among the most important and could run counter to the behavior necessary for promoting these other traits.[62]

Positing that reputation matters to states, leaders, or audiences in no way signifies it is the *only* thing that matters. Much theorizing on international law acknowledges the likely impact of other factors, carefully considering possible limits to reputation. But none of this should take away from evaluating the role reputation in international law on its own terms.[63] This is especially so since some of the strongest legal skeptics question whether a reputation for reliability is of *any* meaningful value in an already allegedly feeble international legal system. Criticisms of reputation in international law also carry some irony. Much of the larger literature on reputation in international relations is overwhelmingly focused on one specific type of reputation—for resolve, or to steadfastly stick to a particular course of action, such as by being willing to follow through on threats in crisis situations.[64] A broader view of many of these same sorts of crises illustrates that other types of reputation (especially for reliability) can be equally if not more important in shaping audience beliefs, state behavior, and outcomes.[65] The salience of nonresolve-based reputations has likely only grown in the contemporary era—"[i]n an interdependent and interconnected world, a reputation for reliability matters."[66]

There are thus good reasons to at a minimum take a closer look at the potential role of a reputation for reliability as a mechanism in the enforcement of international law. Unfortunately, as a general construct reputation is as elusive as it is important. The beliefs underlying an actor's reputation are often not directly observed, while behaviors and outcomes could be the result of a myriad of alternative explanations. Writing about the study of reputation more generally, Jervis laments "we have neither theoretically grounded expectations nor solid evidence."[67] The dynamic workings of reputations are especially ill-defined, leading to the caution that "we know very little about how reputations are gained or lost."[68]

Hurdles are exceptionally high when it comes to evaluating reputational accounts in the case of the enforcement function of international law. One point shared by both sympathizers and critics of reputation in international law is the dearth of systematic empirical research.[69] Although Guzman develops a nuanced theoretical framework for reputation formation and change, he acknowledges that his approach offers "no way to provide an estimate of the magnitude of reputational sanctions."[70] Others are more circumspect about reputational mechanisms, but make a similar admission: "No one really knows how important reputation is for states, however, and thus how much it accounts for compliance with international law."[71] Empirical indecision has corresponding implications for our ability to theorize about reputation. Speaking about international law, Rachel Brewster warns "Without a means of assessment, any claim about the power of reputation remains non-falsifiable and therefore has less theoretical force."[72] It is to this task that the rest of this chapter now turns—offering an empirical strategy to more readily identify and evaluate key links in the causal chain leading toward reputational consequences, and demonstrate the theoretical import of national publics in the enforcement of international law.

An Experimental Approach to Reputation and Public Opinion

Sorting through divergent claims from existing studies on reputation and international law is challenging due to the nature of how both reputations and international legal commitments are formed. Empirical tests of reputation in international relations are difficult because information about an actor's type is fundamentally unknown, and the ways audiences process and make inferences based on actors' behavior are similarly tough to measure.[73]

Adding international law to the mix introduces further problems. Neither the design nor joining of international agreements are random events, but rather strategic decisions in their own right. States are careful when bargaining over the terms of an agreement, where negotiations can carry across numerous rounds lasting months if not years. Membership is not automatic once negotiations conclude—states weigh the costs and benefits of commitment, reflected in uneven participation in many treaties and varying lengths of time it takes participants to sign on. These selection effects loom large in assessments of the consequences of international law, where it is difficult to determine whether any effects are due to the legal commitment itself, or instead background characteristics and circumstances that led states to design, join, or reject, the agreement in the first place.[74]

Pitfalls are triply compounded when evaluating specific mechanisms like reputation. As one general review warns, "selection bias is especially severe in the study of reputation"[75]—a level of severity perhaps only rivaled by that evident in international law, which when combined makes for an especially toxic inferential stew. Similar processes are likely at play that confound the compliance behavior of states, and judgments about any reputational consequences that do (or do not) ensue. In many cases the decision to comply with (or violate) a legal commitment is strategic, where states take into account the likely costs and benefits of their choices, reputational or otherwise. Observing the absence of reputational sanctions after instances of treaty violation does not necessarily negate the role of reputation, since violators may have deliberately chosen to only renege on those commitments where reputational stakes could be minimized or avoided.[76] On the flipside, it does not automatically follow that observing compliance is proof that the specter of reputational sanctions are hard at work. States might be actively following through on their commitments to avoid damaging their reputations, but their behavior could just as easily be due to a host of motives having nothing to do with reputational hopes or fears.[77] A number of observational studies show promising support for reputational costs from violating legal commitments, but these findings remain vulnerable to charges that they fail to adequately take into account potentially counteracting strategic processes.[78]

To address some of the limits in existing empirical studies of international law, I leverage the use of experimental methods.[79] The core experimental logic is fairly simple—to control and manipulate certain elements of the environment, and then examine how subjects respond to those changes. The control possible through experiments offers a powerful tool for arriving at more reliable conclusions about cause and effect. Random assignment increases the likelihood treatment and control groups are similar to each other on average across all observed *and* unobserved factors. By comparing differences in responses between groups, we can estimate with greater certainty the consequences of international law, reputational or otherwise. Experiments provide a promising design approach to help address problems of strategic selection and nonrandom assignment that hamper much of the existing empirical research into the effects of international law.

Experimental methods also afford crucial advantages in the measurement of both cause and effect compared to observational alternatives. Experiments allow for isolating and manipulating key elements of the presence and design of legal commitments in ways not possible with contemporary or historical data often involving a slew of multiple, overlapping agreements. On the outcome side, experiment have an edge by letting researchers directly examine subjects' beliefs and preferences, whereas observational approaches often need to rely on indirect proxies. Advantages in measurement are especially valuable in the case of reputation, given the beliefs underlying actors' reputations are difficult to observe despite being central to theoretical accounts.

A further benefit is that experimental methods can readily be applied to the public by embedding experiments in opinion surveys. A large body of experimental work studying public opinion has grown across various subfields in political science.[80] Looking at public opinion is especially appropriate for our purposes because the public is in fact the main theoretical actor of interest. Popular international law posits that it is the beliefs, preferences, and actions of ordinary people that matter in important ways for the operation of international legal commitments. Survey experiments allow the use of an effective method on the theoretically appropriate population of interest for evaluating the popular foundations of international law.

Experimental methods are not without their own limits, especially when it comes to external validity and making broader generalizations.[81] The control possible through experiments also means that designs are necessarily reduced to a few key treatments, often implemented over a short time period, compared to the complex and fluid nature of real-world conditions. Subjects may act and think differently in experimental settings compared to more commonplace situations. Yet the trade-offs between experimental and observational approaches are not nearly so stark as sometimes portrayed, and there are ways experiments can be conceived to maximize their benefits while minimizing downsides.[82] Ultimately, the value of any method should be a function of how well it addresses the particular empirical challenges posed by the phenomenon under study compared to available alternatives. In one appraisal, experimental methods are most beneficial, "where theory, observational studies, or policy concerns generate contested causal claims and when potential problems such as two-way causation and omitted variable bias plague the statistical analysis of observational data."[83] As the prior discussion makes clear, this exemplifies much current research on international law and the role of reputation in particular, making an experimental approach especially attractive.

A Reputational Research Design

To evaluate the conjecture that the public can serve as an important actor in the enforcement function of international law through reputational sanctions, I designed and fielded a series of survey experiments. All surveys queried respondents drawn from the US public about their beliefs regarding the reputation of foreign countries. The United States is an appropriate venue because the US public offers a hard test due to more deep-seated skepticism toward international institutions compared to many other national populations.[84] Moreover, the US public is an especially relevant population because of the continued pivotal place of their country in the international legal order. As a result, real or threatened refusal by the United States to cooperate (or only on more onerous terms) that could ensue in part through public reactions would prove extremely costly for many foreign countries, raising the salience of reputational sanctions.[85]

The main reputation survey (which also informed the design of a second follow-up study discussed further below) was administered online in 2011 to a sample of 2,929 adults.[86] As a national probability sample, survey participants were representative of the wider US population.[87]

Because an actor's reputation is a function of others' beliefs, the survey examines US public attitudes toward a foreign country.[88] The survey refers to a hypothetical country to reduce the likelihood respondents are influenced by idiosyncrasies concerning any particular country or region.[89] After a general introductory prompt, participants are randomly presented additional information that manipulates the issue area, type of prior commitment and its level of obligation, and compliance behavior of the foreign country. As summarized in figure 3.1, the study can be thought of as a 2 (Issue Area: security/economic) × 3 (Commitment: none/soft law/hard law) × 2 (Compliance: violate/comply) factorial design, where the treatments are fully crossed so that all possible combinations of each condition are included—12 in total. The complete instruments for this and subsequent experiments are available in Supplementary Online Materials.

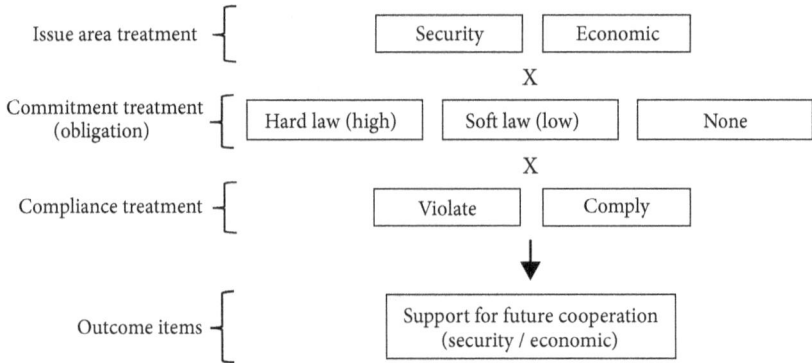

FIGURE 3.1. Reputation survey experiment #1 structure

Notes: Factorial design where all treatments are fully crossed. Survey conducted by Knowledge Networks in 2011.

The first treatment, Issue Area, concerns the foreign policy issue in question, differentiating between security versus economic matters. Considerable debate continues over whether international law only carries weight in "lower" politics issues, while being negligible when national security is involved.[90] Facing such skepticism, some legal proponents remain cautious, accepting that international law may have less impact under "high" politics security situations, including for reputation.[91]

Irrespective of the issue area, the scenario was constructed so as to involve issues of greater salience. The security condition touches on territorial disputes and the use of force, which represents one of the most central issues in international law. The territorial integrity norm and prohibitions against forceful changes to borders is foundational to the modern UN system, but with vestiges going back centuries.[92] The scenario concerns a contested island in another region where natural resources were recently discovered, with the danger that one or more states would use force to take control of the island. Focusing on territorial disputes, which are both frequent but also volatile and more likely to escalate militarily,[93] contributes to making the situation more realistic compared to an uncommon or completely abstract scenario. An island dispute also lessens the likelihood participants associate the scenario with a particular country or region—similar quarrels have taken place across several regions, including the South China Sea, the Middle East, and Latin America at the time the survey was fielded.[94]

The economic scenario, in turn, deals with trade relations between countries. The scenario describes countries in the region facing economic problems, increasing prospects for trade barriers against outside products to protect domestic industries. A generic trade scenario was crafted to similarly guard against respondents attributing events to a particular country or region. Commercial disputes are fairly common, especially with rising membership in the World Trade Organization (WTO), along with preferential trade agreements. Trade also represents a particularly noteworthy economic issue. While some research suggests public preferences toward trade are not very well formed, others point to coherent mass opinions around free trade and protectionism, with matters of reputation and credibility figuring prominently.[95]

All other general elements of the two scenarios were kept as similar as possible to ensure any differences in results were due to the issue at hand rather than other distinguishing features. Both scenarios present a foreign country facing circumstances where it may have incentives to engage in transgressive behavior (either military or economic).

The second treatment, Type of Commitment, deals with whether the foreign country made a commitment not to pursue the relevant policy, and the nature of the obligation if it choose to do so. For the security scenario, the pledge was to refrain from resorting to military force to take control of the contested island. In the economic situation, the promise was to abstain from raising trade barriers against outside products. Both scenarios thus involve a "negative" commitment, or promises *not* to take particular actions, as opposed to a "positive" commitment where a country pledges to take active steps to engage in a given behavior.

Positive and negative commitments are common across a variety of international laws, with many agreements containing both types of provisions. For instance, alliances can take the form of defensive pacts involving a positive commitment to aid a partner under attack, as opposed to nonaggression pacts more akin to a negative commitment where the pledge is not to attack other signatories. The 1949 Geneva Conventions proscribe a range of abuses against vulnerable groups like prisoners and civilians, but also require armed forces to take certain steps to improve their training and operations.[96] Positive and negative commitments may have different reputational implications, since compliance with the former usually necessitates taking some observable action, while the latter require a country only to refrain from engaging in a particular deed. Yet existing research suggests that, if anything, negative commitments should provide a more conservative estimate for the reputational consequences of noncompliance and thus an even tougher test for our purposes.[97]

The commitment treatment involves three experimental conditions: a control group involving no commitment, a soft law (low obligation) treatment, and a hard law (high obligation) treatment. Groups receiving the "none," or no commitment, condition were told the foreign country had not previously made any agreement dealing with the relevant promise (use of force for the security scenario; trade barriers for the economic scenario). The experimental design choice mirrors the key comparison in observational studies between parties versus nonparties to an agreement, where no commitment is the reference group.[98] For the control, I use the generic term "international agreement" so as not to lead respondents to presume the country refused to join a specific type of instrument, especially since the other two conditions vary the level of legal obligation.

The two treatment conditions introduce a prior commitment by the foreign country not to engage in the relevant transgressive behavior. Participants in the "hard law" treatment are told the commitment represented a binding legal obligation, where the country "had previously signed an international treaty where it made a formal promise" to refrain from the applicable action.[99] Higher levels of obligation are correspondingly expected to raise the reputational consequences for violating a legal commitment.[100]

Yet legal commitments come with varying degrees of obligation. A second "soft law" treatment presents a lower nonbinding commitment—respondents in this group are told the foreign country "had taken part in a regional meeting that created guidelines recommending countries" to refrain from the unwanted action.[101] Various organization have adopted recommendations of this sort, such as the African Union on territorial disputes, or the Group of Seven (G7) on various economic policies. As discussed in chapter 1, the status of "soft law" is debated, but these commitments should still be considered as possessing a degree of legal obligation, even if more modest compared to formal treaties. In this first survey, I chose to focus on varying the level of obligation because this element of legalization remains the most widely studied and often seen as being of greatest consequence (a second study detailed later includes other legalization dimensions).[102] While precision or delegation are also sometimes referred to when speaking of an agreement as harder or softer in terms of its legalization, as a shorthand I use "hard law" or "soft law" to describe the level of obligation (high or low) when discussing the experimental results.

The third and final treatment, Compliance, concerns how the foreign country subsequently acted with regards to its (non)commitment in the security or economic scenario. Respondents receiving the "violate" condition were told the country ended up deciding to engage in the transgressive behavior—either using military force to take the island (security scenario), or raising trade barriers (economic scenario). By contrast, those in the "comply" condition were told the country either did not use military force, or did not raise trade barriers. It is important to stress that references to either the "violate" or "comply" are only used as labels here to facilitate discussion of the country's subsequent behavior. Technically speaking, for the "no commitment" control group, neither violation nor compliance could have occurred since the country had not made any prior commitment for it to later follow (or not follow). The actual language received by all participants only presents in plain terms the course taken by the country, avoiding overly pejorative or praiseworthy descriptions that might unduly bias participants.

By both necessity and design not all factors that might be of relevance can be included in the scenario.[103] Increasing the number of treatments can weaken the statistical power of experiments, while introducing complex interactions among conditions that can be difficult to reliably model.[104] Taking a balanced approach, this experiment constructs a situation with readily apparent real-world analogies that engages survey participants across the most pertinent theoretical and empirical dimensions of interest. Whether involving higher (or lower) politics, the military (or economic) issues under dispute are intended to be salient, involving potential security, financial, and symbolic stakes reminiscent of comparable events that have happened at various points in the past and likely to recur in the future.

International legal commitments are not out of place, but rather loom large in these sorts of altercations. The WTO and its rules are frequently invoked in burgeoning trade quarrels, garnering outsized media coverage.[105] In territorial disputes like those between China and several of its neighbors in the South China Sea, various UN conventions, along with judicial bodies like the Permanent Court of Arbitration, figure prominently.[106] More dramatic events, such as Russia's 2022 invasion of Ukraine, has likewise been described as much in legal terms as concerning military or diplomatic dynamics.[107] This attention does not fall on deaf ears, as ordinary people have been shown to respond to this coverage, actively seeking out further information on legal-related matters across a range of issues.[108] The experiment thus seeks to approximate real-world dynamics in ways that allow us to assess how reputational concerns play out among ordinary people.

After considering the scenario that varied across these three treatments, participants are then asked to answer a series of questions regarding support for future US cooperation with the foreign country. Reputational arguments in international law primarily focus on other actors' expectations of a country's trustworthiness to uphold its commitments, and how these beliefs might (or might not) change based on the country's past promises and record of compliance. One observable implication entails examining possible changes in the public's willingness for their government to cooperate and negotiate future agreements with the relevant country. Unlike observational studies relying on indirect and rougher proxies, one of the advantages of an experimental approach mentioned earlier is in providing more precise measurement of the primary theoretical quantities of interest.

Nonetheless, it is important to note what such a design can (and cannot) capture. The experiment is *not* able to show the actual final reputational costs/benefits involving a definitive change to the US government's cooperation with the foreign country. Being in a position to obtain such policy responses is beyond the means of almost any experiment; and would raise enormous ethical issues even if it were possible. What the present study can show is the impact of (non)compliance with legal commitments on the US public's support for cooperation with the foreign country. The chain of responsiveness from mass opinion to government policy may be long and fraught.[109] But the public's attitudes and beliefs are the building blocks to popular international law and an ordinary actor-centered account of the enforcement of legal commitments through a reputational mechanism.

The main outcome variable concerns public support for their government to conclude a future international agreement on a related issue with the foreign country. For the security scenario, participants are told, "The United States is currently thinking about signing an agreement with this country that would involve cooperation over military issues." Those receiving the economic treatment are instead presented with an analogous question about "cooperation over trade issues." The wording refers to a generic "agreement" so that respondents are not cued toward a particular type of legal commitment. Participants are then asked how much they would support or oppose (on a five-point scale ranging from "strongly support" to "strongly oppose") the United States concluding the associated agreement with the foreign country matched to the issue area presented to them.

To capture the possibility of spillover effects to reputations in other issue areas, participants were also asked a corresponding question about support for cooperation with the foreign country in the opposite issue area to the one covered by their scenario (trade cooperation from the security situation; military cooperation for the economic situation). The experimental design thus provides an opportunity to generate more reliable estimates of reputational dynamics in the enforcement of international law, but also identify potential spillover effects which have proved especially complicated to capture.[110]

Finding Reputation

Because respondents were randomly assigned to different versions of the scenario based on the three treatments (issue area, commitment, compliance), the experimental design increases the likelihood that each group differs on average from each other only with respect to the relevant treatments.[111] As expected, balance tests indicate groups were comparable across many observed confounders

that could affect individual support for future cooperation.[112] Sampling procedures also ensure that empirical results are unlikely to be a function of peculiarities to the sample, but rather representative of attitudes held across the wider US
public.[113]

Turning to the analysis, randomization alleviates the need for complex statistical models relying on a battery of controls that characterizes much observational
research on international law. In what follows, I observe commonly accepted best
practices and choose to report relatively straightforward cross-tabulations and
difference-in-means.[114] Nevertheless, results are robust to including standard
socio-demographic covariates commonly associated with individual foreign
policy preferences.[115] For ease of presentation and interpretation, values for the
main outcomes and all subsequent items are rescaled to range between 0 and 1,
so that effect sizes indicate first differences in the percentage-point change in
support for US cooperation with the foreign country—our primary measure for
reputational consequences.[116]

To provide an initial sense of general attitudes, figure 3.2 reports raw levels
of support for international cooperation within each issue area, separated out
by compliance condition but aggregated across all types of commitments. The

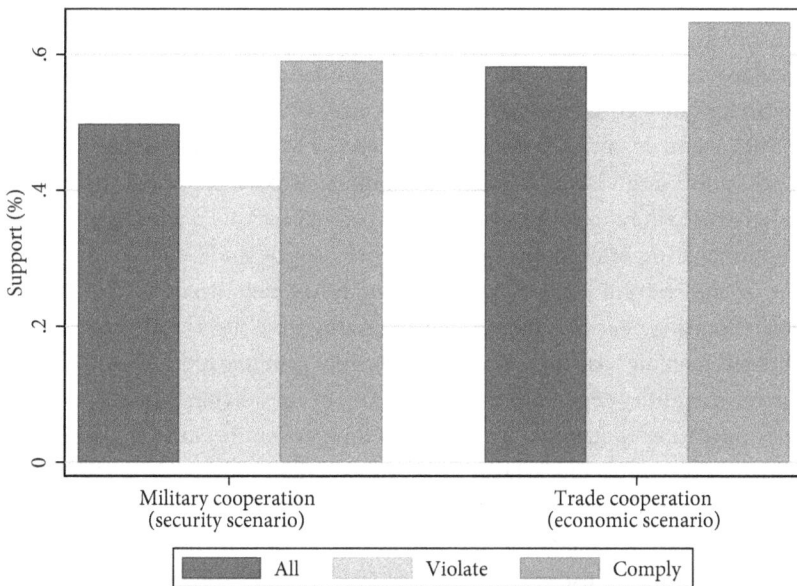

FIGURE 3.2. Overall support for future cooperation, by issue area and compliance

Notes: Support for future cooperation in relevant issue area (military for the security scenario; trade for the economic scenario) separated by compliance conditions. Responses are pooled across all commitment conditions.
Data from reputation survey experiment #1.

US respondents are generally less supportive of their country cooperating with others in military affairs compared to economic matters, and the difference is statistically significant at conventional thresholds.[117] Contrasts in overall support for cooperation across issue area likely reflects greater public concerns over sovereignty and security interests involved in matters of high politics compared to what may be seen as more mundane commercial relations.[118] Participants also appear to use past behavior as a guide in their support for future cooperation. "Violating" actions (using force, raising trade barriers) by foreign countries lead to weaker support for future US cooperation compared to more "compliant" deeds (not using force or raising barriers). The gap between violators and compliers in support for cooperation is wider in the security scenario (decline of 18%) compared to the economic scenario (13%), but the effect is statistically significant in both cases.

These findings are suggestive that public opinion responds in systematic ways to different features of the scenarios. However, the main question of interest for reputational accounts is whether the specific type of commitment previously made by foreign countries affects attitudes toward future international cooperation. Is there a reputational cost among the US public that comes from violating legalized obligations; correspondingly, do reputational returns accrue for adhering to those same commitments? Figure 3.3 shows the reputational consequences of legal commitments in the security and economic scenarios respectively; vertical lines display the 90% and 95% confidence intervals illustrating the uncertainty around each effect. The figure reports the percentage-point change in support for future cooperation (military or trade) with the foreign country resulting from a hard or soft law commitment (high or low obligation) not to engage in the relevant transgressive behavior (using military force, or raising trade barriers), relative to the control group where the country had not made any prior legal commitment. Importantly, the subsequent behavior by the foreign country is the same in the relevant condition—employing force/trade barriers (the lefthand "violate" pairing of each subfigure), or refraining from force/trade barriers (the righthand "comply" pairing).[119] Yet the behavior's *meaning* in the eyes of US participants may differ depending on the presence of a prior commitment. Negative values refer to a reputational "cost" for the foreign country in terms of reduced willingness of participants to favor future cooperation, while positive values indicate a reputational "benefit" of support for enhanced cooperative possibilities.

Looking first at violators in the security scenario (that the foreign country eventually decided to use military force over the islands) confirms that legalized commitments carry greater reputational stakes. Respondents who were told the foreign country had violated a hard law commitment previously made through

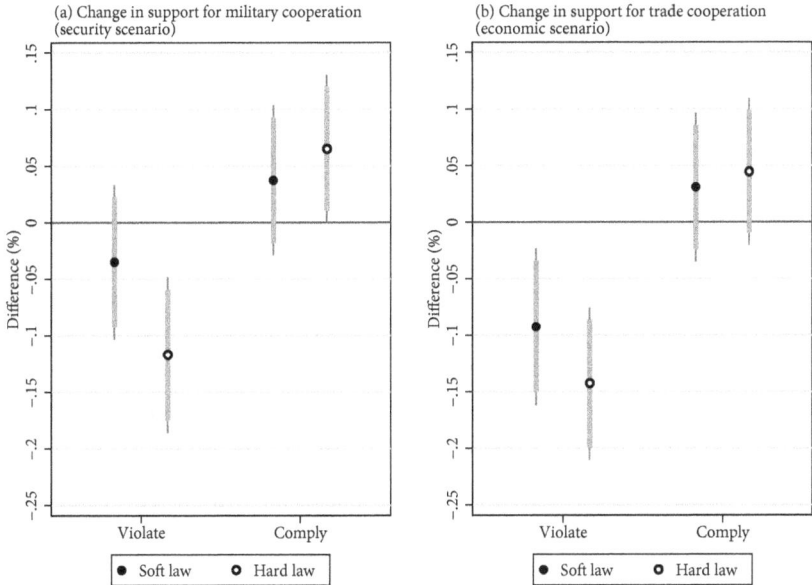

FIGURE 3.3. Reputational effects of legal commitment on support for future cooperation, by issue area

Notes: First differences (with 90% and 95% confidence intervals) between the legal commitment treatment for obligation type (soft law [low] or hard law [high]) and control group (no commitment) on support for future cooperation in the same issue area. Outcome is support for future military cooperation in the security scenario, and future trade cooperation in the economic scenario. Data from reputation survey experiment #1.

a formal treaty were around 12% less likely to favor future military cooperation compared to situations where the country resorted to similar military force but had made no previous legal obligation. The decline was slightly more pronounced in the economic scenario with a drop of 14% in support for trade cooperation. In both scenarios the effect on the relevant form of cooperation from violating a hard law was statistically significant as the confidence intervals do not include zero, or no apparent effect. Consistent with reputational accounts, treaty commitments appear far from costless—there is a price to be paid among the public for noncompliance.

The results go on to suggest, however, that not all pledges are treated equally in the eyes of the public. The level of legal obligation shapes reputational stakes. For the security scenario, violating softer nonbinding guidelines recommending the nonuse of military force results in a decrease in support for future military cooperation, but the effect is much smaller (around 3%) and fails to be significantly different from zero. In the economic situation, the soft law effect is more pronounced (9%) and statistically significant, though still smaller than the decline from violating harder obligations. Legal commitments exhibiting lower levels of obligation thus do not appear to generate the same extent of reputational consequences, which is in line with some expectations from the legalization literature.[120]

In the bigger picture, we should still not make too much of the relative differences in the effects of softer versus harder obligations.[121] Even if they differ in size and significance, violations of all forms of legal commitments are associated with some damage to a foreign country's reputation for reliability.[122] Equally clear in both scenarios is that a foreign country violating a formal treaty comes with sizable reputational consequences in the eyes of the US public. Comparisons across issues reveal some modest differences with reputational costs slightly larger when violating economic versus military commitments. This disparity may reflect a common understanding that security concerns are more likely to trump (but not negate) legal commitments when matters of high politics are under dispute.[123] In this way, interpretations of both commitments and compliance may be filtered through the public's preexisting outlook. If baseline expectations of compliance are lower for security issues, then this may already be factored in somewhat by audiences, meaning reputational consequences for subsequent violations involving the use of force should be less acute. Yet reputational consequences for different substantive commitments are still a matter of degree and not of kind. It is instructive that in both military and economic circumstances, the prospect of public feelings in withholding future cooperation from a violating country are present.[124]

Turning to the right-side values in each subfigure indicates that foreign countries are unlikely to gain much of a corresponding reputational premium among US audiences by adhering to their commitments (i.e., choosing *not* to use military force, or raise trade barriers, respectively). Public support for future military cooperation does rise, as expected, when a foreign country complies with either harder or softer security promises compared to engaging in the same policy in the absence of a prior commitment. However, the size of the effects (7% for hard law, and 4% for soft law) are generally weaker than the negative reputational repercussions from violating those same commitments. The treatment effects for compliance are also generally not statistically significant, except for hard law at the 90% level. The pattern is even more tepid for adherence to economic promises, where increased support for future US trade cooperation is only 4% for hard law and 3% for soft law commitments accordingly.

Lackluster reputational benefits from compliance may be explained in part by referring back to the oft-quoted maxim by legal proponents like Henkin that countries comply with "almost all" of their promises.[125] Reputations are subject to greater change in response to actions that are more informative for audiences.[126]

A foreign country's observance of a prior commitment to refrain from military force (or trade protection) may offer little new information to the US public regarding the country's likely propensity to comply with future promises, help-ing account for the weaker ensuing reputational benefits. In line with past work suggesting that states tend to only join agreements they intend to follow, the US public may be unfazed by records of compliant behavior, disinclined to see the country as more trustworthy or deserving of further cooperative opportunities. By contrast, those same baseline expectations mean that noncompliance may be seen by audiences as more revealing about the foreign country's trustworthiness. As a result, the reputational sanctions for violations should be proportionally greater, which is exactly what is observed.[127]

The combined results from figure 3.3 point to important bounds around what international law can and cannot do. The purpose of international law is less to reward those who meet their commitments with ever greater reputational ben-efits. Rather, one of the primary functions of international law is to serve as an enforcement device to punish those who fail to follow through on their promises. Countries may gain in the short term by reneging on their commitments, but do so under the shadow of longer-term and more diffuse costs, including the pos-sible loss of future cooperative opportunities and foregone collaborative benefits, beginning with public disapproval of their actions.

Why would countries be willing to take on such commitments if the ben-efits seem slight relative to the costs? As formal signaling and bargaining models demonstrate, it is precisely the potential to suffer ex post costs that can improve the credibility of *present* commitments.[128] The experimental findings presented here thus provide strong micro-level support for these models in general, and in particular for the enforcement function of international agreements (for both softer obligations, and especially harder formal treaties) by raising the reputa-tional stakes involved, thereby making violations less attractive and commit-ments potentially more credible.

This overall picture continues to hold when considering possible conditional effects. One worry with the findings so far is that they may mask important dif-ferences across certain subgroups. Of particular concern is whether the effects of legal commitments are limited only to those groups who: 1) already have a favorable view of international law; or 2) may be less active or consequential politically. In other words, is international law simply preaching to the choir, or those unwilling or unable to do much about it? Further analyses reveal a similar reputational story, where neither concern comes into play. On the first point, for US groups commonly thought to be skeptical of international legal commit-ments, such as conservatives or Republicans, the size of reputational effects are actually slightly *stronger* compared to their liberal or Democratic counterparts.[129]

On the second point, across various measures of political participation (e.g., voting, activism, and interest in politics), those more engaged politically are just as much, if not more, influenced by reputational concerns as less-involved citizens. Segments of the public best able to hold governments to account thus prove more than willing to support the enforcement of international legal commitments through reputational channels.

Reputations Spilling Over

This experimental study further offers the opportunity to address an additional hotly debated question in international legal circles—whether reputational consequences extend beyond the matter at hand. Some proponents contend that reputations are far reaching, where compliance has implications for a country's image of reliability outside the initial policy arena. Reputational "ripples" may be greatest in the immediate purview of the commitment's substance, but like a stone dropped in a still lake can be felt farther afield.[130] Acting in bad faith on a trade agreement may not only affect a country's future commercial relations, but lead to a "breakdown of cooperation in other games with other partners."[131] If reputations are evaluations of an actor's disposition, then the question is whether (non)compliance can shape assessments of their commitment to legal rules more generally. Some scholars suggest violations of "one rule or the other" are informative of a country's support for the entire "system of customary international law," signaling whether they have "an overriding interest in maintaining the overall system."[132] Should international laws and related principles have normative underpinnings, then these rules confer a "moral status" that "[n]either superpowers nor states on the periphery of international society can afford to ignore."[133]

Skeptics counter that (to the extent reputational consequences exist) it is better to think about a country's multiple *reputations* instead of a single holistic reputation.[134] Reputational ripples are likely to be minor, as any spillover is limited to circumstances where the correlates of compliance are tightly connected.[135] The information supposedly supplied by compliance with legal commitments is at best confined to the immediate issue.[136] Despite different theoretical claims, both proponents and skeptics agree that testing these competing spillover positions is challenging and remains an open question.[137]

To assess reputational spillover, we can look at the follow-up question asked in the experiment, which queries support for future cooperation in the *other* policy from the one presented to respondents—support for trade cooperation for the security scenario; and support for a military agreement for the economic prompt.[138] Figure 3.4 reports the percentage-point change in US public support for future cooperation in the opposite issue as a function of (non)compliance with each type of legal obligation (hard or soft) relative to the same baseline control of no prior commitment.

The results reveal a more nuanced picture regarding the potential for reputational consequences to stretch to other issues. Consistent with skeptics' expectations, figure 3.4(a) indicates that (non)compliance with economic commitments has little bearing on the willingness of participants to approve of US cooperation on military matters. Raising trade barriers does reduce participants' support for a military agreement in the context of violating either a hard or soft law commitment (both around 3%), but neither is statistically significant. Complying by refraining from imposing such barriers continues to have minimal influence—for soft law the effect is actually slightly negative (−2%), while for hard law the difference is positive (4%) but likewise not significant. Although the reputational sanctions from violations are quite large *within* the context of trade (refer back to figure 3.3[b]), any enforcement dynamics do not appear to extend *beyond* commercial relations. The results so far seem to confirm skeptics' claims that, even if international law heightens reputational stakes, those consequences do not carry over to other areas.

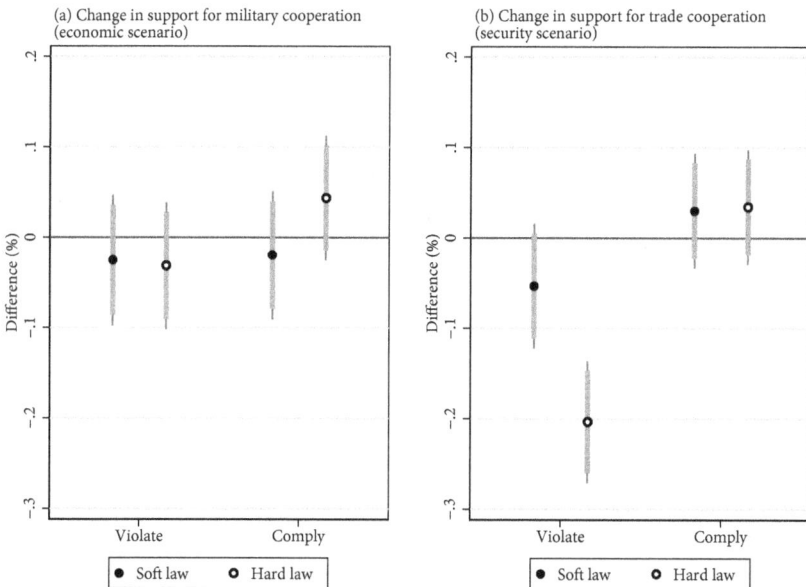

FIGURE 3.4. Reputational spillover effects of legal commitment on support for future cooperation, by other issue area

Notes: First differences (with 90% and 95% confidence intervals) between the legal commitment treatment for obligation type (soft law [low] or hard law [high]) and control group (no commitment) on support for future cooperation in the opposite issue area. Outcome is support for future military cooperation in the economic scenario, and future trade cooperation in the security scenario. Data from reputation survey experiment #1.

Spillover effects may not be universal, but shifting our gaze to the broader implications of security commitments shows they can still be quite substantial. Figure 3.4(b) shows that violating a hard law treaty promise by using force leads to a more than a 20% drop in public support for future trade cooperation with the offending country. This spillover is noteworthy because it is almost double the original decline (12%) in support for cooperation within the same military sphere. This effect is even starker when viewed in relative terms—violating a hard law security commitment generates a percent change decline of almost one third in support for trade cooperation compared to a situation where the country engaged in the exact same behavior without any prior legal commitment.[139] Like the within-issue results, however, similar noncompliance with a soft law commitment is associated with a weaker decline (5%) in trade cooperation, a difference that also just fails to be statistically significant. Meager reputational benefits either within or outside of military affairs persist when complying with those same commitments.

The full results from figure 3.4 suggest an asymmetry in the potential for reputational dynamics to flow from one issue to another. Large spillover effects from security commitments into support for economic cooperation may be explained by the signals such conduct communicate to audiences regarding the foreign country's trustworthiness. General expectations of compliance may be lower for security commitments, but a country showing itself willing to renege on such high-stakes promises may then be viewed as even more prone to violating commitments involving lower politics, such as for trade. Noncompliance in this context is relatively more informative, leading audiences to update their beliefs and willingness to endorse cooperation accordingly. Because security issues are often more salient in the public's eyes, prospects for reputational spillover may be greater for security commitments compared to economic promises even if the latter have more pronounced intra-issue consequences.

The impact of reputation on public attitudes toward international cooperation may be more substantial for economic affairs, evidenced by both the direct and spillover effects on future trade cooperation. Past research has shown more generally that security factors play an important role in either facilitating or inhibiting economic cooperation.[140] Results from this experiment illustrate a domestic pathway through which the public may express stronger support for cooperation on economic fronts with foreign countries who have proven more reliable (or less unreliable) in keeping their legal promises in matters of national security. Mass support for military cooperation may instead follow a slightly more pragmatic logic, where security is of foremost concern with weaker implications for compliance from unrelated promises. But any baseline differences appear slight— even in harder cases of "high politics," international law proves able to fulfill an enforcement function by the imposition of substantial reputational costs that are understood by, and potentially performed through, ordinary members of the public.

Investigating Mechanisms and Alternative Explanations

The results so far offer compelling evidence of reputational consequences among the public for international legal commitments, especially ones rooted in hard law treaty obligations with effects that can even spill over to outside issues. Nonetheless, several questions linger regarding whether these findings are in fact due to a reputational logic as opposed to alternative motivations or modes of enforcement.

To start to address these issues, as part of a second study I conducted a pair of follow-up surveys in 2014 on a total sample of 2,113 US respondents recruited using Amazon's Mechanical Turk (MTurk) service. MTurk allows access to a large subject pool by offering compensation in return for completing a task, in this case filling out a survey. While less representative than national probability samples, participants recruited via MTurk are generally more representative of the US population compared to many common convenience samples and even some broader survey initiatives.[141] MTurk samples do tend to skew in certain directions, such as drawing respondents who are younger, more educated, and lean liberal. Yet as the conditional (non)effects involving political ideology or partisanship noted in the first study make clear, these compositional differences should have little impact and may pose an even *harder* test for detecting reputational consequences.

Our main outcome variable in the original survey involved public support for future cooperation with a foreign country based on its prior commitment and compliance decisions. This measure captures one of the core observable implications from changes in reputation—the willingness to approve of future cooperation with that country. However, the item does not directly gauge *why* publics may feel this way about cooperation, which could be due to reevaluations of trustworthiness, but possibly other desires like simply to punish the offending country.

For the second reputation study, I nested a modified version of the original survey experiment alongside several added treatments and a battery of other items to further probe respondents' reasons behind their attitudes toward future cooperation. The study was fielded in two separate waves with the initial batch centered on the security scenario, followed by a separate sample receiving the economic scenario.[142] Each wave was identically structured except for the issue area under dispute. Because the compliance condition did not yield any significant treatment effects, the follow-up study only presents situations where the foreign country engaged in the relevant "violating" behavior (using force, or raising trade barriers). The survey continues to vary the nature of the commitment and its level of obligation (none/soft law/hard law; there is also an alternative "no mention" control that is not used in the main analysis).[143] Additional treatments on the two other dimensions of legalization concerning precision and delegation are also included, and discussed in greater detail further below. Unlike the first study, the follow-up survey is not a full factorial design—some treatments are only applied to certain groups depending on their assignment to specific experimental conditions. Figure 3.5 summarizes the full structure of this second study.

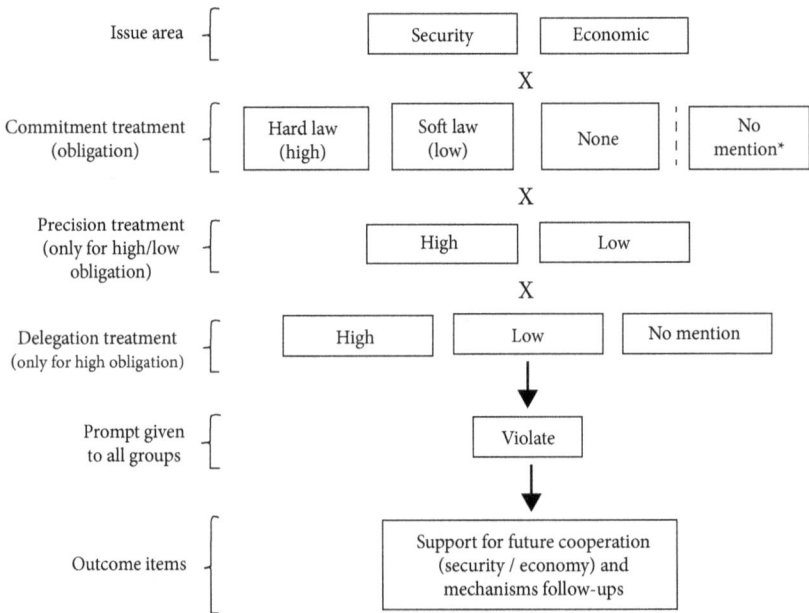

FIGURE 3.5.   Reputation survey experiment #2 structure

Notes: Each issue area (security or economic) was fielded as a separate survey wave with all subsequent design elements remaining identical. The Commitment treatment included an additional alternative "No Mention"* control group (i.e., no prompt given on any form of commitment). However, to facilitate comparisons to the first reputation study, all analysis is conducted with the "None" condition (i.e., prompt that the foreign country had not made a commitment) as the baseline control, which was also used in reputation survey experiment #1. Modified factorial design where Precision and Delegation treatments are only given to certain Commitment conditions as specified in the structure above. All groups were given the "Violate" prompt (use of force in the security scenario/ raising tariff barriers in the economic scenario). Survey conducted using Amazon's MTurk in 2014.

After receiving the same main support for cooperation question as in the first study, participants were then asked, "How likely do you think this country will keep promises on [military/economic] issues in the future?" based on the relevant issue area. Possible answers were on a four-point scale ranging from "very likely" to "very unlikely." This item offers a more direct measure of whether changes in individual beliefs about the foreign country's willingness to uphold its prospective commitments are based on its past behavior, as expected in reputational accounts.

The first pair of values in each subfigure from figure 3.6 reports first differences between the obligation treatments (soft law/hard law) and no commitment control condition, measured as the percentage-point change in beliefs that the foreign country will keep future promises for the security or economic scenario respectively.[144] Negative consequences for the foreign country's trustworthiness is evident for both security and economic commitments with declines of around 32 to 36% for hard law commitments, and smaller but still pronounced drops of a little over 20% for softer obligations. Participants dramatically update their beliefs about the trustworthiness of a foreign country when it violates legalized promises, which is consistent with a reputational argument for the motivations behind support for ex post sanctions from international law.

Figure 3.6 also examines a related question of whether international law activates particular normative beliefs. Beyond the specific behavior being regulated, international law is embedded in a broader set of foundational principles, or metanorms, the foremost being pacta sunt servanda ("promises must be kept"). The desire for reputational sanctions may be driven in part by greater moral sentiments engendered among audiences from violations of legalized commitments. An additional follow-up item asks participants whether the foreign country had a "moral obligation" to refrain from the behavior in question (use military force/raise trade barriers) on a five-point scale ranging from "strongly agree" to "strongly disagree." The second pairs of values in figure 3.6 report first differences from violating each type of legal obligation, again separately for the security and economic scenarios. Results confirm that respondents are more likely to believe countries have a moral obligation to eschew behavior regulated by a legalized commitment compared to when no prior promise was made. Similar to the overall reputation findings from the original study, effects are more marked in the case of trade policy (increases of 41% for hard law and 29% for soft law) relative to military force (around 15% for both obligation types). On matters of national security, where international legal calculations may figure less prominently, both forms of commitment still generate significant moral calculations among members of the US public. While both hard and soft law obligations have

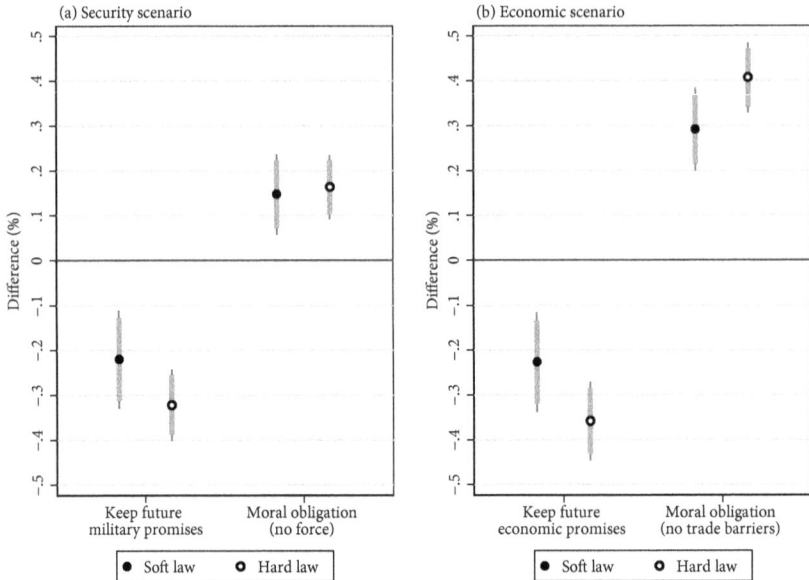

FIGURE 3.6. Effects from violation of legal commitment on expectations of future compliance and moral obligations, by issue area

Notes: First differences (with 90% and 95% confidence intervals) between the obligation treatment (soft law [low] or hard law [high]) and control group (no commitment). Outcomes are beliefs that foreign government will keep future promises, and moral obligation not to engage in relevant violation, respectively. Data from reputation survey experiment #2.

similar moral effects for military matters, violating formal treaties has somewhat more pronounced effects on normative beliefs over trade policy.

The results indicate the normative underpinnings of even many purportedly rationalist mechanisms like reputation.[145] Violations of legal commitments provide greater information to audiences regarding the disposition of foreign countries, but the results confirm international law helps produce a *principled* form of information that appears more likely to trigger reputational concerns within national publics.

We can gain further insight into the public's reasoning through an open-ended question posed to all participants asking them to expand on their answer to the main support for cooperation item. The type and prevalence of words respondents chose to use help illuminate the impact of the relevant commitment condition on their thinking.[146] While words like "trust" or "trusted" were mentioned infrequently by those in the no commitment control, variants of "trust" were among the top ten most common words identified in responses from the hard law group. Mentions of "trust" occurred less often for those receiving the soft law prompt, but was still among the twenty most common terms for this group, which is somewhat expected given the lower level of obligation involved.

A reputational logic was also evident in the fuller explanations many participants gave for their unwillingness to cooperate with a foreign country that violated a formal treaty. As one subject stated: "I feel like the country would go against the agreement eventually. They did it before and I believe that they would do it again. The country doesn't seem very stable or trustworthy." Another response touches on similar themes, but ties their opposition to a deeper sense of honor (or lack thereof): "Because this country, based on its past actions, does not honor agreements. So I would not trust them to honor any agreements it made with the US." Even those not explicitly mentioning trust still thought about obligations in normative terms, including one participant from the hard law group who said, "There is no good reason to invade it [the island]. It is morally wrong to take over another country or island or land that is not yours." Those in the control group who rejected future cooperation justified doing so more out of considerations like the substantive actions taken by the foreign country, or objecting wholesale to US cooperation with anyone. While similar sorts of explanations could sometimes be found in the legal commitment treatment groups, they were less pervasive. The presence of international law thus appears to not only influence overall support for international cooperation, but also ordinary people's reasoning with evaluations of trust being especially prominent, as reputational accounts expect.[147]

Despite these findings regarding the role of trust and moral beliefs in enforcement through reputation, perhaps it is the case that the public is not responding to the particular legal obligations but rather some other characteristic shared by these sorts of commitments. Legal commitments vary not only in terms of their level of obligation (the main empirical focus so far), but can also differ along other dimensions of legalization, including the precision of provisions, or the degree to which powers are delegated to third parties like international courts. These three dimensions—obligation, precision, and delegation—can vary independently with some agreements scoring higher (or lower) on certain components than others.[148] It is possible, however, that the public assumes certain components are more likely to be present with a given level of obligation.[149] The potential role of delegation, in particular, suggests that rather than reputation serving as a more decentralized enforcement mechanism rooted at least in part in domestic actors like the public, findings observed in the original experiment may instead reflect the lurking role of enforcement from a higher authority. This may especially be of concern with the international trade regime where the WTO looms large, but also for territorial disputes like the security scenario where organizations like the International Court of Justice (ICJ) have been active.

To assess these possibilities, the follow-up study continued to directly manipulate the level of obligation (none/soft law/hard law), but also incorporated separate treatments for two other core dimensions of legalization. Precision (low/
high) is a binary treatment that varies the degree of specificity in the commitment. Participants in the high precision group were told the foreign country's
commitment unequivocally prohibited the unwanted conduct "under any circumstances." Greater ambiguity was instead introduced into the low precision
control, where there "was a lot of debate among experts" about what the commitment really meant and "what types of actions are allowed."[150] Delegation (no
mention/low/high), in turn, varies the presence of an international court that
could prosecute the foreign country for its behavior. The delegation treatment is
threefold: one group (high) receives a prompt on the existence of an international
court with prosecutorial powers; another group (low) is instead told a court with
such powers does not exist; and the control group (no mention) is given no additional delegation prompt. The three legalization dimensions ultimately involve
a modified factorial design, where the treatments are not fully crossed, meaning not all possible combinations are included. Because precision and delegation
refer to specific dimensions of a commitment's legalization, neither treatment
was applied to the obligation control groups involving no promise (explicit or
otherwise). Additionally, delegation treatments were only assigned to those in
the hard law (high obligation) treaty group; in practice, it is unusual for enforcement authority to be transferred to third parties over softer rules that are not
legally binding.[151]

Figure 3.7 returns to the main outcome item measuring public support for
future cooperation in the relevant issue, reporting average treatment effects for
each of the legalization dimensions relative to the relevant control group.[152] First
off, the findings for obligation are largely consistent with those from the original
experiment, despite different samples and time frames. The follow-up study provides further confirmation of public support for reputational consequences from
international legal obligations, indicating the results are not an artifact of a single
survey. This also suggests any further findings from the second study are unlikely
to be due to peculiarities in the respondent pool or research setting.

Although incorporating these other dimensions does not negate the findings for obligation, they do suggest other pathways through which legal commitments may shape public support for reputational sanctions. Violating more
precise agreements is associated with declines in the willingness of participants
to approve future cooperation in both issue scenarios—the size of the decline
(around 6–7%) is more modest compared to that for obligation (especially for
formal treaties), but the effects are still statistically significant. The finding offers
support for various conjectures that the precision of a commitment, irrespective

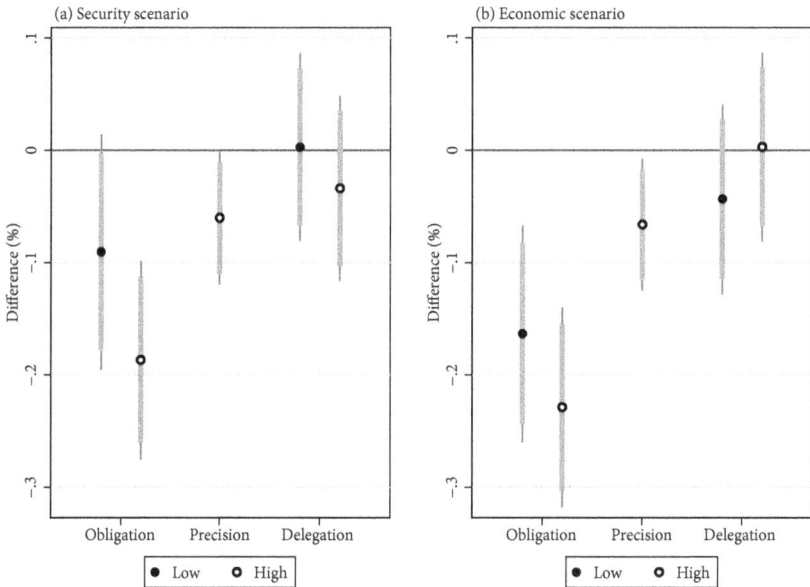

FIGURE 3.7. Reputational effects of legalization from violation of legal commitment on support for future cooperation, by issue area

Notes: First differences (with 90% and 95% confidence intervals) between the relevant legalization treatment and control groups: Obligation (soft law [low]/hard law [high] obligation vs. no commitment); Precision (low vs. high precision; only for those groups receiving a soft law [low]/hard law [high] obligation); and Delegation (no court [low]/court [high] vs. no mention of international court; only for those groups receiving a hard law [high] obligation). Outcome is support for future military cooperation in the security scenario, and future trade cooperation in the economic scenario. Data from reputation survey experiment #2.

of its formal level of obligation, heightens reputational stakes.[153] Greater vagueness in provisions, in turn, introduces uncertainty over the nature of the commitment, reducing potential support for enforcement.[154]

However, delegation (or at least the prospect of punishment by an international court), does not appear to have much impact on a foreign country's reputation as a trustworthy partner among the public. While some results are in the opposite than expected direction (e.g., the slightly positive effect for the presence of a court in the economic scenario), all first differences are of modest size and none are statistically significant. The legalization findings together suggest that formalizing obligations is not the only route to creating a more enforceable agreement. Nonbinding rules can still make reputational considerations more salient, as can crafting more precise provisions. By contrast, frequent handwringing over the powers of international courts—both by supporters and opponents—may be misplaced, at least from a reputational standpoint. Delegation may matter for other functions of international law like preference change, a question I will return to in chapter 5. Nonetheless, the evidence presented here suggests reputational dynamics can operate in a more decentralized fashion, informed by matters from below involving the beliefs of ordinary people on the streets, rather than by what is happening on the benches of international courts.

The prospect of "courtly" punishment does not turn out to figure prominently, but perhaps the public is thinking more about other sorts of penalties when confronted with violations by foreign countries. Reputational sanctions are fairly indirect in the sense that such costs are felt as the loss of foregone, or less advantageous, future cooperative opportunities. Yet as the "Three Rs" of enforcement introduced in chapter 1 point out, punishment can involve more direct retaliatory measures imposing immediate and proximate costs upon nonconforming countries.[155] Even if present to some degree, reputational consequences may be beside the point if the main thrust of public reactions is to support more point-blank retaliatory actions.

An enforcement function for international law may exist, but may not operate solely (or even primarily) through reputational channels. To evaluate this possibility, participants in the second study were asked in a separate set of follow-up questions on whether they supported the United States taking any of the following actions against the violating country: the US president publicly condemning the foreign country's conduct, imposing economic sanctions, or intervening with military force. The three choices represent a range of retaliatory actions—diplomatic, economic, and military.

In absolute terms, overall approval declined with the relative costliness of the punishment, which is not surprising given the costs would be borne not only by the foreign state, but also by the respondent's own country—presidential condemnation was most popular, followed by economic sanctions, while participants were not terribly eager to endorse military intervention. Raw levels of support for retaliation were also on the whole higher in the security scenario, a reasonable pattern given the relative stakes involved in the foreign country's violation of territorial integrity compared to a trade dispute.[156]

Turning to the role of international law, figure 3.8 reports first differences for the main hard and soft law obligation treatments relative to the no commitment control for each form of retaliation. For the security case, despite higher baseline support for punishment, inclinations toward retaliation are generally not heightened much further when a foreign country violates legalized commitments. While all first differences are positive, they are mostly of modest size, and only the effects for economic sanctions are statistically distinguishable from zero. Support for retaliatory consequences are more apparent in the economic scenario, though more so for harder than softer obligations, and mainly at the lower end involving condemnations and sanctions. Like the main reputation findings, the general pattern for retaliation shows that changes in the willingness to approve imposing costs are slightly higher when economic commitments are violated compared to security ones, but differences are not pronounced. Support for retaliation using military force is statistically significant at the 10% level for economic matters, which may seem somewhat surprising. However, we should not read too much into the notion that the public enthusiastically supports replying to trade barriers with bombs. The effect is of moderate size (+5%) and would be unlikely to have much discernable impact on any public debate given raw support for military force in the economic scenario hovers in the low teens among participants overall.

Results from figure 3.8 suggest that retaliatory impulses may be present in the public, but perhaps serve as a complement to popular pressures for enforcement through the sorts of indirect longer-term reputational sanctions that follow from foreign countries violating their legal commitments. Rather than substituting for reputation, dynamics surrounding retaliation are of smaller (or at best

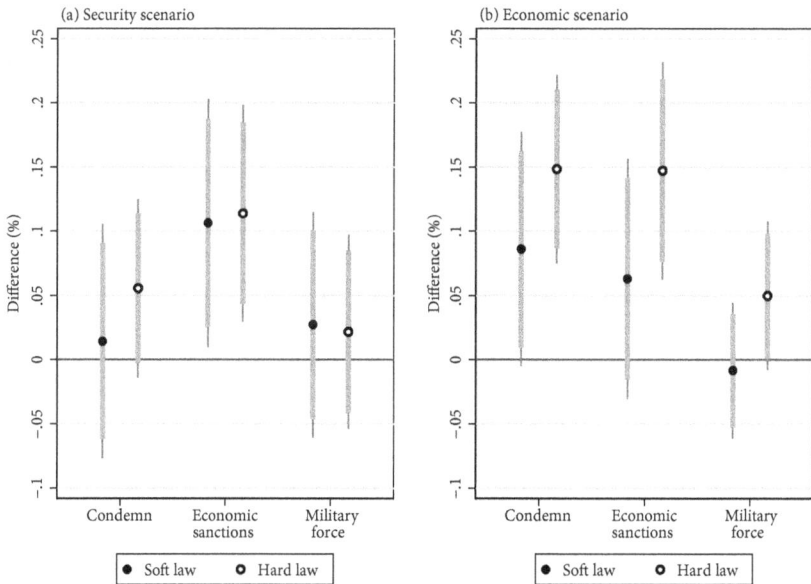

FIGURE 3.8. Effects from violation of legal commitment on support for retaliation, by issue area

Notes: First differences (with 90% and 95% confidence intervals) between the obligation treatment (soft law [low] or hard law [high]) and control group (no commitment). Outcomes are support for different types of retaliation. Data from reputation survey experiment #2.

comparable) size to public support for more diffuse but nonnegligible costs to violators from harm to their image as trustworthy partners along with the potential loss of future cooperative opportunities.[157]

In this chapter, I leveraged experimental methods to investigate whether reputation may serve as a tool of enforcement in international law where more ordinary (and commonly overlooked) actors can play an important role. A series of survey experiments yielded several insights into the relationship between legal commitments, enforcement, and the public. First, legalized obligations do increase the reputational stakes for foreign countries taking transgressive actions across domains of both higher and lower politics. Among regular members of the US populace surveyed, people were consistently less willing to support future cooperation with countries who violated a legal commitment compared to those engaging in the same behavior absent any prior promise. Second, while consequences for cooperation increased with the level of legal obligation, both harder and softer commitments showed the potential to generate support for sizable reputational sanctions, especially in economic matters. Other dimensions of legalization could also play a role, where the precision of an agreement's provisions raised reputational stakes, though delegation figured less prominently.

Third, international law appears to primarily serve an enforcement function by dissuading violations rather than rewarding obedience. Compliance with prior promises was not compensated with similar reputational premiums in the public's eyes. Despite this asymmetry in (non)compliance, the threat posed by ex post costs for defection points to a pathway through which international law can make expectations of adherence toward *current* commitments more credible. Fourth, a further asymmetry is evident in the possibility of support for reputational sanctions spilling over into unrelated issue areas. While economic violations have little effect on evaluations of future military cooperation, the same cannot be said for the inverse. Breaching a security commitment not only damages a country's reputation in military affairs, but extends to the public's willingness to cooperate with them on economic matters too. Lastly, underlying all these findings, international law fundamentally shapes audiences' evaluations of the trustworthiness of foreign countries, where legal commitments animate and are grounded in particular normative understandings of the rules and actions involved.

The experimental findings together bolster the *popular* understanding of international law laid out in chapter 2. Members of the public prove able to discern the fundamental qualities enshrined in different sorts of legal commitments, and respond in ways that facilitate the enforcement of international law. While enforcement mechanisms like reputation are commonly conceptualized as horizontal in nature with an emphasis on state-to-state interactions, the evidence presented here shows a potentially important role for ordinary domestic actors in how ex post costs are created and levied.

The results offer a corrective to skeptics' reservations that "Reputation matters, just not so much as some might like."[158] Looking back to this chapter's title, we may not go so far as the former tennis player Andre Agassi's celebration that "Image is everything,"[159] but reputation seems to be at least "something" in the operation of international law. Support for reputational sanctions can be sizable across a wide range of circumstances. Trade-offs highlighted by some skeptics like Morgenthau—where the ultimate choice "is not between legality and illegality, but between political wisdom and political folly"—may miss the mark.[160] Given the costs that can arise from violations, conducting oneself in a legal manner may also turn out to be politically prudent—legal obligation and self-interest are not innately in tension, especially when accounting for the responses of publics (and not just princes).

The advantage of the experimental methods employed in this chapter is that they allow us to cleanly and carefully control the nature of commitments and directly measure participants' attitudes. Demonstrating the capacity for ordinary members of the public to understand these legal commitments with the potential to serve as agents of enforcement is a promising first step. Like most experiments, however, these findings are vulnerable to worries over generalizability, particularly whether publics react similarly in real-world situations, or whether their beliefs and actions actually matter in the functioning of reputational sanctions. Building on the groundwork made possible by these experimental results, it is to the more concrete workings of international law, reputation, and the public that the next chapter now turns.

4

REPUTATION AND ENFORCEMENT II

The United States, the Laws of War, and
the War on Terror

The previous chapter employed a series of survey experiments to study potential popular foundations for the reputational consequences of international law. By carefully controlling the nature of legal commitments and compliance, the surveys were able to identify how ordinary people understand the costs associated with violating agreements, and the ways the public may be able to facilitate the enforcement function of international law. As promising as these experimental results may be, they leave many questions unanswered—in particular, whether ordinary actors would think similarly when confronting such events in their regular lives, and whether the public could have a meaningful impact on policies and outcomes. This chapter looks to extend the insights gleaned from the experimental data through an examination from recent history of foreign publics and the enforcement of international law. To do so, I investigate the United States' fraught relationship with its international obligations in the early years after 9/11—the War on Terror—and the consequences for the country's reputation.

The War on Terror may seem like an odd place to search for the enforcement of international law, reputational or otherwise. Facing extreme threats from transnational terrorism, many legal skeptics thought it obvious that international obligations would be given short shrift.[1] Even those sympathetic to international legal principles at times came to similar conclusions. Dismayed by how quickly the United States dispensed with several longstanding commitments, the period was portrayed as an all-out "assault" with international law "lapsing into irrelevance."[2]

This assumption was shared inside and outside of the United States. Days after the 9/11 attacks, the vice president Dick Cheney described how the country would need to work "the dark side," "spend time in the shadows," and "use any means at our disposal, basically, to achieve our objective."[3] International law seemed to matter little in US counterterrorism calculus, as the White House counsel (and later attorney general) Alberto Gonzales concluded, "This new paradigm renders obsolete Geneva's [referring to the 1949 Geneva Conventions] strict limitations . . . and renders quaint some of its provisions."[4] It is perhaps of little surprise that such sentiments were expressed by a country possessing the military and economic preponderance of the United States, making it well-placed to absorb any repercussions. If stronger countries are presumed to be less sensitive to the costs of violating international law, then the world's hegemon might reasonably be considered immune. Lamenting the rejection of core international agreements, the German chancellor Gerhard Schröder despaired, "the law of the more powerful has replaced the law."[5]

There is no doubt international law was seriously challenged after (and in many respects before) the 9/11 terror attacks. But replaced? In this chapter, I instead contend that a closer reading of the War on Terror actually illustrates the essential *relevance* of international law as a tool of enforcement. The issue is not so much whether international legal rules could fully prevent the United States from engaging in violations. The more appropriate question is whether significant costs were imposed on the United States by members of the international community for its disdain for key tenets of the international legal order. Rather than reflecting law's feebleness, the War on Terror reveals that even a superpower like the United States, confronting a genuine security threat, faced substantial fallout from violating international obligations.

The particular ways in which these costs were generated and manifested show the importance of reputation and the specific role of ordinary people in the imposition of sanctions. Damage was especially evident to the overall reputation of the United States, as foreign publics updated their beliefs about the country's motives, trustworthiness, and commitment to legal principles. Through pressure on their own leaders, as well as more direct measures, the collective actions of countless ordinary people came to place significant constraints on the United States. Reputational sanctions could be detected across numerous dimensions, from the country's general image in the world to the many ways weakening beliefs in the credibility of US commitments undermined international cooperation, ultimately complicating its counterterrorism and counterinsurgency efforts. Complementing the experimental findings presented in chapter 3, the case study evidence provides further support for a *popular* international law, where publics can play an important part in enforcing legal rules.

Given the prevailing security threats, an in-depth examination of the War on Terror offers both a hard test and an opportunity to evaluate in action the public's penchant to support the enforcement of international law observed in the survey experiments. Outside of the cleaner experimental setting, I trace the extent to which reputational consequences were felt by the United States during this period and the role played by ordinary people. With the United States encountering a body of international laws germane to the use of force already firmly in place for years, the case avoids some of the trickier problems of self-selection. Compliance calculations were thus largely separate from commitment decisions, which in most instances had been made decades earlier by preceding administrations. The War on Terror also provides the chance to turn the (inter)national tables. While the experiments drew on surveys of the US public evaluating other countries, it is the commitments, compliance, and reputation of the United States in relation to foreign publics that is put under investigation here.

For many, the War on Terror harkened back to the Roman statesman and philosopher Cicero's oft-quoted maxim inter arma enim silent leges ("in times of war, the law falls silent"). The issue addressed in this chapter is whether the US experience during this period proves, or disproves, the relevance of international law as a tool of enforcement. The George W. Bush administration sought to silence international law as part of a wide-ranging counterterrorism strategy. But as it turns out, international law would not remain so quiet with foreign publics often furnishing the loudest voices.

Background: Old Rules and a New Kind of War

It is difficult to exaggerate how much the 9/11 attacks fundamentally altered the worldview of the United States. Planned by the al Qaeda terror group led by Osama bin Laden, attackers highjacked passenger planes to target the World Trade Center in New York City and the Pentagon in Washington, DC, killing almost 3,000 civilian deaths and injuring scores more. While deadly attacks took place before, 9/11 was qualitatively different in the destructiveness wrought by a small number of assailants on US soil. After a decade of preponderance and relative tranquility since the end of the Cold War, the superpower faced a new and existential sense of vulnerability.[6] Fears were compounded by the nature of the enemy, which differed from the traditional Cold War adversarial model between recognized governments, predicated on conventional military capabilities and deterrence. The United States instead confronted a smaller, fragmented, and ideologically driven foe willing to employ extreme and irregular tactics, and whose members were difficult to identify or destroy.

The emerging narrative was one of the United States facing a new kind of enemy, which called for fighting a new kind of war. In an administration already skeptical of many international laws, it remained to be seen where existing rules would fit. Speaking in New York City less than a month after the attacks, Vice President Cheney described 9/11 as "a day like no other we have even experienced, requiring a war like no other we have ever waged."[7] Later comments in the same speech boded ill for international rules:

> We cannot deal with terror. *It will not end in a treaty.* There will be no peaceful coexistence, no negotiations, no summit, no joint communique with the terrorists. The struggle can only end with their complete and permanent destruction . . . and in victory for the United States and the cause of freedom [emphasis added].

Cheney's feelings echoed those of his commander in chief. Beyond the number of Americans killed, it was the way al Qaeda and other terror groups organized and perpetrated violence that was so appalling. The laws of war—also known as international humanitarian law (IHL)—are traditionally predicated on expectations of good faith and reciprocity between warring sides.[8] During a Pentagon visit a week after the attacks, President Bush contrasted terrorists with past US foes, denouncing "an enemy that likes to hide and burrow in . . . There are no rules. It's barbaric behavior."[9] Against an adversary refusing to follow conventional laws of international society, what rules would the United States follow? Foreshadowing the approach his administration would eventually take, Bush continued, "But we're going to smoke them out. And we're adjusting our thinking to the new type of enemy . . . it's a new type of war, it's going to take a long time to win this war."

Government threat assessments and the need for a robust response were felt equally by large swathes of the US public. Polls conducted in the period immediately after 9/11 showed large numbers fearful of further attacks, and accepting of more aggressive policies that could come into tension with existing laws, both international and domestic.[10] According to the popular international law framework developed here, not all national publics will always favor compliance with legal obligations at all times—the balance of opinion within the US public during this episode illustrates this overwhelmingly. But what ultimately matters for the larger international order is whether there are sufficient numbers of ordinary people—at home or abroad—who respond to international rules in ways that foster enforcement to maintain a rules-bound system.

What were the "adjustments" alluded to by the president, and eventually supported (or at least tolerated) by significant portions of US elites and the masses? The policies that came to be formulated were forceful in a number of respects.

As one senior official said about orders to the Central Intelligence Agency (CIA), "The gloves are off . . . The president has given the agency the green light to do whatever is necessary. Lethal operations that were unthinkable pre-September 11 are now under way."[11] Yet many of the subsequent actions undertaken not only by intelligence officials, but also the armed forces on up to the highest echelons of the political leadership would turn out to be of questionable validity under international law.

The place (or lack thereof) of international law in the War on Terror remains hotly debated.[12] My purpose is not to disentangle the multitude of opposing viewpoints to arrive at a definitive judgment on the international legality of US actions from the period. My aim is more limited, yet still ambitious—to examine whether and how international commitments produce reputational consequences, traces of which may be observed in this episode. We need not delve too deeply into legal intricacies. Rather, it suffices to establish the general contention that the United States was widely viewed as violating certain international laws, and that such claims were accepted in many foreign countries by their leaders, and especially their publics. After all, a country's reputation is a function of *other* actors' beliefs regarding its character. It follows that any reputational consequences will primarily flow from *other* actors' perceptions about the country's compliance with its international legal obligations.

Even before 9/11, the Bush administration already had an uneasy relationship with international law. Skeptical strains toward global commitments have always been present in American politics,[13] but the aftermath of the 2000 election brought new heights of suspicion for instrumental and ideological reasons.[14] With naysayers at the highest levels, the new government struck a sour tone toward many international obligations from the start.[15] A spate of prominent treaty exits followed, including withdrawing US signature from the Kyoto Protocol to reduce greenhouse gases less than two months into his tenure, followed in the ensuing year by a similar move with the Rome Statute establishing the International Criminal Court (ICC), as well as completely pulling out of the decades-old Anti-Ballistic Missile (ABM) Treaty.

Despite these actions, in practical terms the Bush administration initially represented less of a departure from prior presidencies. The new commander in chief styled himself a "compassionate conservative," which included working through multilateral institutions.[16] On continuing challenges like dealing with Saddam Hussein's Iraq, the Bush administration largely followed the United Nations (UN)–based containment policy put in place during the earlier George H. W. Bush and Bill Clinton presidencies.[17]

Looking at the initial period on its own terms, a deeper challenge to the international legal order was far from inevitable. It took an extreme event like

9/11 to rupture the country's approach to legal commitments. The United States had the capability, but now also a greater willingness, to act with less regard for prevailing international rules. The War on Terror unshackled certain preexisting ideological predilections, bringing them to fuller fruition. As one account of this period concluded, "September 11 would constitute the final shock that allowed the critics of international law to triumph."[18]

What areas of international law were put to the test? It is important to first note that the United States did not reject any and every international obligation all at once. The country's political and military leaders took great care to follow many rules, including attempts to minimize (however imperfect) civilian casualties, and refrain from using particular weapons.[19] The United States was also not alone in those laws it did violate. Other countries engaged in questionable behavior in counterterrorist or related operations, leaving the United States in good (or, depending on one's view, poor) company. But as a key architect of the post–World War II order, the sight of a United States turning its back on elements of that same order struck many members of the international community as especially troubling.

The Bush administration would be condemned in particular for its actions in two core areas of international law dealing with the use of force. International laws governing armed conflict fall into two general categories, closely following the ethical tradition of just war theory—*jus ad bellum* and *jus in bello*.

First, *jus ad bellum* ("right to war") refers to rules regulating the initial recourse to force. Under the UN system, rules were put in place for the peaceful settlement of disputes and rejecting the resort to military force. Enshrined as one of the guiding principles of the UN Charter, Article 2(4) states "All Members shall refrain in their international relations from the threat or use of force against the territorial integrity or political independence of any state, or in any other manner inconsistent with the Purposes of the United Nations." The UN legal framework, in turn, tightly circumscribes when it is permissible for members to employ such force. Chapter VII of the UN Charter delineates that it is the purview of the UN Security Council (UNSC) to collectively determine when and in what form force may be used.[20] The UN framers envisioned some circumstances allowing force absent security council approval, providing in Article 51 for "the right of individual or collective self-defense," though its use was intended to be highly restricted.

Early U.S. military operations were on firmer legal footing. The day after the 9/11 attacks, the UNSC unanimously adopted Resolution 1368 condemning the attacks, calling on the international community "to take all necessary steps . . . and to combat all forms of terrorism." The US invasion of Afghanistan in October 2001, after the Taliban regime refused to hand over bin Laden, was generally accepted as permissible under a more expansive understanding of Article 51 in the Charter, despite the lack of initial UNSC authorization.[21] General (though not unanimous) support for US actions emerged, reflected in subsequent UNSC resolutions creating a transitional administration and multinational postconflict force.[22]

More problematic were US choices leading up to the invasion of Iraq in March 2003, which took place absent explicit UNSC authorization and widespread international opposition. The war was a culmination of what became known as the Bush Doctrine, a preventive strategy to destroy foreign threats before they materialized, acting unilaterally if necessary.[23] Going well beyond the charter's strict delimitations on force only in response to actual or imminent attacks, the doctrine raised far-reaching legal and moral questions.[24]

The lack of international support for war in Iraq meant the second pillar of the international legal order on the use of force would similarly be lacking— UNSC authorization. The Bush administration did make some initial attempts to gain security council approval. But as diplomatic negotiations stretched out, and perceived costs of inaction mounting by the day, the United States ultimately decided to act without the council's blessing.[25] Military operations by the United States and a "coalition of the willing" began in earnest on March 20, 2003. Alongside its main British ally, the United States tried to mount a legal defense by pointing to expanded rights of self-defense and invoking prior UNSC resolutions.[26] Showing that international law is not nearly as malleable as some critics contend, the rationale was overwhelmingly rejected and the invasion deemed contrary to international law by many members of the international community. Reflecting a little over a year after the invasion, the UN secretary-general Kofi Annan declared, "From our point of view and from the charter point of view *it was illegal*" (emphasis added).[27]

Much attention has focused on these aspects of US decision-making in the lead-up to the Iraq War, and ensuing consequences from violations related to *jus ad bellum*.[28] Equally important were repercussions flowing from the actual *conduct* of the United States, alongside related policies both before and after the Iraq invasion as part of the wider War on Terror. The United States also engaged in breaches of a second main body of law, which governs the behavior of belligerents during war—*jus in bello* ("right in war"). Concerns over US conduct covered a number of areas. Legal details for some, such as torture and drone strikes, are discussed at greater length in later chapters (5 and 6, respectively). For our present purposes, attention was often directed most intently toward issues involving captured enemy combatants.

Legal concerns over US detainee policies came to the fore well before the 2003 Iraq War, crystalizing earlier during the war in Afghanistan. The status of captured fighters from the Taliban and al Qaeda became a pressing legal issue.

Neither armed group fit neatly into traditional definitions of combatants under the laws of war, especially the 1949 Geneva Conventions. Geneva law, along with attendant rules and customs, were nonetheless considered by the international community to apply broadly—the default being to accord rights and protections to most, if not all, captured combatants.[29]

The Bush administration took a different stance, declaring by early 2002 in an unclassified presidential memo that "none of the provisions of Geneva apply to our conflict with al Qaeda in Afghanistan or elsewhere throughout the world."[30] Acknowledging Geneva law theoretically applied to the Taliban (as the nominal government of Afghanistan), the memo judged its fighters failed to meet the conditions to qualify as formal prisoners of war, instead falling under a more nebulous category of "unlawful combatants." In the same memo, the president went on to emphasize that his government would still ensure the humane treatment of detainees, even if the country was under no legal obligation to do so:

> As a matter of policy, the United States Armed Forces shall continue to treat detainees humanely and, to the extent appropriate and consistent with military necessity, in a manner consistent with the principles of Geneva.

Despite such assurances, the US decision was widely condemned. Human Rights Watch denounced what it saw as attempts to "eviscerate many of [Geneva's] most important protections," while other commentators warned prisoners entered a "legal black hole."[31] Many of these criticisms were levied *before* revelations later surfaced of indefinite detention, rendition to secret black sites, and systematic torture. The early choice not to be bound by Geneva law was the "Original Sin," sowing the seeds of subsequent abuses.[32]

In the face of multidimensional violations of the use of force, the following question was posed to the international community—what would be the consequences, if any, to the United States? US preponderance, in combination with the perils posed by terrorism, suggests foreign audiences might grudgingly eschew sanctioning the superpower for its actions. Leading up to the 2003 Iraq War, the historian Michael Ignatieff hinted at just this outcome, "America's allies want a multilateral order that will essentially constrain American power. But the empire will not be tied down like Gulliver with a thousand legal strings."[33]

Ignatieff's metaphor is apt, but I contend that a different process was taking shape. Consistent with insights from chapter 3's experimental evidence, US violations harmed the country's reputation, spilling across a number of domains. Confrontation was not always direct, but through various decisions made (and not made) costs were imposed by members of the international community.[34]

The United States would come to feel a web of strings wrapping around the country—many pulled tighter by multitudes of ordinary people around the world. Even in this new war, old laws remained relevant.

Reputational Repercussions: An Inevitable Reaction?

In hindsight, it may be easy to surmise that the international fallout suffered by the United States was a foregone conclusion. Opposition could simply have been the unavoidable result of the United States becoming the dominant player in the global system.[35] Rather than unilateralism or the substance of US actions, international condemnation was just another downside to hegemony, where "resentment comes with the territory."[36] Research on anti-Americanism instead suggests a more complex dynamic driven in part by animosity related to the country's power and what it represents, but also due to specific policies and practices.[37]

The 9/11 attacks and subsequent War on Terror provide a case in point. Far from rejoicing or instinctively resisting the United States, a range of international actors expressed sympathy, initially offering their support and cooperation in various ways.[38] The North Atlantic Treaty Organization (NATO) activated collective defense provisions under Article 5 of the alliance's charter, the first time in its history.[39] NATO's pledge was more than symbolic, and served as a basis for several members' participation in the war in Afghanistan with the alliance taking the lead in the postconflict International Security and Assistance Force (ISAF). The Organization for American States (OAS) similarly passed a resolution expressing members' support, describing the US attacks as "attacks against all American states."[40] The United States received further support from bodies with which it did not always have warm ties. The Organisation of the Islamic Conference,[41] counting almost fifty Muslim-majority partner states, condemned the terror attacks, while refraining from censuring US military operations in Afghanistan, a fellow member.[42] The Vatican too acknowledged that the United States could be justified in resorting to the use of force against terrorists.[43]

A groundswell of support was also evident among foreign populations. People the world over took to the streets to show solidarity with the United States with 200,000 Germans marching in Berlin alone. France's paper of record, *Le monde*, summed up how many felt, "*Nous sommes tous américains*" ("We are all Americans").[44]

Backed by large portions of their publics, expressions of support in many foreign countries became more than just words. Several governments offered access to their airspace and territory, and others troops and equipment, for conducting counterterror operations, unlike past instances like the 1998 embassy bombings in Kenya and Tanzania.[45]

The US administration was cognizant of favorable foreign opinion during these early days. In the same October 2001 speech mentioned previously, Vice President Cheney remarked:

> On the diplomatic side, we have found great support in every part of the world. Tonight President Bush is in Shanghai meeting with leaders from Asia and the Pacific who have been cooperating in this global effort. . . . Different nations are helping us in different ways, but nearly all grasp the enormity of this situation.[46]

Hostility toward the United States was thus not immediately forthcoming. Members of the international community generally understood the rationale behind the invasion of Afghanistan, even if they were not thrilled with this militarized turn. As noted earlier, the Afghan War generally rested on firmer legal grounds. The war would not see the same backlash as the Iraq War (at least not initially), but the conflict was far from universally popular. Various polls showed a preference for more diplomatic means, but foreign public opinion remained fairly muted and less of a constraint on responses to US military operations in light of the lingering shock of the terror attacks and the Taliban regime's general isolation.[47] And the UNSC would come to endorse US actions with international backing for postconflict operations.

Initial reactions to 9/11 and attitudes toward the Afghan War show that international audiences were not impulsively antagonistic toward US counterterrorism operations. The United States would eventually adopt a more unilateral tack, but was by no means alone from the start. What shifted international opinion would be those subsequent US decisions over *how* it waged the War on Terror in contravention of prevailing international obligations.

The remainder of this chapter delves into the historical record to ascertain what, if any, were the consequences to the United States. As will become evident, the ramifications qualified as much more than "any," encompassing a wide range of reputational sanctions. In the sections that follow, I begin at the most general level of the United States' overall image, working down to more specific but equally consequential ways in which US reputation was hurt by its posture toward international law.

Harm to General US Image and Credibility

Countries care about their image, prestige, or status, and how they are perceived by others, not only as an end in itself, but also as means for achieving other objectives.[48] A healthier image can help make others go along with exercises in harder military and economic capabilities, but is also part of "softer" forms of power necessary for persuasion and leadership.[49]

On this score and across various foreign polls, the general image of the United States declined precipitously as the War on Terror progressed. Disentangling the exact sources of this discontent is difficult for two main reasons. First, various factors feed into a country's image; a reputation for upholding legal commitments is just one of many contributors. Second, surveys of this sort are not asked frequently enough with consistent fielding across countries, especially compared to the monthly, weekly (or for US presidents, almost daily) polling of some national publics about their leaders. Sparse coverage makes it more challenging to determine the impact of factors like compliance, since other events may intervene between polls.

Albeit imperfect, the available evidence suggests violations of international law started early on to have a discernable impact on the US image in the world, and endured for some time. Figure 4.1 summarizes several polls conducted

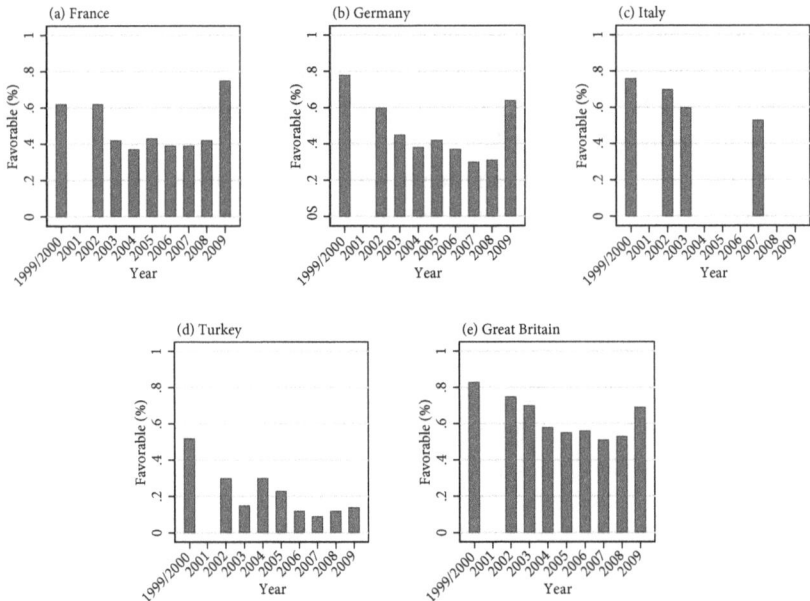

FIGURE 4.1. International image of the United States in selected foreign countries, 1999–2009

Notes: Favorability ratings (percent with a "very" or "somewhat" favorable opinion) of the United States. Surveys were conducted on national samples in various foreign countries for the years 1999 to 2009. Data for 2002 to 2009 are from reports by the Pew Research Center Global Attitudes Project. Data for 1999 to 2000 are based on figures from the Office of Research, US Department of State.

by the Pew Research Center's *Global Attitudes Project*, gauging foreign publics' feelings of favorability toward the United States from 1999 through 2009.[50]
Because of coverage issues, I focus on countries that were queried more routinely, especially during the early years of the War on Terror. The figure also
centers on countries that are US allies, as the United States may be more sensitive to their opinions.

A few trends emerge. One that has already received a great deal of attention
is the immediate impact of events surrounding the invasion of Iraq—from 2002
to 2003, the image of the United States declined in every single one of the countries reported. While feelings were already anemic in Turkey, support dropped
substantially elsewhere with France and Germany moving from solid majority to
minority approval in just one year. Other work suggests that much of this discontent was due to the unilateral approach taken by the United States against Iraq
in contravention of UN obligations.[51] So deep was the opposition that among
those signing on to the US-led "coalition of the willing," such as Britain, Italy,
and Spain, majorities of their publics wanted no part in the war.[52] An unprece-
dented disjunct opened up between US success on the battlefield in routing Iraqi
forces (initially at least), versus a weakened image in the court of public opinion.
Reflecting feelings in both capitals and on the streets, one commentator noted
"Whereas U.S. military prowess may be at an all-time high, Washington's political
and moral authority has hit a new low."[53]

Looking at polling data both before and after the war reveals harm to
the US image was not solely—or, in some cases, even primarily—driven by
the UNSC–Iraq dynamics. In particular, the image of the United States had
already begun to slide *before* the 2003 invasion of Iraq. Except for holding
fairly steady in France, US favorability ratings weakened noticeably between
2000 and 2002, coinciding with the turnover from Clinton to Bush. In fact,
the United States witnessed a bigger absolute drop in its image in 2002 for
Germany, the United Kingdom, and Turkey, than would take place during the
seemingly more definitive events of 2003. While the Iraq War was a salient
episode, the United States already appeared well down the road to tarnishing
its global goodwill.

What accounts for this decline? Perhaps Iraq still loomed large, and the
2002 drop was in anticipation of the invasion the next spring. But for much
of that year, the United States was open to a multilateral route on Iraq, continuing more than a decade of work through the UN.[54] Rather what appears
to better explain the initial fall were the various encroachments by the Bush
administration against international laws. Even before the 9/11 attacks, feelings toward the new US president were quite low across many countries—an
August 2001 Pew Research Center poll showed that publics in many European

countries reserved their harshest judgement for Bush's rejection of the Kyoto Protocol and objections to other international treaties.[55] These feelings seemingly only deepened in the ensuing year, particularly around detainee rights and US repudiation of the Geneva Conventions, which were already put in place by early 2002.

Looking at the period after the Iraq invasion also suggests more was going on than simply a one-off failure to obtain UN blessing. One might expect the US image to at least recuperate somewhat as time passed, even if failing to return to prewar levels. Figure 4.1 instead shows a hangover for years to come, reversing only in 2009 with the transition to the Barack Obama presidency. US favorability remained frail in France and Turkey, while actually declining at equal or greater levels in Germany and the United Kingdom. Sentiment among ordinary Turks was not unique in the region, and had a lot to do with the perceived international legal gap between US words on deeds. A 2009 survey of several Muslim countries found that, "The US is widely seen as hypocritically failing to abide by international law, not living up to the role it should play in world affairs, disrespectful of the Muslim people, and using its power in a coercive and unfair fashion."[56]

Perhaps the international community was holding a grudge over the way the United States entered Iraq. The power vacuum left by Hussein's removal and an intensifying insurgency likely did not help. Yet far more consequential was the way in which the United States was fighting the war and breaching its international obligations, highlighted by the steady disclosure of abuses from Abu Ghraib to Guantanamo.

A similar view eventually emerged within segments of the US government concerning international repercussions. A report by the Senate Select Committee on Intelligence a decade later offered one of the strongest rebukes, specifically denouncing detainee policy: "The CIA's Detention and Interrogation Program damaged the United States' standing in the world, and resulted in other significant monetary and non-monetary costs."[57] Even those closer to the administration worried about longer-term implications. According to the Republican campaign strategist and White House policy adviser, Karl Rove, "it will take a generation to repair the damage to America's image in the Middle East" after the fallout from Abu Ghraib and similar scandals.[58]

Harm was not limited to general impressions of the country's image, but also affected its credibility in related areas like human rights. As one study of the US interrogation program observed, "[T]he use of torture diminished the United States' ability to be a respected advocate for human rights around the globe."[59] The gap between stated humanitarian principles and observed behavior created a "double standard," which denied "the US the moral high ground it needs to censure other nations in the future for human rights abuses."[60] The Senate Select Committee likewise saved some of its most stinging criticism for damage done to the traditional US role as a leading advocate for human rights:

> More broadly, the program caused immeasurable damage to the United States' public standing, as well as to the United States' longstanding global leadership on human rights in general and the prevention of torture in particular.[61]

Violations of international laws can thus produce lasting legacies for a country's image and a daunting undertaking to repair. Despite its importance, something as diffuse as international image may not present a sufficient cost, especially in the face of seemingly immediate security benefits. The experimental evidence showed that reputational sanctions could translate into public support for more tangible consequences that could impair cooperation. Cooperation can prove beneficial in general, but especially when looking to combating a transnational threat like terrorism. Other facets of the War on Terror suggest far more palpable ramifications for the US ability to cooperate internationally that followed from its disregard for international law.

Lowered Participation in US Military Operations

Perhaps the ultimate indicator of cooperation is the willingness of states to fight alongside each other, risking blood and treasure in the process.[62] The international community's corresponding reluctance to unite behind the US mantle was most evident in the size and nature of the "coalition of the willing" that invaded Iraq in 2003. The Bush administration played up the coalition's multilateral credentials, praising the thirty or forty–odd countries (exact numbers depended on the criteria) offering their backing. Closer to the truth was that most participants' involvement was symbolic, providing little material assistance.[63] Palau granted access to its harbors and airports, but were of little use as the tiny island nation lay 6,000 miles from Iraq.[64] Others had no armed forces of their own, including Costa Rica, Iceland, the Marshall Islands, Micronesia, and the Solomon Islands. Only Britain furnished military capabilities that could make a difference on the battlefield. In addition to 250,000 US troops, the initial invading force comprised 45,000 British, 2,000 Australian, and 200 Polish combat personnel.[65] By deciding to go it alone in taking on Iraq, the United States found itself largely on its own once the fighting started.

Part of the rationale for the lack of military cooperation can found in the relationship between international law and foreign publics. Harm to the general US image from violations may have equally affected foreign publics' support for the war, including the willingness to countenance material contributions by their home countries.[66] In response to Bush's ultimatum to Hussein just days before the eventual invasion, the French president Jacques Chirac accused the united States of "favoring force over law."[67] Chirac's words were not simply a case of elites leading the public, but rather channeled views already deeply held by millions of ordinary French citizens, many of whom participated in dozens of protests involving hundreds of thousands of demonstrators in the preceding months. In contrast to Le monde's calls for solidarity with the United States after 9/11, the editor of the weekly Nouvel observateur, published an apt rebuke capturing the feelings of the masses, "Nous ne sommes pas tous américains" ("We are not all Americans").[68]

Even foreign governments initially supportive of the war came to be constrained by domestic pressures. Political leaders in Italy, Spain, and Poland all had to significantly scale back, or withdraw, their contributions to the coalition.[69] The largest partner, Britain, continued both publicly and privately to implore the United States to take a more legal route through the UN in order to bolster public support.[70] Growing domestic opposition to the British prime minister Tony Blair's rule illustrates the dangers of defying public opinion on such matters.[71] Legal perceptions of foreign public were cited by many political commentators as a key factor driving many governments' opposition to the Iraq War.[72]

The earlier 1990 to 1991 Persian Gulf War in response to Iraq's invasion of neighboring Kuwait shows that weak international support for the 2003 Iraq War was not a foregone conclusion. The Gulf War was a mirror image of its Iraqi successor in several crucial respects, while at the same time sharing some important similarities. Both wars were waged by Republican presidents (with the same surname) against the same Iraqi dictator with similar power differentials. Where they diverged most starkly was on the different legal choices of the two US administrations, where in the first instance President George H. W. Bush pursued a more multilateral route, obtaining security council approval.

A number of studies have compared the two Iraq conflicts to test a variety of arguments, where the pairing offers "a natural laboratory from which to draw conclusions for theory and policy."[73] Much of this work has focused on decision-making in the lead-up to the fighting. The conflicts differed markedly not only with the US approach to international laws involving UN authorization (jus ad bellum), but also subsequent wartime conduct (jus in bello), providing an opportunity to trace divergent trajectories resulting from (non)compliance with various obligations. Iraq's own violations may have been clearer in 1990 compared to 2003, but legal cases against the Hussein regime could be, and were, still made in both instances. Widespread international support for the US position in 1990 (and opposition in 2003) was by no means automatic, instead depending in large part on the superpower's disparate rhetoric and actions during each episode.[74]

On firmer international legal footing, the United States in 1990 to 1991 overcame initial skepticism to eventually benefit from a groundswell of international public support, opening greater space for the policies of other foreign governments. Going into the Gulf War, the United States enjoyed an impressive multinational coalition. Unlike the modest number of auxiliary forces outside of Britain in 2003's "coalition of the willing," close to forty countries contributed armed forces and/or military equipment. *Who* those countries were was indicative of the breadth of the coalition assembled. While taking the lead in opposing US action in 2003, France provided almost 15,000 combat troops for Gulf War operations. Facing the uncomfortable prospect of fighting against a fellow Muslim country, Saudi Arabia still provided 100,000 troops and use of its territory, with several fellow Arab states making substantial military contributions as well.[75] In addition to troops, countries made enormous financial offerings totaling more than $50 billion, meeting almost all of the estimated $60 billion price tag for the war.[76] By contrast, just over a decade later in 2003, the United States received meager cash assistance, leaving it to shoulder almost the entire financial burden of the war.

Differences in the willingness of the international community to cooperate could in many ways be traced back the senior Bush administration's commitment to obtaining security council approval. By doing so, military intervention could be genuinely framed as compatible with international law and achieving *compliance* with various UNSC resolutions calling for Iraq to cease aggression against Kuwait. Taking the costly steps of going through the UN certainly provided information to foreign audiences of US intentions and the merits of the intervention, especially among those suspicious of the superpower and/or sympathetic to Iraq's position.[77] More specifically, it was the *principled* nature of the information signaled by UN endorsement that provided a resource and a rationale for others to trust US motives and be willing to cooperate militarily.

Cooperation after the end of conventional hostilities continued to show different trajectories. US objectives in the Gulf War to dislodge Iraqi forces from Kuwait were admittedly more modest compared to the foreign-imposed regime change pursued in 2003. Nevertheless, postwar policies would come to include no-fly zones monitored by US and allied aircraft over large portions of the north and south of the country, ground troops remaining for quite some time in both regions, punishing economic sanctions, and an intrusive weapons inspections regime. Each of these policies was controversial and could have instilled fear, mistrust, and opposition from other countries. Continuing to work through multilateral channels, the George H. W. Bush administration ensured a robust legal framework was put in place for postconflict Iraq. The United States enjoyed significant international support, as well as military and financial contributions, to administer this system for quite some time afterwards, though various tensions later developed over the sanctions and other elements of the containment policy.[78]

By contrast, comparable levels of cooperation were never achieved at any point during the postconflict situation in Iraq from 2003 onward. US preponderance ensured the initial conventional phase of the fighting progressed relatively smoothly. On May 1, 2003, just over two months after the opening shots, President George W. Bush landed with great fanfare on a returning aircraft carrier to declare "Mission Accomplished." Despite the pronouncement, an insidious insurgency was already brewing. In this new and deadlier phase, US forces would find themselves largely fighting alone. The United States was able to obtain UNSC Resolution 1484 of May 22, 2003, affirming the status of it and Britain as occupying powers. A few countries were induced into making some modest military contributions, but a year later the bulk of occupying forces came from the United States (110,000), Britain a distant second at less than 10,000 troops, and other national contingents smaller still.[79] Casualties in the burgeoning insurgency were correspondingly felt disproportionately by US forces.[80] Financial contributions were similarly less than forthcoming, meaning reconstruction costs depended lopsidedly on US coffers.[81]

Foregoing the UNSC certainly hung over the initial postconflict period, yet the broader wartime conduct of the United States further contributed to international unease. The Abu Ghraib prison abuse scandal that broke a year later in spring 2004, alongside further criticisms of US detention policies, played a role in constricting already low levels of international goodwill. Over the course of 2004, a number of countries who had pledged or sent troops either withdrew or announced their impending departure. Many specifically cited public opposition to the US-led war effort as the main driver. Reflecting the feelings of his fellow citizens and many others around the world, the Hungarian prime minister at the time, Ferenc Gyurcsany, conceded, "To stay longer is an impossibility."[82]

In these various ways US violations of international law undermined military cooperation and contributed to turning the few countries initially willing to participate increasingly into a "coalition of the *unwilling*" with more and more of the burden placed on US forces. Although the United States may not have needed others to get into Iraq, international help proved much more essential—and genuinely missed—as the conflict worsened. A similar story would repeat itself in other dimensions of the War on Terror.

Dwindling Cooperation in Other Areas of Counterterrorism

Widespread refusal to provide troops and money serves as one of the most visible markers of the cooperation costs felt by the United States. But in subtler ways, reputational sanctions spilled over to other areas where cooperation was equally (if not more) important to longer-term US counterterrorism objectives. Military operations in Afghanistan and Iraq garnered a disproportionate share of the attention, but were insufficient on their own to defeat diffuse transnational terrorist groups. With financing, recruiting, and planning activities spread across loosely connected networks, one of the main challenges was obtaining information necessary to identify individual terrorists and exploit vulnerable nodes in their organizations.[83] Progress in the War on Terror really came down to success in the battle for intelligence.

Because of al Qaeda and similar groups' transnational character, successful intelligence operations were beyond the control of any single country—even one with formidable resources like the United States. The White House recognized as much in its core counterterrorism doctrine: "Success will not come by always acting alone, but through a powerful coalition of nations maintaining a strong, united international front against terrorism."[84]

Like the Iraq War, however, the United States found a far from a united front. The collaborative chill was not simply a holdover from US unilateralism at the UN in the lead-up to the invasion. Resistance also grew more directly out of various US detainee policies detailed earlier, including refusing to offer terror suspects protections under the Geneva Conventions. In some areas like terror financing, US officials enjoyed greater multilateral support.[85] But in other matters, harm to cooperative efforts was already being felt by early 2002 in response to serious misgivings over US violations. Lack of international support was especially evident in two areas—1) human intelligence related to assistance with the detention and transfer of terror suspects; and 2) general intelligence sharing among national intelligence communities.

Looking first at human intelligence, detention policies figured prominently in early US counterterrorism planning. Less than a week after the 9/11 attacks, CIA operatives were tasked with identifying overseas facilities for holding large numbers of expected detainees.[86] US-controlled foreign military bases initially held the majority of detainees, from longstanding facilities like Guantanamo Bay, to others later administered in conflict zones, such as Bagram Airfield in Afghanistan and Abu Ghraib prison in Iraq. The CIA operated a complementary worldwide network of secret "black sites" for transporting and interrogating terror suspects. In conjunction with its own operations, the Bush administration developed an extraordinary rendition program, transferring suspects to other countries where they could be subjected to more coercive treatment—essentially "outsourcing torture."[87]

While many Bush administration officials believed harsh interrogation techniques were indispensable, doubts remain over their effectiveness in yielding reliable information.[88] Less refutable is that torture and indefinite detention are violations under international law. The vast US detention program required the consent and help from a critical mass of countries to function properly. How then would the US reproach to international law affect prospects for such cooperation?

Any pushback appeared relatively muted initially. The United States leveraged existing economic and security relationships to gain assistance, especially from autocracies with fewer qualms about human rights.[89] Pakistan abetted US counterterrorism policies, especially in locating and apprehending Taliban and al Qaeda forces fleeing Afghanistan, including one of the 9/11 architects, Khalid Sheikh Mohammed, who would eventually be waterboarded hundreds of times.[90] Other countries, such as Egypt, Morocco, Syria, and Jordan, became popular destinations for suspects subjected to more "rigorous" interrogations.[91] Fellow democratic regimes also initially proved willing to help, or at least turn a blind eye to, US detention activities conducted on their territories. Eastern European countries like Lithuania, Poland, and Romania joined a "clandestine archipelago of 'black sites'" for high-value CIA detainees.[92]

Pointing to instances of getting help from some countries is not inconsistent with the United States still suffering reputational repercussions. Reputational fallout does not mean an offending country will obtain *zero* cooperation. Rather, in line with the experimental findings from chapter 3, a violator should be expected to find fewer cooperative opportunities, which may be harder and costlier to conclude. Notable cooperative successes paper over the denominator problem of the many countries refusing to do so, which limited the effectiveness of US activities. As the Senate Select Committee on Intelligence remarked, "From the beginning of the program, the CIA faced significant challenges in finding nations willing to host CIA clandestine detention sites."[93] Reluctance was partly driven by foreign governments' worries over reactions from their publics of being implicated in US detention operations. The cooperation that was achieved was also extremely expensive, involving furtive transfers of millions of dollars to governments to obtain oftentimes grudging support.[94]

Later developments in those initial cooperative countries further demonstrate how reputational dynamics operated. While several of these governments—autocracies and democracies alike—may have had few moral misgivings, their assent ultimately relied on secrecy and covert US activities being conducted in their backyards. As details of the program were exposed, governments who had made deals with the United States began to feel serious public ramifications (and for democracies, electoral costs) that had deterred so many other countries from the start.[95]

The Abu Ghraib scandal of 2004 served as a catalyst for deepening media investigations into wider detention policies. Criticism over US methods accelerated, and by the fall of 2005 crucial details on CIA black sites began to be uncovered.[96] Concerned over reactions from both domestic and international public opinion, several foreign governments quickly changed tack. After news broke in late 2005 that Romania was home to a CIA black site, its government demanded the facility be closed immediately; a center in Lithuania likewise shuttered in short order.[97]

Amid intensifying pressure, in September 2006 President Bush publicly acknowledged the existence of the CIA program, ordering all remaining suspects in CIA custody to be transferred to Guantanamo Bay, effectively bringing the program to an end.[98] The policy shift was driven less by any change of heart, or recent Supreme Court decisions invalidating components related to the program and broader US detainee policies.[99] Rather, the drying up of international goodwill made the program unworkable. Referring to the president's reversal, the Senate Select Committee on Intelligence concluded, "The CIA required secrecy and cooperation from other nations in order to operate clandestine detention facilities, and both had eroded significantly before President Bush publicly disclosed the program on September 6, 2006."[100] The report stressed the depths to which international cooperation had sunk, where with the odd exception: "the CIA was forced to relocate detainees out of every country in which it established a detention facility because of pressure from the host government or public revelations about the program."[101] Detainees would continue to be held at Guantanamo and other US military facilities in countries like Afghanistan and Iraq, but the scale of the program was severely circumscribed due to other countries' refusal to supply needed cooperation. The stance taken by foreign governments, in turn, was in large part shaped by public opposition rooted in responses to US violations.

Second, international reluctance spilled over to the more general relationships between foreign intelligence communities and the United States. Not just limited to terrorism, the increasingly globalized scope of illicit activities made cooperation among intelligence agencies ever more vital. US violations threatened delicate relationships as foreign governments encountered public pressures against cooperating with US intelligence agencies, and being implicated in any resulting abuses.[102] The Senate Special Committee on Intelligence saved some of its most scathing criticism for the long-term harm done to carefully crafted ties with foreign intelligence partners: "The CIA's Detention and Interrogation Program created tensions with U.S. partners and allies, leading to formal *demarches* [political initiatives] to the United States, and damaging and complicating bilateral intelligence relationships" (emphasis in original).[103] Complications could be seen in palpable ways. Continuing on detention, US authorities found their extradition requests were frequently denied by foreign counterparts fearing suspects would face legally questionable treatment. Even when the United States already held a suspect, the lack of cooperation extended to other crucial tasks, such as gathering testimony, corroborating information, and similar forms of assistance.[104]

At the same time, intelligence sharing shows certain limits to reputational sanctions. The 9/11 attacks represented a threat not only to the United States, but the wider international system, heightening incentives for collaboration and downplaying legal or policy differences.[105] Fragmented and insular, the structure of intelligence communities also makes them more immune to public pressures, sometimes leading to disjuncts between official policy and actual operations. Just as the public rift was widening between Bush and French president Chirac, agents from both countries were working closely together on covert operations. As one intelligence expert remarked, The Franco-US case "underlines the way in which the 'low politics' of intelligence co-operation is often disconnected from the high politics of foreign policy and strategy."[106] Reflecting a business-as-usual atmosphere, the CIA's deputy director of operations reportedly stated in a closed 2005 hearing that each of the thousands of kill or capture operations of terror suspects would not have been possible without help from other agencies.[107]

Revealing instances of intelligence cooperation—as impressive as these may be—is not sufficient for claiming there were no reputational costs. It is small wonder that the United States would be able to draw on its formidable resources and existing intelligence relationships to obtain outside assistance. Rather, the better question is what would that cooperation have looked like if the United States had not disregarded international obligations?

Conclusively answering this counterfactual is daunting, which is one of the reasons for employing experimental evidence in the prior chapter. Nevertheless, a closer look at the historical record points to traces of significant reputational sanctions. First, like national leaders, many foreign intelligence agencies were less worried from an ethical standpoint about cooperating with the United States. What they wanted instead were guarantees that any involvement with the United

States could be kept confidential.[108] Yet secrecy became precarious as US policies came under growing scrutiny. With scandals already erupting from existing US violations of the laws of war, any subsequent disclosures risked greater reputational repercussions for any country found participating in US counterterror activities. Many intelligence agencies may have thus been deterred from cooperating as deeply, or at all, with their US counterparts out of fear of being similarly tainted.

Second, evidence suggests that agreements US agencies were able to negotiate ended up being costlier in terms of stricter stipulations than had previously existed. When Switzerland concluded a new agreement on counterterror cooperation with the United States in 2006, negotiators insisted on provisions ensuring more stringent legal safeguards, especially concerning joint interrogations or the use of any intelligence gathered. While Swiss officials portrayed the new terms as simply clarifying technical rules, they also appeared worried over post-9/11 US activities.[109] Third and related, cooperation with foreign agencies also came under greater international constraints, particularly in Europe. After revelations of torture, rendition, and secret prisons—many involving countries from the continent—several European bodies conducted extensive inquiries. Of particular note, the Venice Commission of the Council of Europe invoked member states' duty to ensure all provisions of the European Convention on Human Rights were applied in their collaborative intelligence operations.[110]

For reasons having to do both with their own discomfort with US methods, but also constraints imposed by national and supranational political actors, the concluding remarks in 2006 from Gijs de Vries, then EU counterterrorism coordinator, now appear an understatement, "Abu Graib, Guantánamo and CIA renditions have damaged America's standing in the world and have compromised our common struggle against terrorism."[111] Instead of a liability, greater attention by US authorities to the rule of law—both domestically and internationally—may be seen as a precondition for achieving deeper international counterterror cooperation.[112] Short-term benefits from rendition and abuse came at potentially greater long-term costs inflicted on international intelligence collaboration.

The sections so far have examined how US violations of international law during the War on Terror affected the country's image and support for various types of cooperation. Mass publics were able to constrain their governments' policies, limiting in crucial ways the assistance the United States was able to obtain. Yet it would be in the reactions of ordinary people on the ground in active conflict zones where reputational costs would be most damaging.

Cooperation within Warfighting:
A Longer, Rougher Road

War is often portrayed as an all-out clash between opposing armies, ending only with one side utterly exhausted and vanquished. Or, as the Union general William Tecumseh Sherman put it bluntly, "War is hell."[113] However, cooperation between adversaries in the midst of war is generally the rule rather than the exception.[114] Beyond convivial moments like the Christmas truces that broke out along portions of the Western Front during the First World War,[115] enemies have good reasons to coordinate to avoid the worst excesses of war, making it a bit less hellish. The very existence of laws governing armed conflict presupposes a minimum level of agreement among belligerents on certain restrictions—a point recognized even by skeptics of such rules.[116] The laws of war reflect common expectations about how wars should be fought. Shared beliefs do not guarantee rules will be followed, but still matter by informing opinions of adversaries choosing to comply (or not).[117] These dynamics impact not only leaders, but also ordinary soldiers and civilians on the ground, the latter of whom are increasingly viewed as pivotal for the course and conduct of war.[118]

An assumption that drove certain US violations, such as rendition and coercive interrogations, was that they would on net yield substantial material benefits in prosecuting the War on Terror. US conduct produced several consequences, but ones that made warfighting more, rather than less, difficult overall. The following sections look at three areas in particular: 1) reduced propensity of enemy combatants to surrender; 2) difficulty in winning hearts and minds of local populations; and 3) contributing to the very rise and intensity of insurgencies. Some of the particular dynamics differ, but what they shared was the role of US violations in undermining the country's reputation as a credible partner in the eyes of local populations, reducing the potential for cooperation, and making conflict longer and costlier for all sides.

Declining Surrender Propensity

Deciding to surrender is risky. Soldiers who lay down their weapons and raise their hands leave themselves in one of the most vulnerable positions on the battlefield. One study estimated the average chance for soldiers in modern conflicts to be given quarter was at best a coin flip.[119] Even for those able to successfully surrender, a bevy of abuse can await them in captivity, including harsh living and working conditions, torture, or summary execution.[120]

Soldiers face a menu of options on the battlefield, and may calculate their chances of survival are better by fighting rather than accepting the dangers posed by surrender.[121]

What choice soldiers make is affected by various factors, such as how their forces are doing militarily, ideology, or punishment by their own side for deserting or trying to surrender. But historically, one of the strongest considerations is how well soldiers believe they will be treated in captivity.[122] Scaled up, if properly treating enemy combatants induces others to surrender, humane conduct can undermine the enemy's warfighting capacity. One historian of the First World War argued "it was capturing not killing the enemy that was decisive," as countries like Germany found it next to impossible to continue fighting as their ranks shrunk through surrenders.[123] On the flipside, abuse can engender a sterner foe, where enemy soldiers prefer to fight on knowing the fate awaiting them should they be captured, as occurred in gruesome fashion on the Eastern Front during the Second World War.[124]

Belligerents thus have good strategic reasons to encourage surrenders by trying to convince enemy soldiers they will be treated well. Promises of humane treatment reflect another type of commitment; one that has become deeply embedded in the laws of war. Surrender, in turn, represents an interrelated form of cooperation between captive and captor. The just war theorist Michael Walzer makes this relationship explicit: "A soldier who surrenders enters into an agreement with his captors: he will stop fighting if they will accord him what the legal handbooks call 'benevolent quarantine.'"[125] The ability to assure enemy combatants of proper treatment is affected by a range of considerations, but democracies like the United States have tended to make their commitments more credible due to domestic political culture and institutional constraints.[126] Yet tendencies are just that, and when democracies have engaged in abuse these violations can be particularly informative of a belligerent's intentions.[127] Once a reputation for abuse takes hold, changing the minds of enemy soldiers to believe any subsequent promises becomes much harder.

Dynamics between would-be captors and prisoners were on display at various stages of the 2003 Iraq War. Earlier US refusal to honor the Geneva Conventions applied only to irregular combatants like al Qaeda and the Taliban, meaning regular Iraqi armed forces would in theory still qualify for legal protections. But to justify the invasion, the Bush administration tied Iraq to the wider War on Terror, alleging connections between Hussein's regime and transnational terrorists who could be supplied with weapons of mass destruction. Questions continued to be raised about general US commitments to the laws of war. The US precedent on the inapplicability of Geneva law was well-known to both Iraqi troops and the public.[128] Despite initial US pledges to abide by international laws governing prisoners in the coming Iraq War, it is not surprising that such promises could be met with skepticism.

Events on the ground largely bore out these expectations. Operationally, the US military and its "coalition of the willing" easily rolled over poorly equipped Iraqi units. What was peculiar were the relatively small numbers of Iraqi soldiers giving themselves up. Only around 8,000 Iraqi troops surrendered during the few months making up the conventional phase of the invasion.[129] From the usual menu of options, most Iraqi military units did not put up much of a fight, except for a few pockets from the elite Republican Guard. Rather, many soldiers apparently deserted, taking off their uniforms to blend into the surrounding population and avoid captivity.[130]

Conduct toward those prisoners taken was initially in keeping with international standards.[131] Most captured conscripts were quickly released, while officers were held for further interrogation. Yet worrisome trends began to emerge. Poor postwar planning, combined with little regional assistance, meant US forces lacked sufficient resources to properly care for prisoners. Logistical deficiencies were one of main reasons US officials made the fateful decision to repurpose existing Iraqi prisons to hold prisoners of war. Beyond violating Geneva law,[132] using Abu Ghraib and similar facilities played poorly with the prisoners and local populations as the prisons represented potent symbols of the repressive Hussein regime.[133]

Not everything could be blamed on scarce resources. While regular Iraqi armed forces were initially accorded official prisoner of war status, subsequently captured irregular and foreign fighters were denied Geneva protections in a manner similar to Taliban and al Qaeda detainees.[134] A combination of resource constraints and policy decisions created an environment conducive to abuse.[135] This pattern of systematic prisoner mistreatment from the earliest days of the war would later make headlines in a leaked 2004 report from the International Committee of the Red Cross (ICRC), in which the normally reserved organization publicly confirmed the authenticity of its charges that US behavior toward many detainees was "tantamount to torture."[136]

US conduct before and after the invasion meant any promises of good treatment were less credible to ordinary Iraqi combatants. Choosing between surrendering versus deserting or fighting on, many opposing forces refused to leave themselves at the mercy of US captors who had developed a reputation for not being very merciful. Low levels of initial surrenders foreshadowed a general reluctance among regular Iraqi troops—and later insurgents—to trust US forces. As the insurgency intensified, the United States found itself fighting a more resolute enemy, heightening battlefield suffering for both sides. Indeed, the vast majority of US casualties took place *after* President Bush declared an official end to hostilities.[137] Violations were certainly not the only factor, but US troubles in demonstrating its intentions to abide by the laws of war meant capturing fewer prisoners, and thus fighting more foes.

The Persian Gulf War offers a similar setting but again a study in contrasts. The US-led UN Coalition provided meticulous care for Iraqi prisoners, going so far as to prepare culturally appropriate meals, and even outfitting prisoners with gas masks in anticipation of threatened chemical weapons attacks by the Hussein regime.[138] Unlike modest numbers of prisoners in 2003, during the Gulf War the coalition accepted over 80,000 Iraqi surrenders in just four days of fighting, with 60,000 taken by US forces alone.[139]

The Gulf War's mass surrenders were not happenstance, but a deliberate strategy to induce enemy soldiers to give themselves up, thereby shortening the fighting. In the lead-up to ground operations, coalition air forces dropped millions of leaflets on Iraqi positions in Kuwait with promises of humane treatment and "Arab hospitality."[140] The leaflets' message appeared to get through despite ardent Iraqi counter-propaganda to deter surrenders by convincing its soldiers the leaflets were poisoned and they would be mistreated in captivity, along with deploying death squads to punish would-be defectors.[141]

The multilateral nature of the coalition, alongside strenuous US assurances of decent conduct, meant that commitments of human treatment were viewed more credibly by ordinary Iraqi soldiers. In post-capture interviews, almost all prisoners reported seeing the leaflets, and close to three-quarters said they informed their decision making.[142] Allied messaging went beyond the wildest expectations of military planners and was almost too successful—surrenders actually slowed down the coalition's offensive in many areas.[143] Unlike ICRC criticisms that came to light a decade later, in 1991 the organization dispensed with its usual discretion to praise US conduct, declaring "treatment of Iraqi prisoners of war by U.S. forces was the best compliance with the Geneva Conventions by any nation in any conflict in history."[144]

Credible promises of good treatment helped increase the propensity of Iraqi soldiers to surrender, hastening the end to fighting with less bloodshed on either side.[145] In contrast to the resentment from 2003 onward, in 1991 many Iraqi prisoners reported better treatment than what was afforded by their own army.[146] So content were many prisoners that over 13,000 refused to return home, applying for refugee status.[147] For the vast majority of prisoners who would be repatriated, the United States sought to send them back home as soon as possible, so they could tell family and friends of their decent treatment, bolstering

US credentials. This goodwill was especially important for the postconflict process; even with limited aims, a significant US military presence would remain. As one official military history remarked:

> The United States had to demonstrate to the World—and to Iraq—that it played by the rules and treated its prisoners with respect and humanity. This was essential to influence global public opinion positively toward US policy and US-led actions against Iraq.[148]

The highest echelons of the US military drew similar conclusions regarding the net benefits of following international law. In an extensive review, the Department of Defense contrasted their troops' conduct with the various violations committed by Iraqi forces against prisoners as well as Kuwaiti civilians and property:

> no Iraqi action leading to or resulting in a violation of the law of war gained Iraq any military advantages. This "negative gain from negative actions" in essence reinforces the validity of the law of war.[149]

Unfortunately, just over a decade later US leaders would not heed these same warnings.

An Uphill Struggle in Winning Hearts and Minds

Insurgencies like the ones fought by US forces in Afghanistan and Iraq are often described as "population-centric warfare."[150] Success is measured less on the battlefield; rather, the ultimate prize is the loyalty, or "hearts and minds," of local civilians. Often dismissed as an afterthought, civilian populations are essential to the course of insurgencies. Rebel groups often rely on civilians for everything from food and shelter, to concealment from government forces. Incumbents also desire the locals' support, especially for disclosing rebels and their supporters. "Hearts and minds" may connote attitudes or feelings, but it is the behavioral implications that most interest (counter)insurgents. Obtaining deeper forms of collaboration essentially entails a form of cooperation between belligerents and ordinary people in conflict zones.

Of course, civilians may choose to collaborate for reasons having little to do with sympathy or warm feelings toward a warring side. Many armed groups, from the Vietcong in Vietnam to opposing factions in the Spanish Civil War, gained adherents less out of respect or love, than fear.[151] Yet it is difficult to deploy violence in the ways necessary to selectively target only fence-sitters or those supporting the adversary, while sparing one's own supporters.[152] Foreign powers fighting in unfamiliar surroundings often lack the local knowledge and networks needed; force that is used tends to be more indiscriminate, counterproductively driving civilians further into rebels' arms.[153]

The spread of international law intensifies this calculus, raising expectations of compliance, and thus costs of violations. Reputational repercussions are increasingly difficult to escape as the laws of war become more firmly entrenched.[154] These beliefs can filter all the way down to the hearts and minds of ordinary civilians, with international laws making the conduct of armed actors more salient.

US counterinsurgency doctrine has correspondingly recognized the importance of taking great care when wielding violence. A higher premium is placed on restraint, and instead engaging in service provision and other activities that have the potential to foster goodwill.[155] Awareness of the benefits from limiting violence could be seen even in the Vietnam War, which witnessed many abuses by US forces and their South Vietnamese ally. The Lyndon B. Johnson administration understood the value of applying Geneva law broadly. During the conflict's early days, Chester L. Cooper, a member of the National Security Council staff, described the importance of US conduct:

> We were dealing with a deeply important problem that goes beyond public relations. At issue here is *how* the war should be fought. We should examine carefully the usefulness of such actions as bombing raids by the VNAF[156] and our own planes against Vietnamese villages. Our object is not so much to destroy an enemy as to win a people. We must make sure our military operations are in fact productive. If burning a village provides the VC with a hundred additional recruits then that action is counterproductive in basic military terms [emphasis added].[157]

Doctrinal concerns that violations undermine attempts to win hearts and minds, pushing civilians into the arms of rebels, became a running theme. Foreshadowing the War on Terror, the Department of the Army's 1992 field manual, FM 34–52, dealing with interrogating prisoners was similarly circumspect regarding abuse and its knock-on effects, adding a dose of worry over possible retaliation:

> Revelation of use of torture by US personnel will bring discredit upon the US and its armed forces while undermining domestic and international support for the war effort. It also may place US and allied personnel in enemy hands at a greater risk of abuse by their captors.[158]

The army's later 2006 counterinsurgency manual, FM 3–24, stressed the nexus between legal, moral, and instrumental considerations in wartime conduct:

> The principles of discrimination in the use of force and proportionality in actions are important to counterinsurgents for practical reasons as well as for their ethical or moral implications. Fires that cause unnecessary harm or death to noncombatants may create more resistance and increase the insurgency's appeal—especially if the populace perceives a lack of discrimination in their use.[159]

Experiences from the War on Terror show these lessons were not always heeded. An important point to remember it that the United States frequently did follow the laws of war during this period. US forces often took great care in targeting and other use of force decisions, with military lawyers (judge advocates) involved extensively.[160] Despite meticulous planning in many respects, broader allegations of indiscriminate (or lackluster attempts to avoid such) attacks were also levied, weighing heavily on international and local attitudes.[161]

The mistreatment of prisoners played an outsized role in damaging the image of the United States among the Iraqi populace and the wider Arab world.[162] A Gallup poll fielded a year after the war found most Iraqis welcomed the end of the Hussein regime (especially among Shiites and Kurds), but already a plurality (46%) thought the US invasion did more harm than good.[163] Mixed feelings were tied to occupation policies, with 58% saying US troops conducted themselves poorly; 85% believed little to no effort was made to spare civilians. A majority of Iraqis (57%) favored the immediate departure of coalition forces; a price they were willing to pay even as a similar proportion (53%) acknowledged any withdrawal would likely leave them less safe. General unpopularity carried darker consequences—52% believed insurgent attacks against US forces were at least sometimes justified.

Dim views of the United States were already evident before the Abu Ghraib scandal broke, or controversial counterinsurgency operations in Fallujah and elsewhere. Graphic images of abuse only inflamed tensions, further alienating locals and arousing greater sympathies for insurgent factions. Reflecting on the consequences, the security analyst Anthony Cordesman remarked, "Those Americans who mistreated the prisoners may not have realized it, but they acted in the direct interests of Al Qaeda, the insurgents, and the enemies of the U.S. . . . These negative images validate all other negative images and interact with them."[164]

Images from Abu Ghraib intensified preexisting resentment (and a growing willingness by many Iraqis to do something about it) rooted in the occupying forces' broader warfighting policies. Bitterness was particularly intense around the well-known deprivations suffered by many prisoners. A journalist's interview with a former Abu Ghraib prisoner illustrates the feelings—and more importantly, subsequent actions—kindled by time spent in US captivity:

> But he [the prisoner] remained mystified and wounded by the terrible living conditions in the prisons, which had seemed needlessly primitive and humiliating. Every Iraqi detainee he met, he told me—including those who had not been opposed to the Americans before their arrest—had become determined to fight them in one way or another upon their release.[165]

If the aim was gaining the loyalties of the civilian population, then US conduct in Iraq did much to lead to the opposite. Evidence for this can even be seen in cases of seemingly successful cooperation. Much has been made of the vaunted "Sunni Awakening." Beginning concertedly in 2006 in Anbar province, US forces partnered with local Sunni self-defense councils, an effort that spread to eventually include almost 100,000 fighters. The Awakening Movement was widely credited in helping turn the tide in relations with the Iraqi population, encouraging local collaboration that dramatically improved counterinsurgency efforts in conjunction with the 2007 "surge" of additional US troops.[166]

The origins and evolution of the awakening have been "mythologized" in many respects; a deeper look reveals just how hard it can be to obtain local cooperation.[167] The reasons behind many Sunnis' willingness to work with US forces were complex—especially as some had sided with the insurgents earlier.[168] Partially following the logic that "the enemy of my enemy is my friend," some Sunnis were motivated less by warm feelings toward the United States, but rather growing fears of other groups, especially al Qaeda in Iraq (a precursor to the Islamic State).[169] In line with other episodes from this chapter, the costs to secure this cooperation were significant; by 2008, the United States was paying $16 million a month on fighters' salaries alone.[170] The councils were eventually disbanded, though the decision to do so was partly driven by the Shiite-controlled Iraqi government, which worried over threats to its authority. Indicative of the lack of any fundamental shift in feelings toward the United States, reports soon emerged of former Awakening members switching back to fighting for the insurgency.[171]

As foreign occupiers in a country devastated by war, crushing sanctions, and the legacy of a repressive regime, US forces already faced a daunting task. Whatever expediency came from violating international laws, however, appeared more than offset by negative repercussions. As the insurgency gathered momentum in 2004, Human Rights Watch arrived at a telling conclusion about the local and global reputational consequences, "Ironically, the administration is now finding that it may be losing the war for hearts and minds around the world precisely because it threw those rules out."[172]

Wartime Violations and Insurgency Onset

Violations also contributed to the initial risk of an insurgency breaking out, putting US forces in the position of needing to win hearts and minds in the first place. The Iraq War illustrates how breaking international law can have immediate effects, but also leave embers conducive to further conflict. The onset of insurgencies is driven by a multitude of factors—economic, political, social, geographic, among others.[173] The dangers posed by foreign-imposed regime change (like Iraq in 2003) can be particularly menacing, though not all interventions that turn into occupations are doomed from the start.[174]

The bigger question belligerents face is not only if they will prevail in war, but whether they will win the ensuing peace. *Jus post bellum* ("right after war") receives less attention than its earlier just war siblings on initiation (*ad bellum*) and conduct (*in bello*), but raises fundamental questions about what makes for a virtuous postconflict environment.[175] Questions of justice are important because the destructive nature of war for victor and vanquished alike can create conditions begetting ever more fighting. *How* the prior war began and was fought can have a direct bearing on evaluations of justice once the fighting stops, and the risk it returns.

Formal combat operations may cease, but former adversaries are not operating from a blank moral slate, informed by respective beliefs about the origins and course of the war just fought. Prior conduct can prove pivotal—positively or negatively—for postwar stability. Historical figures have appreciated the longer-term dangers posed by wartime abuses. Napoleon Bonaparte, not exactly known as a humanitarian, saw the merits of some limits, "The natural law . . . forbids us to multiply the evils of war indefinitely."[176] Just war theorist Walzer points to practical benefits from conforming to restrictions, to help "leave behind no festering resentment, no sense of scores unsettled, no deeply felt need for individual or collective revenge."[177] Rancor has rarely dissipated quickly for victims of abuse ranging from the Spanish Civil War to Stalinist mass murders, and can carry over for generations.[178] Awareness of unintended downstream effects is evident in early US understandings of the laws of war. The Lieber Code written for Union troops during the American Civil War allowed a wide berth for using force. Eyeing war's end, however, Lieber's Article 16 insisted on certain bounds, cautioning that "military necessity does not include any act of hostility which makes the return to peace unnecessarily difficult."

Wartime violations complicate relations not simply because abuse breeds anger and resentment. By breaching shared expectations of appropriate conduct, perpetrators undermine their own credibility to uphold future promises. Cease-fires and peace treaties represent an especially important class of commitments that engage belligerents' reputations; success depends on each side sufficiently trusting the other.[179] Various factors shape this trust, but often overlooked is how compliance *during* the war may affect how credible commitments will be viewed *after* the fighting stops.

Calculations of credibility are intensified by the spread of the laws of war.[180] By setting clearer standards against which belligerents' actions are measured, the meaning ascribed to conduct can change.[181] The legalization of warfare generates greater stakes for belligerents' reputations, carrying over into the postwar period. Raising expectations and constructing a vocabulary for grievance, responses may intensify when the laws of war are more firmly established. When reacting to violations, ordinary individuals may be willing to take increasingly bold actions; the riskiest being to join others in armed insurrection, rather than cooperate and acquiesce to the perpetrator's rule.

Indications of a violations-to-insurgency pathway were evident in the 2003 Iraq War and its aftermath. The United States already faced a tall order of stabilizing a country wracked by three disastrous wars since 1980, more than a decade of sanctions, and a power vacuum left by the fall of the Hussein regime. Lack of adequate US postwar planning made a bad situation worse, as neoconservatives presumed peace and democracy would automatically flourish in Iraq.[182] Armories and abandoned Iraqi military hardware were left undefended, allowing huge quantities of small arms and explosives to fall into the hands of nonstate actors.[183] Orders No. 1 and No. 2 of May 2003, issued by the US-led Coalition Provisional Authority (CPA), dismantled much of the existing Iraqi administrative and security apparatuses—removing officials from their posts, disbanding over 300,000 troops, and prohibiting any officer at the rank of colonel or above from serving again.[184] Denying thousands of Iraqi soldiers employment, or even pensions in many cases, exacerbated misgivings toward the US occupation.[185] Although a fresh start might seem appealing, the combined decisions went against lessons from prior regime transitions showing the value of working with existing elites and members of the establishment, giving them a stake in the new system instead of fighting to hold on to the old one.[186]

Postconflict policies created a pool of individuals with the skills and means to rebel. A further spark would come through US wartime conduct. Many Iraqis believed the United States was bent on recolonizing their country like earlier European empires.[187] Refusal to go through the UN Security Council was taken as proof of the malign intentions of a liberator-turned-occupier. US treatment of

detainees in the War on Terror and early stages of the Iraq invasion further confirmed the country could not be trusted. It is not surprising that those most loyal
to Hussein—members of the elite Republican Guard or fighters close to his home
city of Tikrit—fought against the US presence from the start. For insurgency to
take hold, however, required larger numbers of fighters, and came to include
many groups opposed to, or at least ambivalent about, the prior regime.[188] US
conduct, in particular failing to live up to international legal obligations, provided some of the glue necessary to bind disparate groups behind a common goal
of fighting the US occupation.

The Persian Gulf War continues to offer a useful contrast. As noted earlier,
US objectives in this earlier conflict were more limited, but the creation of no-
fly zones and a substantial number of coalition troops operating on Iraqi soil
presented potential targets for would-be insurgents. The ceasefire line crossed
Iraqi territory with several US divisions temporarily deployed throughout
southern portions of the country.[189] In response to Iraqi repression of Kurdish
uprisings in the north, the US-led coalition initiated Operation Provide Comfort in April 1991, deploying 5,000 US troops and thousands of allied soldiers
to the area to supply protection and humanitarian relief.[190] Throughout these
postconflict operations, US and allied forces did not encounter much meaningful local opposition.[191] Rather than resisting the US presence, many Iraqi
soldiers continued to surrender to coalition forces even after most fighting
had stopped to avoid instability within their own country.[192] Proper treatment of Iraqi prisoners in accordance with international obligations was thus
not only morally sound, but also contributed to US strategic interests after
the conflict.

How much do the downstream effects from violations on the risk of insurgency extend beyond Iraq? One observable implication is that a belligerent's conduct during the conventional phase of a war should be associated with changes
in the likelihood of opponents rising up in rebellion after initial hostilities have
ceased.[193] Additionally, consequences from wartime conduct should be greater in
more legalized periods because of the way international law can shape the beliefs
and expectations of state and nonstate actors alike.[194]

One way to assess this conjecture is to examine whether any relationship
exists between wartime conduct and postwar stability. To do so, I look at the
aftermath of all interstate wars, beginning in 1898 with the Spanish-American
War continuing up to the 2003 Iraq War.[195] The turn of the twentieth century
is a useful starting point, as it marks the advent of greater codification of the
laws of war like the 1899 Hague Conventions, and because data on wartime
conduct is less reliable and available for earlier conflicts.[196] This set of wars is
then cross-referenced against whether an insurgency broke out against a given

belligerent within two years of the end of conventional hostilities—a time window allowing dynamics to play out while still being closely tied to the original war. An insurgency is defined as a protracted struggle by armed nonstate actors pursuing political objectives—including independence, greater autonomy, or overthrowing the regime—against existing political authorities, which could include a foreign occupier.[197] I only include interstate wars with a reasonable chance of insurgency onset, defined as meeting one of the following criteria: 1) occupying and maintaining a troop presence on the adversary's territory; 2) maintaining troops on adjoining territory that remains contested; or 3) forcibly installing a friendly (or puppet) government on the adversary. This avoids including conflicts with little meaningful risk of an insurgency, such as after the 1982 Falklands War where Argentinean forces were hundreds of miles from the disputed islands.[198]

The main explanatory variables concern the conduct of belligerents toward civilians and prisoners of war respectively during the interstate war.[199] Several control variables are also included to take into account other factors that may be associated with wartime conduct and insurgency onset.[200]

Looking across this period yields twenty-five instances of insurgency onset after interstate wars out of just over 128 potential episodes.[201] This suggests postwar insurgencies are an infrequent (20% of possible cases), but not unusual, occurrence. The analysis reveals that the Persian Gulf War and 2003 Iraq War episodes are not unique, but reflect a discernable relationship between wartime conduct and risks of subsequent insurgency. Figure 4.2 reports the probability of insurgent onset at different levels of prisoner abuse across the entire time period, as well as separately for the pre- and post-1949 period, using the Geneva Conventions as a common cut-off ushering in a new era in the laws of war.[202] Across the entire period, violations against prisoners are associated with a significant increase in the likelihood that the victimized side will later take up arms—almost doubling in relative terms (from 15% to a little under 30%) the probability of an insurgency.[203] While other work suggests brutality can pay off by cowing an occupied population into submission,[204] the results point to a counteracting menace. Interestingly, targeting civilians alone does not have a similar association, suggesting that at least some of those victimized need to come from former troops who possess the military and organizational skills necessary to fight an insurgency.[205]

Figure 4.2 further shows that the consequences of wartime conduct are not constant over time. While prisoner abuse has little discernable impact in the pre-1949 period, after the advent of the Geneva Conventions the blowback from violations appears more severe, tripling (from around 10% to over 30%) the chances of insurgency. These findings should only be taken as suggestive as

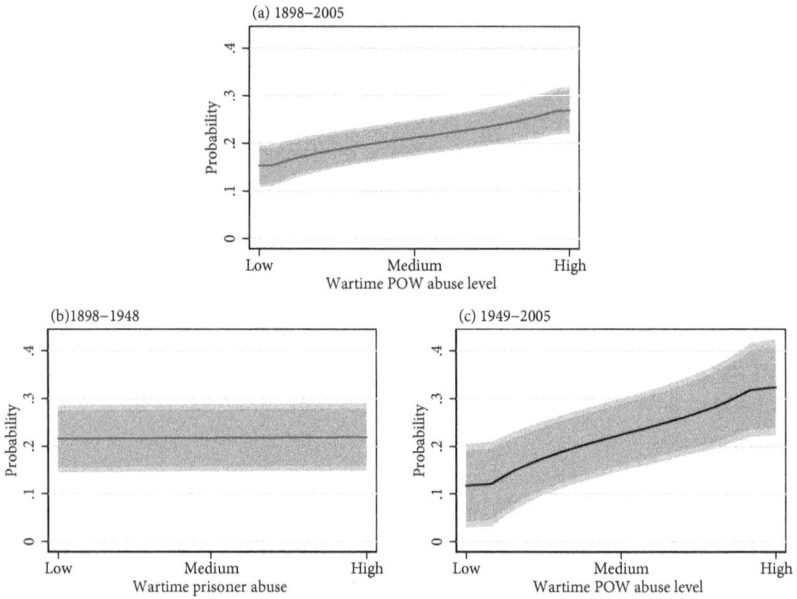

FIGURE 4.2.   Wartime prisoner abuse and the probability of postwar insurgency onset, 1898–2005

Notes: Probability of postwar insurgency onset at different levels of prisoner abuse during prior interstate armed conflict. Analysis covers armed conflicts for the years 1898 to 2005, restricted to conflicts where postwar circumstances displayed a reasonable possibility of insurgency. Probabilities calculated using kernel-weighted local polynomial smoothing. Shaded areas indicate 90% and 95% confidence intervals.

other dynamics could be operating in general and over time. Nevertheless, the results are consistent with the case study evidence from the two US wars in Iraq— violations of the laws of war can spill over and lead to further conflict, and these forces seem to solidify as international rules become more legalized.[206]

Did Reputational Consequences Ultimately Matter?

This chapter has outlined the wide-ranging reputational consequences from US contraventions of international law during the War on Terror. Ramifications included damage to the image of the United State in world opinion in general and around issues like human rights in particular; other countries' objection to contribute troops to US military coalitions; similar reluctance to help in other areas like US intelligence and detention operations; and various dynamics that undermined US warfighting capacity on the ground, making conflict rather than cooperation more likely. These repercussions were evident across various domains and at different levels. What they shared in common was an unwilling-ness of actors (especially ordinary ones) to support cooperation with the United States partly in response to changes in beliefs informed by US violations. It was not simply that foreign actors found US actions odious, but also that the United States was breaking rules embedded in international law, revealing deeper con-cerns over the credibility of its commitments.

An important point still remains—did reputational consequences ultimately mean anything? This gets back to one of the central questions of this book about better understanding how international law matters. If "mattering" denotes whether prospective or actual reputational sanctions stopped the United States from engaging in violations, then the answer is admittedly a definite "no." The very presence of an extensive record documenting questionable US con-duct in the War on Terror shows the risk of international legal consequences was not enough to dissuade the Bush administration from breaching these rules at the outset.

Another interpretation of international law "mattering," however, concerns whether reputational harms (assuming they exist) exceeded the advantages accrued through violations. From a pure cost-benefit standpoint, international law would seem to count for little if what is earned from breaking obligations eclipses any losses incurred. Many Bush administration alumni continued to uphold the core policies that received so much international condemnation—sometimes defending their legality, but almost always rationalizing that infrac-tions were necessary for effectively combating terrorism.

This pattern of denial and vindication is evident in the most contentious of counterterrorism policies—the detention program. Forced to acknowledge the existence of CIA foreign black sites in 2006 amid growing revelations, Presi-dent Bush still championed their value, "By giving us information about ter-rorist plans we could not get anywhere else, this program has saved innocent lives."[207] John Yoo, one of the legal architects of detention policies in the Office of Legal Counsel in the Department of Justice, sought to draw a direct line between enhanced interrogations his memos helped usher in, and the intel-ligence for later locating and killing bin Laden.[208] Shortly after leaving office, Vice President Cheney summarized his position on interrogations: "They were legal, essential, justified, successful, and the right thing to do . . . [T]hey pre-vented the violent death of thousands, if not hundreds of thousands, of inno-cent people."[209]

Administration officials' belief that the bin Laden mission offered vindica-tion presaged a continuing debate over whether US violations were "worth it" and yielded indispensable dividends. A high moment in this controversy came with the release in 2014 of the Senate Select Committee on Intelligence Report investigating the CIA's interrogation program, referenced at various point in this chapter. While many key sections were redacted for security reasons, the report sought to dispel on almost every single count the alleged utility of the agency's torture and rendition program. In response, a flurry of statements by key Bush administration personnel and their supporters put forward a vigorous defense.[210]

Disagreements over detention and other elements of the War on Terror endure. It is beyond our present scope to settle the debate over whether the advantages from violating international law during the Bush era outweighed the many drawbacks detailed here. Searching for definitive answers faces a corresponding counterfactual problem to the study of international law—what would have been the consequences (e.g., to US image, cooperation with others, or counterinsurgency efforts) if the Bush administration had taken a more restrained legal approach? Yet for our purposes this is in many respects the wrong question to ask. It likely exceeds any reasonable expectations for international law, or much else for that matter, to be able to control the actions of an aggrieved and threatened superpower. Rather, a more useful line of inquiry is whether contravening international legal obligations resulted in substantial counteracting effects. On this score, this chapter has presented compelling evidence that the United States suffered for the Bush administration's choices during the War on Terror, and this was most apparent across a variety of reputational consequences.

Much of the fallout was anticipated early on by more moderate voices. In a January 2002 memo to the president during a pivotal period of internal discussions over whether to apply the Geneva Conventions to captured enemy combatants, the secretary of state Colin Powell warned of likely repercussions, including "negative international reaction," with the result of "undermin[ing] public support among critical allies, making military cooperation more difficult to sustain."[211]

It is hard to know whether subsequent defenses by administration officials were sincerely felt, or merely post-hoc excuses hiding private misgivings over what unfolded. Yet looking at the evolution of US practices suggests government officials came to realize the significant costs associated with prior stances. Along with closing secret CIA sites, in later years the Bush administration placed greater constraints on interrogation techniques.[212] Diagnosing the sources of failures from protracted fighting in Afghanistan and Iraq, a sea change took place in US counterinsurgency doctrine, centering efforts more on local populations. In so doing, emphasis shifted to the need for US forces to take the "moral high ground" and act in accordance with international law.[213] The US

Department of Defense later formulated a concerted public relations campaign to communicate these and other changes with a primary objective "To improve U.S. credibility."[214]

It is indicative of how toxic the original detention program had become that one of the first executive orders signed by President Obama revoked several of his predecessor's policies, requiring interrogations by all US personnel to follow prior standards "to ensure compliance with the treaty obligations of the United States, including the Geneva Conventions."[215] Alongside signing another order that same day pledging to close the Guantanamo Bay detention facility,[216] the newly inaugurated president framed his actions in the context of US obligations:

> This is me following through on not just a commitment I made during the campaign, but I think an understanding that dates back to our founding fathers, that we are willing to observe core standards of conduct, not just when it's easy, but also when it's hard.[217]

The War on Terror was no doubt a new kind of war against a new kind of enemy. Yet the question remained what should be the appropriate response— both militarily and legally. Reflecting at the time on those first few defining years of this new war, a 2005 public letter by the general John Shalikashvili and other retired military officers foreshadowed Obama's later words by situating US conduct within the country's larger history of warfighting:

> Repeatedly in our past, the United States has confronted foes that, at the time they emerged, posed threats of a scope or nature unlike any we had previously faced. . . . But we have been far more steadfast in the past in keeping faith with our national commitment to the rule of law.[218]

Recent developments suggest that upholding legal commitments raises more than simply moral considerations, but also has instrumental implications. Although not necessarily celebrating the link, the legal scholar Jack Goldsmith observed a growing trend whereby "Lawful action . . . had become more than a demand of honor or morality . . . it had become a military imperative."[219] Coming from a more approving standpoint, fellow legal scholar Jens Ohlin remarked, "In the war on terror, international law is our best friend, not our worst enemy."[220]

Confirming this pattern, the War on Terror illustrates the many repercussions that can arise when a country does not follow its international commitments.

These effects were not limited to a single source or domain, but extended across numerous areas involving a multitude of actors. Responses were especially evident among mass publics as a whole, and ordinary people individually, who demonstrated how enforcement can take place against violations of international law. This does not mean that all national publics, or segments within a given society, will respond to legal rules in similar ways. In the War on Terror, reactions and enforcement actions were much stronger from foreign populations compared to domestically for citizens within the United States. But as the next two chapters illustrate, the potential for international legal obligations to influence underlying policy preferences—in sometimes direct, but other times more nuanced, ways—may take place even around hard issues and among a seemingly skeptical US public.

FROM LAW TO PREFERENCES I

Experimental Evidence of a Tortured Relationship

> When we engaged in some of these enhanced interrogation tech-
> niques, techniques that I believe and I think any fair-minded person
> would believe were torture, we crossed a line. And that needs to be
> understood and accepted . . . [T]he character of our country has to
> be measured in part, not by what we do when things are easy, but
> what we do when things are hard.
>
> —President Barack Obama (2014)

> Torture works. OK, folks? You know, I have these guys—"Torture
> doesn't work!"—believe me, it works. And waterboarding is your
> minor form. Some people say it's not actually torture. Let's assume it
> is. But they asked me the question: what do you think of waterboard-
> ing? Absolutely fine. But we should go much stronger than water-
> boarding. That's the way I feel.
>
> —Then-candidate and future president Donald Trump (2016)

These words from two recent US presidents illustrate the stark divide not only in
the United States, but across many countries, as to whether their societies should
condone or even celebrate the use of torture. Exactly which acts do, or do not,
constitute torture remain highly contested, but Article 1(1) of the 1984 Convention against Torture (CAT) provides a generally agreed-upon definition of torture as "any act by which severe pain or suffering, whether physical or mental, is
intentionally inflicted on a person."[1] Probably more than any other form of abuse,
the pain and damage wrought on victim and perpetrator alike—individually and
collectively—makes torture a window into a community's values.[2] Torture raises
profound moral questions about what rights should be accorded to prisoners,
counterbalanced against concerns of security for information gleaned through
such harsh techniques that might save innocent lives. Enthusiasm might not
quite reach the levels touted in former President Trump's verdict. Philosophers
have grappled with these trade-offs—Jeremy Bentham, one of the most renowned
liberal political theorists, pondered the conditions under which "torture might

be made use of with advantage."[3] More than a century later, the just war theorist Michael Walzer similarly acknowledged circumstances meriting the use of torture, though lamented doing so meant accepting "dirty hands."[4]

The potential for international law to intervene might seem quite limited when it comes to torture, where engaging in such extreme actions is contemplated precisely because matters of national security and public safety are at stake. That democracies have a long history of engaging in (and innovating on) torture indicates that publics can themselves be avid supporters.[5] A wealth of research suggests that citizens are willing to approve of more repressive and aggressive practices when facing or perceiving threats to their security.[6]

In the face of these challenges, a number of international laws have developed that seek to place limits on interrogation techniques, or prohibit torture outright. These rules are prevalent in the laws of war, but also in international human rights agreements applicable both inside and outside of armed conflict. Alongside enforcement through the imposition of various reputational sanctions examined in the previous two chapters, another main function of international law can be to shape actors' underlying policy preferences. Torture, in turn, offers a particularly hard test for the notion that international legal commitments are able to fulfill this preference function.

In the next section, I provide a general overview of how legal rules in general, and international laws in particular, may influence policy preferences. Much of the rest of the chapter investigates the extent to which international law can shape attitudes around a particularly troublesome and controversial topic—the use of torture against enemy combatants. I begin by surveying the long relationship between torture and various international legal instruments. What has been written down on paper has not always been met in the beliefs and practices of many actors, including the wider public. The remaining sections employ a series of survey experiments to examine how exposure to information regarding these laws may shift support for torture among members of the US public. The results reveal that international law can have an appreciable impact on attitudes toward torture, but these effects differ based on the design of the agreement and the broader conflict context. The evidence also points to some important differences among certain segments of the population, but not necessarily in ways we might initially think. In particular, international laws might *most* affect those who at first sight seem *least* predisposed toward legal appeals. As the recent history of the US interrogation program recounted both here and in the prior chapter shows, international law may not be able to determine policy and practice on its own. Yet by influencing public attitudes, these rules can play an important role in changing broader national preferences, perhaps helping at least blunt some of society's worst impulses during trying times.

Preferences and International Law:
A Theoretical Overview

Although the role of enforcement is important for the operation of legal orders (both international and domestic), law is not reducible to the threat or imposition of sanctions alone.[7] Pure coercion represents an expensive and brittle approach to maintaining legal orders, dependent on constant monitoring alongside the availability and willingness to use scarce resources for punishment.[8] An additional function of law is a more persuasive one—transmitting to actors a set of expectations of what is appropriate, and what sorts of policies and practices should be viewed as being in their interests.[9] Law can be seen not just as a menacing cudgel, but also a guiding tutor of what preferences should be adopted. While law can function as a deterrent through threats of material punishments, actors often frequently abide by legal principles because they view these rules as legitimate, and compliance as consistent with their core interests.[10]

Law's enforcement and preference functions should be seen as complementary in many respects. Legal principles may be able to shape policy preferences on average. But in those instances where it is more difficult to do so, the possibility of enforcement can prove useful for encouraging compliance. And stronger preferences to follow particular rules can reduce the need for enforcement, while improving the readiness of actors to take the costly steps necessary for sanctioning those violations that do occur. Nevertheless, the overall logic behind the two functions is distinct, and it is important to consider the relationship between international law and preferences on its own terms, both theoretically and empirically.

For many skeptics, there is little or no connection between international law and preferences. The realist scholar Hans Morgenthau once recounted, "From that iron law of international politics, that legal obligations must yield to the national interest, no nation has ever been completely immune."[11] Not only do interests trump international law from this perspective, but legal commitments have no role to play in determining what those interests are in the first place.[12] Consistent with many rational choice approaches, an actor's preferences are assumed to be exogenous and mostly fixed. Even some legal proponents adopt a similar view on the separate sources of preferences, where the operation of international law is primarily found in other functions like enforcement.[13] An analogous outlook is evident among some domestic legal scholars, with questions of law kept completely separate from public interests.[14] Law may constrain, but actors' preferences are largely given, created, and endure outside the confines of legal principles.[15]

Against this perspective, and sometimes falling under labels like "constructivist" or "reflectivist," is the view that international laws and norms can transform actors' interests.[16] Rather than entirely divorced from one another, legal obligations are closely tied to actors' understandings of their self-interests.[17] Yet we do not need to go so far as to assert that actors have an inherent propensity to comply with any and all international laws as a general end in itself.[18] An agreement's particular institutional design or substantive content matters in ways that can be more or less impactful. The more modest claim here is instead that the qualities of international law can influence the particular policy preferences of actors, leading them to adopt positions more in line with those laid out in legal commitments.

As with the examination of reputation and enforcement in prior chapters, various arguments have been put forward for the specific ways in which international law functions to influence preferences. Many of these accounts focus on states as the primary site for preferences, either through direct state-to-state interactions or by other actors like international organizations.[19] The notion of popular international law put forward in this book instead calls for taking seriously the role of the public and their preferences vis-à-vis international legal commitments. National publics as a whole, or certain subsets, can serve as important "constituencies" with the potential to bolster (or undermine) particular international laws from the local to the global levels.[20] While we may "only know what is appropriate by reference to the judgments of a community or a society,"[21] popular international law suggests it is incumbent to understand the collective judgments of ordinary citizens in national societies for grasping the operation of rules in the larger international society.

In what ways does international law hold the potential to shape ordinary individuals' policy preferences? Or how exactly is it that "Treaties can *inform* interests and change values" (emphasis added)?[22] Information is important in my account of preference formation and change, but it is not simply technical details coming from monitoring or other agreement provisions.[23] Rather, information generated by international law is more *principled* in the sense that it creates new meanings and activates novel understandings among citizenries. Just as principled information can facilitate the enforcement of international agreements, so too can it help shape people's underlying policy preferences. A large part of the way it can do so lies in the deeper set of values embedded in international laws distinguishing them from other forms of rules or norms. When international legal scholars talk about "fidelity" to, or the "compliance pull" of, international law, they are crediting particular values rooted in these laws that have different effects on audience beliefs compared to nonlegal alternatives.[24]

A parallel pattern is evident in the role of the particular pedigree of domestic and especially constitutional laws in shaping citizens' understandings of their interests. Domestic laws possess a similar lineage of legitimacy leading actors to believe that following the substantive content of these rules is appropriate and in their interests.[25] With this particular authority in hand, "the educative role of the law" means that domestic laws (like their international counterparts) can influence the "desires, wants, and interests" of ordinary citizens in terms of what is expected in their societies.[26] Legal rules communicate multiple types of "messages" to individuals—these include the risk of enforcement against potential violators, but also in a more normative sense that it is "*wrong* to disobey" (emphasis in original).[27]

When popular constitutionalism describes constitutional law as "popular law," it does so in several respects—not only regarding the role of the people in upholding the Constitution, but also law having a distinct impact on popular actors.[28] It is not an exaggeration to say that a distinct morality taking on quasi-religious tones, or a "constitutional faith," undergirds how constitutional rules can occupy a central place in many people's basic thinking about right and wrong, legal and illegal.[29]

Like their international counterparts, the "principled" nature of constitutional rules makes them more likely to "win public approval."[30] A common educational function can be identified across both constitutional and international law, and their respective capacities to shape actors' preferences.[31] Rather than fixed or externally determined, the preferences of actors may thus be endogenous to legal rules. And just as popular constitutionalism emphasizes the role of constitutional law in shaping the public's interests, so too should we take seriously this potential under popular international law for international legal commitments.

None of this is to suggest that all international laws will be able to equally sway all members of the public at all times. As has been noted at various points throughout this book, international laws differ immensely in their design and overall levels of legalization, with potential implications for influencing policy preferences. Legally binding treaties exhibit much higher degrees of obligation compared to softer laws; being more deeply embedded in international legal principles, these rules may yield greater effects as a result. In particular, formal treaties may have a stronger impact on domestic audiences compared to more informal instruments.[32] However, support for less binding laws can be surprisingly impressive, where actors come to accept harder and softer legal obligations in similar ways.[33]

The level of precision in an international agreement may also have implications for actors' preferences. Given the importance placed on information, more precise agreements should send clearer signals of the prescribed or proscribed rules, and thus may be more informative.[34] By contrast, more flexible or ambiguous laws may be less likely to be followed, either as a cynical way to evade obligations, or out of a genuine lack of awareness of what is required.[35]

One final dimension of legalization points to possible areas of complementarity between the preference and enforcement functions of international law. As discussed in the follow-up reputation experiments in chapter 3, agreements can differ markedly in how much power is delegated to third parties like international courts for punishing violators. The prospect of direct sanctions from violating an agreement with high levels of delegation may make actors more willing to abide by the content of the rules. However, over time this seemingly straightforward cost-benefit calculus may give way to a gradual process whereby the rules become internalized to the point where actors view it to be in their interests (or even identity) to follow them.[36] Numerous pathways thus exist where different dimensions in an agreement's legalization come to bear on actors' preferences.

Alongside differences across international agreements, the public itself may differ collectively, or among subgroups, in important ways in their sensitivity to international laws. The general appeal of international legal commitments may vary based on citizens' political ideology, partisanship, or other key factors in line with general research on public opinion and foreign policy.[37] Combined with predispositions for or against the substantive policies in an agreement, the ability of international law to influence those same groups' preferences is far from guaranteed. This is especially the case in the United States, where a number of studies suggest wide swathes of the population are comfortable with a realpolitik way of thinking, and willing to hold legal obligations at arm's length.[38] Even findings consistent with international laws and institutions may be driven by more instrumental concerns rather than deeper changes in underlying preferences.[39] International laws may thus find it harder to change policy preferences in national contexts like the United States, and especially for certain segments of the population.

Doubly worrisome is that the ability of international law to influence preferences may be particularly challenging for policies in some issue areas compared to others. The experimental findings from chapter 3 on enforcement suggested that international law could function in domains of both higher and lower politics, though reputational sanctions were on the whole more modest for security compared to economic issues. The outlook for international law may be even more dire for preferences given the focus here is more on the policies and practices of citizens' own governments instead of foreign countries.

A wealth of research seems to confirm that international laws and norms have few impacts in situations where national security is paramount, especially the proving ground of armed conflict.[40] The record for democracies—where publics should be expected to play a more pronounced role due to the greater account-ability of their leaders—is decidedly mixed. While some studies suggest democracies exhibit a greater preference for restraint,[41] other work argues there is no real difference with autocratic regimes, or even a *greater* penchant for democratic belligerents to engage in abusive behavior at home and abroad during armed struggle.[42] Indeed, national publics have at times been fervent advocates of fairly brutal behavior, for whom calls of "bashing the foreigners" have resonated loudly in many instances.[43] Members of the public are an important constituency, but when facing severe threats they may form "pro-violation constituencies" rather than serving as a bulwark in defense of legal rules.[44]

That international law may be less welcome on matters of national security has been acknowledged even among some of the regime's staunchest proponents. The legal scholar Louis Henkin ceded a fair amount of ground when he said, "It was not a cynic who once suggested that international law established order in unimportant matters but not in important ones."[45] And yet there are good theoretical reasons to believe that the principles embedded in international laws inform citizens and leaders alike in meaningful ways, changing their preferences around matters both unimportant and important. In some ways the potential may be even greater in those "harder" cases where the principled information offered by international laws may be especially illuminating of different considerations and values than those normally held in security affairs. In a symmetry to the hedging by some legal proponents, several skeptics admit that it remains an open empirical question whether international laws are actually able to influence policy preferences in general, and for security issues like torture in particular.[46] In the next section I take up this question by first examining what are the relevant international laws surrounding torture, and how harsh interrogational practices have been approached by governments and their publics.

Background on the Treatment of Prisoners: Of Laws, Policies, and Publics

Probably no issue in recent years has garnered greater controversy, or led to more doubts about the relevance of international law, than the use of torture. Painted in broader brush strokes in chapter 4, the War on Terror begun under the George W. Bush administration largely came to be defined by, and decried for, the (mis)treatment of enemy combatants, epitomized by revelations of torture ordered or condoned at various official levels.[47] The United States has not been alone; a range of other regimes in the preceding and succeeding years have resorted to torture against both captured combatants and political prisoners, from India to Syria to Myanmar.[48]

At first blush the prevalence of abuse might seem puzzling from a lawyerly standpoint. In many respects, torture occupies a privileged place in the corpus of international law.[49] Figure 5.1 lists some of the more notable international agreements banning the practice. A full accounting, including many regional instruments,[50] would yield dozens more, reinforcing the sentiment that torture represents an affront that "shocks the conscience."[51]

One strand of this legal regime prohibiting torture developed as part of a wider modern trend in the codification of various norms and informal customs related to armed conflict, which came to be known as the laws of war, or international humanitarian law (IHL). On the eve of the twentieth century, the Annex to the 1899 Second Hague Convention did not refer specifically to torture, but disallowed it implicitly by mandating in Article 4 that all prisoners of war "must be humanely treated."[52] The successor 1907 Fourth Hague Convention reiterated the same generic obligation concerning prisoner care. Later agreements became more precise in their expectations for how prisoners should be treated. The 1929 Geneva Convention was the first multilateral treaty devoted solely to prisoners of war.[53] Article 2 continued in the tradition of its Hague predecessors by requiring prisoners "be humanely protected." Article 5 on interrogations went further, declaring, "No pressure shall be exercised on prisoners to obtain information," and they "may not be threatened, insulted, or exposed to unpleasantness or disadvantages of any kind whatsoever."

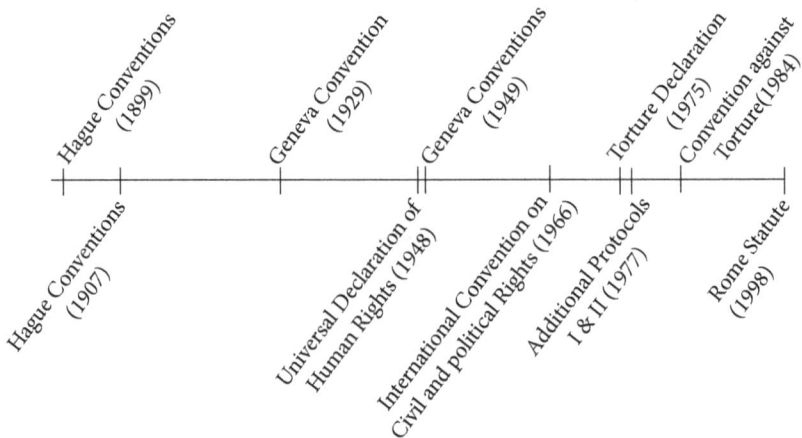

FIGURE 5.1. Major international agreements prohibiting torture

Twenty years later, the 1949 Third Geneva Convention dealing with prisoners specifically outlawed torture across numerous areas, including interrogation (Article 17) and penalties (Article 87), going on to denounce "torture or inhumane treatment" as qualifying as "grave breaches" (Article 130) constituting war crimes.[54] Although prevailing laws at this point in time primarily regulated fighting between states, the odiousness reserved for the practice meant "cruel treatment and torture" were prohibited in the Conventions' Common Article 3 regulating internal and more irregular conflicts "not of an international character." The ban on torture was strengthened in the later 1977 Additional Protocols. Additional Protocol I further refined the laws governing international conflicts, forbidding "torture of all kinds, whether physical or mental" comprehensively "at any time and in any place whatsoever, whether committed by civilian or by military agents" (Article 75[2][a][ii]). Additional Protocol II, the first agreement specifically regulating civil wars and other "non-international armed conflicts" included protections against "cruel treatment such as torture" as one of its "Fundamental guarantees" (Article 4[2][a]). Two decades later, the 1998 Rome Statute establishing the International Criminal Court (ICC) formalized these rules further, mandating that torture constitutes not only a war crime (Article 8[2][a][ii]), but also a crime against humanity (Article 7[1][f]) when part of a widespread and systematic campaign.

Alongside the laws of war, the outlawing of torture figures prominently in the separate but related body of international human rights law, which seeks to guarantee certain rights and protections inside and outside of armed conflict.[55] One year before the 1949 Geneva Conventions, members of the United Nations agreed to the Universal Declaration on Human Rights (UDHR), whose Article 5 includes the now common language that "No one shall be subjected to torture or to cruel, inhuman or degrading treatment or punishment." While technically nonbinding, the UDHR became a cornerstone of the larger human rights legal regime. Of particular note, the 1966 International Covenant on Civil and Political Rights (ICCPR) made the general prohibition against torture (Article 7) binding, and which could not be derogated from (unlike many other rights) even in times of national emergency (Article 4[2]).

Finally, what perhaps most demonstrates the legal centrality of torture is that the practice was eventually viewed by the international community as meriting its own treaty, the 1984 Convention against Torture (CAT). The CAT provides the consensus starting definition for torture (Article 1) described at the beginning of this chapter. It also represents one of the strongest human rights agreements currently in existence.[56] Prohibitions on torture were reaffirmed and expanded (e.g., Articles 2–4), and parties took the additional step of delegating away a significant amount of sovereignty through the principle of universal jurisdiction (Article 5).

Universal jurisdiction allows any state to arrest and try an individual suspected of committing torture, regardless of the nationality of the accused, the victim, or the country where the offense took place.[57] Torture thus occupies a proud place in international law. Some proponents even contend that prohibition of the practice has obtained the rarified status of jus cogens("compelling law"), or a peremptory norm binding all actors from which no derogation is ever permitted.[58]

The prominence of international rules outlawing torture is matched by a seemingly equally large gap between legal principles on the one hand, and the actual practice and rhetoric of many countries on the other.[59] Higher levels of repression are especially common when governments (including democracies) face war or other severe threats—exactly the time proponents hope legal rules would matter most.[60] Yet obstacles to drawing reliable inferences regarding the role of international law in shaping preferences toward torture and other forms of abuse remain formidable in similar ways to those discussed in chapter 3 on reputation and enforcement. In addition to selection effects from commitment and design decisions, directly measuring preferences is difficult; many observational studies instead rely on proxies or inferring preferences from behavior.[61] As with empirical research on reputation, one pattern that has emerged is various promising, but inconsistent, findings for the relationship between international agreements—either concerning the laws of war, or human rights treaties—and the resort to torture or other forms of violence.[62]

Although aggregate patterns are mixed, the actions and rhetoric of various political leaders points to laws against torture seemingly holding little sway. In a crackdown beginning in 2016 as part of a self-described "war on drugs," security forces in the Philippines engaged in a systematic campaign of kidnappings, torture, and murder of thousands of citizens, which the ICC determined was evidence of crimes against humanity.[63] The Filipino president at the time, Rodrigo Duterte, went so far as to advocate torture against anyone standing in his way, including government auditors, when in 2019 he said, "Let's just kidnap people from COA [Commission on Audit]. Let's bring them here, then we will torture those sons of w*****."[64]

Not to be outdone, then-presidential candidate Trump promised not only to keep the prison for terror suspects in Guantanamo Bay open, but expand its capacity and "load it up with some bad dudes."[65] And in a statement eerily similar to the former attorney general Alberto Gonzales's reasoning on the irrelevance of existing laws in the War on Terror noted in chapter 4, Trump called for changing laws to explicitly permit torture:

> We have an enemy that doesn't play by the laws. You could say laws, and they're laughing. They're laughing at us right now. I would like to strengthen the laws so that we can better compete.[66]

Alarmed by this turn by leaders in the United States, the Philippines, and elsewhere, the UN high commissioner for human rights, Zeid Ra'ad al-Hussein, in 2017 warned, "There is no longer any pretence. They are breaking long-held taboos. . . . The dangers to the entire system of international law are therefore very real."[67]

Dangers to the international legal system may come not only from elites, but also the masses. When confronting threats to their security, citizens across various political orientations have been willing to sacrifice core civil liberties.[68] Punitive tendencies apply to even extreme abuses like torture, where threat in combination with dehumanization of the enemy can make the unthinkable not only acceptable but mainstream.[69] Accountability to a fearful public might actually have the pernicious effect of leading democracies to be *more* willing to engage in torture.

Conventional polling indicates that a sizable portion of the US populace does not seem immediately repulsed by the harsh interrogation of detainees. Figure 5.2

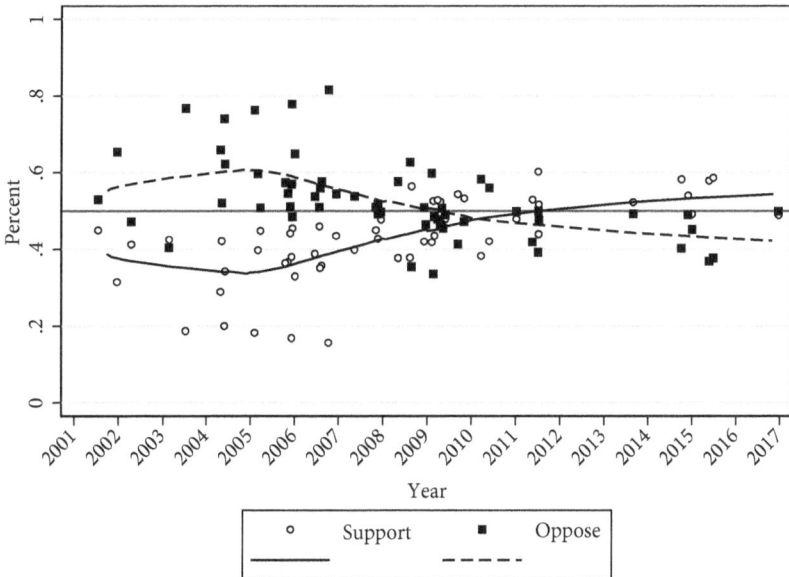

FIGURE 5.2. Public support for torture against suspected foreign terrorists, United States, 2001–2016

Notes: Surveys asking about support for use of torture against suspected foreign terrorists/militants/extremists. Surveys conducted by various polling agencies of national samples in the United States during the years 2001 to 2016. Only the percentages "Support"/"Oppose" or their equivalents are reported. Answers of "Neutral/Undecided," or "Don't Know/Refused," are not shown. Lines indicate locally weighted smoothing of the "Support" and "Oppose" survey responses respectively.

shows trends in US national opinion toward the use of torture against suspected foreign terrorists for the period 2001 to 2016.[70] For each poll, the figure shows the percentage of respondents supporting or opposing the use of torture.[71] Lines are based on estimates from a locally weighted smoothing (LOWESS) function to illustrate temporal trends in support/opposition to torture.

Aggregate opinion was weighted more toward opposing torture during the earlier years, but levels of support actually rose gradually from 2006 onward to become a slight majority view, though any upward trend largely flattened out after 2010. Widely covered outside developments, such as the 2004 Abu Ghraib prison scandal or notable Supreme Court cases going against the Bush administration's detainee policies,[72] do not appear to have appreciably shifted opinion (at least at the aggregate level) one way or the other.[73] Despite some modest movements, the overall picture reveals a public pretty evenly divided over torture. Keeping in mind the usual volatility across individual polls, the gap between opponents and proponents of torture was fairly modest, and if anything narrowed over time. On the whole, torture represents a closely contested issue, despite the fact that (or perhaps because) it raises fundamental questions over trade-offs between human rights and national security. Situations where both sides are evenly matched are precisely those where even small changes in public opinion can have outsized impacts by altering the center of gravity on the issue.[74]

Nevertheless, there is only so much we can glean from existing polling. Although figure 5.2 was limited to questions involving similar situations of torture against suspected foreign terrorists, making comparisons is problematic because of differences in sampling procedures, question language, and answer options used by various polling firms. Even identifying overall levels of support is challenging, since the public has been less approving of specific practices, such as waterboarding or sexual humiliation, relative to generic references to torture.[75] Despite some differences, many widely cited polls share a number of explicit or implicit frames tending to bias respondents toward greater expressed support for torture.[76] The threat posed by prisoners and torture's efficacy are largely taken as given despite notable disagreement on both counts. Especially important for our purposes, legal rules are rarely mentioned, or only in ways downplaying their significance. One study looking at framing in surveys on torture "found no instances where respondents were primed for compliance with the law."[77]

A more systematic examination of public attitudes toward torture is thus essential for a number of reasons. First, data on public opinion are frequently used to make larger claims about the strength of international rules and norms. The absence of "social constraints" makes it easier to justify and engage in violations.[78] In the case of coercive interrogation, several studies point to the available public sentiment in the United States as evidence of "norm regress," where torture has allegedly gone from "perhaps the ultimate taboo and made it part of the landscape," as the practice became widely viewed as "simply necessary to prevent greater evil."[79] Second, investigating policy attitudes offers a direct means for assessing one of the core functions of international law—to shape and change preferences. And *public* opinion is particularly important on this point because of the centrality of ordinary actors under popular international law. Looking at torture provides a particularly hard test for international law not only because contending security concerns are at play. If it is true that rules against torture are indeed weakening and near death, then international law should matter little. Seeking answers to these questions is the undertaking for the remainder of this chapter.

International Law and Torture: Research Design

Following a similar strategy to chapter 3 on reputation and enforcement, I employ a series of survey experiments to examine the role of international law in shaping policy preferences among the US public toward torture. Random assignment ensures experimental groups are fairly similar to each other on average, mitigating issues of selection effects and allowing us to estimate with greater certainty the impact of international law on people's policy preferences. Another benefit from experiments is the greater ability to directly measure the relevant outcome of interest and underlying functions—whether that be enforcement in previous chapters, or preferences in this and the following chapter. Just as observational studies of reputation and international law often have had to rely on rough proxies or behaviors, much of the research into preferences described earlier either employs similar indirect measures, or turns to the limited conventional polling available. The experiments designed and presented here offer the opportunity to more systematically evaluate the role of international law in influencing individual preferences. Focusing on the United States also continues to make sense given the country's centrality in debates over prisoner treatment, and as a challenging context for expectations that international law could have much impact on popular sentiment.

The first main survey was administered online between October and November 2008 to a nationally representative sample of 2,817 US adults.[80] Timing is always an important consideration, but a survey like this one that was fielded several years ago still has the potential to yield important insights. As figure 5.2 indicates, aggregate opinion toward torture has been fairly stable and evenly split between supporters and opponents over the years. Later surveys conducted as part of this and related studies also confirm similar overall patterns in opinion toward torture, suggesting there is nothing unusual about this particular survey.[81]

The timing of the survey being in the field over the course of the 2008 presidential election also offers certain benefits. A frequent criticism of experiments remains their generalizability, especially concerning how seriously participants take the scenarios and are willing to change their beliefs. The survey took place during a period of high political salience. Foreign policy issues figured prominently on the campaign trail with ongoing conflicts in Afghanistan, Iraq, and the larger War on Terror. On the specific matter of torture, the two main presidential candidates did not differ markedly in their positions, meaning space was available on the issue despite an increasingly polarized partisan environment. The Republican nominee, John McCain, was a former prisoner of war from the Vietnam War who had personally been tortured. Democratic nominee and eventual president Obama espoused similar antitorture views.[82] The survey thus provides a valuable setting for examining the role of international law in influencing attitudes toward a charged policy during a time of high stakes domestically and internationally.

The scenario was designed to resonate sufficiently with participants, while staying general enough to minimize conflict- or crisis-specific factors that could bias responses in any one direction. All subjects were first presented with an opening prompt containing the following common background information:

- In conflicts ranging from World War I to the present, the United States has often captured combatants from the opposing side. These combatants may have information of interest for the conflict, such as plans for future attacks. Some US officials believe interrogating these combatants through a variety of methods is a useful way to obtain information.
- The interrogation methods would involve torture, meaning they would cause severe pain or suffering.
- The information may, or may not, be accurate or relevant.

A few points regarding the choice and phrasing of this background information. Although the vignette subsequently presented is hypothetical and does not focus on a particular adversary or conflict, to introduce greater realism the first part of the prompt invokes the country's long history of fighting and capturing foreign foes.[83] I avoid constructing the sort of "ticking time bomb" situations commonly portrayed by television shows at the time like *24*, which could overly predispose people to favor torture.[84] Yet the suspect is still depicted as potentially possessing actionable intelligence, meaning the resort to torture could in theory be instrumental for some wider end rather than simply being punitive or sadistic. I also point to official beliefs about the potential usefulness of harsh interrogation methods to remain consistent with widely accepted views within prominent government circles during this period.[85]

Considering heated debates over what does (or does not) constitute torture, in the second point I employ the "severe pain or suffering" descriptor that has attained the minimum consensus in prevailing international agreements like the CAT.[86] While avoiding overly inflammatory language, the scenario still offers a clear sense of what is at stake personally for prisoners. I chose to directly use the term "torture," instead of more subtle or indirect euphemisms like "enhanced" or "coercive" interrogation techniques, to remain in line with much of the polling at the time but also to tie attitudes to this concrete concept. In the third point, I present a neutral stance on the effectiveness of torture in obtaining accurate or actionable information. This does represent a conscious departure from most traditional polling from this period, which tended to implicitly or explicitly frame torture as inherently successful in extracting intelligence.[87] I elected for a more balanced posture reflecting the actual state of controversy over torture's effectiveness.[88]

After presenting everyone with the same background information, the experimental component then involves randomly providing respondents with additional pieces of information regarding the scenario for them to consider. Three elements were varied—international law (no mention/law), type of enemy combatant (insurgent/regular soldier), and reciprocity (no mention/enemy abuse). As summarized in figure 5.3, since all three treatments are binary, the study represents a $2 \times 2 \times 2$ factorial design, generating eight total groups once the treatments are fully crossed with all possible combinations for each condition.[89] Full details for the design of this and all other instruments discussed in the chapter can be found in Supplementary Online Materials.

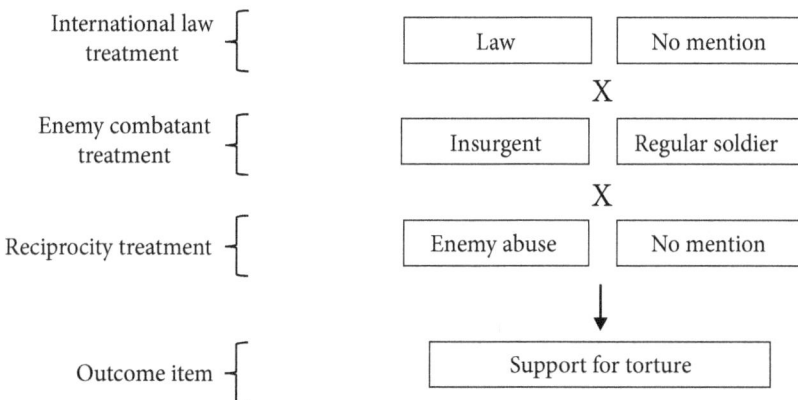

FIGURE 5.3.   Torture survey experiment #1 structure

Notes: Factorial design where all treatments are fully crossed. Survey conducted by Knowledge Networks in 2008.

For the key International Law treatment, the treatment group was given the following statement:

> The interrogation methods would violate international law. The United States has signed international treaties that do not allow the use of these methods under any circumstances.

The treatment states in clear terms that any torture would be contrary to existing US international legal obligations.

The choice for the International Law control group was taken with great care in this particular situation. Unlike the reputation experiments from chapter 3, in the present study the control group was not given a corresponding prompt asserting the United States had refused to join any international treaties prohibiting torture. Part of the reason for not doing so is pragmatic—such a statement of noncommitment would be factually incorrect. The United States has ratified many of the IHL and human rights agreements outlined earlier in figure 5.1, in particular the 1949 Geneva Conventions and the CAT (though not the Rome Statute establishing the ICC). And even though the country had not joined the 1977 Additional Protocols, US officials have accepted key provisions as customary international law.[90] The situation presented in the experiment may be abstract, but the country involved (the United States) and its obligations are not. Experimental conditions should ideally conform more closely to actual fact patterns for purposes of greater realism, which were less of a concern with the more purely hypothetical scenarios in the reputation experiments earlier.

Setting aside matters of experimental realism, telling some survey participants that the United States was not bound international laws would be deceptive. There is a great deal of debate over the merits and trade-offs of deception, with different professional norms across disciplines.[91] Ethical concerns are especially heightened when dealing with sensitive issues. Surveys have been shown to not only measure existing attitudes, but in their construction can also socialize participants into holding certain positions, a dynamic especially prevalent in polling on torture.[92] In addition to ethical dilemmas, misleading participants is problematic for drawing reliable inferences, especially in studies like this one where we want to understand public attitudes toward an actual policy.

Facing these constraints, I decided the International Law control group would receive no mention of any additional legal prompt. While this differs from the main control used in the earlier reputation experiments, the construction of such a null, or "no mention," control group based on the absence of the treatment remains a commonly accepted approach.[93] One potential worry about the null of receiving no legal prompt is that we may be unsure about what beliefs participants already hold, or may infer and carry forward in the study. For instance, the control group likely contains some people who knew about, and consequently may have been influenced by, international legal principles prohibiting torture despite not directly receiving the legal treatment. The flipside is that the treatment group may similarly include individuals who were already aware of the relevant international laws, where the legal prompt may provide little in the way of new information (though it offers a direct reminder).[94] If anything, such dynamics would provide an even harder test by *underestimating* possible effects of international law by narrowing actual differences between the treatment and control groups. And participants' prior legal awareness does not pose a threat to internal validity; randomization ensures that on average such knowledge should be unrelated to an individual's treatment assignment.

The International Law condition is perhaps best viewed as priming the treatment group by highlighting the international legal obligations involved, compared to the absence of exposure for the control group.[95] Ultimately, there is no single decision rule on the best construction of a control group, or treatment for that matter. What is appropriate should be driven by theory and the demands of the research question. The approach taken here provides an ability to assess how exposure to international law (relative to the null of no mention of a legal prompt) may affect preferences toward the use of torture.

The study also included two other contextual treatments to enrich the vignette and incorporate other relevant details that could influence support for torture. Enemy Combatant varies the type of prisoner in custody. Past research shows belligerents tend to employ more extreme violence when fighting insurgencies compared to conventional adversaries; a pattern that extends to prisoner treatment.[96] Motives to abuse insurgents may be stronger for a variety of reasons, including the perceived illegitimacy of their fighting tactics, or beliefs they hold more valuable intelligence compared to ordinary troops. For Enemy Combatant, the treatment group involved captives who were insurgents, while the control group concerned regular armed forces. For the actual treatment language, terms like "insurgent," "guerilla," or "terrorist" were avoided because of their pejorative connotations and potentially priming on other prisoner attributes, which could bias responses. To mitigate these concerns while still capturing basic differences across combatants, I used more neutral language with the treatment group told the prisoners "are not regular combatants," while informing the control group they "are regular combatants."[97]

The second contextual treatment, Reciprocity, varies whether information is provided about the adversary engaging in abuse against captured US troops. Retaliatory pressures figure prominently in historical accounts as well as formal models of wartime behavior, including in the context of international law.[98] To assess possible retaliatory motives, the Reciprocity treatment group was told the adversary was abusing US prisoners, while the control group was given no mention of such a prompt. International law may be less constraining in situations where the enemy is discovered to be torturing one's own soldiers, reducing desires to comply with IHL obligations and instead respond in kind.[99]

After reading the full vignette randomized across these three treatments, respondents were then asked about their support or opposition to torture. Everyone was presented the following item: "To what extent do you agree or disagree with the following statement: The United States should use interrogation methods involving torture on captured combatants." Answers were on a seven-point scale ranging from "strongly agree" to "strongly disagree," where higher values indicate greater approval for torture. In line with the measurement strategy used in chapter 3, values for this main outcome and all subsequent items are rescaled to between 0 and 1 to facilitate presentation and interpretation. Effect sizes indicate first differences in the percentage-point change in support for torture. Rates of nonresponse were low and under 1%.

International Law and Torture: Results

To first get a sense of general opinion, raw levels of support for torture across the entire sample were around 43%. The overall share is generally in line with many past polls, especially those from years around when this survey was fielded (refer back to figure 5.2). While some polls recorded slightly higher support, this is not entirely surprising. Unlike my survey, and as noted earlier, questions asked in many conventional polls presented certain elements as given that tend to raise approval, such as torture being effective, or failing to mention legal considerations. Nonetheless, a general correspondence with existing polling suggests the survey's sample was not unusual and fairly representative of the US population, meaning we can be more confident in inferences about wider public preferences.[100]

Turning to the experimental component (and as expected due to randomization), a series of balance tests indicates groups assigned to the various treatment conditions were comparable across a range of characteristics likely to influence opinion on torture. The survey thus offers a more direct approach for estimating preferences toward torture, in particular the influence of international law. If being informed of prior treaty commitments can shape domestic publics' subsequent policy preferences, then respondents exposed to the international law treatment should be less supportive of the use of torture compared to those in the control group not receiving this legal prompt. On the other hand, if skeptics are correct that legal rules have little impact, or public attitudes are idiosyncratic and unstable, then we should observe no meaningful differences.

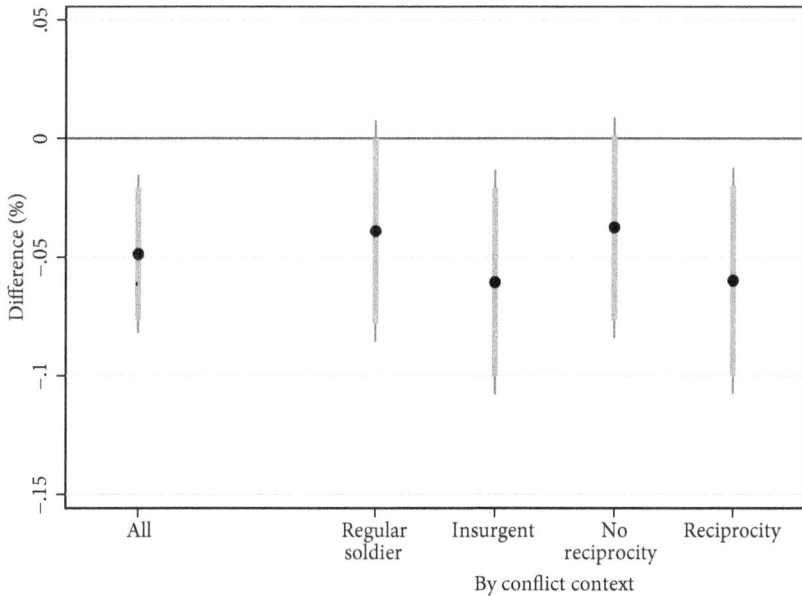

FIGURE 5.4. Effects of international law on support for torture

Notes: First differences (with 90% and 95% confidence intervals) between the international law treatment and control group (no mention) on support for torture. Data from torture survey experiment #1.

Figure 5.4 goes some way toward resolving these differing viewpoints on the influence (or lack thereof) of international law on policy preferences. Using simple difference-in-means tests, the figure reports the percentage-point change in support for torture between the international law treatment and "no mention" control group in general, and separated out by conflict context treatment (combatant type and reciprocity).[101] Confidence intervals (both 90% and 95%) are indicated by vertical lines around each effect.

The results provide support for the impact of international legal appeals on citizens' policy preferences. Exposure to international law reduces approval for torture by around 5% compared to those in the control group receiving no prompt regarding international legal obligations.

Like some other studies described in this book, a 5% decline is admittedly not enormous, but for this survey remains statistically significant and in line with effect sizes from other experimental studies examining attitudes toward a variety of policies.[102] The substantive significance of a result also needs to be put into broader context. Even a modest effect is impressive given the wartime circumstances involved, the potential value of intelligence, and other elements of the vignette designed to dim the prospects for international legal appeals. And in the case of prisoner abuse, seemingly small changes in aggregate opinion may translate into outsized consequences, tipping the balance given the narrow gap separating supporters and detractors in the United States. Far from relegated to the realm of "low politics," international law appears to influence public preferences even in an area like wartime conduct.

Under the trying circumstances characterizing armed conflict, international law continues to have a marked impact when incentives for violations are especially acute. Demands to dispense with legal niceties may be higher when facing insurgents who do not fit the conventional wartime mold, or when the enemy is explicitly reported to be torturing captured soldiers from one's own side. Although not presented here, groups who were told the prisoners were insurgents were on average more likely to approve torture (a 5% increase) compared to when captives were from regular armed forces. There was also some minor evidence for "tit-for-tat" dynamics, where groups informed the adversary was torturing US soldiers were slightly more likely to approve torture (a 2% increase) compared to those receiving no such prompt, though the difference is not statistically significant. Despite these weaker effects, this should not be taken to mean that reciprocity does not play an important role in wartime.[103] The public appears to be fairly deliberative in evaluating particular incentives for or against abuse, reflected in patterns of their (dis)approval of torture.

Keeping these average effects in mind, the righthand side of figure 5.4 reports the effects of international law on attitudes toward torture, conditional on the conflict's context. Each value shows the change in support for torture between international law treatment and control groups, separately for each of the combatant type and reciprocity conditions. On the whole, respondents appear committed to considering legal principles when faced with varying wartime circumstances. International law turns out to be slightly more influential (6%) in situations like holding insurgent prisoners or a foe already reportedly engaging in torture, where pressures toward abuse should be heightened. Conditional effects for international law are correspondingly somewhat weaker for the regular soldier and "no mention" of reciprocity situations (both 4%), though even here both are at or near statistical significance around the 10% level. International law may thus act as somewhat of a brake on retaliatory desires, or when facing less legitimate foes.[104] To be fair, tests for differences across these conditional effects do not achieve standard levels of statistical significance. It is nevertheless instructive that international law has at least an equal (if not greater) impact in more threatening situations where pro-torture motives should be at their peak. Rather than simply operating when there are few incentives for violations as many skeptics claim, international law appears to work hardest when it is needed most.

From International Law to Legalization: Research Design

The evidence so far provides an opening into international law's promise, but also some boundaries, in affecting the policy preferences of mass publics. Yet the first experimental study admittedly conveyed a fairly generic legal appeal, which is either present (treatment) or absent (control group). Less clear is how the public would respond to commitments differing in their level of legalization. As chapter 3 indicated, the reputational consequences for violators can diverge markedly based on the design of agreement that was breached. Legalization may have similar implications for international law's other functions, including our focus here on policy preferences.

To investigate more fully the role of institutional design, I conducted a second experiment that tests the causal effects of the three main dimensions of legalization—obligation, precision, and delegation—on preferences toward torture. Like the first study discussed above, the survey was conducted in collaboration with Knowledge Networks. The survey was fielded online in the summer of 2010 to a representative sample of the US adult population, resulting in 6,101 total participants.[105]

The overall scenario resembled the first study, where the United States had captured enemy prisoners and the government was deciding whether or not to use torture. To concentrate on institutional design, I curbed the number of moving parts in the vignette by not varying any of the contextual treatments from the initial experiment. Any reference to reciprocity and torture by the adversary against US troops was dropped, since this treatment did not figure prominently in the first study. However, all respondents were told the prisoners were insurgents, or not regular forces. I made this choice to heighten the scenario's realism in light of the main types of wars and adversaries the United States was facing, alongside the prior experimental results showing heightened support for torture against insurgents.

After laying out the basic contours, all respondents were then given an additional prompt introducing some form of international legal rules against torture to which the United States was subject. Because the main objective of this second experiment is to investigate how changes in institutional design affects public preferences, a control group receiving no mention of any international law prompt was not included.

The main treatments instead varied three different dimensions in the legalization of international agreements prohibiting the use of torture. Conceptually speaking, each dimension operates on a continuum ranging between higher and lower levels of legalization for an agreement.[106] But on pragmatic grounds, employing more finely grained differentiations across three separate components would greatly increase the number of experimental groups, quickly becoming unwieldy.[107] A series of binary treatments—representing high versus low levels of obligation, precision, and delegation, respectively—offers a more reasonable, though still useful, approach. Keeping with chapter 3 and for ease of discussing the design and results, I use "hard law" or "soft law" to refer specifically to (high or low) levels of obligation, even though both terms are sometimes employed in the literature when referring to the other legalization components.

The design and language choices for the legalization conditions generally aligned with those from the main follow-up reputation study in chapter 3, though with a few important differences.[108] Like reputation study #2, the present torture survey also involves a modified factorial design where not all treatments are fully crossed. Delegating a large amount of authority to third-party actors like international courts does not really exist in practice when the agreement's obligations are not legally binding.[109] Investigating individuals' reactions to purely imaginary instruments may be an interesting theoretical exercise, but takes us farther away from our central purpose here to better understand how the public's policy preferences are influenced by actual international laws. All permutations of the three legalization treatments were thus included as separate experimental groups except for any combinations involving high delegation and low obligation, which results in a total of six experimental groups. Figure 5.5 summarizes the full structure of the second torture study.

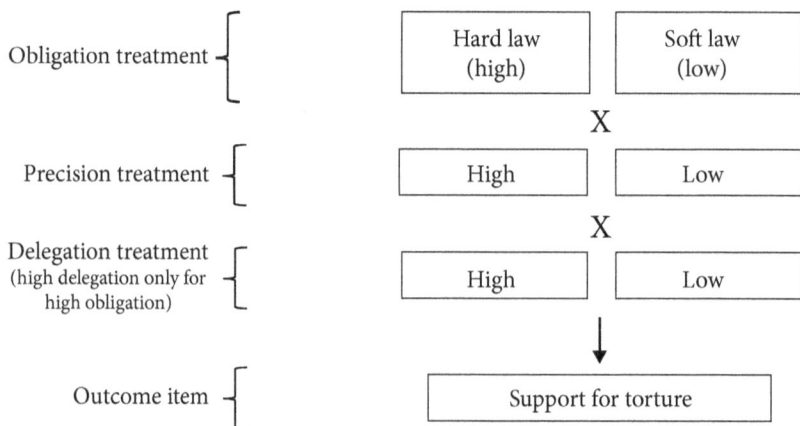

FIGURE 5.5.   Torture survey experiment #2 structure

Notes: Modified factorial design where "High" Delegation treatment is only given to the "High" Obligation condition as specified in the structure above. Unlike torture survey experiment #1, all groups are told the prisoners are insurgents (or "not regular combatants"), while there is no reference to reciprocity (or abuse by the enemy). Survey conducted by Knowledge Networks in 2010.

For Obligation, and unlike in the reputation experiments or first torture study, no baseline control is included (whether a null "no mention," or an explicit "none" no commitment condition), since all groups in the follow-up torture experiment involved some form of legalized commitment. As in many substantive areas, instruments governing torture vary in their level of obligation. For instance, the 1975 Declaration against Torture denunciated the use of torture, yet as a resolution adopted by the UN General Assembly (UNGA) did not place any binding obligations upon member states.[110] The 1975 Declaration acted as a precursor to the 1984 CAT negotiated less than a decade later. The CAT codified and expanded many of the declaration's prior provisions, but packaged in a formal treaty states had to ratify and were legally bound to follow.

Although torture-related instruments of varying obligation have existed historically, more complicated is how to depict US commitments at the time the survey was fielded in 2010. As with the choice in the first torture study for a control condition absent any mention of international law rather than falsely declaring the United States was not bound by any legal rules, care must be taken in the present survey when deciding how to most appropriately convey different levels of legal obligation. The high obligation "hard law" treatment is fairly straightforward, using similar language to the reputation studies earlier in chapter 3 and the first torture study above. Respondents in this hard law group were told the "United States has signed international treaties" involving some form of prohibition against the use of torture (the exact formulation depends in part on the precision and delegation treatments discussed further below).

More challenging was crafting the low obligation "soft law" condition. Stating the United States was solely bound by softer nonbinding rules against torture would be factually incorrect, as the country ratified the CAT in 1994. Even the legal status of the prohibition against torture in the immediate years after the 1975 Declaration is up for debate. The 1966 ICCPR, whose Article 7 created a binding obligation forbidding torture, formally entered into force just a few months later in early 1976.[111] And this is setting aside if or when torture may have achieved standing as customary international law, or even a peremptory norm (jus cogens).

Given the desire to reflect the existing state of play and avoid deception, the construction of the low obligation "soft law" condition thus differs slightly from the phrasing used in the reputation experiments in chapter 3, which referred to "guidelines recommending" against resorting to particular actions. The language instead adopted in the present torture experiment was to inform those in the low obligation condition that torture was against "general international values," to which the United States was subject. Although it might be ideal to keep the exact same formulation of treatments across all surveys, this is not always possible, nor necessarily desirable. Just as the appropriate conceptualization of control groups may differ, constructing treatments should be guided by the study's purpose.[112] Despite some differences between the prior reputation and present torture surveys, what the two phrasings for lower-level obligations share in common is the lack of any explicit reference to formal legal commitments, distinguishing them from the high obligation "hard law" treatment.

One question is whether the "general international values" described in the low obligation condition could have multiple connotations, from more informal "international norms" to blending into a somewhat harder rule if potentially understood as customary law. Of course, such concerns could apply to almost any construction; a perennial worry among experimentalists is whether a given treatment captures the theoretical quantity of interest.[113] Norms can be more or less "institutionalized," or exhibit stronger or weaker "robustness."[114] Nonbinding declarations from bodies like the UNGA have sometimes been used as evidence for the existence of harder customary laws.[115] And even though customary law is generally seen as binding, there is disagreement over whether customs do or should occupy the same pride of place as formal treaties.[116] What matters for our purposes is that the two experimental conditions reflect meaningful differences in emphases on the perceived level of obligation. It should also be remembered that any lack of differentiation between experimental groups creates a more conservative test for the role of legal obligation in affecting attitudes toward torture.

More briefly, the treatments for the other two legalization dimensions closely follow the constructions used in the follow-up reputation experiment from chapter 3. Precision here deals with the extent to which provisions narrowly proscribe the use of torture, irrespective of whether the rule is legally binding. Just as with other areas of international law, the laws of war vary greatly in clarity over what acts are considered violations.[117] Across both the laws of war and human rights law, much of the debate in the United States and elsewhere during the War on Terror concerned the precise international legal meaning of "torture." To capture this difference experimentally, the higher precision treatment condition declares conclusively that relevant rules "do not allow the use of torture under any circumstances against prisoners." By contrast, the lower precision control primes respondents with some uncertainty, qualifying that the terms "might, or might not, allow for the use of torture against prisoners. But there is a lot of debate among experts about what" the relevant rules (treaties or values) "really mean." The expectation is that more precise agreements should exert a greater influence on policy preferences.

The third and final dimension, delegation, concerns the degree to which a third party has the authority to punish officials for authorizing torture. The treatment focuses on the power of international courts, which seems reasonable in light of continued debates over the effectiveness of bodies like the ICC to reduce war crimes and human rights abuses.[118] The high delegation treatment condition makes the prospect of an international body intervening salient, informing respondents that "If US officials used torture, then an international court could prosecute them for war crimes." By contrast, the low delegation control highlights the alternative (and generally more common) situation involving no effective international judicial actor, qualifying that "Even if US officials used torture, no international court could prosecute them for war crimes."

At the time of the survey, the United States was not party to the ICC (which is currently still the case). The earlier Bush administration also negotiated a series of bilateral nonsurrender agreements with many countries (including many parties to the Rome Statute), which effectively shielded US nationals from the ICC's grasp.[119] Nonetheless, an argument can still be made that the United States could become subject to the ICC's purview—one of the reasons why US critics so vociferously opposed the court and similar tribunals at the time.[120] Because the focus of this second torture experiment is on directly estimating the effects of different legalization components, a separate control group without any mention of delegation (whether high or low) was not included. Investigating the effects of delegation provides an opportunity to integrate insights from enforcement into the preference function of international law. The prospect of material punishment means the presence of an international court may be expected to reduce support for torture compared to the absence of any real outside legal remedies.

After receiving the common opening prompt alongside one of the six combinations of the three legalization components, respondents were then asked the same question as in the first experiment on their support or opposition to the use of torture against prisoners. Rates of nonresponse remained low at less than 1%.

International Legalization and Torture: Results

Looking first at overall opinion across the entire sample, 47% expressed approval for the use of torture. These raw levels are slightly higher than the 43% support from the first torture experiment, though are not entirely surprising since all respondents in the present survey were given the insurgent prompt, which tends to raise support.[121] General attitudes across the two surveys continue to track with conventional polls during this period (refer to figure 5.2), suggesting neither involves some unusual sample. Rather, both studies are capturing sentiments among the wider US public with results that can be readily comparable.

The setup allows for a more fine-grained analysis of how the particular institutional design of an agreement, rather than simply the presence/absence of

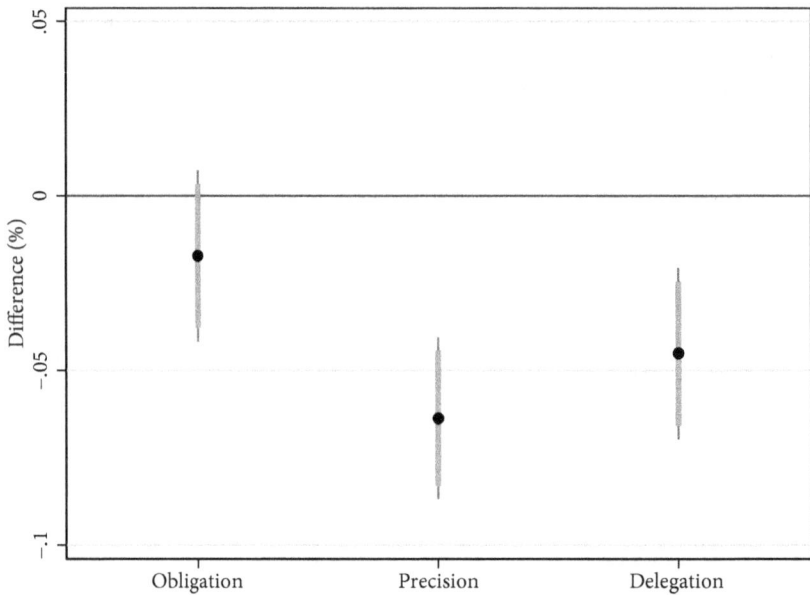

FIGURE 5.6. Effects of international legalization on support for torture

Notes: First differences (with 90% and 95% confidence intervals) between the relevant international legalization treatment and control groups: obligation (soft law [low] vs. hard law [high]); precision (low vs. high); and delegation (no court [low] vs. court [high]; high delegation only given to those groups receiving a hard law [high] obligation). Outcome is support for torture. Data from torture survey experiment #2.

international law, may shape policy preferences. Figure 5.6 shows the average effect (measured in percentage-point terms) on support for torture when moving from lower to higher levels of legalization for each dimension, respectively. Vertical lines indicate 90% and 95% confidence intervals.

Beginning with obligation, respondents appear similarly swayed by both harder and softer legal appeals. The corresponding implication is that more formalized treaties do not have much greater impact than informal commitments—the 2% decline in support for torture for harder obligations is in the expected direction but is not statistically significant. While the difference across the two types of legal commitments is smaller compared to what was generally observed in chapter 3 for reputation, both sets of experimental findings suggest the public can be influenced by obligations across the range of legalization, whether regarding enforcement or changes in underlying preferences. Comparing results should still be treated with caution, especially because of some of the necessary differences in language for certain conditions discussed above.

This apparent nonfinding for obligation still has important implications for popular international law and the role of the public. In assessing the resonance of different sorts of commitments, results from figure 5.6 suggest the public may not always make subtle distinctions across different levels of obligation.[122] The implication is less that legal considerations do not matter, so much as that the public reasons in similarly principled ways across the obligation spectrum. Once within the realm of some legalized agreement, relative gradations of obligation do not appear to figure prominently in the public's calculations of its preference. While obligation is often viewed as playing the dominant role among legalization components due to the "special quality of treaties,"[123] the findings suggest that softer nonbinding rules can still generate quasi-obligatory impulses.[124]

If the "general international values" invoked in the lower obligation condition are instead thought to reflect notions of custom, then the experimental findings may also offer lessons for the role of ordinary people in the functioning of customary international law. Although customary law is frequently mentioned alongside formal treaties,[125] skeptics of international law are especially skeptical of the relevance of such customs.[126] Others counter that custom—even if not formally written down—is embedded in the same underlying normative framework as treaty law, creating a similar sense of obligation.[127]

Yet the more diffuse nature of customary law makes it even more challenging to empirically test and adjudicate between these contrasting views.[128] The experiment here offers one opportunity for investigating whether international custom may influence preferences in similar ways to more concrete, written-down treaties. With little separating the more customary-like "international values" from the "treaty" obligation in figure 5.6, the public appears to view customary rules as comparably influential to even "harder" written agreements.[129] If governments take into account domestic preferences when evaluating a previously ratified treaty, then it follows that they may likewise keep in mind the public's interests when it comes to broader customs. Because beliefs of legal obligation (*opinio juris*) are a crucial element to the very existence of a customary law, public preferences may thus represent an important source in the creation and evolution these rules. With even some legal skeptics acknowledging that, when it comes to customary law, the United States occupies a privileged place due to its material and institutional capabilities, then the preferences of the US public, as gauged in these experiments, can correspondingly matter a great deal.[130]

The lack of distinction across various understandings of obligation does not mean the public is completely unmoved by different dimensions of legalization. Figure 5.6 goes on to show that precision exerts a substantial impact on policy preferences. Respondents in the high precision treatment—those told torture was a definitive violation of international law—were less likely (6% decline) to condone torture than those receiving the lower more indeterminate prompt, an effect that is statistically significant. If international law can be thought of as a principled form of information, then the less ambiguous are the rules the clearer any signals should be. It follows that more specific laws should have a greater ability to alter preferences, which is borne out in the experimental data.[131]

Uncertainty can undermine the preference function of international law in two related yet distinct ways. First, audiences may be bewildered and at a loss over what exactly international law requires. Vagueness can create situations where actors genuinely believe a given policy is consistent with legal commitments. This line of thinking fits with the managerial school of compliance, which views imprecision as one of the key drivers of most violations.[132]

In a second more strategic pathway, leaders, elites, or other societal groups can cynically take advantage of imprecision to "evade" legal obligations, and promote an alternative narrative where their behavior is consistent with international legal principles.[133] The rhetoric of legality can be marshalled to disarm potential compliance constituencies, even turning them into abettors.[134] Such tactics appear to have figured prominently in the formative period of the Bush administration's detention program through a series of writings by various officials in the Department of Justice (DoJ) that became commonly known as the "Torture Memos."[135] Debates over the CAT's meaning of "torture" noted earlier became weaponized. In one of the most notorious opinions, Jay Bybee, the head of the Office of Legal Counsel in the DoJ, argued that the "severed pain or suffering" limit under Article 1 of the CAT could be interpreted so narrowly as to include only "serious physical injury, such as organ failure, impairment of bodily function, or even death."[136] The Bush administration subsequently conducted a concerted disinformation campaign to muddy the legal waters over depictions of its interrogation practices, and public understandings of the country's obligations.[137]

This episode highlights the often-overlooked importance of precision and how it can shape public attitudes and the operation of international law. Often relegated to the least consequential component of legalization,[138] the experimental results instead indicate precision has the strongest effects on public preferences across the three dimensions. When it comes to forming policy preferences, the public thus appears particularly attuned to the rules' exactness. The crucial role of precision may also help explain why for issue areas like the laws of war, greater attention has often been devoted to clearing up the risk of misunderstandings or subterfuge by reducing ambiguities in existing rules, rather than necessarily attempting to create new or more binding rules.[139]

Turning to the third and final element of legalization, figure 5.6 shows that delegation also significantly shapes public attitudes toward torture. Individuals in the treatment group who were informed that an international court could prosecute US officials were around 5% less likely to support the harsh interrogation of enemy detainees compared to those in the "low" group told that no such international court existed. The effect size for delegation is not quite as large as for precision, but the first difference does reach standard thresholds of statistical significance.

The finding offers an interesting point of comparison to chapter 3, where the prospect of punishment by an international court did not have any added effect on more decentralized reputational sanctions. Here we instead see that vertical "enforcement from above" can influence the preference function of international law. The public does appear to take seriously the possibility (even if not the certainty) that an external court can intervene when forming their policy attitudes. Domestic actors thus offer a different route for international courts to have an impact on outcomes, in place of the more external direct enforcement effects of international courts debated by many skeptics and proponents.[140] The delegation result is all the more remarkable given the discourse during this period (and even to this day) in the United States toward international courts. The Bush administration vilified the ICC and similar tribunals, taking active steps to undermine them. Obama sought a more constructive relationship, but still a distant one due to domestic cleavages, which only seemed to harden with the advent of Trump's outright rejection of the court. Biden subsequently took a softer tone, but active collaboration with the court remained a remote possibility. Based on this survey, the US public appears swayed in important ways by the court's powers in adjusting their preferences.[141]

Nevertheless, putting the results from the two torture experiments together indicates that preferences are not reducible to the threat of enforcement. Delegation appears to be but one pathway to shaping preferences, not the only or even necessarily the most important one. The role of precision matters equally (if not more so),[142] and the general presence of obligation and the principles accompanying legal commitments appear to fundamentally affect how publics conceive of their own preferences, and by extension those of their governments.

Conditional Effects of Law and Legalization

Everything presented up until now has been for the US public as a whole, yet there are good reasons to think that the impact of international law on preferences may vary across different groups, especially around such a charged issue like torture. Chapter 3 indicated little divergence among domestic societal groups over the willingness to impose reputational sanctions in response to legal violations, but the scenario involved more general policies and actions of a foreign country.

Although still hypothetical, the experiments in this chapter put the spotlight on a high-stakes conflict situation involving respondents' own government, concerning a practice where members of the public may have strong views. International laws are not abstract sets of rules, but in the end are tied to substantive policies—individuals may react differently to those issues and legal commitments based on whatever their priors may be.

To investigate how people's backgrounds may affect their reactions to international legal appeals, figure 5.7 reestimates the main treatment effects from the two torture experiments, separated for various societal subgroups. The choice was a function of existing research on factors that tend to be associated with general attitudes to wartime violence and international legal principles. For instance, conservatives have generally been found to prioritize order and security over individual rights and liberties (and specifically are more supportive of torture),

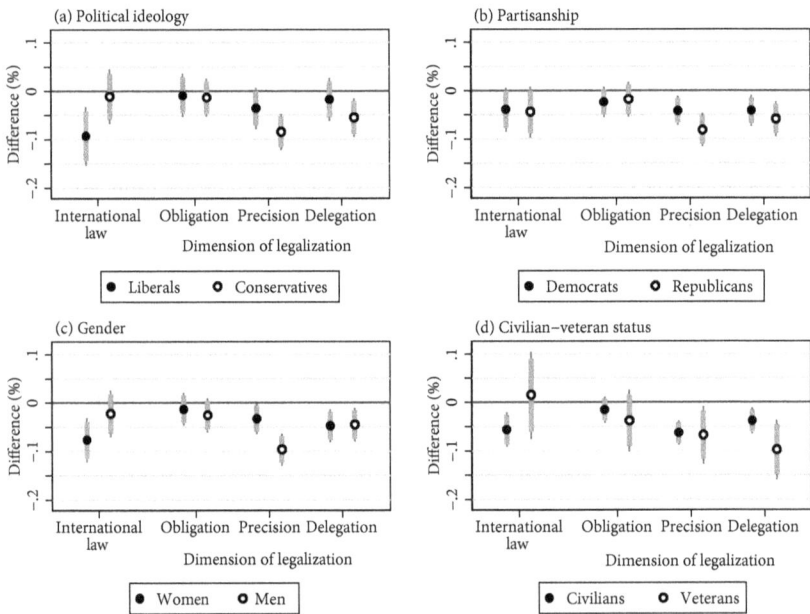

FIGURE 5.7. Effects of international law and legalization on support for torture, conditional on certain political and socio-demographic traits

Notes: First differences (with 90% and 95% confidence intervals) between the relevant international law/legalization treatment and control groups, conditional on specified political or socio-demographic traits. The first pair of values in each subfigure refers to first differences between the international law treatment and control group (no mention). The three subsequent pairs of values refer to first differences between the relevant international legalization treatment and control groups: obligation (soft law [low] vs. hard law [high]); precision (low vs. high); and delegation (no court [low] vs. court [high]; high delegation only given to those groups receiving a hard law [high] obligation). Outcome is support for torture. Data from torture survey experiments #1 and #2.

while at the same time skeptical of international law and institutions.[143] As political ideology has become closely connected to partisanship, Republicans likewise have shown themselves strongly supportive of torture alongside being suspicious of international commitments.[144] On gender, a wealth of research shows important differences between men and women on matters of violence and war.[145] The gender gap is especially evident on questions on the use of force, as well as relative commitment to multilateral institutions.[146] And a large literature demonstrates important gaps between civilians and military veterans across a range of foreign policy issues.[147] Indeed, in both of the torture experiments, raw levels of support for torture were higher among conservatives, Republicans, men, and veterans compared to their liberal, Democrat, female, and civilian counterparts.[148]

Existing dispositions may shape the capacity for international law to change groups' policy preferences. Those more enthusiastic about their government employing torture may be impacted little, if at all, by international legal prohibitions. The left-hand pairs of values from each of the subfigures in figure 5.7 suggest just such a dynamic may be going on, where societal groups differ markedly when exposed to a general international legal prompt. Each pair represents the first differences in the initial torture experiment between the international law treatment and the "no mention" of any legal prompt control for each set of societal subgroups. Those who may already be wary of torture—liberals, women, civilians, and to a lesser extent Democrats—become even more so once they are explicitly presented with the practice's international illegality. First differences are statistically significant for each of these subgroups (for Democrats only at the 90% level), and for some like liberals the effect size is almost double that seen across the entire sample. By contrast, those already liable to condone torture are mostly unaffected by these initial international legal appeals. First differences for conservatives, Republicans, and men are not statistically significant, while the effect for veterans is actually slightly positive though only weakly so (meaning those receiving the law treatment were a bit more likely to support torture relative to the control).

The first set of results in figure 5.7 should temper even the cautious enthusiasm offered by the earlier overall analysis. The positive impact of international law on attitudes toward torture across the US population as a whole is still there, but hidden behind are noticeable differences in how certain segments are seemingly unfazed by international legal rules. While conditional effects are less apparent by partisanship,[149] notable differences stand out in the effect (or noneffect) of international law within the other subgroups. If anything, international law widens gaps between opponents and proponents of torture, serving as a further source of polarization in an already divided citizenry on this issue and others. Limits seem to exist in the promise of international law to offer an avenue toward convergence in attitudes around fundamental questions of human rights.

A more complex story emerges when we incorporate findings from the second torture experiment. Recall that the initial experiment just looks at the general presence or absence of international laws prohibiting torture, while the second study delves more deeply into specific dimensions in the design of these rules. It is important to remember that baseline levels of support remain similar across the two experiments, with conservatives/Republicans/men/vetrans more approving on the whole of torture compared to liberals/Democrats/women/civilians.

What happens when these various subgroups are exposed to agreements with different levels of legalization? As in the case of the entire sample, none of the subgroups differ dramatically when informed of prohibitions involving softer versus harder levels of obligation. When turning to the relative influence of the other dimensions of legalization, however, an intriguing pattern surfaces. Conditional effects for precision and delegation are often equal or greater for those traditionally skeptical groups compared to their seemingly more accommodating counterparts. Differences are often starkest for precision, where the effect of high versus low precision agreements is appreciably greater for conservatives, Republicans, and men relative to their opposite numbers. Precision is less differentiable by military experience, but for delegation veterans are much more likely than civilians to alter their preferences toward torture when informed an international court could come into play. Conditional effects for delegation are also noticeable by ideology, and to a lesser extent for partisanship and gender. But the overall story is one where more skeptical groups reacted much more strongly to highly legalized appeals, even if the first experiment initially suggested the opposite of little receptivity toward general legal appeals.

What accounts for these seemingly contradictory results across the two experiments? While still keeping the other subgroups in mind, I concentrate on investigating the liberal–conservative divide because it is the starkest in some respects but also speaks to broader theoretical debates about the impact of political ideology on understandings of the law (international and domestic).

For liberals, moving along the spectrum of legalization may lead them to hit some form plateau effect.[150] When faced in the first experiment with an international agreement prohibiting torture versus to the absence of any legal commitment, liberals' deeper general attachment toward international society led them to respond more keenly to international law. This communitarian commitment, however, might paradoxically make liberals *less* susceptible to subsequent differences among legalized instruments. When the existence of international rules was taken as given, liberals' preferences shifted only marginally in response to different degrees of obligation, precision, or delegation. The legalization non-findings do not necessarily nullify liberals' attachment to international law. Integrating results from both experiments suggests that liberals are influenced by *any* form of agreement. What matters is simply the existence of some form of legal rules; their actual design is less consequential.

A similar pattern of reversal in the conditional effects of international law and legalization is present, but not nearly as clear-cut for the other societal subgroup pairings. Like liberals, women and civilians are more affected by the initial legal appeal compared to the generally more skeptical subgroups of men and veterans. Unlike liberals, certain components of legalization also have a significant impact on women and civilians, though the relative effects are more modest compared to their male and veteran counterparts. The general impact of international law does not differ much by partisanship, but again Democrats are relatively less affected by legalization compared to Republicans, even if the first differences for precision and delegation are significant for both partisan groups. The absence of the same sharp reversal observed for political ideology, however, is not wholly surprising. The baseline divide on the merits of torture was widest between liberals and conservatives than for any other subgroup pairing. Political ideology is also associated with distinct understandings of legal rules. Across all subgroups to varying degrees, a second part of the puzzle that needs answering is why those who are *less* enthusiastic about general legal appeals nonetheless show themselves to be as much, if not *more*, affected when those rules are highly legalized.

Turning to conservatives suggests a corresponding threshold effect when moving from weaker to stronger types of legalized agreements. Conservatives are generally found to hold more skeptical views of international commitments.[151] This coolness is supported by the first torture experiment, where the initial international law prompt did little to move their attitudes toward torture. Once exposed to higher levels of precision or delegation, however, some of these legal inhibitions appear to be overcome, and conservatives (and to varying extents other skeptical subgroups) are *more* influenced by legalized appeals than their liberal (or more welcoming) counterparts.

The combined set of findings for political ideology are in many ways consistent with expectations from motivated reasoning, a phenomenon widely identified in psychology. Instead of updating in a relatively efficient and unbiased manner, theories of motivated reasoning instead posit that people's preexisting beliefs affect how they interpret and incorporate new information.[152] New developments consistent with prior viewpoints will be readily accepted, while contradicting information will be strenuously resisted. This latter disconfirmation bias means that "people will spend more time and cognitive resources denigrating and counterarguing attitudinally incongruent than congruent arguments."[153]

Motivated reasoning has been shown to operate with equal vigor in legal matters—research demonstrates that individuals tend to judge the merits of domestic case law in terms that are compatible with their prior preferences.[154] A similar dynamic may be operating when scaled up to international rules. Because of a skeptical predisposition toward international law, conservatives may discount and ignore the sorts of general legal appeals invoked in the first experiment. The ambiguity inherent in the low precision condition from the second experiment likewise provides conservatives with sufficient room to rationalize away any critiques, reasoning that the resort to torture is legally justifiable (perhaps even allowable). Yet tendencies behind motivated reasoning are just that; even extreme biases have limits when confronted by sufficiently compelling outside forces.[155] For instance, faced instead with a highly precise and unequivocal legal prohibition against torture, the discretion in conservatives' reasoning appears greatly reduced, and their preferences consequently more affected by international law.

A different, yet complementary, process may be playing out in the case of the larger effects for delegation. When stakes are raised with individuals subjected to greater accountability for their choices, the power of motivated reasoning and similar biases tends to weaken considerably.[156] The prospect under the high delegation treatment of an international court with authority to punish US officials represents a stark cost, appearing to push even resisters to think twice before supporting abusive practices.

In their own ways, precision and delegation can shape the preferences of more skeptical audiences like conservatives (and to a degree similarly situated subgroups like men, veterans, and Republicans), but only at higher levels of legalization. The (non)findings for liberals (and comparable subgroups) suggest motivating reasoning may also guide their own tendencies toward international law. Liberals' lack of responsiveness to different levels of legalization may reflect a sort of confirmation bias given their higher affinity with legal appeals.[157] Even modest levels of legalization appear sufficient to activate liberals' opposition toward torture, meaning additional hardening of the laws is unlikely to yield further changes in their preferences. Legal rules and prior preferences may be interwoven in complex ways, but the experimental results demonstrate that under various conditions international law can have sizable impacts on policy preferences for different segments of the public.

The conditional findings between international law and political ideology also mirror in intriguing ways debates over contending interpretations of domestic legal principles. The notion of popular international law put forward throughout this book (that ordinary people are important actors in the operation of international law) builds off the thesis of popular constitutionalism (that ordinary people are important actors in the operation of constitutional law). It follows that how actors of different ideological bents understand and apply the Constitution may have a bearing on how they approach international laws as well.[158]

Views on appropriate ways to interpret the Constitution and other core domestic laws are often arrayed along comparable liberal–conservative lines. More conservative legal philosophies, such as textualism, call for a circumscribed method of interpretation based solely on the plain meaning of statutory language with little weight accorded to contextual considerations.[159] Consistent with this philosophy, ordinary conservative citizens surveyed in the torture experiments were influenced by international law only when the language of such rules was more precisely specified such that prohibitions against torture became plainly unambiguous.

Ordinary liberals instead appear willing to entertain ideals contained in broader international agreements more open to interpretation (and thus less precise). This penchant parallels the liberal-leaning domestic legal philosophy commonly known as the "Living Constitution."[160] Unlike textualists' narrow emphasis on the fixed meaning of statutory language, these approaches see fundamental laws like the Constitution as inherently dynamic, akin to a living being capable of change.[161] To take one prominent example, evolutionary understandings have come to the fore over the Eighth Amendment to the US Constitution, which bars "cruel and unusual punishments," but the exact meaning of those key words was left unresolved since its original passage in 1791.[162] In the landmark case *Trop v. Dulles*, the Supreme Court ruled the amendment's words "are not precise and that their scope is not static," and consequently meaning must draw on "the evolving standards of decency that mark the progress of a maturing society."[163] The court's ruling overturned the federal government's decision to revoke the plaintiff's citizenship. Interpreting the government's policy as "cruel and unusual," in a fitting connection to this chapter's substantive focus, the chief justice Earl Warren opined this represented "a form of punishment more primitive than *torture*" (emphasis added).

A similar form of reasoning appears to guide ordinary liberals' approach to international law. It is not that liberals are unresponsive to legalization; rather they are *equally* affected by both more and less legalized rules, highlighted by the precision findings. While conservatives were only influenced by highly precise commitments, liberals expressed similar levels of disapproval toward torture even when dealing with vaguer international values. Faced with a more open set of potential meanings, liberals nonetheless interpreted less precise international obligations as a legal duty to refrain from employing torture in no uncertain terms. Likewise, liberals did not require additional punitive consequences from greater delegation to be influenced by international law. A corresponding "Living

International Constitution" may be operating, at least among certain segments of domestic US society, and with implications for the larger international society.

This chapter offered further support for popular international law, and the interplay between international rules and ordinary people in fulfilling another key legal function of influencing underlying policy preferences, even in the challenging context of national security. Through a series of survey experiments, the evidence shows that international law generates discernable impacts on attitudes toward torture. Different dimensions of legalization can leave a further imprint on preferences, though the effects are more apparent for some dimensions (precision and delegation) than others (obligation). The results also show some important conditional effects, where particular segments of society are more affected by certain types of international laws. Even those groups who on the surface may be most skeptical of international legal commitments can be swayed by legal appeals, especially those that are highly legalized.

As with chapter 3 on reputation and enforcement, we should not stop here on the "preferential" workings of international law. The torture experiments were tied to an animated policy issue, but the general setup for the scenarios was largely hypothetical even with efforts to evoke greater salience and realism, while possible trade-offs and counteracting forces were not directly considered. The next chapter builds on these findings through a combination of both experimental and more conventional surveys to further investigate in more real-world settings the potential and limits of international law to shape preferences around vital policy areas.

6

FROM LAW TO PREFERENCES II
Droning on about War

The previous chapter offered a first look at the potential for international law to serve another key function—influencing actors' underlying policy preferences. Through random assignment, a series of survey experiments demonstrated that international laws of various designs were able to generate causal effects in changing support for torture. Given the controversial nature of a topic where national security concerns should predominate, the experiments represented a fairly hard test. Consistent with popular international law, the ordinary public understands and engages with legalized commitments in ways that can bolster the operation of the international legal system.

Nevertheless, there are a few reasons why we should want to build on these findings. First, as salient as torture may be for both publics and international law, the proper treatment of detainees still represents a single issue whose findings may or may not translate to other arenas. Examining the role of legal commitments in additional areas allows us to better assess whether the preference function of international law generalizes to other domains. A second related matter of generalization involves some of the limits of solely experimental evidence. Although experiments can be very effective at isolating causal effects, there are reasonable worries over whether these findings carry outside of the immediate survey setting.[1] These questions may be especially pressing for the experiments from the prior chapter, which leaned more heavily toward hypothetical scenarios all while still trying to introduce elements that would resonate with audiences.

This chapter seeks to extend the experimental evidence already presented by broadening the subject matter under investigation and introducing greater doses of realism in several ways. I do so through two complementary sets of studies that continue to examine the preference function of international law. The first continues with randomization, but involves a series of survey experiments modeled directly off of the real-world policy debate over drone strikes where matters of international law figured prominently for critics and defenders alike. The second half of the chapter then shifts outside the experimental setting to investigate how people's actual exposure to, and understanding of, legal principles affect their preferences toward a range of wartime behaviors related to the laws of war. Although different in their particular subject matter, both studies continue in the realm of high politics, where international law's promise is usually most questioned.

Law's Impact . . . *Compared to What?* Insights from Drone Strikes

Demonstrating that international law can have some discernable impact on public preferences—even, as shown in chapter 5, around controversial issues like torture, and even among harder-to-convince subgroups—may not sufficiently satisfy legal proponents or their detractors. Implicit (and oftentimes explicit) are claims not simply about the role of international law in isolation, but its impact relative to competing forces. The question then is not just whether and how international law matters, but "compared to what?" Indeed, across a range of issues, "the most challenging questions for both political elites and mass publics occur when fundamental principles or values are conflictual."[2] Such trade-offs are not unique to international law, but are especially salient in adjudicating its relevance. For many skeptics, international rules may shape actors' beliefs and behavior in some circumstances, but are quickly dispensed with when contending matters of power and security arise.[3] A range of studies seem to confirm that when directly confronted with strategic considerations like military success and effectiveness, international laws and norms quickly fall by the wayside.[4] To the question on the role of international law "compared to what?" the answer seems to be "well, not much."

The torture experiments from chapter 5 offer an initial retort to stronger versions of the position that the impact of international law is minimal when core state interests are at stake. Yet admittedly, that evidence did not directly examine international law in relation to opposing arguments, especially in a real-world situation where such trade-offs can be highly salient. The purpose of this section is to provide just such an assessment through an experimental evaluation of the debate over drone strikes at a time when competing considerations were being contested in the marketplace of ideas.[5] I do not take a position on the larger question of whether the advent of drones, or unmanned aerial vehicles (UAVs), represents a transformational military technology or is "just another platform" incrementally building on existing thinking and capabilities.[6] What is useful about looking at drones, however, is that real-world disputes over the technology's use were frequently couched in legal versus strategic terms, providing an opportunity to gain further insight into the relative role international law can play in shaping public preferences.

Background on Drone Strikes: Law, Military Effectiveness, and the Public

Attempts to create autonomous weapons systems operating on the ground but especially in the air go back at least as far as both world wars.[7] More concerted US efforts began during the Vietnam War with later deployments in a series of conflicts in the 1990s, which mainly involved using drones for surveillance and reconnaissance. But the main controversy over drones became their weaponization for the purpose of targeted killings during the War on Terror. The first reported use of a UAV to try to kill a terror suspect took place in the opening days of the 2001 War in Afghanistan against the Taliban leader Mullah Omar.[8] In the years since, the United States has launched over 10,000 drone strikes (and counting) against suspected militants in a range of countries, including off any formal battlefield in places like Pakistan, Somalia, and Yemen, killing more than 10,000 people, thousands of whom were civilians by some estimates.[9] The strategic use of drones to go after militants from afar has been a bipartisan affair. Beginning under the George W. Bush administration, rising dramatically under Barack Obama, spiking at times under Donald Trump with the 2020 killing of the Iranian general Qasem Soleimani as one of the most contentious strikes, and continuing in important respects under the Joe Biden administration. US counterterrorism policy has always been multifaceted—with important military, diplomatic, and intelligence pillars—but drone strikes became a "key feature."[10] Even as he became one of the technology's most prolific users, Obama cautioned against jumping to the conclusion of "drone strikes as a cure-all for terrorism."[11] Others have been less qualified in their support. On the campaign trail in the lead-up to the 2016 election, Trump declared his preferred strategy was to "quickly and decisively bomb the hell out of ISIS [the Islamic State]," a promise he kept once in office.[12] The United States has not been alone, as drones have proliferated across a number of countries, but US practices have set important precedents on views regarding *how* these technologies can and should be used.[13]

The prominence of US drone strikes has been matched by their controversy. Legal concerns figured prominently from the start with denunciations by UN officials and human rights groups like Amnesty International questioning the legality of the US drone program on numerous grounds.[14] Critiques mirror in important ways the discussion in chapter 4 of related practices begun under the Bush administration in fighting the War on Terror, which were considered violations of two key streams related to international law—*jus ad bellum* (rules concerning recourse to the use of force) and *jus in bello* (rules governing wartime conduct).[15]

In terms of *jus ad bellum*, some critics charge that several areas where US drone strikes have been most frequent and prominent—places like Pakistan, Somalia, Yemen—are illegal because the United States is not directly at war with these countries' governments, but rather insurgents like al Qaeda or the Islamic State located within their borders.[16] While Article 51 of the UN Charter allows military force for purposes of self-defense, the justification for drone strikes in such off-the-battlefield circumstances is even more tenuous than the US–UK attempt to use a similar rationale for the more conventional invasion of Iraq in 2003. It is questionable whether militants targeted in many strikes pose a sufficiently serious, impending, and direct enough threat to justify the recourse to force. According to one study, just 2% of those suspects attacked represented "high-level targets" and most were "neither presently aggressing nor temporally about to aggress."[17]

On top of concerns over whether drone strikes are allowable under most counterterrorism operations, *jus in bello* criticisms focus on the manner in which strikes are conducted. One of the foundational rules of the laws of war is the principle of distinction, that civilians should be distinguished from combatants and protected from direct attack.[18] The precision so often lauded in the surveillance and targeting technology employed by drones betrays a reality that civilians are often caught in the line of fire, dying at disproportionate rates relative to the value of the militants being targeted. Official US figures report low civilian fatalities, but are based on restrictive criteria. A meta-analysis of a number of independent investigations "found far more civilian casualties than administration officials admit."[19] As the US drone program went on, targeting restrictions that could put civilians at risk became more, rather than less, permissive in some respects. Beginning in 2008, specific identification of the individual was no longer required for an attack to proceed; rather, behaviors or other elements resembling "signatures" of militants were sufficient. The shift to these so-called signature strikes was condemned for being associated with sizable increases in civilian deaths.[20] Some greater restrictions were put in place in later years of the Obama administration, but loosened under his successor with a perhaps not surprising jump in civilian deaths in Trump's first year in office.[21]

Yet one interesting element of the drone debate is that detractors not only attacked the US program on legal terms, but questioned the strikes on military grounds as well. The asymmetric nature of drone warfare, where a more technologically advanced power attacks lightly armed and largely unaware victims from a safe distance, can play directly into militants' hands. Harkening back to biblical stories, "the disparity in power between the parties . . . reinforces popular support for the terrorists, who are seen as David fighting Goliath."[22] Living in constant fear of attacks from above, or witnessing the deaths of friends and family members up close, drone strikes can become a powerful recruitment device for militants among resentful local populations.[23] In a 2015 open letter, several former US service members pleaded with the Obama administration to reconsider its reliance on strategies that "fueled the feelings of hatred that ignited terrorism and groups like Isis, while also serving as a fundamental recruitment tool similar to Guantánamo Bay."[24]

The US government under various administrations has not stood silently in the face of criticism. As Obama declared in a May 2013 speech, "dozens of highly skilled al Qaeda commanders, trainers, bomb makers and operatives have been taken off the battlefield . . . these strikes have saved lives."[25] Confirming the former president's claims, several empirical studies suggest drone strikes are effective not in only eliminating individual terrorists, but also degrading the operational capabilities of militant organizations.[26] On the legal side too, the US government launched a robust defense of its drone program as being consistent with *ad bellum* and *in bello* obligations. Summing up the US government's perspective on claims by its various critics, Jay Carney, at the time White House press secretary to President Obama, stated unequivocally, "U.S. counterterrorism operations are precise, they are lawful and they are effective."[27] And despite Trump's later brash and sometimes alarming statements, administration officials reaffirmed the country's drone program rested on firm strategic, moral, and legal grounds in terms of where strikes were conducted and protecting civilians from harm.[28]

Just as critics have launched their attacks in the public sphere, one of the reasons the US government was so vocal in defending its actions is the recognition that "no counterterrorism strategy can succeed over time without public support."[29] General Michael Hayden, former director of the CIA and the National Security Agency, acknowledged that "no president can do something repeatedly over a long term without that broad popular support."[30]

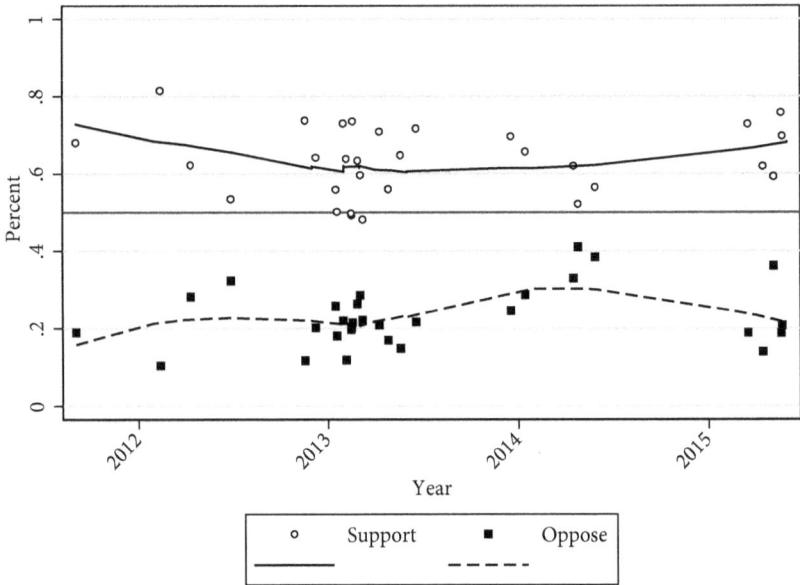

FIGURE 6.1. Public support for drone strikes against suspected foreign terrorists, United States, 2011–2015

Notes: Surveys asking about support for drone strikes against suspected foreign terrorists/militants/extremists. Surveys conducted by various polling agencies of national samples in the United States during the years 2011 to 2015. Only percent "Support"/"Oppose" or their equivalents are reported. Answers of "Neutral/Undecided," or "Don't Know/Refused," are not shown. Lines indicate locally weighted smoothing of the "Support" and "Oppose" survey responses, respectively.

As in the last chapter on torture, we can get an initial sense of US public sentiment by looking at conventional polling on drone strikes. Figure 6.1 summarizes opinion toward the use of drone strikes against foreign militants during the years 2011 to 2015.[31] This was the period public debate was at its height, coinciding with when most polling was conducted. The lines are estimates from a locally weighted smoothing (LOWESS) function to illustrate trends in support and opposition respectively.

Overall support for drone strikes among the public as gauged by these polls is somewhat higher than what was observed for torture, hovering around the mid-60% mark, but still far from universal. A good deal of noise is evident in the data, where some polls conducted in close succession showed discrepancies of twenty points or more in support, ranging from mid-70% to at or less than 50%. Some of the usual concerns over different samples, question wordings, and answer options limit comparisons. But as with the torture polls, a more fundamental qualification against what we can glean are tendencies in the questions asked that in many respects primed respondents toward support for drone strikes. Most items focused on the targeting of militants with little or no indication of risks posed to civilians. And mentions of international law were almost wholly absent or toed the government line.[32] The seemingly stronger support for drones strikes observed may be as much a function of how questions were asked as reflecting actual opinions.

In the few instances where respondents were called upon to consider some of these issues, a different picture emerges. A pair of Pew Research Center polls fielded first in 2013, and then again 2015, asked respondents how concerned they were about certain facets of the US drone program. Figure 6.2 shows that US citizens were far from unquestioningly enthusiastic, taking many of these concerns seriously (even if not equally). Foremost were worries over civilians with 80% in both surveys expressing fears over risks to noncombatants. More pragmatic concerns were also evident over possible retaliation against the United States, but these were around similar levels as questioning the legality of the strikes. Interestingly in light of several of the earlier chapters, reputational consequences were present but somewhat lower compared to other issues at stake.

Although the results from figure 6.2 are suggestive, neither such multidimensional questions nor standard polling on overall support can provide much

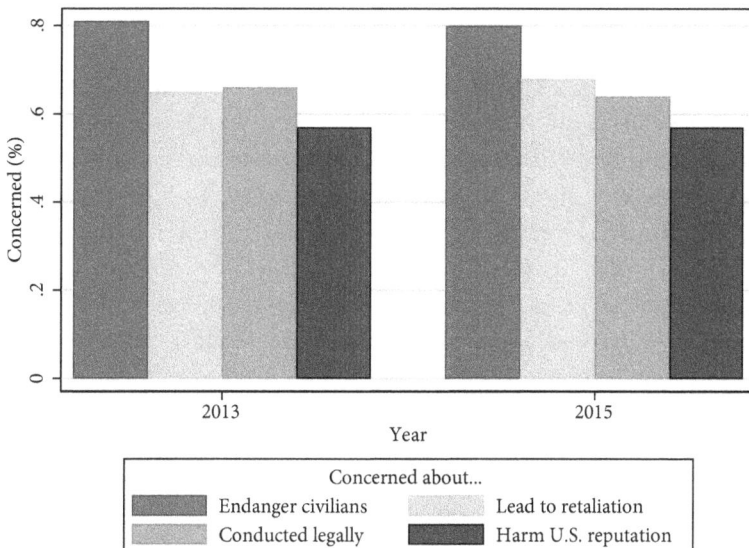

FIGURE 6.2. Concerns over consequences of drone strikes

Notes: Concerns over various consequences from the United States engaging in drone strikes. Data from national polls conducted by the Pew Research Center in the United States in 2013 and 2015.

insight into: 1) the sources of the public's attitudes toward drones, and 2) which of the considerations frequently mobilized in favor of, or in opposition to, drone strikes they find most persuasive, especially concerning the complementary (though still distinct) lines of argumentation regarding legal versus military-strategic calculations. As with other general functions of international law, an experimental approach offers a way to more reliably estimate the *relative* effect of international law on policy preferences, though here in the more real-world context of the actual drones debate.

Debating Drones: Research Design

The main survey experiment was designed to probe how exposure to particular legal versus military arguments, which have been made in the larger discourse around drones, may affect mass attitudes toward such strikes. The experiment was conducted online in September 2013 to a nationally representative sample of 2,394 US adults.[33] The timing of the experiment coincided with a period where debates over drone strikes were particularly salient in the public sphere, as evidenced by the clustering of polls around this time (see figure 6.1 above). In contrast to hypothetical scenarios or surveys conducted with some distance from contemporary events, the study provides an opportunity to investigate public attitudes at a charged moment.

All subjects were first given the same background information: "There has been a lot of recent discussion about the use of unmanned aerial vehicles, also known as drones, by the United States to target suspected militants." The control group only received this initial prompt; other groups were randomly assigned additional information based on the following two sets of treatments.

To inject greater realism, the substance and language chosen for the treatments reflected actual arguments put forward in public debates at the time. The first treatment varies the particular issue frame based on two of the main arguments made for or against drone strikes discussed in the previous section: (1) whether strikes are effective at eliminating militants; and (2) whether they are consistent with prevailing international legal commitments. Each issue frame also varied whether the position was favorable or critical of the legal/effectiveness merits. Respondents receiving the pro-effectiveness condition were told drone strikes were "instrumental in killing suspected militants and making Americans safer," while the critical version emphasized that strikes "trigger anti-US sentiment and help militants recruit new members, making Americans less safe."

In line with multipronged legal criticisms, the international law conditions were disaggregated into two separate branches involving either concerns over respect for the target country's sovereignty (*jus ad bellum*), or taking appropriate steps to prevent civilian deaths (*jus in bello*). The critical *jus ad bellum* treatment indicated "these strikes violate international law because they break the sovereignty and territorial integrity of the country where the attack takes place"; the pro version instead stated "these strikes do not violate international law because they are an act of self-defense against individuals plotting attacks against Americans." Because contending claims were particularly heated on the question of civilian casualties, more measured language was chosen that, if anything, should underestimate the effects for civilian concerns. The *jus in bello* violation condition stated that "these strikes violate international law because they do not take necessary measures to prevent the death of civilians," while the pro version declared "these strikes do not violate international law because they take necessary measures to prevent the death of civilians." All issue frame conditions were constructed such that the language was as similar as possible—both across issue frames, but also for the pro/con pairs—except for the substantive argument put forward.

The drones debate was defined not just by the stark substance of the arguments, but also the particular voices behind these positions. Arguments for or against drone strikes did not exist in a vacuum, and were often tied to specific actors. To further reflect the nature of the debate at the time, a second treatment associated each issue frame with a particular elite voice that had been active on the issue. Given credibility is seen as an important ingredient in shaping opinion, actors were chosen who were seen as particularly credible—those possessing knowledge germane to the topic and generally trusted.[34] Three elite actors were selected who have been especially vocal on drones, and drawn from the international organization (IO), nongovernmental organization (NGO), and national government policymaking communities. For NGOs, Human Rights Watch was chosen for reasons of external validity, given it was one of the most outspoken nongovernment critics.[35] The UN Special Rapporteur for Counter-terrorism and Human Rights was selected as the IO source given this office's prominence in evaluating various merits of US drone policies. Lastly, for the government voice, the Joint Chiefs of Staff (JCS) was selected because members of the military should be seen as especially credible by the public—this also provides a harder test for the less recognizable IO/NGO voices.[36]

Theoretically, each elite source could hold multiple and contrasting positions, yet in practice they were remarkably consistent in their respective messaging. To keep the design in line with real-world policy debates, the government JCS voice was associated with the "pro" position for each of the effectiveness and legal issue frames, while the IO/NGO were both assigned the "con" position that strikes are ineffective or violated legal obligations.[37] The overall approach takes the form of a modified 3 × 3 design summarized in table 6.1, which involves nine

TABLE 6.1 Drones survey experiment #1 structure

	ISSUE FRAME		
	INTERNATIONAL LAW		MILITARY EFFECTIVENESS
ELITE SOURCE	SOVEREIGNTY	CIVILIANS	
IO/UN†	Con	Con	Con
NGO/HRW‡	Con	Con	Con
US Government/JCS*	Pro	Pro	Pro

Notes: An additional baseline control group receives none of the source or issue frame treatment combinations.

† The international organization (IO) source is the United Nations (UN) Special Rapporteur for Counter-terrorism and Human Rights.

‡ The nongovernmental organization (NGO) source is Human Rights Watch (HRW).

* The US Government source is the Joint Chiefs of Staff (JCS).

Source: Survey conducted by GfK in 2013.

separate treatment groups for each of the issue frame-elite source combinations, alongside the control group receiving no additional prompt. This approach balances limiting the complexity of the experimental groupings, while still allowing a focus on the main quantity of interest—the role of international law (whether supportive or critical) relative to military (in)effectiveness on public preferences toward drone strikes.[38] Full details for the design of this and all other instruments discussed in the chapter are included in Supplementary Online Materials.

After being randomly assigned to a given scenario, for the main outcome respondents were then asked to gauge their support for drone strikes on a five-point scale ranging from "approve strongly" to "disapprove strongly," where higher values indicate greater approval. As in earlier empirical chapters, values for the outcome and all subsequent items are rescaled to range between 0 and 1. Effect sizes indicate first differences in the percentage-point change in support for drone strikes. Rates of nonresponse were low at less than 1%.

Looking for Law vs. Effectiveness: Results

Across all respondents, the raw support for drone strikes was 64%. Overall approval rates were comparable to those in the conventional polling on drone strikes reported earlier in figure 6.1. Alongside closely following population benchmarks, congruence with general opinion indicates the sample is not unusual, but rather representative of prevailing attitudes at the time. That approval appears fairly strong and stable suggests any treatment effects are unlikely to be either impulsive or spontaneous. The tenor of the debate at the time and the consistency of mass opinion should make it particularly difficult for critical voices, such as those pointing to international legal concerns, to alter public preferences.[39]

Turning to the experimental component, a series of balance tests indicates groups randomly assigned to the various treatment conditions were comparable across a range of observable characteristics likely to affect attitudes toward drone strikes. Figure 6.3 uses difference-means-tests to calculate the percentage-point change in support for drone strikes between each issue frame-elite source treatment condition and the baseline control group who were only given the generic background prompt. Separated by issue frame, the first estimate combines together the two critical IO/NGO voices, while the latter three show the individual effects for each IO, NGO, and progovernment voice, respectively. Confidence intervals of 90% and 95% are indicated by vertical lines around each effect.

The figure reveals several patterns consistent with results from the previous preferences chapter, though with some caveats. Broadly speaking, appeals by either IOs or NGOs to international law (whether regarding violations of sovereignty or civilian protections) lead to a 5% reduction in support for drone strikes among ordinary actors. The size of the effects is in line with those seen

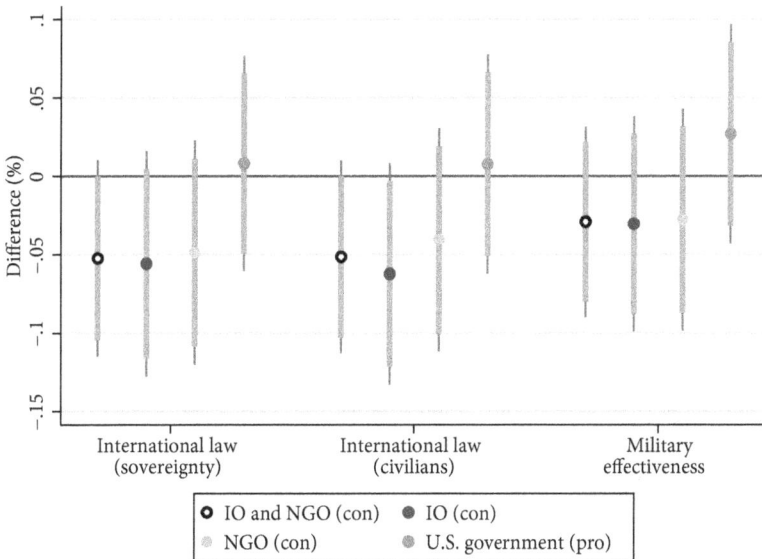

FIGURE 6.3. Effects of issue frame and elite source on support for drone strikes

Notes: First differences (with 90 and 95% confidence intervals) between each issue-frame/elite source treatment and the control group (no mention) on support for drone strikes. Elite sources are an IO (United Nations Special Rapporteur for Counter-terrorism and Human Rights), an NGO (Human Rights Watch), and the US government (Joint Chiefs of Staff). The position for each issue frame depends on the elite source: in favor (US government), or against (IO or NGO). Data from drones survey experiment #1.

in the earlier experiments on preferences toward torture, as well as some other related studies on drones.[40] However, overall variance in estimates for the first differences in the drones study is larger, which is reflected in wider confidence intervals, meaning some of the effects are only significant at the 10% level. The effects are thus less sharp compared to several studies from earlier chapters, but continue to show that criticisms centered on violations of international law can have discernable impacts on preferences among the US populace.

Figure 6.3 also offers an opportunity to evaluate the relative effects of criticisms grounded in international law compared to legal defenses as well as military-based (counter)arguments. In contrast to effects alleging violations of sovereignty or targeting civilians, government justifications that the US drone program complies with these two branches of international law barely budge public opinion. First differences for both legal defenses are in the expected positive direction, but are miniscule at less than 1%. Keeping in mind that confidence intervals do overlap somewhat, a certain asymmetry is evident with arguments emphasizing breaches of international law landing harder among the public compared to claims of adherence to legal standards.[41]

Voices from within the US government are slightly more persuasive when making their case on military grounds—arguments that drone strikes help keep US citizens safe are associated with just under a 3% rise in approval for the program, though this effect remains weak statistically. Criticisms by IO/NGO sources on strategic grounds that drone strikes are militarily ineffective, or even counterproductive, exhibit similarly modest declines of around 2% to 3% in approval. Effectiveness-based arguments thus do not appear terribly efficacious at moving public opinion on way or the other.

Looking across the results from figure 6.3 offers confirming (though more modest) evidence that international law can play a role in shaping attitudes around controversial policies like drones.[42] While the torture experiments from chapter 5 focused on examining international law on its own terms, the present study on drones suggests that international law can also stand on its own feet when up against competing considerations. Legal and normative factors are often discounted or dismissed when it comes to questions concerning the use of force.[43] Yet the evidence suggests international legal criticisms are at least equal to (and potentially greater than) strategic factors in shaping public preferences.

Differences in effects for particular arguments (even if they are not drastic) point to a public that is not blindly following whatever various voices in the drones debate are saying. If the public were simply paying attention to *who* was talking rather than the message's content, then effects for a given source should be similar irrespective of the specific argument put forward. Instead, IO and

NGO sources appeared slightly more impactful in their legal messaging, while the Joint Chiefs of Staff moved opinion little except somewhat weakly for reasons of military effectiveness. Moreover, the relative credibility of each voice in the public's eyes seemed to have little bearing on their assessments of drone policy.[44] As part of the survey, I include a follow-up item asking respondents how credible they found the elite voice making the argument to which they were exposed. Respondents actually saw the Joint Chiefs of Staff as much more credible than either the IO or NGO voices, even though government claims did little to move opinion. What seems to matter most to the public is *what* is being said about drones, rather than who is saying it—with criticisms pointing to violations of international law holding somewhat greater sway.

Putting the Results in Their Outside Context: Bringing in Media Coverage

What may be going on to account for these various results? To summarize so far, this experiment was designed to examine the relative role of international law in the midst of a prominent public debate over the merits of drone strikes. Although the study offered some evidence for international law compared to military factors, the effects were more modest compared to several of the surveys described in prior chapters. One of the strengths of experimental approaches is the ability to carefully craft and control particular treatments, in our case involving exposure to international law. Yet it is important to remember that survey participants are not blank slates and often arrive with prior beliefs and knowledge, which might affect how they respond to the design.[45] Participants' cognitive "baggage" is present to some extent in most surveys, but may weigh especially heavily in the present study which was explicitly modeled on real-world debates.

Given this charged environment, citizens' prior exposure to particular messages may have played a role in the differential effects observed for government versus critical voices. A possible explanation for the government's seemingly limited persuasiveness despite its credibility, or vice versa for the UN and NGO, could have something to do with how much members of the public had already heard such messages and voices.[46] And for a controversial issue like drones, this messaging may have been particularly widespread.

On matters of national security, governments traditionally enjoy an informational advantage over other actors, both domestic and international.[47] This edge may be especially sharp for classified programs like drone strikes, where details on the accuracy, circumstances, and even the number of attacks remain closely held and selectively released. Independent initiatives can seek a more open accounting, but remain at a disadvantage relative to official government sources.

Examining media coverage confirms the privileged place occupied by the US government in the drones debate. I conducted a content analysis of US newspapers to measure the relative frequency of mentions in drones-related stories of the three main sets of voices from the experiment—the US government, IOs (with a focus on the UN), and NGOs.[48] The analysis focuses on January 2009 to December 2013, coinciding with President Obama's entry into office and increasing salience of drones in public discourse. In addition to overlapping with when the main survey experiment was fielded in September 2013, this also represents a period during which the public was exposed to broader arguments and voices in the drones debate.

Figure 6.4 summarizes the results across all US newspapers.[49] The first panel displays the raw number of news stories on drones by month mentioning each of the three categories of elite sources. To give a better sense of the relative coverage, the second panel reports the percentage of stories on drones from that month featuring each voice.[50]

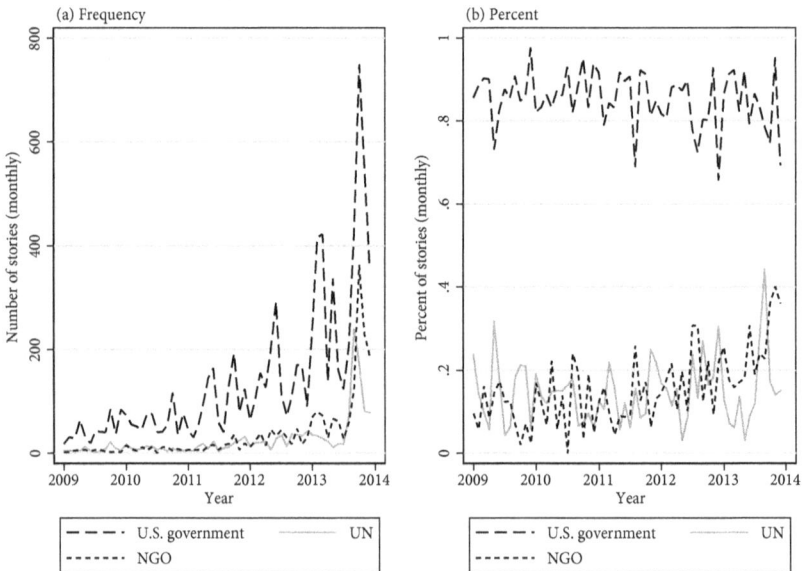

FIGURE 6.4.   Coverage of elite voices on drones in US newspapers, 2009–2013

Notes: Subfigure (a) reports the monthly number of articles in US newspapers mentioning drones and each of the specified sources of elite voices. Subfigure (b) reports the corresponding percentage of all news articles on drones each month mentioning each elite source. Because news articles may mention more than one elite source, the total percentages across sources for a given month may sum to more than 100%. Media coverage data based on the Factiva News Database for the years 2009–2013.

The left-hand panel in figure 6.4 shows ebbs and flows in coverage across US newspapers, though with discernable increases from 2011 onward and peaking in late 2013 as more details about the Obama administration's drone program emerged. Against these fluctuations in the frequency of stories, the US government consistently remained the dominant voice on drones. The pattern is highlighted in the righthand panel, where the US government regularly appeared in 80% or more of all stories on drones mentioning one of these three groups. NGO and UN sources did gain a foothold toward the latter half of 2013, likely from the wide release of several critical reports.[51] As denunciations launched by NGO/UN sources became more regular, however, the US government's media presence rose in lockstep. Throughout the five years of coverage, the share of stories featuring the UN or NGOs was usually 40 to 60% lower than official US sources.

The US government's media advantage means that members of the public were likely more aware of the official administration's position on the drone program's merits—both in strategic and legal terms. Looking back to the main survey experiment, the government's justifications may have broken little new ground in the public's mind, resulting in only small differences from the control group where similar views were already baked in. By contrast, criticisms highlighted by IO and NGO sources would present newer information to respondents, with a greater potential in turn to influence their preferences.[52] Yet the fact that not all criticisms hit in similar ways suggest that the content of the message still matters. Consistent with the view of popular international law, international legal commitments appeared to offer *principled* information, which can have an impact not simply by being newer, but also by activating specific beliefs and values.

Getting at Legal Mechanisms

A follow-up drones experiment was conducted to investigate what sorts of considerations may be triggered within the public by international law. This second survey was fielded in November 2013 a few months after the original experiment, and involved a sample of 601 participants recruited via Amazon's Mechanical Turk (MTurk) service.[53] To simplify matters, the experiment focuses on a single international law treatment involving the targeting of civilians, since this represented the most salient and frequent legal criticism of drone strikes. Harsher language was chosen for the civilian treatment, telling respondents that US drone strikes had led to civilian deaths, in place of the initial survey's more oblique reference to failing to take necessary protective measures. A stronger treatment was adopted to better reflect the more strident tone of several notable NGO reports released after the first survey.[54] To further limit the number of experimental conditions, the source was fixed as generic "human rights groups," since the first experiment did not show dramatic differences between IO and NGO criticisms. Respondents were thus randomly assigned to one of two conditions—the control group received the same general background prompt as in the original experiment, while the treatment also highlighted violations of international law resulting from civilian deaths.

Everyone was then asked the same question gauging approval for drone strikes. A series of follow-up items then probed additional considerations that may be raised when international law is invoked. On the more normative side, respondents were asked whether or not they believed drone strikes were "morally wrong." Continuing themes discussed in chapter 3 on reputation, another question asked about beliefs over whether or not drone strikes hurt the "image" of the United States in the world. To evaluate more firmly strategic considerations, another item asked respondents if they believed the strikes were counterproductive by helping militants to recruit new members. While the first experiment treated international law and military effectiveness as largely separate, it could be that strategic concerns are only activated once the public is exposed to reports of alleged legal violations. Lastly, to address possible pressures for substituting between different types of military force, respondents were asked how much they would favor using special forces in place of drones in more military missions, even with increased risks to US troops.[55]

The effects of international law on general preferences toward drone strikes, as well as these additional considerations, are summarized in figure 6.5. Alongside each of the first differences between treatment and control groups, vertical lines indicate 90% and 95% confidence intervals. The effect for international law is larger (a more than 10% decline) compared to the first experiment, though this is not entirely surprising given the treatment's stronger language.

Normative concerns appear to figure most prominently in the public's evaluation of drones. Being informed of the questionable international legal basis leads to almost a 10% increase in evaluations that the US drone program is morally wrong. In line with prior survey results, international law seems to engender a form of normative reasoning, leading individuals to attach deeper meanings to particular policies and practices. Reputational worries over US violations also shape public opinion, though the first difference is almost half the size of moral concerns. The effects of international law on public preferences do not appear to be reducible to reputational dynamics, rather serving as a complementary though distinct function in the operation of international law.

More instrumental concerns were inconsistent. Violations of international law moved public worries that drone strikes would serve as a recruitment tool for militants modestly (a 3% increase) and the first difference was statistically indistinguishable from zero, or no apparent effect. International law also had no

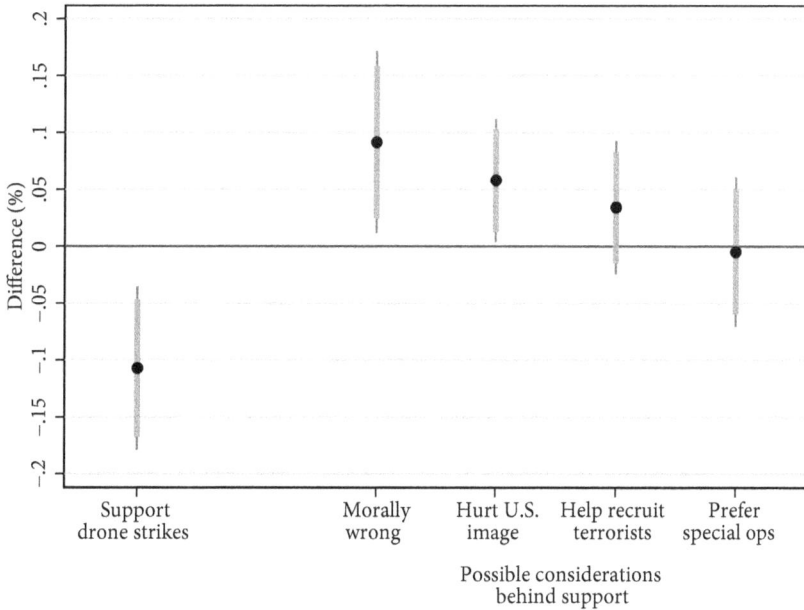

FIGURE 6.5.   Effects of civilian deaths under international law on support for drone strikes and related considerations

Notes: First differences (with 90% and 95% confidence intervals) between the international law (civilian deaths) treatment and control group (no mention) on support for drone strikes and related considerations. Data from drones survey experiment #2.

meaningful effect on the desire to switch to special forces for sensitive operations, pointing to some pragmatic limits on the willingness of the public to put US troops in harm's way even when informed of legal breaches.

We should be careful not to conclude too much from results in this second experiment, especially since the first differences for the various follow-up items overlap somewhat. Fully disaggregating distinct normative versus instrumental mechanisms presents a constant challenge, since certain survey items likely blend together in some respects.[56]

What the combined results across the pair of drones experiments do reinforce is that arguments rooted in international law seem to have a different impact on the public than other sorts of assertions, even ones emphasizing more strategic calculations. International law appears to have this influence on policy preferences in part by activating first-order concerns over normative principles, even if members of the public may also at times consider second-order instrumental consequences ensuing from such normative transgressions.

Trying to tackle an issue like drone strikes in the midst of heated debates points to the promise, but also limits, of experimental designs to answer questions about the role of international law in shaping public preferences. People's prior beliefs and knowledge likely matter a great deal for how they approach and understand policy questions, especially those with important legal implications. Rather than treating individuals' baseline understanding as a nuisance to be controlled for, the remainder of this chapter moves outside of the experimental mold. The sections that follow go beyond the laboratory to investigate how real-world knowledge of international law affects people's opinions across a range of abuses at the core of contemporary debates over what belligerents should (and should not) be allowed to do during wartime.

Real-World Knowledge of International Law and Preferences toward Wartime Conduct

How does exposure to international laws regulating wartime conduct shape individual attitudes toward violence? This question animated the prior chapter on torture and the analysis up to this point on drones. The experimental evidence marshalled so far suggests legal principles can meaningfully move ordinary people's preferences around a number of controversial policies, as expected under a popular approach to international law. Yet as I have readily acknowledged throughout this book, the clarity experiments bring in more reliably identifying causal effects comes with significant limits, continuing to raise questions for fully understanding the consequences of international law.

The experiments examining the preference function presented situations that were more or less hypothetical, or provided legal manipulations varying in their strength or directness. They share a common approach to seeing how exposure to legal ideals of various forms in an experimental setting may shape subsequent preferences around a single specific policy. Yet the one-shot nature of each of these surveys, in conjunction with the short time lapse between when survey participants received the legal treatment and were then asked about their attitudes, can make it difficult to know how ingrained or longer-lasting feelings about international law and policy preferences may actually be.[57] The ever-constant incursion of the real world also poses challenges for ascertaining whether any findings (and nonfindings) revealed in carefully controlled experiments generalize to how people actually think and feel when they interact with matters of law and a wider range of policies in their normal lives. As with the two-step approach to reputation and the enforcement function of international law in chapters 3 and 4, incorporating nonexperimental data can offer a better picture of how legal rules influence preference formation and change over the long haul.

A More "Knowledgeable" Design: Survey Evidence of International Law and Violence

A survey by the International Committee of the Red Cross (ICRC), *The People on War Report*, fortunately offers a way of addressing some of the concerns with purely experimental data.[58] The survey was commissioned by the ICRC in 1999 to mark the fiftieth anniversary of the signing of the Geneva Conventions, which set out a core series of legal obligations providing various protections for victims of armed conflict. Unlike much conventional polling that focuses on a single issue, the ICRC survey is unique in its wide coverage of questions related to wartime violence. Equally vital, the survey queried respondents on their actual knowledge of the Geneva Conventions, providing an opportunity to assess how people's real-world exposure to the laws of war (or international humanitarian law, hereafter IHL) and the humanitarian impulses embedded in the conventions may shape general preferences toward violence.

There may be some hesitation about what we can learn from a survey fielded over two decades ago. Beyond the length of time, other notable developments include the emerging norm of the Responsibility to Protect (R2P), as well as the creation of the International Criminal Court (ICC). There are several reasons why insights gleaned from the ICRC survey remain relevant for our purposes. It is true the ICC did not officially come into being until 2002, but the Rome Statute establishing the court opened for ratification in July 1998, well before when the survey was fielded. Important precedents had also been in place beforehand, such as the special tribunals for crimes committed during conflicts in Rwanda and the former Yugoslavia.[59] Similarly, discourse surrounding R2P began concertedly in the mid to late 1990s in the aftermath of the Rwandan genocide and Balkan atrocities.[60] Although it is difficult to know a priori whether findings based on the ICRC survey would be stronger, weaker, or the same as similar polling conducted in the present day, the data nonetheless provide a useful reference point for thinking about the relationship between international law and individual attitudes toward wartime violence. Other work has likewise profited from using historical survey data to examine questions of contemporary relevance regarding public opinion and the use of force.[61]

Of course, the ideal situation would be running a cross-national panel questionnaire of most countries of the world conducted across multiple waves in the manner of the World Values Survey (WVS), or regional projects like the

Afro- and Eurobarometers. Yet the sheer breadth of questions asked about both wartime conduct and IHL position the ICRC survey as one of the most promising sources available for examining public attitudes toward a wider range of wartime abuses.[62]

The ICRC project was cross-national in scope with surveys conducted in the United States, several other UN Security Council members, as well as a range of countries that had recently experienced, or were still experiencing, armed conflict.[63] Given this book focuses on the United States, the analyses below are limited to the US sample. However, in other work I show that similar patterns between knowledge of law and preferences toward violence hold in other settings like the conflict countries surveyed.[64] The survey was designed and fielded by the ICRC, in tandem with the survey firm Greenberg Research, using a stratified multistage cluster sampling method.[65] For the US sample, subjects were contacted by telephone with 1,009 participants completing the survey.

OUTCOMES: ATTITUDES TOWARD VIOLENCE

US respondents were asked a battery of eleven items dealing with wartime violence, which fell into two main categories based on the nature the victimized group—civilians and prisoners. The measures provide a nice point of comparison to the torture and drones experiments, dealing with these same broad groups though the ICRC survey covers a wider range of behaviors. Table 6.2 summarizes the items, which are all rescaled so that higher values indicate greater levels of approval for abuse. The five civilian measures focus on preferences toward attacks against civilian versus military targets, as well as strategies that disproportionately harm noncombatants, such as land mines. For instance, the phrasing for the first civilian item is as follows: "When combatants attack to weaken the enemy, should they . . ." Respondents were then given the following answer options in declining order of willingness to accept violence against civilians: "Attack enemy combatants and civilians"/"Attack enemy combatants and avoid civilians as much as possible"/"Attack only enemy combatants and leave the civilians alone."[66]

The six prisoner abuse measures cover a variety of common violations associated with the capture and detention of enemy combatants, ranging from torture to denying access to outside observers. For example, for the first prisoner item, respondents were asked "Would you save the life of a surrendering enemy combatant who killed a person close to you?" Respondents could then answer either yes, they "Would save," or no, they "Would not save." The full text for these and other relevant questions is included in Supplementary Online Materials.[67]

I then use these items to construct a series of summary indices measuring each respondent's general attitudes toward wartime abuse rather than relying

Table 6.2 Questions used to construct attitudes toward wartime abuse indices

ITEM

Civilian abuse
- General willingness to attack enemy combatants vs. civilians
- Deprive civilians of food, medicine, or water
- Attack enemy combatants in populated areas
- Plant land mines even if endangers civilians
- Take civilians hostage to get something in return

Prisoner abuse
- Refuse to save the life of surrendering enemy combatants
- Prohibit prisoners from contacting relatives
- Torture prisoners
- Prohibit visits to prisoners by outside representatives
- Kill prisoners in retaliation
- Prisoners deserve to die

Notes: All items from 1999 ICRC Survey.

on each item individually. An overall index was created using a principal factor analysis of respondents' answers to the eleven items, which uncovered a single common underlying dimension reflecting preferences toward abuse.[68] Loadings generated from the factor analysis were then used to create the Overall Abuse index. Because past research points to important differences in the treatment of various groups during war,[69] separate indices were also created for violence toward civilians (Civilian Abuse) and prisoners (Prisoner Abuse) using the relevant items. As in other analyses in this book, to facilitate subsequent estimation and interpretation, each index was rescaled to range between 0 and 1, where higher values indicate greater support for wartime abuse.[70]

Figure 6.6 is a histogram overlaid with a smoothed kernel density plot, which presents the distribution of values across the three abuse indices. Aggregate attitudes are weighted toward the lower end of support for violence. Yet less than 5% of US respondents professed the lowest levels of support, meaning a large share felt at least some situations warranted denying protections for (or outright targeting of) civilians and prisoners.

The second and third panels of figure 6.6 indicate that lower-end values are more prevalent when distinguishing between the separate civilian and prisoner indices, but support for higher levels of abuse remains noticeable. Those who abhor wartime violence are not necessarily the same when it comes to the treatment of civilians versus prisoners. Although the two victim-specific indices are positively correlated among US respondents overall, they are actually negatively

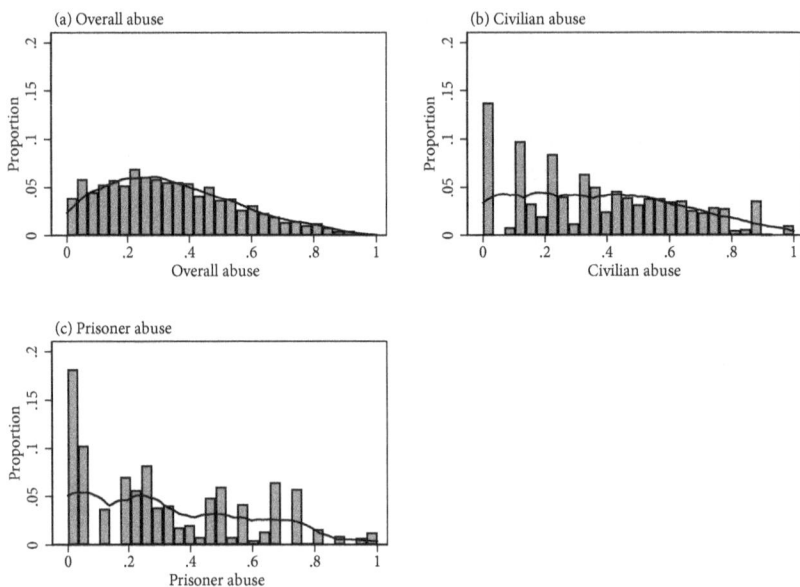

FIGURE 6.6. Summary of support for wartime abuse indices

Notes: Histogram for each abuse index overlaid with a kernel density plot. Data from 1999 ICRC Survey, US respondents.

related at the lower ends for values less than or equal to 0.1 on each index.[71] This pattern points to the importance of considering the possibility that determinants of support for violence may differ depending on the victim. This localized negative relationship between the two indices also helps account for why the proportion of cases falling at the lower ends is more pronounced for each victim-specific index individually compared to the overall abuse index.

The average value of support for violence is actually slightly higher for the civilian abuse index (0.37) than for prisoner abuse (0.32). This may seem surprising given the general emphasis in much discourse on rights for civilians, along with the lesser threat or blame generally attributed to noncombatants that could be used to justify violence. Yet differences in the distributions within each index are likely more a function of their respective constituent items—several of the prisoner questions were more forthright, such as torturing or killing combatants, while a number of civilian items involved less direct actions (denying food, planting land mines) or emphasized "attacking" rather than more charged language of "killing."

Directly comparing absolute values across the various abuse indices is difficult. It might be preferable if the survey items were exactly the same except for the group being victimized. But closer congruence would come at the cost of ignoring the most relevant types of violence directed against civilians versus prisoners, which differ in important respects.[72] Ultimately for our specific purposes, absolute levels of support for various forms of wartime violence are less central than are *differences* in individual preferences based on key attributes, in particular understandings of international law.

MAIN EXPLANATION: KNOWLEDGE OF INTERNATIONAL LAW

Turning to international law, the survey takes a different strategy for investigating the relationship between legal principles and policy preferences. Rather than manipulating exposure to international law in the vein of the experiments presented up to this point, the ICRC survey includes a set of questions to more directly measure individuals' legal knowledge, specifically their understanding of IHL. Consistent with the multimethod approach of this book, combining insights from this observational survey with earlier experimental data provides the opportunity to both cross-check the experimental findings while at the same time giving a fuller appreciation of individual attitudes toward international law.

To capture real-world exposure to IHL, I rely on a pair of questions posed to all respondents about their comprehension of the 1949 Geneva Conventions. Although the IHL regime complex is composed of a host of international agreements regulating a broad array of weapons and behavior, the Geneva Conventions represent the foundation for the contemporary laws of war.[73] Protections afforded to civilians and prisoners under the Geneva Conventions codified many prior rules and customs, while serving as a basis for later laws, such as additional protocols to them, as well as the 1998 Rome Statute establishing the ICC. As such, understanding the conventions introduces individuals to basic legal principles of humanitarian restraint at odds with violations at the heart of the abuse outcome indices.

For the international law measure, respondents were first asked, "Have you ever heard of the Geneva Conventions?" For those who answered affirmatively, this was followed by an open-ended question "Could you tell me what the Geneva Conventions are about?" to ascertain their actual understanding of the treaties. Interviewers then recorded whether or not the response accurately identified the main purpose of the conventions, such as references to placing limits on wartime conduct. I use these items to construct the binary variable "Know about Geneva Conventions," which equals 1 if a respondent had heard of the conventions and correctly identified their purpose, and 0 if respondents had either not heard of them or incorrectly described what they were about. Clear differences exist in baseline international legal knowledge among US respondents—just under half

(49%) possessed a basic understanding of the conventions, suggesting exposure to basic IHL principles is widespread but not universal.[74]

This measure is unable to make fine-grained distinctions in a person's relative awareness of particular rules of warfare, much less the minutia of various legal technicalities occupying the attention of international lawyers. Nevertheless, the variable offers a number of distinct advantages. First, the second item is open-ended, requiring respondents to provide an answer in their own words, making guessing and false positives less of a worry compared to closed-ended questions. Second, the generality of the construct is beneficial by not being directly linked to specific items gauging preferences for or against abuse, mitigating concerns over consistency bias between responses. Third, the two Geneva Conventions questions were asked well after the items used to construct the abuse index outcomes, helping minimize worries over question ordering and contamination.[75]

Because the data are not experimental, I also include a number of other items that past research suggests should have some bearing both on people's propensity to know about international law as well as their foreign policy attitudes more generally. These include socio-demographic indicators like age, gender, and education, but also military experience, media consumption, and whether they tend to take sides when following conflicts abroad.[76]

Legal Knowledge and Wartime Preferences: Results

What do these more conventional survey data tell us about the relationship between greater real-world exposure to international law and people's preferences toward a range of wartime abuses? Figure 6.7 reports the coefficients from a series of regression models estimating the determinants of attitudes among US respondents for each of the three violence indices—overall, civilian, and prisoner abuse. Since all indices are continuous, models were estimated using ordinary least squares (OLS). Because each index was rescaled between 0 and 1, interpreting coefficients is relatively straightforward—positive (negative) values indicate a given percentage-point increase (decrease) in support for abuse. Horizontal lines indicate the 90% and 95% confidence intervals around each coefficient.

The figure shows some intriguing findings in general and across the three abuse indices. Looking first at overall abuse, those "knowers" with prior awareness of the Geneva Conventions were associated with 6% lower support for wartime abuse writ large compared to their counterparts (or "unknowers") who were unaware of these foundational IHL agreements. We should be careful not to automatically describe these as *causal* effects, since results come from more traditional survey questions rather than the sorts of experiments

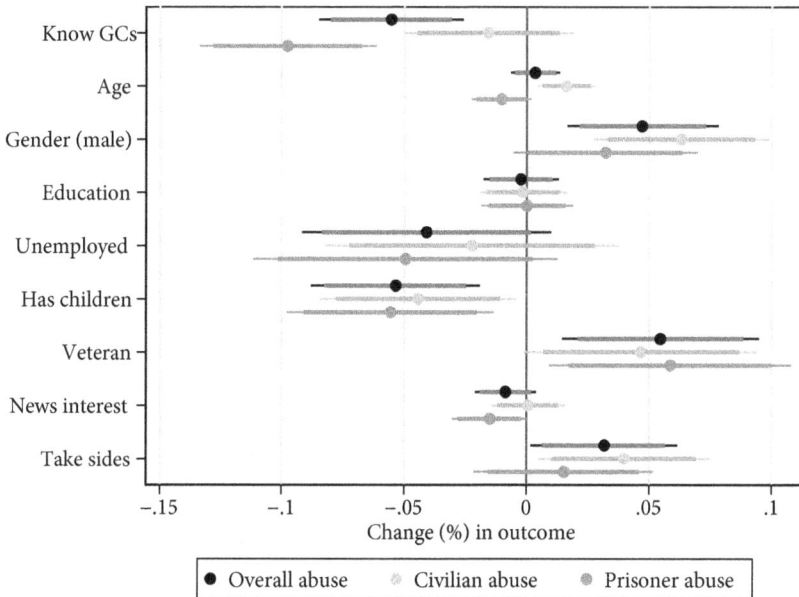

FIGURE 6.7. Determinants of support for wartime abuse

Notes: Coefficient plot (OLS) indicating percentage-point change in support for each abuse index. Lines indicate 90% and 95% confidence intervals. "Know GCs" refers to knowledge of Geneva Conventions. Data from 1999 ICRC Survey, US respondents.

described earlier in this chapter and chapter 5. Nonetheless, the ICRC data point to a statistically significant relationship between international law and attitudes toward wartime conduct that reflects many similarities to the experimental benchmarks already established.

Equally important, this relationship holds even after taking into account common competing factors like gender, education, and military experience. Education is especially relevant since more educated individuals may differ systematically in both their preferences and baseline legal knowledge. In particular, those holding higher levels of education tend to take more liberal positions on many foreign policies.[77] However, the relationship between schooling and political violence is much less settled; some research suggests education plays a constraining role, while other argue it can actually enable abuse.[78] If respondents who know more about the Geneva Conventions are also the most educated, then any observed relationship between awareness of IHL and preferences toward violence may be spurious and simply a function of educational attainment. Figure 6.7 suggests this is not the case, since the association between IHL "knowers" and preferences toward violence remains significant even after controlling for education.[79] I also conducted a range of additional robustness and specification tests, which provide further confidence that the relationship between knowledge of international law and greater opposition to overall acts of wartime violence is genuine.[80]

Beneath the results for the overall abuse index hide some important differences, and the role of international law does not appear to be constant across all types of abuse. Most glaring, in the case of violence against civilians, the association with IHL knowledge disappears; the coefficient for "knowers" is still negative but diminishes both in size (under a 2% drop) and statistical significance. By contrast, those in the United States with greater IHL knowledge are associated with almost a 10% decline in support for abuses directed toward prisoners. These patterns hold across various alternative specifications. For instance, the role of international law actually appears stronger for less grave or more indirect forms of abuse compared to graver or more direct violence, at least in the case of prisoner treatment (though both forms remain negative and statistically significant).[81]

In many ways, these differential impacts based on the severity of violations are consistent with the contention under popular international law that legal rules can provide new information to the public—information that is more credible, principled, and meaningful. Building on the torture experiments from chapter 5, many members of the US public may already have some sense that torturing or killing captured enemy combatants is wrong; knowing the precise legal rules prohibiting these practices may further shape and reinforce their preferences. Nevertheless, knowledge of the Geneva Conventions is associated with a proportionately greater difference in attitudes toward more moderate forms of abuse, such as detainees' rights to outside communications and visits, which may be less obvious in the general public's mind.

In a corresponding manner, the consistent nonfinding for the association between IHL knowledge and civilian abuse does not necessarily mean US respondents are completely uncaring toward noncombatants' plight. Rather, these weaker results may actually point to the possibility of a more widespread *acceptance* of underlying norms of civilian protections, taking on a certain taken-for-granted status.[82] Of course, individuals may still condone the targeting of civilians for strategic reasons, even while acknowledging that limits likely constrain such actions in principle. Discrimination between combatants and noncombatants, and by extension protecting civilians, remains one of the foundational tenets of the laws of war and just war theory, and may thus be more commonly accepted in mass opinion.[83] Possessing more specific IHL knowledge may bring little new to the minds of such "knowers" and, in turn, do little to change their preferences toward targeting civilians relative to IHL "unknowers."

By contrast and as chapter 5 made clear, the appropriate treatment of prisoners may be less settled given the uneasy status of combatants who have been fighting, or potentially even perpetrating abuses, not long before capture.[84] US experience in the War on Terror, as detailed in chapter 4, highlights how countries can brutalize enemy combatants, while treating civilians at least somewhat more humanely.[85] Even if international law does provide a *principled* form of information, to have an independent impact on preferences that information still has to contain something novel. To the extent the Geneva Conventions and similar laws disseminate beliefs about appropriate treatment of detainees, or bolster existing suppositions with heavier legal gravitas, it follows that IHL knowledge may have a greater association with changed preferences in less formulated areas like prisoner abuse.

Returning to the results as a whole, differences in support for both overall and prisoner abuse among Geneva Conventions "knowers" versus "unknowers" are of comparable sizes to those found in experimental studies presented in this and earlier chapters. Especially noteworthy, the 10% decline in support for prisoner abuse among IHL "knowers" is almost double the drop reported in the first torture experiment from chapter 5 for those US respondents who were treated with an international law prompt. This corroboration helps address a common complaint that causal estimates gleaned from experimental studies do not travel well to real-world situations and may overstate effect sizes. The results here instead suggest that experimental studies may sometimes *underestimate* the effects of international law. By considering the more gradual and longer-term exposure of ordinary individuals to legal principles in an observational setting, we can develop a greater appreciation for the ways international law can shape public preferences.

Looking at the results within figure 6.7 from a relative standpoint, the coefficient for knowledge about the Geneva Conventions is also of equal or greater size to those for many common individual-level drivers of attitudes toward violence. In fact, IHL knowledge represents the single largest coefficient among those estimated in the prisoner abuse model. The substantive importance of prior awareness of international law is thus in line with existing research and impressive when compared to alternative factors. Many of the other explanatory variables are consistent with existing research, with men and those with prior military experience generally expressing greater support for wartime abuses, while parents were usually less supportive.[86] Other factors, such as age, education, and media consumption, instead appeared to have less bearing on attitudes toward wartime violence.

Conditional Relationships between Legal Knowledge and Preferences

The results so far suggest that exposure to international law in the real world has a comparable (or even greater) effect on policy preferences. Of course, one of the key questions raised throughout this book is whether international law only works in easier situations, or with those actors already predisposed toward legal principles. The continued focus on harder contexts like armed conflict counters the contention that international legal rules are quickly dispensed with when national security is at stake. But are all citizens equally influenced, or are legal rules simply preaching to the choir? In other words, *who* does the law influence most? If legal rules can operate not just with saints but also with potential scofflaws, this would provide an even firmer basis for acknowledging the potential of international law.

Figure 6.8 offers a window into possible differences in the operation of international law across several US subgroups. The subfigures report the observed relationship between IHL knowledge and the three abuse indices by estimating

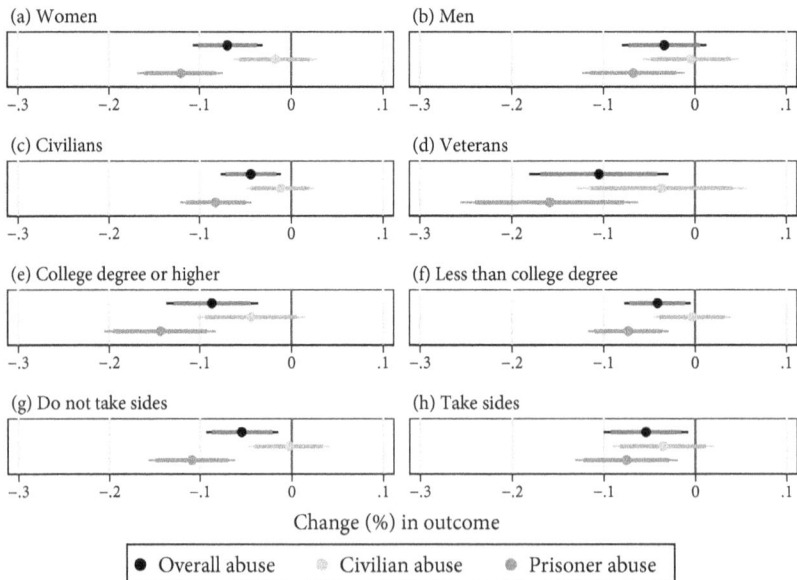

FIGURE 6.8.   Knowledge of Geneva Conventions and support for wartime abuse, conditional on certain political and socio-demographic traits

Notes: Coefficient plot (OLS) for knowledge of Geneva Conventions indicating percentage-point change in support for each abuse index, conditional on specified political and socio-demographic traits. Lines indicate 90% and 95% confidence intervals. Data from 1999 ICRC Survey, US respondents.

separate models for each of the relevant subsamples while holding all other variables constant.[87] Although the ICRC survey includes a rich set of items on law
and violence, the questionnaire did not ask US respondents about their partisanship or ideological leanings. This unfortunately precludes a direct comparison
to some of the conditional effects discussed in chapter 5 between international
law and preferences toward torture. Nevertheless, the ICRC survey captured a
number of other individual attributes. Figure 6.8 focuses on gender, education,
military experience, and the tendency to take sides versus remaining neutral in
armed conflicts, which may be important factors conditioning people's foreign
policy attitudes.

The subfigures indicate that the relationship between international law and
preferences toward wartime abuse is not limited only to those already inclined
toward legal principles. While men, veterans, and those inclined to take sides
during conflicts do tend to be more supportive of abuse in general (as was evident
earlier in figure 6.7), these groups' weaker humanitarian impulses do not then
mean they are insensitive to international legal appeals. The influence of international law in reducing support for abuse between IHL "knowers" versus "unknowers" is largely the same across the various subgroup pairs, such as between men
and women. If anything, international law may exert a slightly *stronger* pull on
some subgroups like veterans, who at first glance may presumably not be very
welcoming to humanitarian appeals compared to those without military experience.[88] Those holding a college degree or higher are more influenced by knowing about international law than college graduates with no understanding of the
Geneva Conventions, though again the relationship between law and support
for violence is not terribly different among their less educated counterparts. The
results from figure 6.8 confirm a remarkable consistency in the popular foundations of international law by shaping the preferences of a variety of segments of
the US population who may approach violence and legal principles from radically different starting points.

Investigating Mechanisms and Additional Implications

All of the results from the ICRC survey discussed so far point to international
legal appeals resonating among the US public even on issues as controversial as
wartime violence. This influence of international law is evident not only for the
population as a whole but also across wide segments of society. With the role of
actual knowledge of international law on real-world policy attitudes reasonably
established, one final way in which we can take advantage of the survey is by
gaining a better appreciation of *how* and *why* international law can shape public
preferences, and with *what* additional implications.

What may be the reasons why those previously exposed to IHL differ in their policy attitudes from people less aware of the principles underlying the Geneva Conventions? Beyond being less willing to condone the actual resort to abuses in wartime, IHL "knowers" may simply be more likely to believe that certain limits exist in wartime. The laws of war can provide a clear focal point for expectations of allowable actions through their specificity and more obligatory nature. People who have not had similar experiences with international law may still also come to believe that limits exist on fighting. But such conclusions may be less prevalent within this group of "unknowers" since they will not share the same reference point. The survey contained an item that can help investigate this conjecture—all respondents were asked "Is there anything that soldiers and fighters—should not be allowed to do in fighting their enemy?" This was an open-ended question, where respondents could offer their thoughts on what limits should exist, if any. I then simplified those responses into a binary measure of beliefs regarding wartime limits, where either "yes" they felt there were at least some things combatants should not do when fighting, or "no" where fighters were unshackled and pretty much anything was fair game.

This measure admittedly sets a low bar for wartime limits as referring to *any* curbs on fighting, meaning those answering in the negative are implicitly (or explicitly) making an allowance for unrestricted warfare. Not surprisingly, the latter was the minority view, but even here around 30% of US respondents felt there should be few meaningful restrictions on combatants' actions. But what role does international law play in shaping these beliefs? Figure 6.9 reports the association between those who knew about the Geneva Conventions and the probability they believed that limits on fighting should exist. To simplify the presentation of the analysis, the figure only reports results for the knowledge of IHL measure, though the logit model estimated also included a similar set of common socio-demographic covariates to the earlier main abuse models. In substantive terms, the figure indicates that IHL "knowers" are about 17% more likely to believe limits on fighting ought to exist compared to "unknowers," and the difference is statistically significant.[89] While a majority of respondents declared that limits on fighting should exist, the feeling is more widespread among that segment already having a deeper understanding of international legal principles.

Everyone who answered this question affirmatively were then asked a follow-up item looking to find out more about *why* they believed limits on wartime conduct apply. Respondents were offered one of two answer choices tapping into complementary but distinct rationales. One centered on the sense that breaching such limits "just causes too many problems." While the word "problems" was left ambiguous, the language more closely connects to instrumental rationales. The second answer option instead stated categorically that "It's wrong" to engage in

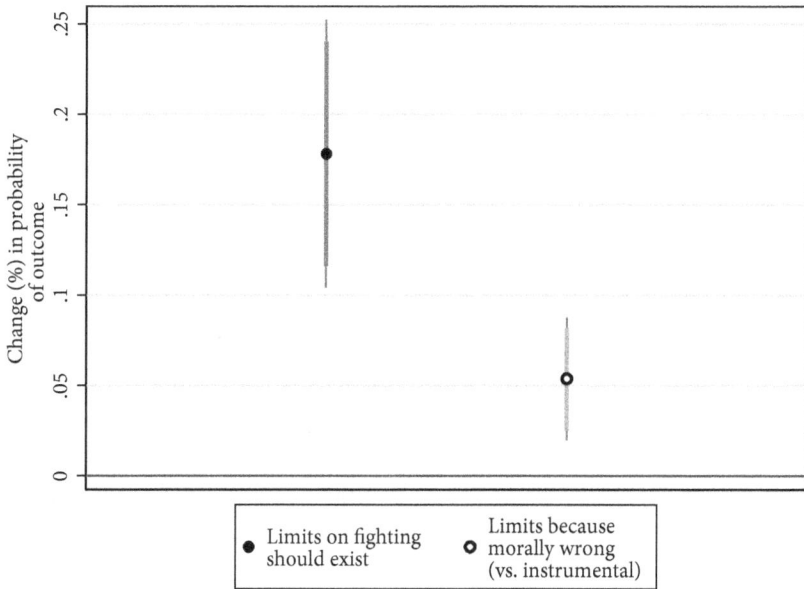

FIGURE 6.9. Knowledge of Geneva Conventions and beliefs about limits on wartime conduct

Notes: Logit estimation separately for each outcome. Average marginal effect (percentage-point change in the predicted probability of the relevant outcome) of knowledge of Geneva Conventions, while holding all other variables at their median values. Lines indicate 90% and 95% confidence intervals. Model for second outcome (reason for limits on fighting) limited to respondents who answered affirmatively the prior item believing that limits on fighting should exist. Data from 1999 ICRC Survey, US respondents.

such actions, following a normative line of reasoning where matters of justice figure more prominently in questions of violence. The answer options are not mutually exclusive—individuals could think of the "problems" caused by violations in moral terms, and breaching such limits could in turn be viewed as "wrong" because of negative strategic repercussions.[90] Yet set against one another, each offers differing instrumental and normative emphases for ordinary people's thinking regarding the sources of limits on wartime conduct.

The second point estimate in figure 6.9 above indicates how much those who have been exposed to IHL emphasize normative over instrumental considerations when justifying their beliefs that limits on fighting exist. Though of more modest size, IHL knowers were around 6% more likely to believe that limits are due to moral rather than instrumental reasons. The two results from figure 6.9 indicate that concerted exposure to the Geneva Conventions does have discernable implications for attitudes toward wartime conduct, and where these legal principles are associated with heightened normative thinking.

The results do not necessarily mean that instrumental motives are completely absent from people's thinking over the proper place of international law during armed conflict. The potential interplay between normative and instrumental dynamics can be seen in other ways in which international law shapes the public's beliefs, especially when it comes to how legal rules are thought to operate during war, as well as what to do with those combatants who engage in violations.

Later in the survey, interviewers described to all respondents—irrespective of whether they already knew about the Geneva Conventions—the key traits of these agreements, stating that "The Geneva Conventions is a series of international treaties that impose limits on war by describing some rules of war. Most countries in the world have signed these treaties." Respondents were then asked to express their beliefs about the consequences of the laws of war, specifically whether they thought the conventions were effective and "Prevents wars from getting worse," or make "No real difference."

This item offers a different take on one of the central issues of this book concerning whether or not international laws have any meaningful impact. In this case, are those people who are exposed to, and know about, international law more likely to believe in its effectiveness? The answer has fundamental implications for thinking about the appropriate role of international law in both domestic and international society. If those who know more about international law believe in its effectiveness, this could provide a basis not only for the spread of international legal beliefs among the wider population, but also in creating a coalition of domestic actors committed to the agreement's goals. Some domestic theories of compliance are predicated upon the assumption that exposure to international law can help mobilize domestic groups to defend and promote these values.[91] International law may have these mobilizing effects not only through changing people's preferences (confirming the experimental and nonexperimental studies from the last two chapters), but also by strengthening a collective sense that mobilization will succeed.[92] In light of often-vocal "pro-violation" constituencies in the face national security threats, beliefs in the power of legal rules may motivate a counterbalancing "pro-compliance" base that can prove pivotal in tipping the balance of governments' human rights and wartime policies.[93]

However, we should not immediately jump to the conclusion that knowing about IHL, or international legal rules more generally, should lead to greater faith in its effectiveness. Exposure to legal rules can have counteracting effects, especially if those institutions do not live up to people's demands in practice. In the related area of constitutional law, greater participation by members of the public in constitutional reform processes can lead to "distrusting democrats"— citizens who exhibit stronger attachments to democratic principles in theory, but are suspicious of democratic institutions as they become more aware of how they actually function.[94] An international corollary may be "distrusting legalists"—aware of the humanitarian principles enshrined in the laws of war, but wary of their limits on the ground. The risk of international legal discourse having perverse negative consequences needs to be taken seriously.[95] If this alternative viewpoint holds, then international law's impact on domestic actors contains the seeds of its own defeat. Exposure to IHL could heighten feelings in the futility of legal constraints on wartime conduct, inhibiting its further spread among populations by confirming its irrelevance in their minds.

The ICRC survey offers an opportunity to adjudicate between these contending views on the relationship between knowledge of IHL and beliefs about its effectiveness. Figure 6.10 reports results from a logit model, where the outcome variable is respondents' beliefs that the Geneva Conventions prevent wars from getting worse (relative to making no difference), using knowledge of the conventions and other standard socio-economic items as explanatory variables. Point estimates indicate the change in the probability a respondent believes the Conventions are effective, while holding all other variables at their median values.

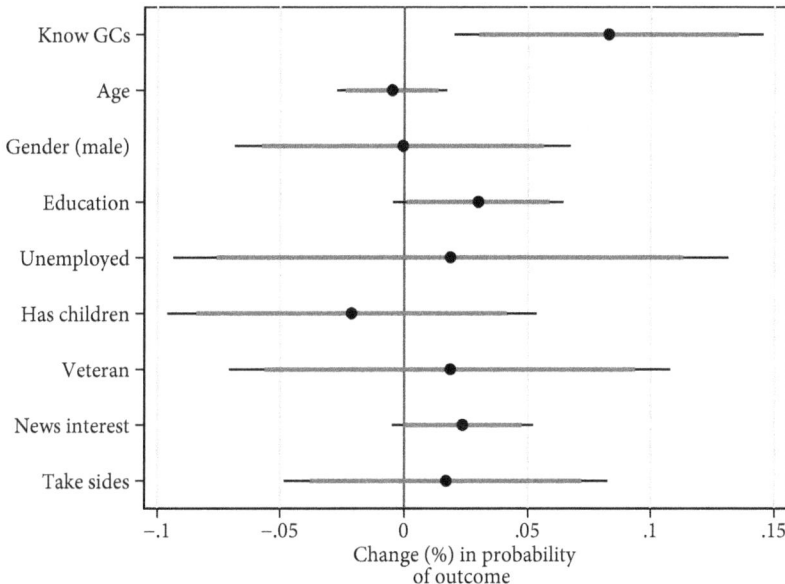

FIGURE 6.10. Determinants of beliefs in the effectiveness of the Geneva Conventions in preventing wars from getting worse

Notes: Logit estimation. Average marginal effect (percentage-point change in the predicted probability of the outcome) of each independent variable, while holding all other variables at their median values. Lines indicate 90% and 95% confidence intervals. "Know GCs" refers to knowledge of Geneva Conventions. Data from 1999 ICRC Survey, US respondents.

IHL "knowers" turn out to be around 8% more likely to believe the agreements succeed in preventing wars from getting worse compared to their "unknowing" counterparts. Moreover, and as a point of comparison, none of the other explanatory variables attain a similar size substantively nor are they statistically significant. Rather than undermining confidence in international law, IHL "knowers" show that greater exposure to these rules is associated with increased conviction in their effectiveness.[96]

Perhaps this is just another manifestation of motivated reasoning, where people tend to interpret information and adopt positions consistent with their preexisting beliefs.[97] As we already know, IHL "knowers" hold stronger preferences against wartime abuses and similar violations. They may correspondingly reason that those same laws must surely be at work in preventing prohibited acts. Yet these more legally imbued people are not naïve or guilelessly optimistic compared to their "unknowing" compatriots.

Analysis of a number of additional survey items reported in figure 6.11 indicates IHL "knowers" hold a fairly sober view of the state of violence in armed conflicts, even as they remain more hopeful about addressing such challenges. The first estimate shows that IHL "knowers" are 6% more likely than "unknowers" to believe that wartime atrocities were becoming more prevalent in recent years. The last point estimate further suggests those with greater knowledge of international law are not wearing rose-tinted glasses, since they were indistinguishable from IHL "unknowers" on perceptions on whether world affairs were heading in the right direction.

Despite this general ambivalence, IHL "knowers" were 7% more likely to express that atrocities are not inevitable and could be prevented. It is not simply a matter of IHL "knowers" putting greater faith in abstract legal principles to reduce abuses, as they also demonstrated greater confidence in certain concrete measures. For instance, peacekeeping has become an important tool not only for deterring the resumption of fighting, but also in protecting civilians from harm.[98] Those exposed to IHL were 8% more likely to believe that strategies like sending peacekeepers are helpful for protecting civilians on the ground. Irrespective of their specific motivations, those who know about IHL are more sanguine that these laws can operate effectively in even the most trying of circumstances. Instead of the law falling silent in the midst of armed conflict, awareness of legal principles has the potential to generate a vocal majority calling for belligerents to adhere to these rules in both word and deed.

Speaking of actions, holding firmer beliefs over what counts as appropriate conduct—and what might be done in response to behavior contrary to those beliefs—offers another chance for thinking about the relationship between the

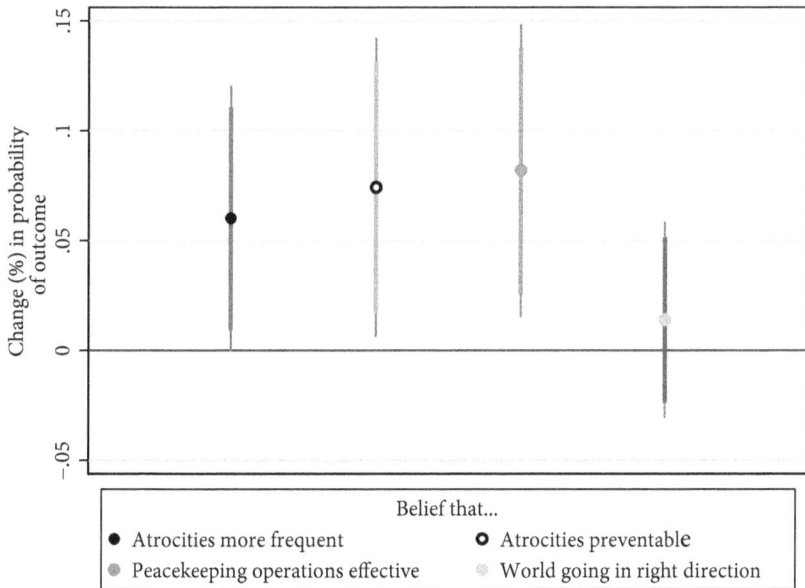

FIGURE 6.11. Knowledge of Geneva Conventions and beliefs about atrocities and direction of the world

Notes: Ordered logit estimation separately for first (frequency of atrocities), third (effectiveness of peacekeeping operations), and fourth (direction the world is going) outcomes. Logit estimation for the second (whether atrocities are preventable) outcome. Average marginal effect (percentage-point change in the predicted probability of the relevant outcome) of knowledge of Geneva Conventions, while holding all other variables at their median values. Lines indicate 90% and 95% confidence intervals. Data from 1999 ICRC Survey, US respondents.

preference and enforcement functions of international law. Throughout the last four empirical chapters, I have mostly treated matters of enforcement as largely separate from underlying preferences toward legalized policies. Those deeper preferences may not be a necessary condition for approving of enforcement, but these sorts of beliefs may facilitate support for sanctions. One of the alleged weaknesses of international law is the challenge of getting sufficient buy-in for the costly actions needed for enforcement. Under popular international law, domestic actors can help to fill this gap by serving as an internal source for the external enforcement of international legal rules.

The question that remains is whether the preferences engendered by international law in fostering "procompliance" constituencies can be activated in such a way that ordinary people can form corresponding "proenforcement" constituencies willing to approve sanctions. The experimental findings from chapter 3, supplemented by the case study evidence from chapter 4, indicated that

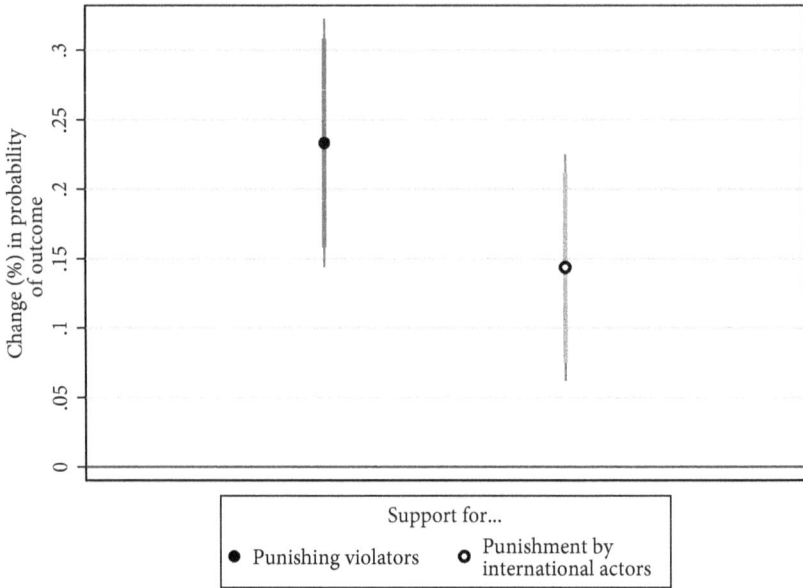

FIGURE 6.12. Knowledge of Geneva Conventions and beliefs about account-ability for violators

Notes: Logit estimation separately for each outcome. Average marginal effect (percentage-point change in the predicted probability of the relevant outcome) of knowledge of Geneva Conventions, while holding all other variables at their median values. Lines indicate 90% and 95% confidence intervals. Model for second outcome (punishment by international actors) limited to respondents who answered affirmatively the prior item that violators should be punished. Data from 1999 ICRC Survey, US respondents.

international law creates greater support for more indirect forms of punishment, such as through reputational sanctions, though the results for direct retaliation were more mixed. Additional items from the ICRC survey allow us to revisit this question in a different context. All respondents were asked a simple yes/no question, but one with deep implications: "Are there rules or laws that are so important that if broken during war, the person who broke them should be punished?"

The results from the first value in figure 6.12 confirm that the thinking of IHL "knowers" continues to diverge from "unknowers" possessing little knowledge of international law. Those who knew about the Geneva Conventions were almost 25% more likely to believe that perpetrators should be punished. Beyond general preferences toward more humanitarian conduct in line with the laws of war, IHL knowers were willing to proverbially "put their money where their mouth is," and support enforcement of those same rules.

Furthermore, exposure to international law creates a corresponding internationalization in the demands for *who* should be taking the reins over enforcement.

Those respondents who answered affirmatively to the initial punishment item were asked in a follow-up, "who should be responsible for punishing the wrong-doers?" Answer options included various domestic actors—including the government, politicians, domestic courts, or the military—as well as an international actor in the ICC. The second value in figure 6.12 indicates that IHL "knowers" were 15% more likely than "unknowers" to prefer international over domestic actors when enforcing IHL against violators. These findings offer micro-level evidence for the increased attention to the authority of international courts to enforce humanitarian and human rights principles.[99] What these results further suggest are important *domestic* sources for such international legal authority.

A reciprocal relationship seems to exist between international organizations, domestic actors, and international law. Just as the second torture experiment from the previous chapter showed that greater delegation to international courts can help change the public's preferences toward torture, the results here show that international law can in turn serve as a basis to strengthen domestic support for international institutions. Looking specifically at the laws of war, this body of rules has been notoriously difficult for finding constructive ways of encouraging compliance and enforcing rules when breaches do occur. Consistent with the expectations of popular international law, the collective evidence from the ICRC survey points to a domestic-centered set of processes that imbue people with stronger feelings that international laws should be followed, and potentially a deeper commitment to enforcement when those laws are not followed.

This chapter offers further evidence for the ability of international laws to shape the preferences of ordinary members of the public. Additional experimental evidence modeled off the larger debate over drones showed that legal considerations could play a role at least equal to (and potentially greater than) more strategic imperatives related to military effectiveness on approval for such strikes. The drones surveys continued to highlight the need to take seriously the role of prior beliefs in ascertaining the effect of international law, even in experimental studies. The second half of the chapter then engaged these sorts of preexisting beliefs more directly by examining how actual exposure to international laws related to wartime conduct affect people's attitudes toward violence. Results from this unique survey showed that those with greater understanding of international laws do differ in important ways in their policy preferences from those without similar knowledge, but the differences were most marked in areas where principles ingrained in legal rules were most informative. Throughout the studies presented in this chapter, we see that international laws continue to operate in trying circumstances, and can shape the preferences of groups who may not seem predisposed to the messages being carried.

In conjunction with the prior experimental chapter, the aggregate results point to an important role for international law in shaping the underlying beliefs of ordinary actors. The particular multimethod approach differs in certain respects from the earlier pair of chapters 3 and 4, which employed a combination of experimental and case study evidence to illustrate the importance of reputation in the enforcement function of international law. But by employing both experimental and observational surveys and related forms of data, this chapter and chapter 5 demonstrate how different types of multimethod designs can help us develop a better understanding of hard-to-study questions like the ways international law can inform and transform policy preferences.

Conclusion

UNDERSTANDING THE PUBLIC AND INTERNATIONAL LAW

> Where there is no vision, the people perish: but he that keepeth the Law, happy is he.
>
> —Proverbs 29:18

> Legal meaning is a challenging enrichment of social life, a potential restraint on arbitrary power and violence. We ought to stop circumscribing the *nomos*; we ought to invite new worlds.
>
> —Robert Cover, "*Nomos* and Narrative" (1983, 68)

To whom does international law belong? Who are the actors responsible for the operation of the international legal order? This book puts forward a theory to answer these important questions. To better understand how the main functions of international law are carried out, we ought to invite in and look more closely at the beliefs, preferences, and actions of ordinary members of the public, embracing what I call *popular international law*.

This statement rightfully merits some suspicion. After all, international law has traditionally focused on states alongside their rulers, diplomats, jurists, and other elites as the main (often only) actors in international legal affairs. Definitionally speaking, inter*national* law, or the law of nations, is often seen from start to finish as involving states, and solely states. Setting definitional questions aside, treaties and other international rules are commonly thought to occupy rarified air, only accessible to elites with the material and cognitive abilities to fully grasp and act upon them. The intricacies and complexities of international legal rules are deemed beyond the comprehension of the simple masses, who possess few channels for influencing the operation of international law in any event. The added fact that many world leaders range from being pleasantly confused to outright dismissive of international legal obligations does not bode well for the faculties or predilections of their citizens.

Against this view, I argued throughout the preceding chapters that there are good reasons to believe that publics have played, and have the potential to continue to play, an important role in international legal commitments. I began this book by pointing to the opening passages of two foundational legal documents—the US Constitution and the Charter to the United Nations (UN). Preambles of these sorts are routinely discounted as largely hortatory, offering a few platitudes before getting to the "real" rules to which societies are supposed to abide. Yet as most any novelist or journalist will tell you, the choice of first words is critical.[1] The focus in each document on "the People(s)" suggests something about who these instruments are for, and what position they, in turn, should occupy in the operation of legal orders domestic and international.

This is not to say that other actors—from leaders, legislatures, and other elites, to states or international organizations and courts—do not play an important and active role in international law. Rather, the appeal is to consider ordinary people in their own right with their own particular beliefs, understandings, and voices in international legal affairs. This is also not to claim that the public (either in whole or in part) will at all times exhibit procompliance tendencies prioritizing the law above all else, or will always determine their government's policy choices. Public attitudes toward international law are nuanced and complex, varying across different issues, circumstances, and periods. But those attitudes are an important part of the larger conversations between ordinary and elite actors over what role international legal commitments should play in national societies and the larger international society.

Summary of Argument and Findings

This book takes several steps in making and testing an approach linking ordinary people to international law. In chapter 1, I began by offering a working definition of international law as *legalized rules that seek to regulate the behavior of internationalized actors who are conferred certain rights and responsibilities*. In this definition, "actors" are purposefully conceived in the broadest sense to extend beyond the standard focus on states to allow for other more ordinary actors, in particular an internationalized role for national publics. Although treaties similarly garner the lion's share of attention, also included under this definition are less formalized softer laws that are increasingly prominent in international legal affairs. What unifies these outwardly disparate instruments is a common set of values that binds together to varying extents all forms of legal commitments. After seeing what international law *is*, the larger objective of this book is to better understand what it *does*. I limit the purview to examining two core functions of any legal order, international or otherwise—enforcement, and the shaping of underlying policy preferences.

With these building blocks in hand, chapter 2 turned to formulating a theoretical framework for investigating the place of national publics in fulfilling these functions of international law. This stands in contrast to theories largely focused on the interplay between states and elites, or those viewing domestic actors and processes as wholly distinct from external mechanisms. Drawing on work from international relations, international law, and political behavior, I instead propose that ordinary publics have the wherewithal to understand core tenets and values of international law, and thereby influence the traditional functions of international legal commitments.

The resulting notion of popular international law is inspired and given further credence by similar arguments made in the field of constitutional law. International and constitutional law have traditionally been seen as fundamentally distinct, with lessons from one having little useful to say about the other. This artificial separation has begun to be bridged in more recent years with greater appreciation of the overlap in form and content between these two sources of law.[2] Recognition of their affinities, however, has been used by skeptics to argue for the general *irrelevance* of both international and constitutional law.[3] I take similar precepts, but arrive at very different conclusions regarding the relevance of legal rules in national and international society, but also which actors are most relevant for the core functions of a legal system. On constitutional questions, popular constitutionalism posits that executives, courts, and other elites are not supreme, but that "the people" are important legal players as well.[4] Likewise, on questions of international law, the popular international law framework developed in this book advances that states, leaders, and other elites are not supreme, but that "the people" are also important international legal players.

I rely on several complementary methodologies and types of evidence in testing different elements of this argument. Chapter 3 examined whether there are popular domestic sources contributing to the traditional enforcement function of international law by taking on the question of whether international legal commitments can have reputational consequences. Leveraging a set of survey experiments involving the US public, the results show how international legal commitments shape citizens' evaluations of the foreign policy behavior of other countries. Violating a legal commitment provides information of a particularly principled form to national publics, leading them to be willing to support the imposition of reputational sanctions like withholding future cooperative opportunities. Reputational stakes are often proportional to the commitment's level of legalization, but the propensity to support enforcement through reputational costs remains to an extent for softer agreements that are still bound up in deeper legal understandings. The findings for reputation are also not limited to a narrow swath of the population, but are evident for more politically active segments who may be most willing and able to influence their governments. Groups of various political leanings—whether more or less amenable to legal appeals or the substantive issues at stake—appear to respond in comparable reputational terms. Popular limits still certainly exist to the enforcement of international law. The size of reputational sanctions is generally smaller for higher politics security issues relative to lower politics economic matters, though noncompliance on security obligations has the capacity to spill over and affect reputations in other issue areas. Support for retaliation through more costly actions is also more modest, suggesting the public favors a more indirect mode of enforcement of imposing punishment through foregoing future cooperation, as general models of reputation would expect.

Chapter 4 supplemented the experimental evidence by examining both the limits, as well as potential, of international law in the context of the United States and the War on Terror. The immediate post-9/11 period demonstrates that not all national publics will automatically serve as a constraint. Overwhelmed by national security concerns, much of the US citizenry appeared to largely defer to the George W. Bush administration's counterterrorism policies. From the unilateral invasion of Iraq to the treatment of detainees, many of these tactics ran afoul of prevailing international rules. Although the US public seemingly played at best a modest role, the response of other foreign populations to US violations illustrated how ordinary people could collectively contribute to the enforcement of international law. As the global image of the United States became tarnished by its repeated rejection of core international rules, pressure from foreign publics played a role in reducing their own governments' willingness to cooperate across a range of US endeavors. The costs of a sullied reputation were perhaps starkest in US warfighting and counterinsurgency efforts. From a comparative analysis of the earlier Persian Gulf War to quantitative evidence of insurgency onset, ordinary individuals showed a capacity to impose multiple costs upon the United States. Of course, by one measure international law was insufficient to prevent the United States from engaging in violations in the first place. But taking a broader perspective, the War of Terror showed how there can be real costs to breaching international laws, which emanate just as much from the streets as the halls of power.

The next two empirical chapters turned to examining another main function of international law concerning its ability to shape underlying policy preferences. I focused on some of these recurrent security issues among a seemingly skeptical US public. Chapter 5 looked into one of the most controversial debates of the past several decades concerning the use of torture, where past polling reports that sizable portions of the US population appear supportive of these techniques. Yet numerous issues have been uncovered in conventional polling questions, which may prime respondents toward condoning abusive practices and discount international law. Constructing a series of survey experiments revealed a more nuanced picture where the presence and design of international legal prohibitions have discernable effects in moving attitudes against torture. Individuals are not blank slates—international legal appeals are filtered through existing predispositions, though not always in expected ways as those most outwardly skeptical of international rules can still be influenced by them. Again, these results can be interpreted in different ways. International laws are unlikely to be able to change avid supporters of torture into diehard opponents. But if the measure of success is to be able move opinion to an extent not possible in their absence, then internationals laws may have a role to play in policy debates.

A more careful and qualified view of international law and the public is reinforced by the findings from chapter 6. Starting with the equally contentious topic of drone strikes, the US government occupied a privileged place (though not necessarily a monopoly) over information regarding the legality and efficacy of using drones to target suspected militants. Even in the midst of such hardened positions, criticisms rooted in international law had the ability (albeit more modest) to shift public support. Furthermore, these legal appeals were relatively more potent than those emphasizing the military liabilities of strikes, which was credited in part to the normative values raised by references to international law. Although facing an uphill battle in a forbidding media environment, tying contemporary events into an experimental design showed how international law can play an important part in conversations around foreign policies. The remainder of the chapter leveraged data from a rich conventional survey to investigate how people's actual knowledge of international law shapes their policy attitudes. Looking at a battery of wartime violations, individuals with a greater awareness of the 1949 Geneva Conventions—the foundational agreements for the modern laws of war—were shown to generally hold more restrained views toward abusive wartime behavior, even when taking into account likely confounding factors. This knowledge premium does not appear to hold across all issue areas. But in those domains where international law can provide new information, the legal rules appeared to do so in principled ways that can shape policy preferences.

In sum, survey experiments, traditional surveys, large-N statistical analysis, and historical case studies collectively confirm the value of using multiple methodologies to assess the impact of international law on the public, and ordinary people's corresponding contributions to the main functions of international legal commitments. Each type of data offers a different way to evaluate particular dimensions of the public's beliefs, preferences, and actions in both theory and in practice. Combined together, the evidence points to the need to take the public seriously in the study of international law, even if important qualifications and questions remain.

Making the Theory Travel: Implications and Extensions

This book admittedly has a number of limitations—some by necessity, others by design. By turning attention to an often discounted and overlooked actor, I largely focused on better understanding the relationship between international law and ordinary members of the public on their own terms. I purposely avoided setting up a "horse race" of the public versus states, leaders, or other usual suspects to see who matters "most" in international law. There is no doubt that states and elites remain central; my point is rather that we should allow a place for the mass public in conversations concerning the functions of international legal commitments. Being attentive to these ordinary voices may tell us something more profound about how international law operates. Looking at some of these functions, I confined myself to focusing on only two—facilitating enforcement and shaping policy preferences. Although these are important, there are other functions of international law, many of which would benefit from greater sensitivity to the place of ordinary actors. The study was also largely circumscribed by the boundaries of the United States, mostly as a source but other times a target in the operation of international law. As I explained in earlier chapters, the United States is a hard and important test for a theory linking the public to international legal commitments. But the book should be seen as providing a blueprint for a cross-national framework for popular international law, while remaining mindful of possible differences in national context. Toward this end, in the following sections, I consider some of the broader implications of the argument and findings, and outline avenues for further work.

Legalization and Institutional Design

Treaties remain the overwhelming focus of scholars and policymakers alike. Questions endure over why governments join (or exit) formal agreements like the Rome Statute to the International Criminal Court (ICC), or whether this or other treaties like the Convention against Torture (CAT) make any difference.[5] Softer instruments are often seen as being of secondary importance, despite some notable exceptions.[6] Yet what has been sometimes stated theoretically often bears out empirically as well—"there is no stark distinction between agreements that are formal treaties and those that are not."[7] Across different issue areas and functions, distinctions in the design and level of legalization in agreements is more a matter of degree than kind. And in those cases where differences exist, the effects are not always as expected. Of the main dimensions of legalization, the level of obligation is often seen as paramount.[8] From reputational stakes to preferences around torture, treaties with their highly obligatory nature do seem to sway mass audiences. The evidence across several of the experiments, however, suggests that technically nonbinding rules can also create a sense of duty—sometimes more muted, but in other cases comparable to more formal commitments. Rather than distinguishing between higher or lower levels of obligation, what may matter more is the common legal principles connecting these instruments, which engenders a particular normative attachment.

The surveys also show that some dimensions of legalization matter in surprising ways. While often relegated to a subordinate position, an agreement's precision can be of great significance, irrespective of the formal level of obligation. In the case of support for torture, it is the relative ambiguity in provisions that seems to most influence people's attitudes. By clarifying the terms of the commitment involved, more precise agreements further influence audience beliefs about the reputational stakes flowing from compliance with international commitments.

However, the prospect of punishment through greater delegation to international courts also makes people think twice, but is hardly a prerequisite for enforcement. In the case of reputational sanctions, involving an international court had no discernable impact one way or another on the public's inclination to update their beliefs about the trustworthiness of foreign countries. The lesson is that we need not always look for solutions involving enforcement from above through empowering international courts or similar bodies. Reactions of the public to international commitments of various stripes suggests alternative pathways of enforcement that instead start from below and build upwards.

The findings also raise interesting questions about the current and future status of the international legal architecture. In recent years, there has been much handwringing over the weakness of many treaties, and the need for updates or negotiating entirely new instruments. In the laws of war, there have been calls for a "Geneva 2.0" to replace the 1949 Geneva Conventions, or dedicated treaties dealing with emerging technologies like drones or automated weapons systems.[9] In light of the logistical hurdles in concluding new treaties, softer commitments hold the potential to make meaningful headway in curbing or at least helping to regulate these new areas. Setting aside a "treaty-or-bust" model, more attention could instead be devoted to the precise language and terms of an instrument (whether of harder or softer form), which could go further in fulfilling its functions. Likewise, less pressure should be placed on involving international bodies, instead empowering domestic actors to take part in more bottom-up relationships. An approach attuned to popular international law thus opens up new possibilities for thinking about institutional design and the reorientation or repurposing of existing agreements.

Investigating Other Sources and Mechanisms

An additional side benefit of the approach developed in this book comes from a more pragmatic methodological standpoint. The main subjects of popular international law—ordinary members of the public—are often easier to access and analyze than the usual focus on states, leaders, or other elites.[10] The public is not simply a convenient proxy, but an actor that can help better understand a host of questions large and small about how different elements of international law operate. Experimental evidence from chapter 3 offered more direct proof of the reputational consequences of violating international law, in particular the conditions under which these effects can spill over to other issue areas; effects that have been long surmised but difficult to ascertain using formal modeling or observational data alone.[11] Other areas could similarly benefit from incorporating evidence and perspectives from the ordinary public.

One particularly fruitful area concerns the study of customary international law. While occupying a prominent place in much legal thinking, systematic empirical studies of customary laws are sorely lacking.[12] One of the biggest obstacles is simply being able to identify the presence, much less strength, of customary laws compared to treaties, where the latter are written down, ratified, deposited, and contain other clearer markers. These difficulties are particularly pronounced in customary law's criteria of *opinio juris* ("opinion of law"), where actors must hold the belief that they are legally obligated to follow a rule. Instead of only relying on indirect measures of state preferences and practices, scholars can query the public for evidence of their beliefs and how these may reflect and reinforce customary obligations.

Precedent already exists in the canon of international law for taking seriously the lawmaking capacity of the ordinary masses. The 1899 Hague Convention, which represents one of the earliest multilateral codifications of the modern laws of war, also contained an important popular element. In what became known as the "Martens Clause" for the Russian delegate Friedrich Martens, who proved pivotal for its inclusion, the preamble stressed that belligerents were bound by "the laws of humanity and the requirements of the public conscience" in the case of any legal gaps in the convention's provisions. While the "public conscience" can be interpreted in different ways, one emphasis is on members of the public in a concrete sense.[13] Attention to the public would not always mean evidence in favor of a given custom; sometimes just the opposite could happen with the weakening or change to customary laws, as some of the mixed evidence on attitudes toward torture or drones from chapters 5 and 6 indicates. Just as work on the robustness or death of international norms points to the importance of taking societal attitudes seriously,[14] a popular international law approach emphasizes the need to be sensitive to the role of the public in customary rules as well.

Alongside understudied sources of law, attention to the public may contribute to research on other functions of international law not covered in as much detail in this book. Matters of enforcement as discussed in several chapters are mostly backward-looking in terms of whether countries face ex post costs for breaching their prior commitments. A related question is whether international law can serve as a forward-looking commitment device, signaling to audiences the country's capabilities or willingness to credibly abide by its promises. These credibility effects may partly be a function of anticipated ex post costs from reputation or other enforcement mechanisms, where the prospect of punitive sanctions deter an actor from engaging in violations. But credibility may also work through ex ante signals sent by the upfront costs or other elements of the initial commitment process.[15] For instance, hurdles to ratification are higher for some countries or for certain types of agreements than others, which could provide different signals of their relative credibility. On the other hand, if legal commitments can transform underlying preferences as suggested by chapter 5 and 6, then legalized commitments may change expectations, irrespective of ex ante or ex post costs. A debate continues over whether international laws screen beforehand, constrain afterward, involve a combination of both, or even some other dynamics.[16] Using experimental data involving the public offers a way to more directly control and manipulate both screening, constraining, and other elements to identify the presence and specific drivers of international law as a commitment device.

Advantages from a greater appreciation of the public in popular international law are not limited to experimental designs. Much of this book focused on the contemporary public over the last few decades, but the implications of popular international law may extend much further back in time. Several insightful histories of the law of nations have been written, but primarily from the perspective of leaders, lawyers, and other elites.[17] The story of the early law of nations seems primarily composed of countries and their rulers with little space for anyone else. In certain respects, attention to elites makes sense, since particular voices, such as "highly qualified publicists," are built directly into the main sources of international law.[18] This discussion on other sources like customary law suggests that voices from the public may have something useful to say for the present as well as the past. Even during earlier periods seemingly dominated by esteemed figures, popular influences were not always far away. Speaking of different legal considerations heading into the attempted reconstruction of the post–World War I legal order, the British attorney general Frederick E. Smith commented that "These things are very easy to understand, and ordinary people all over the world understand them very well."[19] The role of both international law and the public in the First World War may have been subsequently forgotten in ways both deliberate and by happenstance, but does not mean that both cannot be revived. In a similar manner to recent treatments that incorporate marginalized actors outside of the usual Anglo-European players,[20] an "international legal history from below" would provide a welcome inclusion of more peripheral actors like mass publics in key moments and across a longer timeline. One way to read some of the early key works on popular constitutionalism was as a reappraisal of the historical place of ordinary people from the early operation of the US Constitution onward.[21] Historicizing popular international law would similarly seek to offer a chance for investigating the place of ordinary members of nations in the larger law of nations.

Getting a Passport: Overseeing Overseas Publics and Other Actors

Another limit openly acknowledged from the start, but which also presents an opportunity, is the focus of this book mostly on the United States. As a powerful country with a long-running streak for isolationism and distrust of foreign entanglements, the United States presents a particularly difficult case for international legal appeals. Yet just because we find significant effects for international law among the US public across a range of situations and functions does not mean we should automatically conclude that similar or greater effects should hold for other citizenries.

More in-depth cross-national work on international law, especially concerning national publics, is small but growing. What exists so far does not point in any clear direction regarding the generalizability of this book's findings to other countries. The case study in chapter 4 examining reactions to US violations in the War on Terror suggests foreign publics very much are able to think in legal terms and respond in ways consistent with popular international law, such as facilitating enforcement. In other work on policy preferences, I find the ways real-world knowledge of international law shapes attitudes toward wartime conduct carry over to other national contexts facing legacies of armed conflict where such issues loom especially large.[22] More recent data on global attitudes toward the United States and its leaders also appear to contain significant legal components. Overall international confidence in former President Donald Trump during his final year in office leading up to the 2020 election was anemic, but some of the harshest condemnation was reserved for policies viewed as contrary to international legal rules, such as unilateral trade protectionism and withdrawal from the Paris Climate Accord.[23] Favorability toward the former president only improved among more reactionary segments of foreign publics—in other words those sharing his skepticism toward international commitments.

Support for legal mechanisms have found a welcome reception among societal actors in such challenging circumstances as postapartheid South Africa and post-conflict Yugoslavia.[24] Even secessionist rebel groups, despite or perhaps because they are challenging existing territorial boundaries, have shown a particular affinity for abiding by the laws of war in an attempt to bolster their legitimacy.[25] In those cases where public opinion in the United States is directly compared to other countries, considerations of international law are often of comparable (and sometimes even greater) magnitude for foreign publics.[26] Findings from this book based on the United States would seem to bode well for contemplating a similar international legal role for other national publics.

Yet the United States is not unique in its distribution of legal preferences, with other countries containing sizable "pro-violation" constituencies of their own.[27] Abstract appeals of international law may diminish when ordinary people of any nationality are faced with the direct prospect of their own leaders or citizens being targeted by international tribunals, as demonstrated by a recent study looking at the aftermath of violence in Kyrgyzstan.[28] A confrontational stance against international legal proceedings can even become part of a winning electoral strategy for some governments.[29] Genocidal policies against the Rohingya minority starting in 2016 in Myanmar may have been damaging to the ruling regime's international reputation as it faced condemnation and a range of sanctions. But the image of Nobel Peace Prize laureate Aung San Suu Kyi rejecting these charges and defending her country's actions at the International Court of Justice turned out to be immensely popular back home. Despite continued international scrutiny, her ruling party, the National League for Democracy, was not punished domestically and in the subsequent 2020 general election achieved a commanding majority (even if this success was short-lived with a military coup the following year). Support for international law among foreign publics is thus far from guaranteed, especially when other considerations are at play.

Existing research paints a rather complicated picture of the relationship between different publics and international law. In other collaborative work related to cross-national attitudes toward repression, I found that international law can have a constraining effect, no impact, or even enable support for violence depending on the particular national context.[30] The specific conditions and pathways through which international law shapes public opinion remain open theoretical and empirical questions. Comparative work on popular constitutionalism provides hints of the intellectual road to follow. For instance, whether compliance with constitutional limits impacts the credibility of political leaders in the eyes of their publics will depend on the latter's "particular normative stance toward law."[31] Determining whether compliance with international legal obligations will have reputational consequences among foreign publics similarly requires delving into the deeper place and understanding of legal principles among these different societal actors.

Beyond the particular opinions held by foreign publics, a comparative approach also calls for investigating more closely the role of institutional and other domestic features that shape how much different national populations actually matter in legal and policy processes. This has implications across democratic systems, as well as for various nondemocracies where the masses are further removed from power but with different "audiences" drawn from upper echelons being more or less influential.[32] Either instance involves incorporating the role of elites relative to publics in international law, which could come back to offer useful lessons for similar questions in the US context. While some research suggests important gaps between public and elite preferences, other work indicates the two groups are closer in their foreign policy views than commonly assumed.[33] If the two correspond closely, then looking at public opinion would have something useful to say about elite dynamics, even if more work remains to be done. Ultimately, a cross-national framework for popular international law necessitates paying more attention to comparisons in national context and how legal principles are received and acted upon by ordinary (and less ordinary) members of these communities.

Taking Stock: Backlash and Populism in Perspective

Speaking of possible differential effects for international law across other countries raises a related concern about changes over time or among certain groups in their receptiveness to international legal rules. Recent years have witnessed not only skepticism but increasingly outright resistance toward international laws on many fronts. The question may not be so much whether foreign commitments matter, but rather whether they are on net doing more harm than good in terms of the responses they are provoking.[34] Backlash against the legalization of world affairs is not new, especially toward international courts often viewed as meddlesome, issuing rulings from high above with little consideration to local sensibilities.[35] Yet opposition to the international legal order seems to be intensifying in its pace, breadth, and depth. Indications of disenchantment among both elites and the populace can be seen across a range of countries, from the Brexit referendum to leave the European Union to Burundi's exit from the ICC.

We do not need to look even this far afield, as the United States has in many ways been at the vanguard of the backlash. The 2016 election of Trump to the White House was widely seen as a watershed. Stoking grievances around trade, immigration, and cultural divides, one of the constants of his campaign and later presidency was a wholesale attack on the global rule of law, where "President Trump and his supporters appear to hold international institutions and agreements almost in contempt."[36] It is too easy to assign all the credit (or blame) to a single person for these developments, as misgivings about the liberal international order had been festering within many segments of US society. A multitude of labels have been proposed to distill the essence of these animating forces in the United States and elsewhere, but a growing consensus has settled on "populist" as most apt.[37] Backlash against international law and institutions can be seen as an outgrowth of populism gaining traction in the United States and many other countries.[38]

Settling on what exactly constitutes populism is difficult because it remains "a notoriously vague term" leading to many different meanings.[39] One of the most widely accepted defines populism as "an ideology that considers society to be ultimately separated into two homogenous and antagonistic groups, the 'pure people' and 'the corrupt elite,' and which argues that politics should be an expression of the *volonté générale* (general will) of the people" (emphasis in original).[40] Populist leaders assert their legitimacy is derived from embodying the true wishes of the people, irrespective of (or in purposeful opposition to) existing structures of authority.[41] That populists should be unencumbered by domestic institutional or normative constraints, it follows that they and their adherents would show little respect for international rules. Linguistically and conceptually, populism and popular international law would seem to be uncomfortably close in their respective emphases on "the people." Rather than serving as an important actor in the operation of the international legal order, populism seems to suggest that the people would take an active part in its weakening and eventual destruction.

To resolve some of these tensions, we can look to how populism has been evaluated in the context of another body of law and scholarship that informed the approach taken in this book—constitutional law and popular constitutionalism. At first sight, not much would appear to separate populism from popular constitutionalism. Some of the early critiques of popular constitutionalism in fact argued it would descend into a populist form of governance with constitutional rules at the mercy of whatever was espoused by the tyranny of the majority.[42] Early proponents of popular constitutionalism did not help their case by sometimes remaining unclear about the nature of legal commitments underlying the public's beliefs and preferences.[43]

Despite these seeming connections, there are several reasons why popular constitutionalism (and by extension popular international law) does not fit closely with, and in many respects runs counter to, populist impulses. Although ordinary people figure prominently in both accounts, there are fundamental differences in the way legal obligation shape preferences and interactions. Populism remains a "thin-centred ideology" disconnected from any deeper beliefs, legal or otherwise, and as a result tends toward a rejection of constitutional rules and protections.[44] Under popular constitutionalism, the people may play a prominent role, but their beliefs are still informed and shaped by a basic commitment to domestic legal obligations. The history of many social movements has been typified not by a repudiation of constitutional rules, but rather citizens' understanding of their centrality, and the use of opinion and activism to more fully express and give effect to those rules.[45] Often targeted are domestic institutions and elites to better guarantee and uphold basic rights and obligations, rather than attempts to undermine the entire legal edifice.[46] While populism largely denies the relevance of laws for the people, popular forms of legalism (constitutional and international) see the people as inhabiting a normative space where considerations over what is lawful and unlawful are always present, even if their exact nature and boundaries are subject to contestation and change.[47]

Another important difference between populism and popular international law lies in the practical place of ordinary people. The thinness of populism is manifested by constant sloganeering around "the people," but with little actual agency granted to ordinary members of society. The "myth of global populism" is that populist leaders invoke a general will all the while centralizing authority as part of a move toward more authoritarian rule.[48] Popular constitutionalism and popular international law do not view ordinary people as the sole actors; they are part of a broader conversation with elites and other institutions. This stands in contrast to the one-way broadsides by populist leaders claiming to be acting in the people's interest, but where the people themselves act very little. Of course, populism and populist projects do not arise in a vacuum—Brexit and the 2016 US presidential election had important antecedents. Combating populism, however, lies not in relying on other elites or technocrats—however, constitutionalist, internationalist, or well-meaning they may be—as this would only reinforce the narrative populist leaders desire to spread. Rather, greater faith can be placed in "the people," rousing offsetting impulses that serve as a bulwark for the rule of law domestically and internationally.

Traces of a continued general attachment to international rules and institutions can be found in the period of populism's supposed ascent and backlash against the international legal order. These trends are evident even in the United States, where Trump was able to marshal populist forces against foreign commitments such that there were frequent pronouncements that his ideology of "'America First' has won," with consequences outlasting his presidency.[49] Legal scholars of different stripes could agree that the Trump administration represented an "onslaught" engaged in "efforts to break, stretch, or violate international law."[50] A portion of the US electorate certainly seemed to follow in lockstep Trump's approach of unilateral trade policies, dismissing protections for refugees, and other conduct denigrating international obligations.

As vocal as these segments may be, they remained a fairly small minority compared to the bulk of attitudes among the US citizenry toward international law and institutions. While Trump regularly denounced the UN as weak and incompetent, US public approval for the organization actually improved slightly during his presidency, continuing a trend stretching back more than a decade.[51] The wider public further parted ways with Trump on several of the former president's signature foreign policy stances. Almost two-thirds believed the United States should have stayed in the Iran nuclear deal.[52] In retrospect, most US citizens were not sold on the merits of leaving this or other agreements; sizable majorities later favored rejoining the Iran agreement, alongside reversing other exits like from the Paris Climate Accord.[53]

Organizations and agreements consistently lambasted by Trump and other elites have been greeted with greater receptivity by the wider citizenry. In a time when the Trump administration placed sanctions against ICC officials, overall public support only proceeded to grow for developing a more cooperative relationship with the Court.[54] And just as the US trade war was heating up against China and other countries, over half of the US public generally approved of free trade agreements with a plurality expressing skepticism toward unilaterally raising tariffs.[55]

To be sure, there are important differences among members of the US public toward international agreements, with partisanship playing a prominent role. But on some general principles toward international institutions, Democrats and Republicans are not always that far apart and can find common ground. More constant has been a general underestimation by government leaders and other elites of the US public's willingness to support international law and institutions, and their country's place within this system.[56]

Listening more closely to ordinary people outside one's own narrow coalition would reveal a more complex picture regarding attitudes toward international law that are far from reflecting a uniformly populist ethos. The 2020 presidential election is a case in point that can be read a few different ways for what it says about public attitudes toward international law and institutions. Foreign policy was not the only issue on the ballot, but the outcome was a stern rebuke of Trump's overall approach, denying reelection to a sitting US president for only the fourth time in the previous century. Positioning himself as a more internationalist candidate willing to (re)commit to a range of agreements, Democratic nominee Joe Biden garnered more votes (over eighty-one million) than any previous presidential candidate. In contrast, with over seventy-four million votes of his own, Trump collected the second most votes in history, showing that his comportment and policies did not turn off a sizable share of the electorate. The public is not a monolith, and confrontations among these different perspectives are likely to persist. What the preceding years have shown is that the people will play an important role in the direction the country takes toward its legal commitments at home and abroad.

Populist pressures pushing for a backlash certainly exist and will likely endure in some form, but counteracting forces among members of the public show an important place for international law and institutions. Populist attacks on international law have often failed due to a lack of coherent worldview necessary for building a longer-lasting opposition movement.[57] A *popular* international law giving voice to the beliefs and preferences of ordinary people is not an inherent invitation to populism and backlash, but may instead present a source for reestablishing a deeper sense of personal obligation and commitment toward international legal principles in the United States and elsewhere.

Keeping Alert: Potential Downsides to (International) Law

Taking seriously the dangers posed by backlash taps into deeper concerns about the proper place of international law in international and domestic societies. Objections to particular international laws are not always driven by nationalism, nativism, or knee-jerk populist abhorrence of legal rules. What is "legal" and what is "just" do not always neatly overlap, and can sometimes be in direct tension. Criticisms may say more about problems contained in the law itself rather than any deficiencies in the thinking or interests of opponents.

First, far from reflecting a cooperative spirit and forever bending toward egalitarianism, the longer arc of legal history points to how laws at all levels can be a source of worsening inequality, reinforcing the privileges of the powerful.[58] At home in the United States, domestic laws have been frequently deployed to perpetuate white supremacy and racial hierarchy, even under supposedly "progressive" policies of the New Deal era.[59] Beyond broken promises, the history of US treaties with Native American tribes was one of institutionalizing dispossession and marginalization.[60] Nowhere are these forces more evident than with the founding documents of the US republic. Commitment to "Life, Liberty, and the pursuit of Happiness" in the initial Declaration of Independence severely circumscribed to whom it applied, as the Constitution subsequently entrenched the institution of slavery through the notorious Three-Fifths and Fugitive Slave Clauses.[61] The Fourteenth Amendment of 1868 would eventually formally abolish slavery, but did little to prevent the subsequent use of Jim Crow laws to reassert white dominance in the South, and also contained the seeds allowing the spread of modern mass incarceration that systematically targeted communities of color.[62]

Similar dynamics are evident in the history of international law, which may be more soberly viewed "as a regime and discourse of domination and subordination, not resistance and liberation."[63] Agreements from the 1494 Treaty of Tordesillas between Spain and Portugal to the 1848 Treaty of Guadalupe Hidalgo ending the Mexican-American War were meant not to free oppressed people, so much as promote further subjugation through legalizing colonialism and conquest. Many of the rules examined in this book—from the laws of war to territorial nonaggression—may be seen as seeking to constrain certain undesirable actions. Even in these cases, however, what is desirable or undesirable is a matter of perspective. The territorial integrity norm, enshrined in the UN Charter and other instruments, has played an important function in stabilizing borders and reducing the risk of disputes.[64] But the norm ingrained a status quo often reflecting past conquests and the interests of existing states to the detriment of various self-determination movements facing an increasingly fixed international political geography. So too the laws of war may have constrained certain tactics or weapons, but killing could still be permitted or even enabled in ways advantageous to the powerful. In the First World War, much of the carnage was technically consistent with prevailing rules, such that many sought to reject a body of "law [that] got separated from some of the real causes of moral concern."[65]

At a more fundamental level, from the extremes of the battlefront to day-to-day living on an ostensibly more peaceful home front, there is an inherent violence connected to the law. Speaking of criminal law, but in ways that can be generalized to the enforcement function of domestic and international laws, the legal scholar Robert Cover (author of one of the epigraphs to this chapter) remarked that "Legal interpretation takes place in a field of pain and death."[66] Lacking a privileged place, ordinary people too often become subject to the whims of this system of legal violence. In many cases, their beliefs and actions may only serve to reinforce an order that undermines their core needs.

In addition to more purposeful built-in inequities, a second concern is that these rules can have further unforeseen consequences. As I initially put forward in chapter 1, international law should not be defined solely by its effects, but those impacts can nonetheless counteract what may have been originally intended. Greater legalization is not always an unalloyed good, and can lead to perverse incentives, such as trade agreements empowering protectionist interests.[67] More legalized rules can also encourage actors to engage in evasive behavior in ways that create policies farther from underlying normative goals.[68] Attraction to evasion is endemic in the laws of war, where the spread of legal obligations may have had the paradoxical effect of leading many governments to take active steps to avoid those same obligations, such as by refusing to declare war or conclude formal peace treaties.[69]

Evasive tendencies may be most prone by those with more intimate knowledge of legal technicalities, and how they can exploit them for their own interests. After all, in *The Devil's Dictionary*, the nineteenth-century US writer Ambrose Bierce chose to define a "Lawyer—One skilled in circumvention of the law."[70] The elastic nature of what counted as torture in the War on Terror illustrates the complicated role of lawyers, at times constraining but also advancing harsh interrogation techniques.[71] Ordinary people may also be willing to avoid legal obligations at times (taxes being a perennial example). But there may be benefits to commoners' less technocratic understandings of legal obligations, which can foster more genuine beliefs in core principles like pacta sunt servanda ("promises must be kept") to an extent not shared by their elite counterparts.

A third concern that builds on the prior two involves a separate danger of a narrowness in thinking resulting from overly strong attachments to the law. Through its particular attributes, international law may indeed be able to exert a "compliance pull,"[72] but this is not necessarily a welcome development if the law's substance is itself problematic for the reasons discussed above. Closely following the letter of the law should not be an end in itself, and may actually be orthogonal to furthering the actual policy goals at stake. The gap between what the law says and what is needed on the ground may only expand as circumstances change while legal provisions remain fixed.

Domestically, some legal scholars talk of a "constitutional faith," a "wholehearted attachment to the Constitution as the center of one's (and ultimately the nation's) political life."[73] Yet this healthy bond can easily descend into a "cult of the Constitution,"[74] valuing legal principles above all others. A similar tension exists in popular constitutionalism over the proper place of constitutional rules, the menace of an overly restrictive reverence among citizens toward a single document, and how they in turn navigate situations where broader values may come into conflict with existing rules. Popular international law must grapple with these same tensions between publics and their relationships toward international agreements that may be more foul than fair.

Violence may be at the heart of any legal system, but the control law exerts can manifest itself through more diffuse channels. When law is described as an "empire," it is not only through sovereign force, but the ways legal rules infuse all aspects of how actors define their interests and their very sense of selves, collectively creating "liegemen to its methods and ideals, bound in spirit while we debate what we must therefore do."[75] A particular legal consciousness can take root among actors, restricting their thoughts and actions in furtherance of the narrower demands of the legal system.[76]

Legal consciousness is generally conceived in rather critical terms over how the law can subtly but inextricably reinforce inequalities and the hegemony of circumscribed legal thinking.[77] Although legal consciousness may influence all sorts of actors—regular and elite alike—there are reasons to be cautiously upbeat about the role of the public in countering some of these tendencies. Ordinary people may not have the training or technical acumen of leaders, judges, or lawyers, but this might be viewed as an asset not a liability. When important rights and obligations are at stake, other work has shown that ordinary individuals often make better evaluations and arrive at fairer decisions than more esteemed experts.[78] This applies equally to foundational documents like the Constitution, which President Franklin D. Roosevelt described in ways relevant to this day as a "layman's instrument of government," countering "those who would shrivel the Constitution into a lawyer's contract."[79] International treaties are likewise pored over by international lawyers, often claiming their content as beyond the grasp of mass publics. But agreements like the UN Charter or the Geneva Conventions are likewise perhaps better viewed as laypersons' instruments of international governance. More seriously incorporating ordinary people's voices may not be a hindrance, but rather help achieve the aspirations at the heart of these and other agreements.

Closing Thoughts: The Promise of (International) Law and the People

In closing, I wish to return to the final thoughts in the introductory chapter expressing hope that a book mostly about international law might still have something useful to say about the operation of law more broadly. That constitutional and international laws are somehow intertwined has been a driving assumption in the preceding pages. Exactly how these two bodies of law are related to one another, and whether this should be viewed in a positive or negative light, is more hotly debated. Table C.1 outlines four general relationships possible between international and constitutional laws, with different combinations of either body of law being stronger or weaker. These are meant to be ideal types and could operate to varying extents for particular countries, across specific issues, or for respective legal systems as a whole. Each cell represents a way of tying international and domestic laws together, but with very different ramifications.

The upper-left cell is occupied by those who see little impact of law—either domestic or international—on policies or outcomes. These skeptics may agree that international and constitutional laws are structurally similar, in particular the absence of a higher enforcement authority, but this leads them to conclude both sets of rules are largely irrelevant in the face of actors' preexisting power and interests.[80] Legal considerations simply do not enter into the equation when actors are navigating either within or outside their own national borders.

The opposite lower-right cell is where the overall approach taken in this book more closely fits—that constitutional and international laws both matter in some meaningful way even if important limits and caveats remain. The exact relationship between the two bodies of law could be more or less cooperative or conflictual, but the main thrust is that both are tied together structurally and in their operation. Various actors could also be more or less emphasized, but the popular international law framework put forward in this book is that just as ordinary people can play an important role in the operation of constitutional rules, so too can they play an important role in fulfilling international commitments. The multilevel legal system that results is one where both sets of laws are ultimately related to and reinforce one another.

The last two cross-cutting cells are suggestive of a more substitutive relationship between international and domestic laws, though this too can be read a few different ways. On a more constructive front, countries with weak domestic legal systems may turn to "preeminent" international laws in the manner of the upper-right cell to make their commitments more credible or pursue policy objectives that would be difficult otherwise. For instance, countries with less robust domestic judiciaries have been shown to be more willing to join the ICC in order to provide stronger assurances that war criminals will be held accountable.[81] Along similar lines, newly democratic countries have used international agreements to try to "lock in" institutions and policies during the democratizing process when

TABLE C.1 Relationships between international law and constitutional law

		INTERNATIONAL LAW	
		WEAK	STRONG
CONSTITUTIONAL LAW	WEAK	Legal irrelevance	Global legal preeminence
	STRONG	National legal ultra-sovereignty	Multilevel legalism

they are especially vulnerable to internal counterthreats and backsliding.[82] While international laws may initially step in for weaker domestic institutions, the longer-term expectation is that global preeminence will subside as domestic legal systems eventually strengthen so that both sets of laws are operating in a more complementary fashion. Capacity building is inserted into many international agreements for the expressed purpose of supplying resources to institutionally weaker countries for improving domestic compliance systems.[83] Over the longer term, international and domestic laws may then gradually reinforce each and shift to the lower-right cell of a multilevel legal order.

Others see something more nefarious at work in the possible interrelationship between international and domestic laws, and consequently the need to keep the two far apart and on unequal terms. A strain of scholarship in the United States (but also elsewhere) contends that international laws are fundamentally at odds with domestic legal values. For them, the choice is largely between one of the two cross-cutting cells from table C.1—either an "ultra-sovereign" national legal system where domestic rules are always paramount (lower-left cell), or a necessarily more depraved one dominated by global rules (upper-right cell). The supposed "perils of global legalism" come from the latter possibility of according too paramount a place to international law, generating confusion with domestic laws and ruinous costs for governments and their citizens.[84] When denouncing international agreements, some critics do so out of the fear that international rules will supplant domestic ones.[85] An even more fundamental menace posed by international law is to the attachment of leaders all the way down to ordinary citizens toward their own constitutions and national laws.[86] According to this logic, as allegiance to the Constitution falls, a country becomes increasingly vulnerable to international laws contrary to core domestic principles. This was part of the logic behind a draft executive order under the Trump administration calling for an embargo on any new multilateral treaties, charging that "treaties are used to force countries to adhere to often radical domestic agendas that could not, themselves, otherwise be enacted in accordance with a country's domestic laws."[87]

In this zero-sum legal vision, any influence gained by international laws— often depicted as being of an outside, alien, or hybrid character—must come at the expense of longstanding national laws. Rather than mutually reinforcing, international laws are seen as a direct threat to the sanctity and vitality of national legal systems.[88]

Concerns over the substantive content of international laws and how they fit with domestic rules are reasonable, harkening back to the potential downsides of certain legal rules discussed in the prior section. The solution, however, is not necessarily to completely reject foreign commitments for some "ultra" vision of national legal sovereignty (lower-left cell), as this comes with its own risks.

There is a certain irony that some of those same critics of international law have at other times questioned whether constitutions too can or should offer any real constraints.[89] The bigger threat appears to the rule of law more generally at *both* the international and domestic levels.

International and domestic laws are interconnected—what actors think and do in one legal sphere have implications for the other. Rather than operating separately, constitutional and international laws are better viewed as "conjoined efforts to regulate the sovereign state from an 'internal' and 'external' perspective."[90] The danger of attacking laws internationally is that it may lead to similar corrosive pressures against laws domestically. The rise of populist leaders and movements is just one such manifestation that is perhaps best seen as comprehensively anti-legalist.[91] Rejections of international legal agreements may thus carry over into questioning the status of domestic legal principles as well.

Where do ordinary people fit into this discussion? In either embracing or spurning (anti) legal appeals, the public can play a pivotal role in shaping the future of both domestic and international legal systems. A more commonsense approach to legal questions suggests publics have a decent understanding of the stakes involved. As the Cold War ground on, the legal scholar Francis Boyle recognized the role of the US public in the interrelationship between international and domestic laws in ways not always appreciated by their leaders:

> The American people have never been willing to provide sustained popular support for a foreign policy that has flagrantly violated elementary norms of international law precisely because they have habitually perceived themselves to constitute a democratic political society governed by an indispensable commitment to the rule of law in all sectors of their national endeavors.[92]

Looking at the current moment and to the future, this represents a qualified defense for the importance of the public. Much room still appears left open for ordinary people to perhaps condone less "sustained" endeavors or less "flagrant" violations. Publics are far from perfect in upholding legal commitments, showing themselves willing to be swayed by more instrumental considerations toward approving at times quite egregious acts.[93] Even when people's thinking may be consistent with more legal reasoning, their awareness of concrete laws may also leave something to be desired.[94]

Keeping these qualms in mind, the standard should not be whether the public always makes the "right" choice, since the historical record of leaders and other elites toward legal commitments is far from glowing. The question is instead whether ordinary people can sufficiently appreciate legal principles and bring a useful perspective to an area dominated for too long by a small coterie. This book offers some initial thoughts, but more work is needed to understand how popular attitudes toward *both* international and constitutional laws are formed and interact with each other alongside other contextual factors, and how these in turn reinforce or undermine the operation of legal rules of various sorts.[95]

As the legal scholar Lon L. Fuller remarked, "if law exists at all, it exists imperfectly—it is still in the process of being born."[96] A question that arises is who then should play a role in this continual legal work in progress. In this book I have argued that part of the answer lies in paying greater attention to the people—their beliefs, preferences, and actions. In his call for a more prominent place for the public in constitutional affairs, the popular constitutionalist scholar Mark Tushnet concluded, "As [Abraham] Lincoln said, the Constitution belongs to the people. Perhaps it is time for us to reclaim it from the courts."[97] The law of nations may have begun as something belonging more to kings, queens, and emperors—a set of rules even Lincoln once claimed was beyond his grasp. But over time these laws have spread in ways that include ordinary individuals as objects and increasingly subjects possessing their own agency. A closing corollary for popular international law, and a more prominent place for the public in international legal commitments, goes as follows: *International law belongs to the people. Perhaps it is time for us to reclaim it from states and international courts.*

Notes

INTRODUCTION

1. Billias 2009, xv. Though on the US Constitution's waning appeal, see Law and Versteeg 2020.

2. Fassbender 1998.

3. The extreme steps the US government has taken to protect the Constitution and other founding documents point to the tangible value attached to the parchment itself and the ideals articulated (Puleo 2016).

4. Zelikow 1996, 6; Glennon 2001, 2; Weeramantry 2004, 4.

5. Bolton 2000a, 8.

6. Ginsburg, Chernykh, and Elkins 2008.

7. Vanberg 2005, 8–12, 169–73.

8. Staton and Moore 2011.

9. Yoo 2005; Posner and Vermeule 2010.

10. Schwartz 2000, 227.

11. On similarities in the positions of constitutional and international legal skeptics, see Ohlin 2015, 49–50.

12. As one example, Goldsmith and Posner (2005) and Guzman (2008) offer starkly different rational choice accounts (one critical, the other more optimistic) on the effectiveness of international law. Using a rough metric for the relevance of the public, however, neither mentions "public opinion" in their main texts, while references to the "public" as an actor that may have its own interests only show up once in Guzman and a handful of times in Goldsmith and Posner. Both do use "citizens" more frequently, but still relatively sparingly, and often in the context of governments devising international rules that act upon their citizens, rather than as individuals possessing agency. By contrast, almost every single page of both books contains references to "states," "governments," or various leaders and elites. See accompanying Supplementary Online Materials for a fuller content analysis of these and several other prominent works on international law.

13. Kelsen 1948, 89. See also Oppenheim 1908, 322.

14. Goldsmith and Posner 2005; Guzman 2008.

15. Hathaway 2022.

16. Raustiala and Slaughter 2002, 540.

17. Beck, Arend, and Vander Lugt 1996.

18. Finnemore 1996; Keck and Sikkink 1998; Goodman and Jinks 2013.

19. Slaughter 2000; Moravcsik 2017.

20. Dai 2007; Simmons 2009.

21. Almond 1950; Lippmann 1955; Morgenthau 1985, 7.

22. Alexander and Solum 2005, 1607.

23. Achen and Bartels 2016, 7, 9.

24. Tushnet 1999; Kramer 2004b.

25. Although not employing the popular constitutionalist label, and with differing views on the relative agency of publics versus elites, see Vanberg 2005, 14; Staton 2010, 13–15.

26. Graber 2013, 103.

27. Simmons 2010, 280.

28. Slaughter Burley 1993; Keohane 1997; Abbott 2004.

29. For a general discussion, see Whytock 2018.

30. Slaughter 1995; Moravcsik 2017.

31. Reus-Smit 2004, 20.

32. Gourevitch 1978.

33. For a similar view on the cross-national diffusion of domestic social policies, though through a different process from more standard enforcement mechanisms for international law, see Linos 2013.

34. Or, as I describe in greater detail in chapter 2, this represents a "second image re-reversed" approach connecting international law to domestic politics.

35. Populism as employed in the contemporary era refers to a wide-ranging set of movements led by political leaders in a variety of countries (e.g., Donald Trump in the United States, Nigel Farage in the United Kingdom, or Viktor Orbán in Hungary) who espouse a skeptical, even disdainful, view of established norms and institutions, including international laws. I return to the question of populism in greater detail in the conclusion.

36. Whytock 2005; Spiro 2006.

37. Bederman 2001, 84–85.

38. Shelton 2000a. This also differs from John Rawls's concept of the "Law of Peoples," where the people are distinct and the state is not directly involved (1999, 23–30).

39. Donnelly 2012, 163.

40. Kramer 2004, 24–29.

41. Morgenthau 1985, 295; Mearsheimer 1994, 13.

42. Ohlin 2015, 50.

43. Auerswald 1999, 476–77; Hyde and Saunders 2020, 364.

44. Tushnet 1999, 194; Kramer 2004, 229.

45. Schattschneider 1960, 2. Though there are tensions in Schattschneider's book on the agency of the masses relative to elites, and the independent ability of the former to become involved in political conflicts.

46. Kertzer 2017.

47. Gaubatz 1996; Lipson 2003. However, see Gartzke and Gleditsch 2004.

48. Risse-Kappen 1991, 483–84.

49. Weiss and Dafoe 2019, 964.

50. Chakravarty 2012.

51. Thompson 1966.

52. Lüdtke 1995.

53. Rachamimov 2002, 4.

54. Tyler 1990; Gibson 2006.

55. Ohlin 2015, 8.

56. Sands 2006, 221.

57. Janis 2010.

58. Kupchan 2020.

59. Fagan and Huang 2019. Though some of this polling can be read a few different ways with US support for the UN fairly stable and even improving in recent years.

60. Drezner 2008.

61. Young and Kearns 2020; Sagan and Valentino 2017.

62. Dunlap Jr. 2001, 18.

63. Kagan 2002, 3.

64. Verba and Nie 1972, 3–5.

65. Bartels 2008, 7.

66. Kang and Powell 2010; Rasmussen, Reher, and Toshkov 2019.

67. Risse-Kappen 1991, 510.

68. Washington's Farewell Address (1796).

69. Henkin 1996, 175.

70. Parent 2011, 34.

71. Ikenberry 2001; Witt 2013.

72. Chaudoin, Milner, and Tingley 2010.

73. Paine 1894, 99.

74. de Tocqueville 1945, 280.

75. In particular, chapters 3 and 5.

76. Downs, Rocke, and Barsoom 1996, 383.

77. On counterfactuals in international law, see Guzman 2008, 22–23. Challenges to causal inference are not unique to international law, but also plague domestic legal studies (Ho and Rubin 2011).

78. Simmons 2010, 292.

79. Chilton and Tingley 2013.

80. Hyde 2015.

81. Croson 2009.

82. Notable examples include Tomz 2008; Chilton 2015; Chapman and Chaudoin 2020.

83. It is important to note that randomization does not mean that groups will be perfectly balanced, but that any differences essentially cancel each other out, creating groups that can be more safely compared. In one general review of the approach, Diana Mutz notes, "The beauty of random assignment is not that it guarantees equivalence between experimental and control groups on all possible variables, but rather that the expected sum of any differences between groups across all variables is zero" (2011, 138).

84. Hyde 2015, 405.

85. Chilton and Linos 2021.

86. McDermott 2002; Mutz 2011, chapter 8.

87. Gaines, Kuklinski, and Quirk 2006, 9–12.

88. Acheson 1963, 15.

89. Kinder and Palfrey 1993, 1.

90. For more general discussions of the value of mixed-method designs in the context of experiments, see McDermott 2011; Mutz 2011, 135, 141; and Dunning 2012, chapter 7.

91. Dahl 1989, 28.

92. Powell 2004, 91.

93. Shklar 1986, 126.

94. Fuller 1969; Hart 2012.

1. WHAT IS INTERNATIONAL LAW AND WHAT DOES IT (SUPPOSEDLY) DO?

1. Epigraph taken from Segal 1961, 114.

2. One of the main concerns was that by invoking the international law of blockade, Lincoln was conceding to the Confederacy status as a coequal belligerent government rather than a group of secessionist rebels. In contrast, countries like Britain and France greatly preferred a blockade, which still afforded them certain rights as neutral nations, rather than the closure of ports under domestic law that would have been more problematic for foreign vessels. For a historical analysis of the available options, see McGinty 2008, 121–25.

3. Underwood 2008, 20–22.

4. This definition draws partly on the work of Arend, though with some important differences that will become apparent later (Arend 1999, 26).

5. Hurd 2017.

6. Though "esteem" should be evaluated in relative terms as the UN has its fair share of detractors across the ideological spectrum (Mearsheimer 1994, 33–34; Barnett 2002).

7. Unlike tomes written about the 1949 Geneva Conventions protecting victims of war, another Geneva Convention negotiated that same year garnered much less attention—the Convention on Road Traffic. Though by coordinating traffic rules, the latter likely played some role in reducing fatalities of a less dramatic sort.

8. The Security Treaty between the United States and Japan was originally negotiated in 1951. An amended version, the Treaty of Mutual Cooperation and Security between the United States and Japan, was concluded in 1960.

9. Bolton 2000a, 4.

10. Young 1980, 332. For a general discussion of the concept of international institutions, see Martin and Simmons 1998.

11. Abbott and Snidal 1998, 9.

12. This definition comes from the English School (Bull 1977, 74).

13. Bull 1977, 57–59, 72–74.

14. Krasner 1982, 186.

15. Though the boundaries of an issue area can be porous when touching upon many disparate endeavors, as evidenced in "regime complexes" like the one governing climate change, which incorporates economic, environmental, and cultural matters, among others (Keohane and Victor 2011).

16. Young 1980, 332

17. For example, Stein 1982; Keohane 1984. Though for a discussion of certain distinctions between the terms, see Haggard and Simmons 1987, 495–96.

18. Finnemore and Sikkink 1998, 891.

19. This partly helps to explain how different scholars can sometimes use "norms" and "institutions" when referring to outwardly similar phenomena (Finnemore and Sikkink 1998, 891).

20. Katzenstein 1996; Crawford 1993.

21. Ruggie 1982.

22. Keohane 1984, 186–87.

23. As one review remarks, "Institutionalization is not a necessary condition for a norm cascade, however, and institutionalization may follow, rather than precede, the initiation of a norm cascade" (Finnemore and Sikkink 1998, 900).

24. Strange 1982, 484–85.

25. Hasenclever, Mayer, and Rittberger 1997.

26. Abbott et al. 2000, 404. The related rational design literature similarly sought to narrow the understanding of international institutions to "explicit arrangements, negotiated among international actors, that prescribe, proscribe, and/or authorize behavior," though acknowledged this definition remained "relatively broad" (Koremenos, Lipson, and Snidal 2001, 762–63).

27. Barnett and Finnemore 1999; Abbott and Snidal 1998.

28. Kratochwil and Ruggie 1986, 771–74.

29. For a general discussion, see Arend 1996. The same can be said for the general concept of "law" (Hart 2012, 1–17).

30. Bull 1977, 128.

31. McDougal and Lasswell 1959, 120.

32. Kennedy 1980, 367.

33. Krasner 1982, 186.

34. Bull 1977, 54.

35. Keohane 1984, 58. Even using specificity to differentiate norms from rules is not fail-safe, as rules (and laws) can be more or less precise, which represents one of the main dimensions of legalization to be discussed later (Abbott et al. 2000, 412–13). Keohane acknowledges that "The rules of a regime are difficult to distinguish from its norms; at the margin, they merge into one another" (Keohane 1984, 58).

36. Hart 2012, 80–81.

37. Hart 2012, 80.

38. Burke 1999, 126.

39. Abbott et al. 2000, 401–2.

40. Hart 2012, 82–91.

41. Fuller 1969, 46–80; Franck 1990, 166–94.

42. Tyler 1990, 19–27.

43. Finnemore 2000, 703–4.

44. Krasner 1982, 186.

45. Finnemore and Sikkink 1998, 900.

46. Tannenwald 2007. However, some question even the existence of a more informal nuclear taboo (Press, Sagan, and Valentino 2013).

47. Arend 1999, 33.

48. Laws can represent one class of "social facts" (Wendt 1999, 75, 280–81, 314–15).

49. Bull 1977, 136.

50. Shaw 2017, 53–66.

51. Brownlie 2008, 4–5.

52. The importance of consent is accepted even by many who see an outsized role for international law. For instance, Henkin remarks, "General law depends on consensus: in principle, new law, at least, cannot be imposed on any state; even old law cannot survive if enough states, or a few powerful and influential ones, reject it" (Henkin 1979, 23). For an overview of both naturalist and positivist approaches, see Beck, Arend, and Vander Lugt 1996, 34–37, 56–59.

53. Shaw 2017, 84–88.

54. The latter's full name indicates tensions in its legal status: "Non-Legally Binding Authoritative Statement of Principles for a Global Consensus on the Management, Conservation and Sustainable Development of All Types of Forests."

55. See, for instance, the contributions to Shelton 2000a.

56. Abbott and Snidal 1998, 408–18.

57. Szasz 1997, 32.

58. Arend 1999, 25.

59. Weil 1983, 423.

60. This is evident in some definitions. Elsewhere, Arend defines international law in part as "a set of binding rules . . ." (1996, 290). While not speaking specifically about the issue of soft law, Bull similarly describes international law as a "body of rules which binds . . ." where "binding" is understood as "legal" (Bull 1977, 127).

61. Franck 1990, 40.

62. On the "law-like promises or statements" of soft law operating along a wider legal continuum, see Guzman and Meyer 2010, 173–74.

63. Shelton 2000b, 10.

64. Lipson 1991, 498–500; Abbott and Snidal 2000, 423; Guzman and Meyer 2010, 176–78.

65. Schachter 1977, 300–301.

66. An equivalent under many domestic laws is that hateful feelings toward certain groups are not directly outlawed, but hate speech or hate-motivated acts are prohibited.

67. Sen 1997, 54–73.

68. Waltz 1979, 114–16; Mearsheimer 1994, 10–12.

69. Oppenheim 1908, 322.

70. Friedmann 1964, 213. Though there are exceptions, such as the EU negotiating and concluding trade agreements collectively on behalf of member states.

71. Manner 1952, 428.

72. See Article 125 of the Third Geneva Convention governing prisoners of war.

73. Moravcsik 2000, 218.

74. Byers 1999, 5 n6.

75. Although I generally refer to national publics as "domestic" actors as shorthand throughout, they should also be considered "internationalized" for conceptual purposes given their status as objects and subjects of international law.

76. Reus-Smit 2004, 23.

77. DiMaggio and Powell 1991, 2. Hart's distinction between primary and secondary rules is relevant on this point. On one level, secondary rules are essential for the proper operation of the primary regulative rules through processes of interpretation, adjudication, and the like. In addition to this regulative-supporting purpose, however, secondary rules also more fundamentally help to define (i.e., constitute) the relevant actors being regulated and doing the regulating (Hart 2012, 94–95).

78. Coggins 2014.

79. See Article 4(2) of the Third Geneva Convention governing prisoners of war.

80. Abbott et al. 2000, 402.

81. Tuchman 1990, 154.

82. Keynes 1920; Boemeke, Feldman, and Glase 1998.

83. Kissinger 1994, 280.

84. Morgenthau 1985, 295; Waltz 1979, 115–16; Mearsheimer 2001, 363–65. This political realism should not be confused with "legal realism." Both see a close relationship between law and politics, but come to very different conclusions on their relative import (Slaughter Burley 1993, 209 n11).

85. Goldsmith and Posner 2005.

86. Glennon 2001, 2.

87. Leeds, Long, and Mitchell 2000, 687.

88. Crandall 1904, 228–29.

89. For instance, see Section 3, and especially Article 33, of the 1969 Vienna Convention on the Law of Treaties.

90. Yoo 2000, 361; Rivkin and Casey 2000, 38.

91. Bolton 2000b, 188–89.

92. Morgenthau 1985, 295.

93. Henkin 1979, 47.

94. Clark and Sohn 1958, xi–xiii.

95. Boyle 1985, 17.

96. Steinberg and Zasloff 2006.

97. Oppenheim 1908, 355.

98. Henkin 1979, 47.

99. Falk 1964, 230 n72.

100. Chayes and Chayes 1993, 176.

101. Fortna 2003.

102. Hull 2014, 42–43.

103. Hathaway and Shapiro 2017, 313–35.

104. Ikenberry 2001, 160–62.

105. Dancy and Fariss 2017; Reus-Smit 2004, 23.

106. Falk 1964, 211.

107. McDougal and Lasswell 1959.

108. Kennedy 1980.

109. Charlesworth, Chinkin, and Wright 1991.

110. Budiansky 1993, 8. However, this unfairly minimizes professional wrestling, where risks to the health and even lives of these "performers" are equal if not greater than their "amateur" counterparts. An additional disservice is done to the cognitive abilities of young children, which can be quite sophisticated (Gopnik, Meltzoff, and Kuhl 1999).

111. Hobbes 1904, 85.

112. Austin 1832, 138.

113. Both quotes are from Austin 1832, 139.

114. It does not appear Claude ever formally published this formulation, but it became a popular phrasing, Arend 1999, 29–31, 39 n59; Rochester 2011, 47–48.

115. Milner 1991, 68.

116. Waters 2015, 136.

117. Waltz 1979, 88.

118. Reus-Smit 2004, 34.

119. Waltz 1979, 115–16.

120. Austin 1832, 145.

121. Acheson 1963, 14. Perhaps somewhat awkwardly, Acheson spoke these words at the annual meeting of the American Society of International Law. His comments were in reference to a vibrant debate over the relevance of international law in US decision-making during the Cuban Missile Crisis, in particular imposing a quarantine around Cuba. For Acheson, questions over the "legality" of these actions under international law were beside the point.

122. Bolton 2000a, 4.

123. Hurd 2015.

124. Hart 2012, 18–25, 38–42.

125. Dunoff and Trachtman 1999, 30. They go on to acknowledge differences between the two forms of law, but stress this goes both ways. For instance, the doctrine of consideration central to the law of contracts, and which aids in distinguishing legally binding agreements from others, has no equivalent under treaty law. Likewise, the place of reservations in treaties has no real counterpart in contract law.

126. Janis 1999, 9.

127. Tyler 1990, 3–4.

128. *Hamdan v. Rumsfeld*, 548 U.S. 557 (2006).

129. *Furman v. Georgia*, 408 U.S. 238 (1972).

130. Vanberg 2005, 17.

131. Structural similarities between international law and constitutional law turn out to be of great theoretical import. Chapter 2 explicitly draws on constitutional theories to better understand the operation of international law.

132. Rabkin 2005, 240–41, 263–70.

133. Oppenheim 1908, 322.

134. Bull 1977, 131.

135. Kelsen 1948, 49.

136. See, for example, Barkun 1968.

137. Carr 1939, 170.

138. Hart 2012, 214.

139. Hart 2012, 237.

140. Others use "primitive" to describe international politics more generally (Masters 1964). Some reject this comparison, pointing out that the constituent units of the modern international legal system are themselves highly institutionalized, even if no higher authority exists (Hoffmann 1968, 24). For a lengthier retort to Hart's view on the relative level of development in the international legal system, see Franck 1990, chapters 11 and 12.

141. Morgenthau 1985, 295. A contemporary, Aron, took a similar tack in ceding to proponents that international law is law, but still one with minor consequences: "Most jurists reply in the affirmative, and I shall not contradict them. I prefer to show differences between kinds rather than deny membership in the same genre" (2003, 110).

142. D'Amato 1984, 1314.

143. Hart 2012, 27–29.

144. D'Amato 1984, 1301.

145. Brierly 1928, 118–19.

146. Bellamy 2012, 1–3.

147. Hoffmann 1968, 27.

148. Morgenthau 1985, 14. Bolton channels this same sentiment: "There is no legal mechanism—no coherent structure—that exists today on a global level to enforce compliance with treaties, a fact international law advocates flatly ignore" (2000a, 5).

149. Carr 1939, 173, 191; Posner 2009, 25–27.

150. Morgenthau 1985, 295.

151. Spinoza 1854, chapter III, paragraph 14.

152. More specifically, Machiavelli writes, "Nonetheless one sees by experience in our times that the princes who have done great things are those who have taken little account of faith and have known how to get around men's brains with astuteness; and in the end they have overcome those who have founded themselves on loyalty" (1998, 69).

153. Morgenthau 1985, 295, 313; Mearsheimer 1994, 15–16. Though the line between issues traditionally deemed "low" versus "high" politics has become increasingly blurred, as problems like climate change take on near-existential overtones.

154. Krasner 1982, 192.

155. Lipson 1993, 12; Chayes and Chayes 1993, 198–200.

156. Aron 2003, 733.

157. D'Amato 1987, 24–25.

158. Kelsen 1948, 23–26.

159. Kelsen 1948, 58.

160. Guzman 2008, 33–34.

161. One important exception is human rights law, which is discussed in greater detail in chapter 5. For an overview of enforcement challenges in human rights, see Simmons 2009, 114–18.

162. For instance, under Article 60(1) of the Vienna Convention on the Law of Treaties, "A material breach of a bilateral treaty by one of the parties entitles the other to invoke the breach as a ground for terminating the treaty or suspending its operation in whole or in part."

163. Downes 2008, 34; Wallace 2015, 46–48.

164. Axelrod 1984, 3; Morrow 2007, 560–62.

165. To differentiate these first two "Rs," reciprocity is characterized by "tit-for-tat," while retaliation involves a "tit-for-a-different-tat" (D'Amato 1984, 1310–12).

166. Bull 1977, 72; Guzman 2008, 46–48.

167. Glennon 2001, 2.

168. Thompson 2013, 510–13; Ohlin 2015, 105.

169. Schachter 1991, 8.

170. Ikenberry 1998; Holquist 2004.

171. Henkin 1979, 52–53.

172. Tomz 2007, 58.

173. Guzman 2008, 42, 46.

174. Credibility is not only a function of ex post enforcement costs, but can be influenced by a variety of other sources (Simmons 2010, 275–77). Although the empirical chapters do not systematically examine the potential of international law to affect ex ante expectations, I return to this additional function in the conclusion.

175. Goldsmith and Posner 2005, 7–10.

176. Fearon and Wendt 2002, 55.

177. Schachter 1991, 7.

178. Ohlin 2015, 50.

179. Swaine 2002; Norman and Trachtman 2005; Guzman 2008.

180. As Henkin remarks, "To adopt some [cost-benefit] formula like that suggested is, of course, the beginning of inquiry, not the end of it" (1979, 50).

181. Dai 2007, 106.

182. Reus-Smit 2004, 20.

183. Checkel 2001, 553; Finnemore and Sikkink 1998, 913–14.

184. Fearon and Wendt 2002, 52; Keohane 1988, 393.

185. Kocs 1994, 538.

186. Simmons 2010, 277.

187. Oppenheim 1908, 355; Hart 1958, 601 n25. Though in later work Hart qualifies his earlier assertion, acknowledging a place for morality in the law (2012, vi).

188. See, in particular, Fuller 1969. In the opening to *Law's Empire*, Ronald Dworkin affirms the connection between law and morality: "There is inevitably a moral dimension to an action at law, and so a standing risk of a distinct form of public injustice" (1986, 1).

189. Boyle 1985, 175; Cassese 1986, 128–57.

190. As Fearon and Wendt remark, "the boundary between preferences and action . . . is relative and unstable. One researcher's preference over outcomes is another researcher's preference over actions" (2002, 64).

191. Goldsmith and Posner 2005, 225.

192. Goldsmith and Posner 2005, 3, 42–43.

193. Mearsheimer 1994, 7.

194. Henkin 1979, 23.

195. Downs, Rocke, and Barsoom 1996, 382–83.

196. For Carr, the direction of causation was clear, "principles were deduced from policies, not the policies from principles" (1939, 73).

197. Witness the aspirations to outlaw war called for in the opening passages of the Kellogg-Briand Pact, the Covenant of the League of Nations, or the Charter of the United Nations, and the subsequent state of armed conflict. Though as discussed earlier, a gap between ambition and practice alone is not necessarily evidence for the weakness of such instruments, while preambles are not always empty words.

198. Aron 2003, 109.

199. Mearsheimer 2001, 364; Gruber 2000, 10.

200. Courts in authoritarian systems are not always judicial rubber stamps, with some gaining sufficient autonomy to exert significant constraints (Moustafa and Ginsburg 2008, 11–14).

201. Schwarzenberger 1964, 198–99.

202. Steinberg 2013, 146.

203. Carr 1939, 172; Morgenthau 1985, 295; Goldsmith and Posner 2005, 3.

204. Thucydides 1996, 352.

205. Ohlin 2015, 50.

206. For a more general discussion of institutions and endogenous preference formation, see Bowles 1998.

207. Fuller 1969, 41. Applying Fuller's framework specifically to international law, see Brunnée and Toope 2010, 6–7, 29–30.

208. Tyler 1990, 19–27.

209. Franck 1990, 193.

210. Finnemore and Sikkink 1998, 904–5.

211. Koh 1996, 2602–3; Risse and Sikkink 1999, 11–17.

2. THE OPERATION OF INTERNATIONAL LAW

1. Hess 1968; Navasky 2013.

2. J. Edwards 1997, 10.

3. For a copy of Petty's cartoon, see Pataki 2020, or https://justiceinconflict.org/2012/08/28/the-us-and-the-icc-why-a-closer-relationship-isnt-necessarily-a-good-thing/.

4. Chapter 4 examines in greater depth the consequences, particularly reputational, for the United States from its conduct during the War on Terror.

5. Singer 1961, 90–91. However, as will become clear, my framework departs from Singer's exhortation not to integrate explanations across levels.

6. Abbott and Snidal 1998.

7. Chaudoin, Milner, and Pang 2015.

8. Milner 1992, 467.

9. Kelsen 1948, 89. For a historical overview of the state-based focus of many philosophers and legal scholars toward international law, see Aron 2003, 111–12.

10. See, for example, Guzman 2008; Goodman and Jinks 2013.

11. Kelsen 1948, 49; D'Amato 1987, 24–25.

12. Waltz 1979, 114–16; Goldsmith and Posner 2005, 5.

13. Axelrod 1984; Keohane 1984; Ohlin 2015, chapter 4.

14. Guzman 2008, 33.

15. Reus-Smit 2004, 32; Goodman and Jinks 2013, 21–28.

16. Checkel 2001, 556.

17. Coplin 1965, 617.

18. Hurd 2007, 3.

19. Cass 2001, 40–42; Alter 2014, 5.

20. Finnemore 1996, 5–13, 89–92.

21. Keck and Sikkink 1998, 16–25. Strictly speaking, the more diffuse transnational processes associated with international NGOs differ in important respects from the top-down influence in usual accounts of intergovernmental organizations. Nevertheless, both share a commonality in looking to actors outside individual state boundaries.

22. Barnett and Finnemore 1999, 710–15.

23. Hawkins et al. 2006.

24. One exception concerns the rise of emanations—international organizations created by existing organizations—but even here states retain significant levers of control (Johnson 2013).

25. Burley and Mattli 1993; Garrett 1995; Alter 1998.

26. Steinberg 2002, 341.

27. Swanson 2019.

28. Hathaway and Shapiro 2011.

29. Parent 2011.

30. Wendt 2003.

31. Voeten 2005; Chapman 2011; Thompson 2006.

32. Voeten 2013.

33. Keohane 1988, 392; McKeown 2009, 8.

34. Putnam 1988, 427.

35. Stein 1982; Keohane 1984.

36. On different variants of Liberalism in international relations theory, see Zacher and Matthew 1995.

37. Moravcsik 1997, 516–21.

38. Slaughter Burley 1993, 226.

39. Moravcsik 2017, 87.

40. Thomas 2002; Dai 2007; Simmons 2009.

41. Reciprocity's tit-for-tat dynamic entails committing acts in kind to push a violator back into compliance. The prospects for reciprocity would seem higher where actions can impose considerable costs on violators, such as with trade (raising barriers against imports from the violator) or wartime conduct (engaging in similar abuses). Reciprocity's path looks rockier for human rights, which involve a government's treatment of its own citizens. It is not clear how a state "reciprocating" by mistreating its *own* citizens entails any costs for a repressive foreign government, and may even be welcomed by the latter as justifying its own actions.

42. Henkin 1979, 235.

43. Simmons 2009, 114.

44. Dai 2005, 364–65.

45. Slaughter 1995, 532.

46. Moravcsik 2017, 96.

47. Milner 1992, 494.

48. Hart 2012, 61.

49. Reisman 1981, 107.

50. Franck 1990, 39–40.

51. Bull 1977, 136.

52. Simmons 2009, 127–29; Brewster 2003, 504.

53. Milner 1997, 70, 106–8; Martin 2000, 23–24. On voters as a "random factor," see specifically Schimmelfennig 2005, 834–36.

54. Slaughter 1995, 524; Koh 1996, 2602; Powell and Staton 2009.

55. Nuñez-Mietz 2016; Arsenault 2017, 85–116.

56. Witt 2013, 3–4. The full name was Instructions for the Government of Armies of the United States in the Field, originally issued as General Orders No. 100 (1863).

57. Keck and Sikkink 1998, 8–10. Also see the earlier discussion on some of the blurring of the lines between transnational mechanisms and other levels of analysis, which is especially relevant for activist organizations operating inside and outside of states.

58. On norm entrepreneurs, see Finnemore and Sikkink 1998, 893; Price 1998, 616. On epistemic communities, see Haas 1989; Adler 1992.

59. Sandholtz 2007, 71.

60. Finnemore 1996, 73–82.

61. Gourevitch 1978, 881–82.

62. Frieden and Rogowski 1996, 31–32.

63. Rose 1998, 151.

64. Gourevitch 1978, 883; Goldstein and Keohane 1993, 11–13.

65. Slaughter and Burke-White 2006, 327.

66. Cortell and Davis 1996.

67. Waltz 1959, 80–85.

68. Moravcsik 2017, 87.

69. Russett 1993; Lake 2009, 225.

70. A related formulation looks at "first image" (reversed), which connects individuals to international forces (and vice versa; Kertzer and Tingley 2018, 329–30). While individual citizens make up national publics, my account is located more at the level of second image theorizing with a focus on collective domestic actors and processes.

71. The nonreductionist neorealism of Kenneth Waltz probably represents one of the purest visions of international factors as paramount (Waltz 1979, 70–78). But for second image reversed approaches accepting a role for domestic factors, see Gourevitch 1978, 882, 900; Rose 1998, 146–47. Correspondingly, on the potential for systemic dynamics to influence the domestic-centered building blocks of second image theorizing, see Lake 2009, 232.

72. Putnam 1988, 427.

73. Abbott 2004, 18–19.

74. Trachtman 2010, 156.

75. This claim thus departs from stronger Liberal assumptions that "Preferences are by definition causally independent of the strategies of other actors and, therefore, prior to specific interstate political interactions, including external threats, incentives, manipulation of information, or other tactics" (Moravcsik 1997, 519).

76. Rathbun 2004, 21–23.

77. On international security, commercial, and legal factors being treated as exogenous, see, respectively, Gourevitch 1978, 898; Frieden and Rogowski 1996, 26; Simmons 2009, 19.

78. von Stein 2005, 611–12.

79. Even the decision to join an agreement is rarely unitary, as multiple veto players influence the ratification process (Lupu 2015).

80. Koremenos, Lipson, and Snidal 2001, 762–63.

81. Schabas 2011, 16–22.

82. Verdier and Voeten 2015. Some actors can matter more in particular issues, such as the 1945 Truman Proclamation claiming national jurisdiction over the surrounding continental shelf. The United States might have been a powerful catalyzing agent in this case, but still depended on the assent of other countries for a new customary law to take hold (Brownlie 2008, 206).

83. The United States signed the Geneva Conventions almost immediately after they were concluded in 1949, formally ratifying them a few years later in 1955.

84. Carr 1939, 170–71; Hoffmann 1968, 27; Bolton 2000a, 5.

85. Simmons 2010, 275.

86. Morgenthau 1985, 295–96.

87. Waltz 1979, 111–12; Wendt 2003, 491–92.

88. Carr 1939, 180.

89. Hyde and Saunders 2020.

90. Weeks 2008; Mattes and Rodríguez 2014.

91. Auerswald 1999; Baum and Potter 2015, 3–4.

92. Moravcsik 2017, 111.

93. Keane 2003.

94. Moravcsik 1997, 518.

95. Trachtman 2010, 156.

96. Goldsmith and Posner 2005, 193.

97. Waltz 1979, 95–96.

98. Nettl 1968, 564; Evangelista 1997, 203.

99. Madison 1791, 14. On Madison's more nuanced thinking regarding the role of the state versus the people, see Kramer 2006.

100. Bull 1977, 129.

101. Kelsen 1948, 10, 89–92.

102. Obama 2014.

103. Biden 2023.

104. Shaw 2017, 53–56.

105. Meron 2000, 83.

106. Wheatley 2010, 353.

107. von Bogdandy, Goldmann, and Venzke 2017, 116.

108. von Bogdandy 2004, 901.

109. Ohlin 2015, 24. Ohlin further notes that the notion of a quasi-sovereign is also present in domestic law, such as the US Supreme Court justice Oliver Wendell Holmes's dissent in *Southern Pacific Company v. Jensen*, 244 U.S. 205, 222 (1917), when describing common law as "not a brooding omnipresence in the sky, but the articulate voice of some sovereign or quasi sovereign that can be identified."

110. Putnam 1988, 432.

111. A similar understanding of "the people" as active agents is evident in the constitutional theory of popular constitutionalism, which will be incorporated in greater detail later in this chapter (Kramer 2001, 11).

112. Solomon and Steele 2017. An emphasis on ordinary people also shares some commonality with feminist approaches to international relations (Enloe 2014, 27).

113. Milner and Tingley 2015, 69–71.

114. Gowa 1998, 307.

115. Druckman and Jacobs 2015, 3–4; Bartels 2008, 252–82.

116. Risse-Kappen 1991, 479–80.

117. Lindsay and Ripley 1992, 422.

118. Kertzer 2016, 50–51.

119. Quoted in Bryce 1909, 364.

120. Quoted in Manning 1848, 248.

121. Thompson 2009, 51–54; Chapman 2011, 106. The role of international law in the Persian Gulf War, especially in contrast to the War on Terror, is examined in further detail in chapter 4.

122. Canes-Wrone 2015, 149–54; Rasmussen, Reher, and Toshkov 2019, 413–14.

123. Tomz, Weeks, and Yarhi-Milo 2020.

124. Graber 1968, 319; Rathbun 2012, 67.

125. Graber 1968, 318. Several of the case studies explicitly involved international legal matters, such as the 1803 Louisiana Purchase, as well as negotiations with France leading to the 1800 Treaty of Mortefontaine ending their two-yearlong Quasi War.

126. Greenberg 2016, 223–29.

127. Gallup 1938, 8–9.

128. Druckman and Jacobs 2015, 43.

129. Jacobs and Shapiro 2000, 7.

130. Searles, Ginn, and Nickens 2016, 950.

131. Halloran 1984, A5.

132. Powell 2003, 148.

133. Great Britain War Office 1958, 173, para. 619.

134. Simmons 2010, 277.

135. Tufte 1978.

136. Aldrich, Sullivan, and Borgida 1989.

137. Kertzer and Zeitzoff 2017, appendix 2.4.

138. Tomz, Weeks, and Yarhi-Milo 2020.

139. Bartels 1991, 467–68.

140. *The Republic of Nicaragua v. The United States of America* (1986 I.C.J. 14). However, the United States refused to participate in the case, nor abide by the ICJ's ruling.

141. Holsti 1992, 453.

142. Neustadt 1990, 185.

143. The legal scholar Pildes defines credibility as "generalized judgments about presidential performance, such as how well motivated the President is considered to be, how effective his or her actions are judged to be, and how wise or prudent his or her judgments are taken to be" (2012, 1387).

144. Rosenbaum 1993, A1.

145. Rivers and Rose 1985, 193. However, on some of the general conceptual and methodological difficulties of estimating the impact of presidential popularity on legislative activity, see G. Edwards 1997.

146. Key 1961, 413.

147. Reiter and Stam 2002, 199–201.

148. Aldrich et al. 2006, 496.

149. Risse-Kappen 1991.

150. Weiss 2014, 40–41; Bellin 2012. On the rise of various forms of "competitive authoritarianism," with more sensitivity to citizens' concerns, see Levitsky and Way 2002.

151. de Sola Pool 1973, 463; Lynch 2003, 69–70.

152. Weiss and Dafoe 2019, 964; King, Pan, and Roberts 2013, 326–27.

153. In *Of the First Principles of Government*, Hume wrote, "as FORCE is always on the side of the governed, the governors have nothing to support them but opinion. It is therefore, on opinion only that government is founded; and this maxim extends to the most despotic and most military governments, as well as to the most free and most popular" (1993, 16).

154. Hyde and Saunders 2020, 387.

155. Simmons 2009, 150–54.

156. Almond 1950, 54. While Lippmann similarly described the public as susceptible to extreme fluctuations, at other times he attached an "inertia" to the masses, where "[t]he movement of opinion is slower than the movement of events" (1955, 20–21).

157. Lippmann 1955, 18.

158. Almond 1950, 69.

159. Converse 1964, 1970, 175–76. Converse's research represented a more systematic continuation of earlier work questioning the rational basis for the public's attitudes and political choices (Lazarsfeld, Berelson, and Gaudet 1948; Campbell et al. 1960).

160. Almond 1950, 83–84; Lippmann 1955, 24–25.

161. Lippmann 1955, 18, 20.

162. Morgenthau 1985, 7.

163. Dahl 1989, 24–26.

164. Achen and Bartels 2016, 1–20.

165. Caspary 1970, 536.

166. Shapiro and Page 1988, 213.

167. Page and Shapiro 1982, 34; Jentleson 1992, 49–50.

168. Hurwitz and Peffley 1987, 1111; Wittkopf 1990, 21–27.

169. Holsti 2004, 163–239.

170. Rathbun 2007.

171. Holsti 1992, 450. A large literature on political knowledge points to a more nuanced story regarding how relatively informed the public is as a whole toward those issues that matter most to them, especially among certain segments (Delli Carpini and Keeter 1996, 7–8, 17).

172. Conover and Feldman 1984, 96; Popkin 1994, 44.

173. Gigerenzer and Gaissmaier 2011, 454–55.

174. Although not always strictly interpreted in international legal terms, a number of studies offer accounts consistent with the view that international institutions serve as heuristics, shaping public opinion around foreign and domestic policies (Thompson 2009; Chapman 2011; Linos 2013).

175. Zaller 1992, 5–9; Lupia and McCubbins 1998, 4–11; Berinsky 2009, 5.

176. Dellmuth and Tallberg 2021.

177. Bartels 2003, 49.

178. Druckman and Jacobs 2015, 4.

179. Zaller 1992, 96; Druckman and Jacobs 2015, 99.

180. Edwards 2006, 25. For a more middle-ground position on the relationship between elite and public opinion, see Canes-Wrone 2006.

181. Strezhnev, Simmons, and Kim 2019, 1300; Chu and Recchia 2022.

182. Almond's criticism of the public's incoherence does not lead him to praise the faculties of elites, charging the latter with "serious miscalculations" when the public's moods were insufficient to serve as a necessary check (Almond 1950, 85).

183. Shapiro and Page 1988, 213n1; Surowiecki 2005, 10. Though on some of the conditions for, and limits of, the wisdom of the crowds, see Landemore and Elster 2012.

184. Mercer 2005, 94.

185. Waldron 1999, 250–51.

186. Drezner 2008, 57–60; Kertzer and McGraw 2012, 245.

187. Dellmuth et al. 2022b.

188. Kramer 2004b, 962.

189. Stone 1994, 442; Spiro 2006, 447. This is especially the case in the study of courts, where there has been a great deal of cross-fertilization in theories of international and domestic judicial bodies (Staton and Moore 2011, 557).

190. Goldsmith and Posner 2005; Posner and Yoo 2005.

191. Posner and Vermeule 2010; Yoo 2005.

192. Ohlin 2015, 49–50. Pildes reinforces this point, noting both arguments come down to a view "about the nature [or lack thereof] of legal constraints in general" (2012, 1393).

193. Bolton 2000a, 4–6.

194. The "Law of the Land" phrasing goes at least as far back as the Magna Carta of 1215 and shows up in some form in many other modern constitutions.

195. Though it should be noted that not all countries have a constitution, nor at all times. On the general design and prevalence of constitutions, see Elkins, Ginsburg, and Melton 2009, 36–64.

196. Vanberg 2005, 6.

197. Relevant cases include, in order, *Korematsu v. United States*, 323 U.S. 214 (1944); *Roe v. Wade*, 410 U.S. 113 (1973) and its later overruling in *Dobbs v. Jackson Women's Health Organization*, 597 U.S. ___ (2022); and *United States v. Nixon*, 418 U.S. 683 (1974).

The Supreme Court made several rulings related to the War on Terror, but the most notable on detainee rights were *Hamdi v. Rumsfeld*, 542 U.S. 507 (2004), *Rasul v. Bush*, 542 U.S. 466 (2004), and *Hamdan v. Rumsfeld*, 548 U.S. 557 (2006).

198. In *Federalist* 78, Alexander Hamilton pointed to the judiciary's structural weaknesses for why it should be considered the "least dangerous" branch of government:

> The judiciary . . . has no influence over either the sword or the purse; no direction either of the strength or of the wealth of the society; and can take no active resolution whatever. It may truly be said to have neither FORCE nor WILL, but merely judgment; and must ultimately depend upon the aid of the executive arm even for the efficacy of its judgments.

199. *Worcester v. Georgia*, 31 U.S. (6 Pet.) 515 (1832). Jackson's quote is thought to be apocryphal, but Marshall avoided mandating that the federal executive carry out the order to hedge against the risk of the Court being ignored. Importantly, however, Georgia eventually complied, suggesting constitutional law might be enforced in ways other than sovereign decree (Miles 1973, 519–20).

200. Austin 1832, 273.

201. Goldsmith and Levinson 2009, 1795. See also Fisher 1961, 1131–32.

202. Whytock 2005, 158.

203. Goldsmith and Levinson 2009, 1794.

204. Hinsley 1986, 158.

205. Chilton and Versteeg 2015; Cross 1999.

206. For studies offering a qualified defense of constitutions in constraining government repression, see Davenport 1996; Keith, Tate, and Poe 2009; Hill Jr. and Jones 2014.

207. Quotes from *Federalist* 51. On this point, also see Goldsmith and Levinson 2009, 1832.

208. Chayes, Ehrlich, and Lowenfeld 1968, xii–xv.

209. Spiro 2006, 447.

210. Whytock 2005, 170–85.

211. Graber 2013, 174.

212. For instance, as part of its constitutionally vested responsibilities, under Article I Section 8(10) the US Congress is obligated "To define and punish . . . Offences against the Law of Nations."

213. Wildhaber and Breitenmoser 1980, 204. For additional examples, see Arend 1999, 33–34.

214. O'Connell 1965, 49.

215. Quote from decision in *Foster & Elam v. Neilson*, 27 U.S. 253, 314 (1829). Though Marshall went on to differentiate self- versus non-self-executing treaties, with the latter not automatically binding without passage of implementing legislation (Graber 2013, 180).

216. From a historical perspective, it makes sense that international law writ large—not just treaties—would figure into US domestic law. After all, at its founding all relevant international law was customary since the newly formed republic had not yet negotiated any treaties. According to one estimate, even in modern times most US obligations have at least some customary basis (Henkin 1996, 231–32).

217. For one notable critique of international treaties as equal to the US Constitution, see Yoo 1999.

218. Henkin 1996, 235; Graber 2013, 204–5.

219. Graber 2013, 196–97. For instance, in *Trop v. Dulles*, 356 U.S. 86 (1958), the US Supreme Court reversed the government's ability to revoke an individual's citizenship,

drawing in part on outside laws to interpret the Eighth Amendment's prohibition against "cruel and unusual punishments." Later, in *Lawrence v. Texas*, 539 U.S. 558 (2003), Justice Anthony Kennedy explicitly drew on the laws of other countries and common understandings of the European Convention on Human Rights to strike down antisodomy statutes. Not all justices have agreed about the role foreign laws should play. In his dissent in *Roper v. Simmons*, 543 U.S. 551, 18 (2005), which ruled the death penalty for juvenile offenders unconstitutional, Justice Antonin Scalia asserted "the basic premise of the Court's argument—that American law should conform to the laws of the rest of the world—ought to be rejected out of hand."

220. Elkins, Ginsburg, and Simmons 2013; Tushnet 2003, 142.

221. One cross-national analysis questions the usual monist–dualist divide, suggesting a variety of ways to classify national approaches to incorporating international law (Verdier and Versteeg 2015).

222. Knowles and Toia 2014, 33.

223. Schwartz 2000, 226–31.

224. For a summary of these positions, along with the less widespread "compact theory" insisting on the authority of political subunits like US states, see Graber 2013, 110–20.

225. Tushnet 2006, 999.

226. Kramer 2001, 11–12; Kramer 2006, 699.

227. Donnelly 2012, 163.

228. Kramer 2004b, 962.

229. Donnelly 2012, 161–62; Knowles and Toia 2014, 33–36. Kramer acknowledges this diversity, "For there is no one theory. Popular constitutionalism, as such, is just a general concept or broad idea" (2006, 702).

230. Kramer 2006, 702.

231. Hulsebosch 2005, 655.

232. Kramer 2004a, 25–28; Tushnet 1999, 194; Ackerman 1991, 266–94.

233. Kramer 2004b, 959.

234. In response to concerns that government officials could disregard their constitutional obligations, Kramer argues that "federal lawmakers would find themselves facing formidable popular resistance—via elections, juries, popular outcries, or in the unlikely event that all of these failed, by more violent forms of opposition" (2004a, 83–84).

235. Adler 2006, 726–27; Hart 2012, 94–95.

236. Ackerman 1991, 266.

237. Kramer 2004a, 107.

238. Kramer 2006, 699.

239. Knowles 2016, 35–36. Though Knowles notes that in practice many popular constitutionalists were motivated to offer a rejoinder to what was seen as the activism of many conservative judges at the time.

240. Gibson 2017.

241. Dowdle 2012; Hand 2006; Son and Nicholson 2017.

242. Vanberg 2005, 8–9; Carrubba 2009, 56; Staton 2010, 13–14.

243. Stone 1994, 442; Kramer 2004a, 24; Tushnet 2006, 991. Kramer borrows the "political-legal" phrasing when describing the Constitution from Reid 1991, 28–29.

244. Kramer 2004a, 24.

245. Austin 1832, 272.

246. Austin 1832, 272.

247. Posner and Vermeule 2010, 4.

248. Posner and Vermeule 2010, 88.

249. Ohlin 2015, 51.

250. Pildes 2012, 1411. For Pildes, these skeptics commit a fundamental conceptual error: "To avoid acknowledging the role of legal constraints, they relabel as 'political' the kind of constraints that many would characterize as 'legal'" (2012, 1381).

251. Kramer 2006, 700–701; Tushnet 2006, 994.

252. Alexander and Solum 2005, 1602; Posner and Vermeule 2010, 82; Knowles and Toia 2014, 36–44.

253. Kramer 2006, 702.

254. The concept is so loose that even popular constitutionalism has been at times equated as a "stringent form of departmentalism" (Post and Siegel 2004, 1031).

255. See, for instance, Berman 2009; Siegel 2009.

256. Hamilton 2006.

257. Alexander and Solum 2005, 1611, 1613.

258. Brown 1998, 556; Tribe 2004; Powe 2005, 866–84.

259. Examples include Coleman 1982, 148; Marmor 1998, 525; Shapiro 2002, 418.

260. Kramer 2001, 6. This antijudicial supremacy bent is evident in the very titles of notable works on popular constitutionalism (Tushnet 1999; Kramer 2004a). Among constitutional scholars, there is a great deal of debate over the relative place of judicial review (that the courts can play a role in assessing the constitutionality of legislative or executive actions) versus supremacy where courts are the sole judges of the Constitution (Post and Siegel 2004; Graber 2013). A large reason for this goes back to differing interpretations of the landmark Supreme Court case *Marbury v. Madison*, 5 U.S. (1 Cranch) 137 (1803), establishing the principle of judicial review (and for some, the seeds of supremacy) when Chief Justice John Marshall declared "It is emphatically the province and duty of the judicial department to say what the law is." Later cases, including *Cooper v. Aaron*, 358 U.S. 1 (1958) and *City of Boerne v. Flores*, 521 U.S. 507 (1997), only seemed to confirm and extend the court's supremacy on constitutional matters. Not surprisingly, there is a close correspondence between intellectual support for judicial supremacy in some form and opposition to popular constitutionalism (Alexander and Solum 2005; Chemerinsky 2004).

261. Paulsen 1994, 262. Proponents of executive supremacy draw on constitutional history, but with a close eye to contemporary events like the War on Terror, which they believed could only be effectively addressed by an unconstrained unitary leadership (Yoo 2005, 143–60; Posner and Vermeule 2010, 8–10). Some of these accounts rely heavily on the writings of Carl Schmitt, the Nazi philosopher who called for limitless executive power. For an extended review and critique of this position, see Ohlin 2015, chapter 2. On the third main possibility of legislative supremacy, see Farber 1989.

262. Tushnet 2006, 1001–5. For the US Supreme Court, among the most notorious is *Dred Scott v. Sanford*, 60 U.S. (19 How.) 393 (1857) denying citizenship rights to African Americans, described by Kramer as "perhaps the single most reviled decision in the canon of American constitutional law" (2004a, 210). Also high on the list includes *Korematsu v. United States* (1944), which upheld an executive order mandating internment camps for Japanese Americans during the Second World War.

263. Cover 1983, 53; Gibson, Caldeira, and Baird 1998; Waldron 1999, 251.

264. There is a large literature on the impact of public opinion on the US Supreme Court. Notable examples include Marshall 1989; Friedman 2009. Though for counterarguments, see contributions in Persily, Citrin, and Egan 2008. On the impact of public opinion on high courts in other countries, see Vanberg 2005, 8–9; Staton 2010, 13–14.

265. Posner and Vermeule 2010, 82–83.

266. Knowles and Toia 2014, 43; Donnelly 2012, 163.

267. Borrowing from Christianity (but with parallels in many other religious traditions), the legal scholar Sanford Levinson distinguishes between constitutional

"catholics" who hold in part that there is a single "ultimate authority" (usually the Supreme Court), while "protestants" (of which popular constitutionalism would be one variant) believe in the "legitimacy of individualized (or at least nonhierarchical communal)" sets of actors (Levinson 2011, 18–30). Levinson also includes a separate dimension based on the *source* of legal doctrine, based either solely on the constitutional text (protestant) versus the text in addition to unwritten tradition (catholic), which allows for different doctrinal combinations.

268. Waldron 1999, 251–52; Graber 2013, 103.

269. See Powe 2005, 857; Alexander and Solum 2005, 1594.

270. Kramer 2004a, 24–29. A place is even kept open for courts, though in a more balanced position relative to citizens (Kramer 2004a, 249–53).

271. Tushnet 2006, 994.

272. Friedman 2003, 2598–99.

273. Balkin 2011, 246–47

274. The conclusion discusses in greater detail how popular international law speaks to, and can address, the rise of populism in various countries.

275. Slaughter Burley 1993, 228–31; Simmons 2009, 71–77; Mitchell and Powell 2011, 69.

276. Graber 2013, 103.

277. Ohlin 2015, 54.

278. von Bogdandy, Goldmann, and Venzke 2017.

279. Tushnet 2006, 994.

280. Friedman 2003, 2598–99.

3. REPUTATION AND ENFORCEMENT I

1. Liddell Hart 1946, 75–76; Bartov 1996, 5.

2. Pastor 1983, 113–17.

3. Kennan 1979, 3. On the adoption in some historical circles of this German term to describe the war, see Stibbe 2013, 2.

4. Hull 2014, 2.

5. Rachamimov 2002, 69–78, 123–25.

6. Tuchman 1990; Kissinger 1994; Macmillan 2001.

7. Thompson 1966. Examples applying a more bottom-up approach to the conflict include Rachamimov 2002; Keegan 1976.

8. Fagen 1960, 451–52.

9. Hull 2014, 33–43.

10. Holsti 1992, 440.

11. Hoffmann 1968, 27; Morgenthau 1985, 311.

12. Hathaway 2005, 506.

13. Guzman 2008, 33–34, 43, 48.

14. Dafoe, Renshon, and Huth 2014; Brutger and Kertzer 2018.

15. Mercer 1996, 5. I am thankful for several enlightening exchanges with Jon Mercer about various understandings of reputation in international relations more broadly, and implications for international law.

16. Huth 1997; Walter 2009. Works on reputation in other fields include Kreps and Wilson 1982; Raub and Weesie 1990; and Gambetta 1993.

17. Baird, Gertner, and Picker 1994, 181; Posner and Sykes 2013, 32.

18. Abreu and Gul 2000; Sartori 2005; Kertzer 2016.

19. Schelling 1966, 124.

20. Guzman 2008, 33.

21. Mercer 1996, 6–10; Jervis 1982, 8.

22. Brewster 2009b, 235.

23. For this and additional terminology on "types" in the context of international cooperation, see Tomz 2007, 17.

24. Brewster 2009b, 236.

25. Henkin 1979, 52.

26. Morgenthau 1985, 313.

27. Guzman 2008, 33.

28. Hathaway 2005, 506.

29. Keohane 1984, 105–6.

30. Leeds, Long, and Mitchell 2000.

31. Gibler 2008; Crescenzi et al. 2012.

32. Mattes 2012; Miller 2012, 16.

33. Tomz 2007, 58–60; Nelson 2010.

34. Axelrod 1986, 1107–8; Simmons 2000, 819; Leeds 2003, 805.

35. Chapters 5 and 6 examine the extent to which international law can shape actors' underlying policy preferences.

36. This point is acknowledged by both those supportive and skeptical of reputational arguments. For instance, Guzman contends "the theory developed here assumes that states have no particular taste or preference for a good reputation, but rather are concerned with maintaining good standing within the international community only to the extent that changing one's standing or reputation affects payoffs" (2008, 35). While offering a more critical account, Brewster likewise notes "Here, reputation is purely instrumental. States care about their reputations not for reasons of honor or prestige, but because it is a means of securing gains to the state by entering into more cooperative agreements" (2009b, 236).

37. Lahno 1995, 496–99; Goldsmith and Posner 2005, 100–101. This is evident in the very title to Guzman's (2008) *How International Law Works: A Rational Choice Theory*, where reputation figures prominently.

38. Simmons 2000, 819.

39. Guzman 2008, 59.

40. Reus-Smit 2004, 3.

41. Reuters 2020.

42. Probably more than any other mechanism, reputation is situated at the intersection of instrumental and normative approaches to international law. As Simmons concludes, "for these [rationalist] reputational mechanisms to work, there must be widespread social agreement that law creates more serious obligations than other kinds of agreements, a point stressed by constructivist scholars" (2010, 277).

43. Spiro 2006, 447.

44. Whytock 2005, 172–75.

45. Posner and Vermeule 2010, 122–23. Though earlier in the same book they express skepticism that acting in a constitutionally legal manner pays much of a reputational benefit on its own (Posner and Vermeule 2010, 88).

46. Olson 1993.

47. Pildes 2012, 1414.

48. Axelrod 1984, 155.

49. Levi 1997, 107–8.

50. Levi 1997, 16–21. Alongside trustworthiness, Levi argues a second requisite is that people believe a critical mass of other citizens are engaging in "ethical reciprocity," or a willingness to trust the government and cooperate with its policies (1997, 24–27). Ethical

reciprocity is in many ways consistent with the overall argument of this book that the public's broader (even if not unanimous) commitment and buy-in is essential for the operation of legal systems (domestic and international).

51. Levi 1997, 20.

52. Kramer 2004b, 211.

53. Tushnet 1999, 66.

54. Renshon, Dafoe, and Huth 2018.

55. Goldsmith and Posner 2005, 101; Guzman 2008, 73.

56. Brewster 2009a, 327.

57. McGillivray and Smith 2000.

58. Mercer 1996, 6–8; Press 2005, 8–9; Pfundstein Chamberlain 2016, 5–6.

59. Consistent with this view, the historian A. J. P. Taylor remarked that "men use the past to prop up their own prejudices." Quoted in Jervis 1976, 217.

60. Scott and Stephan 2006, 89n8.

61. Aron 2003, 108; Downs and Jones 2002; Goldsmith and Posner 2005, 102–3; Brewster 2009b, 233.

62. Keohane 1997, 497; Swaine 2002, 617.

63. As Guzman notes, "What all this really means is that there are many influences on a state's behavior beyond its compliance reputation. This observation does not, however, undermine the basic point that the compliance reputation is relevant to state decisions" (2008, 117).

64. Kertzer 2016.

65. Miller 2012, 20. For a general critique of scholarly preoccupation with reputations for resolve, see Jervis, Yarhi-Milo, and Casler 2021, 193–94.

66. Chayes and Chayes 1995, 230.

67. Jervis 1982, 9.

68. Mercer 1996, 2.

69. Goldsmith and Posner 2005, 103; Simmons 2010, 292–93.

70. Guzman 2008, 84–85.

71. Posner and Sykes 2013, 33.

72. Brewster 2009a, 324.

73. Mercer 1996, 32–33.

74. Simmons 1998, 89; Shaffer and Ginsburg 2012, 14–15.

75. Dafoe, Renshon, and Huth 2014, 385.

76. On implications of selection effects for understanding the general role of credibility, see Schultz 2001.

77. In addition to this strategic class of compliance rationales, an alternative category put forward by the managerial school views some violations as "involuntary" in the sense that the country does not have the capabilities to comply with the agreement (Chayes and Chayes 1993, 193–95). In these instances, it might be unfair to tarnish a country's reputation as untrustworthy, since noncompliance was not due to some inherent disposition toward unreliability, but rather a lack of necessary resources. If anything, the response by others might be to *increase* cooperation and encourage closer partnerships with the "offender," where violations are seen as a problem to be managed rather than punished. Only by engaging with such involuntary defectors to improve their capabilities could compliance and mutual benefits be achieved in the long run. Of course, the line dividing voluntary and involuntary violations is blurred, giving actors incentives to publicly *claim* their inability to comply with a particular commitment to avoid possible costs of reneging. Distinctions between (in)voluntary violations further demonstrate the empirical challenges of studying reputation in international law.

78. Gibler 2008; Nelson 2010; Crescenzi et al. 2012.

79. The introductory chapter discusses some of the general challenges to the empirical study of international law, and the relative value of experiments versus other methods.

80. Morton and Williams 2010.

81. Shadish, Cook, and Campbell 2002, 86–90.

82. Mutz 2011, chapter 8.

83. Druckman et al. 2006, 7.

84. Kagan 2002; Drezner 2008. The introduction provides a lengthier justification for looking at the United States for examining questions of international law.

85. Although the experiments here focus on US reactions *toward* foreign countries, this does not mean that reputation does not also matter for the United States in terms of the corresponding beliefs of foreign countries *toward* great powers like them. Various scholars argue that image concerns carry significant weight for the most powerful states as well (Schelling 1966, 124–25; Nye 2004, 256–57).

86. The survey was fielded by Knowledge Networks (presently known as GfK) thanks to support from Time-sharing Experiments for the Social Sciences (TESS), an initiative funded by the National Science Foundation (NSF Grant 0818839, Jeremy Freese and Penny Visser, Principal Investigators). From December 8–19, 2011, 4,781 panelists were drawn from the Knowledge Networks panel; 2,929 responded to the invitation, producing a final completion rate of 61.3%.

87. Knowledge Networks offered a probability-based panel covering the entire online and offline US population aged eighteen years or older. Participants were provided internet access if necessary.

88. To facilitate the discussion of the design and results, I describe the country as "foreign" throughout to distinguish it from US participants' home country. However, in the actual survey I refer to countries "in another region of the world" to avoid any negative connotations associated with the term "foreign."

89. There is some debate over using hypothetical versus real-world countries and scenarios in survey experiments, especially for purposes of external validity. However, several studies show more abstract scenarios produce comparable results to richer vignettes across a range of issue areas and designs (Kreps and Roblin 2019; Brutger et al. 2023).

90. Krasner 1982, 192; Mearsheimer 1994, 15–16.

91. Lipson 1993, 12; Simmons 2010, 281.

92. Zacher 2001. Reflecting this rule, Article 2(4) of UN Charter states, "All Members shall refrain in their international relations from the threat or use of force against the territorial integrity or political independence of any state, or in any other manner inconsistent with the Purposes of the United Nations."

93. Huth 1996.

94. In a second follow-up study described in greater detail below, I included an item near the end of the survey asking participants which region they thought most closely resembled the scenario presented. For the security scenario, the most common choice was Asia (39%), followed by the Middle East (31%) with other options receiving between 5% to 10% of responses. For the economic scenario, the Middle East (34%) switched places to be most common, followed by Asia (28%). However, results do not change substantially when limited to perceived regional subsamples, suggesting any regional beliefs were unlikely to be driving participants' answers.

95. Hainmueller and Hiscox 2006; Guisinger 2017; Chen, Pevehouse, and Powers 2023.

96. Lines between positive and negative commitments can also become blurred depending on what is considered the status quo. For instance, Article 11 of the General

Agreement on Tariffs and Trade (GATT) on eliminating quantitative restrictions contains both a positive requirement to reduce and eventually eliminate existing restrictions, but also the negative commitment not to institute or raise new protections.

97. Levy et al. 2015.

98. For representative observational studies, see Simmons 2000; and Fortna 2003. There is a great deal of discussion in the experimental literature about what "control" means conceptually, and what counts as a suitable control group (Harrison and List 2004). In a second follow-up study discussed further below, I included an additional cleaner "no mention" baseline control whose subjects were not given any prompt specifying a prior (non)commitment. Results show little consistent differences in responses for those in this alternative control compared to the more conventional "none" control group explicitly told no prior commitment was made. Ultimately, the design of control groups should reflect the particular attributes and objectives of the research question; some of the experimental designs in later chapters use different formulations appropriate to the specific question under consideration. For the current chapter, however, the main results presented rely on the original direct "none," or no commitment, control as this best matches real-world situations concerning the reputational consequences of international law.

99. Technically, signing a treaty generally does not carry the same obligation as formal ratification or accession, though signatories are still expected to avoid anything that would defeat the object and purpose of the treaty. See Article 18 of the 1969 Vienna Convention on the Law of Treaties. However, one worry was that more technical terms like "ratify" may have led to greater confusion among participants. By comparison, signature is more straightforward yet still carries the desired connotation of making a legal commitment. If anything, the current phrasing underestimates any treatment effect, should some respondents infer a weaker level of commitment from signing alone.

100. Abbott and Snidal 2000, 427; Guzman 2008, 59. As Lipson contends, "The more formal and public the agreement, the higher the reputational costs of noncompliance" (1991, 508).

101. An additional concern is differences in effects between the hard law and soft law treatments may not be due legal obligation, but rather the level at which the agreement was negotiated—"international" for the hard law treaty versus "regional" for the softer guidelines. However, in the second follow-up study, referring to the softer recommended guidelines similarly as "international" (as opposed to "regional") does not significantly change the results.

102. Abbott et al. 2000, 405.

103. Looking to related experimental studies in international relations (Hyde 2015), possible candidates for additional treatments include the regime type of the foreign country, whether the foreign country is an ally or adversary, or the value of future cooperation to the United States, among many others.

104. Druckman 2022, 47–48.

105. Chaudoin 2014a, 882–83.

106. Graham 2016.

107. Hathaway 2022.

108. Pelc 2013; Dancy 2021.

109. Powell 2004, 91.

110. Brewster 2009a, 329; Posner and Sykes 2013, 33.

111. On the logic and benefits of randomization for obtaining more reliable causal estimates, see Mutz 2011, 136–38, 149–54.

112. Full results available in Supplementary Online Materials. Similar balance tests were also conducted for all other experimental studies included in this and subsequent empirical chapters.

113. I compared various socio-demographic characteristics across respondents in the sample to the US population. As a point of comparison, I employed the December 2011 update for the Current Population Survey (CPS), the same month the survey was fielded. The survey sample was largely consistent with CPS benchmarks with an average deviation of only around 3%. Similar procedures were also conducted for all remaining survey experiments discussed in this book.

114. Dunning 2012, 112–15; Mutz 2011, 123–28.

115. Full results available in Supplementary Online Materials.

116. For similar approaches, see Malhotra, Margalit, and Mo 2013; Lupu and Wallace 2019. To further simplify the interpretation of results, levels of support/opposition (whether "strongly" or "somewhat") are aggregated to reflect overall sentiments of (dis)approval for cooperation accordingly. Results do not change substantially when using alternative measures for the relevant outcome variables.

117. All analysis conducted using Stata 15 unless otherwise noted.

118. Economic relations can have fundamental security implications (Kirshner 1995, 3–7).

119. As noted earlier, the labels "violate"/"comply" simplify descriptions here for the foreign country's subsequent behavior in similar terms across the various conditions, even though strictly speaking there was no commitment to comply with for the control group.

120. Abbott and Snidal 2000, 427–28; Guzman and Meyer 2010, 177.

121. For instance, in the economic scenario the difference between hard and soft law effects in figure 3.3(b) are modest though in the expected direction. Although the confidence intervals for hard and soft law overlap for violators in the security scenario, the relative size of the treatment effects between the two types of commitments do appear to be statistically distinguishable as suggested by additional analyses following the recommendations of Schenker and Gentleman 2001. While this should only be taken as suggestive, figure 3.3(a) does indicate that the effect of soft law relative to the control for security affairs is not statistically significant, while the corresponding effect for hard law does achieve statistical significance.

122. Some work contends that violators can deploy various strategies of "image management" to blunt the worst effects, but even here a country's reputation is still best served by complying with their obligations (Morse and Pratt 2022, 2089).

123. Chayes and Chayes 1993, 200. A separate TESS survey fielded in 2013 through GfK indeed suggests that publics expect that foreign countries are more likely (even if only moderately) to violate security commitments compared to economic ones. Though this may not be the only reason for the observed pattern. As noted in figure 3.2, the US public may be less supportive of cooperation on security issues in general due to sovereignty concerns, perhaps creating modest floor effects against further substantial decreases in approval across experimental groups.

124. While the size of treatment effects for soft and hard law are larger in the economic scenario compared to military commitments, the differences across issue area are not statistically significant.

125. Henkin 1979, 47.

126. Guzman 2008, 84.

127. Other explanations may also be consistent with this asymmetry in the reputational consequences of violating versus complying with legal commitments. A large body of work from cognitive psychology points to a strong negativity bias, where people are more affected by negative acts like violations than equivalent positive ones like compliance (Baumeister et al. 2001). Research from social psychology makes related claims about how undesirable and desirable behaviors are interpreted differently by individuals. Extending

these insights to reputation, Mercer argues that undesirable actions are viewed by audiences as due to the offending actor's underlying disposition, while desirable actions by those same actors are interpreted as driven by situational features (1996, 53–55). Because reputation refers to evaluations of an actor's disposition, this means that only undesirable actions should have reputational consequences. Translated to international law, the implication would be that only violations should lead to reputational sanctions, while compliance will have little reputational benefits, which is what figure 3.3 indicates.

Although explanations drawing on cognitive and social psychology are reasonable in many respects, they do not account for the full pattern of findings here. Neither offers firm theoretical expectations for variation in reputational sanctions based on the commitment's level of legal obligation. Furthermore, perceptual biases should be expected to be stronger for particular subgroups. For instance, Mercer generates different expectations for what is viewed as (un)desirable (and thus reputation-affecting) behavior for a country's allies versus adversaries (1996, 65–69). Although the political allegiance of the foreign country is not varied in our main reputation experiment, certain attributes of participants (such as ideology or foreign policy preferences) should be indicative of whether those individuals would view violations as more or less desirable. For instance, conservatives or those with hawkish inclinations may accept violations like resorting to military force as reasonable, having in turn little impact on their reputational evaluations. However, in both this first reputation survey and subsequent follow-up study, no consistent conditional treatment effects are evident for these or related individual characteristics. See the main text for further discussion of conditional effects. Other psychological explanations are thus best viewed as complementary to the account presented here.

128. Fearon 1997. Some evidence from a separate follow-up experiment suggests that legalized commitments are viewed as more credible, raising expectations of future compliance among international audiences.

129. Full results available in Supplementary Online Materials. Chapter 5 on the preferences function offers a more nuanced discussion of the conditional role of political ideology and partisanship, among other factors, on international law.

130. Guzman 2008, 103.

131. Yarbrough and Yarbrough 1997, 136.

132. Trimble 1990, 833; Swaine 2002, 618.

133. Thomas 2001, 36.

134. Goldsmith and Posner 2005, 102. As Mercer notes, "it appears that commitments are more independent than interdependent" (1996, 9).

135. Downs and Jones 2002, S109–S111.

136. Brewster 2009b, 259.

137. Guzman 2008, 100–111; Brewster 2009a, 329; Posner and Sykes 2013, 33.

138. There may be concerns over consistency bias where participants' answers to the first cooperation item will sway their responses on the other issue. However, the two items are only modestly correlated ($r = 0.54$). Moreover, the varying results across different issue areas discussed below suggest such biases are unlikely to account for the patterns observed.

139. The absolute percent support for trade cooperation with a foreign country that resorted to force in the military scenario, yet had made no prior legal commitment, was 63%. By contrast, the equivalent level of support for a country that employed similar force over the island in contravention of a treaty promise was just 42%.

140. Gowa 1994.

141. Berinsky, Huber, and Lenz 2012. MTurk samples have also been widely employed to study public opinion across a range of domains, including foreign policies and commitments, Chaudoin 2014b; Levy et al. 2015.

142. The security wave was fielded in October of 2014, and the economic wave in December that same year. To ensure participants from the first wave were excluded from the second, I followed procedures laid out in Peer et al. 2012.

143. As mentioned earlier, this second study introduced an alternative "no mention" control group that was given no explicit commitment prompt of any kind. Since results differ little irrespective of how the control group is specified, I continue to use the main "none," or no commitment, control (where participants were expressly told the foreign country had not made any prior commitment) in all of the main analyses for this study.

144. More specifically, values refer to beliefs over keeping promises in the same issue area as the scenario presented—military commitments for security, and trade commitments for the economic situation. The analysis presented for this and several other follow-up items reports simple first differences rather than conducting a more formal mediation analysis incorporating the support for cooperation item as the main outcome. While mediation analysis has gained in popularity, these techniques are subject to a number of methodological and inferential limits (Fiedler, Schott, and Meiser 2011, 1235). Nevertheless, employing a common mediation estimation method from Imai et al. (2011) presents a similar picture regarding the role of these additional considerations as mediators between international law and attitudes toward reputational consequences.

145. Simmons 2010, 277–80.

146. Additional details on the content analysis are provided in Supplementary Online Materials. This open-ended item also provides a useful manipulation check of sorts (alongside a more standard series of recall items asked to all participants later in the follow-up survey). Participants in the hard law group frequently referred to "treaties," "laws," or "rules" in their responses, which makes sense since their prompt explicitly mentioned an international treaty. "Treaties" was much less commonly mentioned in the soft law group, but the latter two terms showed up frequently in their explanations. By contrast and as expected, none of the terms appears even once in responses from the "none," or no commitment, control group.

147. Further analysis of the main close-ended support for cooperation outcome shows that other motives receive little support. For instance, vengeful individuals are no more affected by violations of international law than their more forgiving counterparts, despite attention to vengeance as a general source of foreign policy attitudes (Stein 2019). Additionally, personal expectations about the (in)efficacy of enforcement do not condition participants' willingness to impose reputational sanctions, which avoids a potential self-fulfilling prophecy of weak enforcement in actuality. Further details provided in Supplementary Online Materials.

148. Abbott et al. 2000, 404.

149. On general challenges of confounding, or the need for "informational equivalence" across experimental treatments, see Dafoe, Zhang, and Caughey 2018.

150. The construction of the precision and delegation treatments was based in part on prior experiments I designed and fielded on attitudes toward torture. The torture surveys, as well as the role of legalization, are further discussed in chapter 5.

151. Abbott et al. 2000, 406.

152. First differences report each effect relative to the appropriate control group, pooled across all relevant conditions for the other two legalization dimensions. For instance, the high obligation ("hard law" in earlier parlance) treatment measures the first difference with the "none," or no commitment, control group, aggregated across all precision and delegation groups. Precision compares the high precision treatment to the low precision control across all high and low obligation commitments, excluding those in the obligation control groups who received no commitment (since there was no precision to vary). Similarly, high delegation reports the first difference between the high

delegation (court) and delegation control (no additional delegation prompt), aggregated across all precision conditions but limited to those groups receiving the high obligation treatment (since they were the only ones who could receive any delegation prompt). Further analysis does not reveal any consistent conditional relationships among the various legalization components that would undermine the overall patterns reported in figure 3.7.

153. Lipson 1991, 508; Guzman 2008, 93. As Simmons remarks, "treaties also allow a more complete reputational commitment because of their capacity for clarity. Precision reduces the plausible deniability of violation by narrowing the range of reasonable interpretation" (2010, 277).

154. Linos and Pegram 2016, 593.

155. Guzman 2008, 33–34, 46–48.

156. Specifically, average support aggregated across all commitment groups for each type of retaliation in the security and economic scenarios respectively was as follows: condemn (79% and 70%), economic sanctions (65% and 40%), and military force (24% and 12%).

157. Further analysis reveals that it is generally the same individuals supportive of reputational sanctions who are also more approving of most forms of retaliatory actions. Different types of enforcement mechanisms thus appear to run in the same direction.

158. Downs and Jones 2002, S113.

159. Slogan from a 1990 advertising campaign for the Canon Rebel camera.

160. Morgenthau 1985, 588–89.

4. REPUTATION AND ENFORCEMENT II

1. Delahunty and Yoo 2006, 73–75; Posner and Vermeule 2007, 182–85.

2. Belz 2006; Ohlin 2015.

3. Meet the Press 2001.

4. Gonzales 2002, 2.

5. Beste et al. 2003.

6. Pyszczynski, Solomon, and Greenberg 2003, 93.

7. Cheney 2001.

8. Morrow 2014, 62.

9. Bush 2001.

10. Huddy et al. 2005; Berinsky 2009, 155–56.

11. Woodward 2001.

12. Duffy 2005.

13. See the introductory chapter for further background on this more skeptical dimension in the US international legal tradition.

14. Spiro 2000; Rivkin and Casey 2003.

15. Chayes 2008.

16. Distilling the defining traits of a compassionately conservative foreign policy, several commentators settled on three key principles: "commitment, capacity building, and collaboration" (Feaver and Malesky 2000).

17. Thompson 2009, 135.

18. Arsenault 2017, 101.

19. Kahl 2007.

20. Article 39 states that "The Security Council shall determine the existence of any threat to the peace, breach of the peace, or act of aggression and shall make recommendations, or decide what measures shall be taken in accordance with Articles 41 and 42, to maintain or restore international peace and security." UNSC authorization is thus

generally considered a requisite for the legal use of force by any state. Though some critics counter this represents a reinterpretation of how the initial framers of the charter—the United States chief among them—viewed their obligations and ability to employ force absent council approval (Trachtenberg 2005, 217–21).

21. Though there are critics of this military operation as well under international law (Paust 2002).

22. See, in particular, UNSC Resolutions 1378 and 1386.

23. The doctrine was formally spelled out in the 2002 National Security Strategy (Bush 2002).

24. Shue and Rodin 2007.

25. Kreps 2011, 118–19.

26. Yoo 2003.

27. MacAskill and Borger 2004.

28. Thompson 2009; Kreps 2011.

29. Rodley 2009, 3–6.

30. White House, 2002.

31. Human Rights Watch 2004, 1; Steyn 2004.

32. Danner 2004, 42.

33. Ignatieff 2003.

34. Walt 2005, 129–32. Subtle and indirect reactions bear a lot of resemblance to the concept of "soft balancing" as opposed to more traditional balancing behavior. It is indicative that one of the most prominent studies of soft balancing begins by noting the catalyzing role played by US violations of, or withdrawals from, several international treaties (Pape 2005, 7).

35. Kagan and Kristol 2000.

36. Boot 2003.

37. Katzenstein and Keohane 2007.

38. Mendelsohn 2009, 2–3.

39. Article 5 states in part, "The Parties agree that an armed attack against one or more of them in Europe or North America shall be considered an attack against them all."

40. OAS Resolution RC.24/RES.1/01. September 21, 2001.

41. The organization is currently known as the Organisation of Islamic Cooperation.

42. *Economist* 2001.

43. LaFraniere 2001.

44. Bernstein 2003.

45. Beard 2001, 571–72.

46. Cheney 2001.

47. Conetta 2002, 11.

48. Renshon 2017, 2–3.

49. Nye 1990, 31–32.

50. Pew data during the initial period of this time series were sparser with no values available for 2001.

51. Thompson 2009, 180–81.

52. See Pew Research Center, "America's Image Further Erodes, Europeans Want Weaker Ties," March 18, 2003.

53. Asmus 2003, 22.

54. Kreps 2011, 116–19.

55. Pew Research Center, "Bush Unpopular in Europe, Seen as Unilateralist," August 15, 2001.

56. Kull et al. 2009, 15.

57. Senate Select Committee on Intelligence 2014, xxv.

58. Bowden 2004, 37.

59. Arsenault 2017, 168–69.

60. Fogarty 2005, 10.

61. Senate Select Committee on Intelligence 2014, xxv.

62. Wolford 2015, 12.

63. Daalder 2003.

64. Milbank 2003.

65. Pauly and Lansford 2005, 117. Spain and Denmark also supplied small numbers of troops, but were never deployed in combat.

66. Gallup polling showed how the presence or absence of UN approval proved crucial in informing foreign publics' support for the war (Thompson 2009, 189–92). An additional survey experiment I conducted confirms that UN approval is important for public support for military intervention by their country, driven by the legitimating function of the organization rooted partly in international legal principles (Wallace 2019b).

67. McCartney 2003.

68. Bernstein 2003.

69. Beehner 2007.

70. Wallace and Oliver 2005, 170.

71. Kennedy-Pipe and Vickers 2007, 218–19.

72. Trachtenberg 2005, 213–14.

73. Quote from Thompson 2009, 45. See also Saunders 2017; Kreps 2011.

74. For an account for how UN approval (both going through the organization and obtaining approval) is not endogenous to prior international public support, see Thompson 2009, 54–56.

75. Hersh 2005, 181.

76. Bennett, Lepgold, and Unger 1994, 50.

77. Thompson 2009, 47–48.

78. Cortright and Lopez 1999, 750.

79. Pauly and Lansford 2005, 125–26.

80. The Iraq Body Count (IBC) project provides more detailed statistics on various fatalities related to the war.

81. O'Hanlon and de Albuquerque 2004, 15.

82. Dempsey 2004.

83. Shapiro 2005, 254–62.

84. Bush 2003, 19.

85. Mendelsohn 2009, 113–14.

86. Priest 2005a.

87. Mayer 2005.

88. Rejali 2007, 446–47.

89. Hafner-Burton and Shapiro 2010, 416–17.

90. Kronstadt 2003, 10; Filkins 2014.

91. Mayer 2005.

92. Miller and Goldman 2014.

93. Senate Select Committee on Intelligence 2014, xxiv.

94. Miller and Goldman 2014.

95. Cordell 2021.

96. Danner 2004, 215–16; Priest 2005a.

97. Miller and Goldman 2014.

98. Human Rights Watch 2011a, 21–22.

99. Prominent cases include *Hamdi v. Rumsfeld* (2004), *Rasul v. Bush* (2004), and *Hamdan v. Rumsfeld* (2006).

100. Senate Select Committee on Intelligence 2014, xxiv.

101. The CIA spent millions constructing facilities that never ended up housing any detainees "in part due to host country political concerns" (Senate Select Committee on Intelligence 2014, xxv).

102. Fogarty 2005.

103. Senate Select Committee on Intelligence 2014, xxv.

104. Kris 2011, 67.

105. Mendelsohn 2009, 100; Hafner-Burton and Shapiro 2010, 416.

106. Aldrich 2009, 131.

107. Priest 2005b.

108. Kris 2011, 69.

109. Aldrich 2009, 134.

110. Hakimi 2007, 443–47.

111. Quoted in Hillebrand 2012.

112. Hafner-Burton and Shapiro 2010, 415.

113. Quoted in Lee 2011, 239.

114. Chiu 2019.

115. Ashworth 1980, 24–28.

116. Posner 2003.

117. Morrow 2014, 15–19.

118. Kalyvas 2006, 104–6.

119. Holmes 1985, 382.

120. Wallace 2015, 20–22.

121. Ferguson 2004, 149.

122. Grauer 2014.

123. Ferguson 2004, 155–56.

124. Bartov 2001, 115–20.

125. Walzer 2000, 46.

126. Reiter and Stam 2002, 65–69; Wallace 2015, 62–65.

127. Morrow 2007, 566–67.

128. Human Rights Watch 2004, 1–2.

129. Doyle 2010, 314.

130. Keegan 2005, 3.

131. Carvin 2010, 183.

132. Article 22 of the Third Geneva Convention governing POWs states, "Except in particular cases which are justified by the interest of the prisoners themselves, they shall not be interned in penitentiaries."

133. Springer 2010, 198.

134. Doyle 2010, 314.

135. Ricks 2006, 271–72; Carvin 2010, 185–95.

136. ICRC 2004, 3.

137. During the initial conventional phase of the invasion of Iraq from March 20 to May 1, 2003, less than 200 troops from US coalition forces were killed (Clodfelter 2008, 770). By contrast, according to various tallies over 4,000 US service members alone died in the ensuing years fighting the insurgency.

138. Rowe 1993, 198; Vance 2006, 168

139. Springer 2010, 193. For a breakdown of prisoners taken by national armed forces of the UN Coalition, see Doyle 2010, 296–97 n15.

140. Cody 1991.

141. Jones and Summe 1997, 6–7.

142. Mallet 1997, 291.

143. Gordon and Trainor 1995, 363.

144. US Department of Defense 1992, 577.

145. Promises of humane treatment were not the only message contained in leaflets. These promises often followed after leaflets communicating coalition military superiority and the certainty of attack, with the sequence of the two messages having a particularly pronounced impact (Clancy and Horner 1999, 524–25). While there is some debate over the relative role of such promises, the following quote from an Iraqi Brigadier General is telling, "Second to the allied bombing campaign, psychological leaflets were the highest threat to the morale of the troops." Quoted in Mallet, 1997, 292.

146. Springer 2010, 194.

147. Roberts 1993, 161.

148. Brinkerhoff, Silva, and Seitz 1992, 67.

149. US Department of Defense 1992, 624.

150. Schutte 2017.

151. Kalyvas and Kocher 2009; Balcells 2011.

152. Kalyvas 2006, 171–76.

153. Kocher, Kalyvas, and Pepinsky 2011; Schutte 2017.

154. Fazal 2018, 56–58.

155. Kilcullen 2006.

156. Acronym for the Air Force of the Republic of Vietnam (South Vietnam).

157. United States Department of State 1965, document 117.

158. Department of the Army 1992, 1–8.

159. Department of the Army 2006, 7–7.

160. Kahl 2007.

161. Human Rights Watch 2003.

162. Nasr 2009.

163. Burkholder 2004.

164. Quoted in Karon 2004.

165. Anderson 2004, 374.

166. Kagan 2009, 197; Ricks 2010, 66–67. Though the precise role of the surge, Awakening Councils, and other factors in explaining declining insurgent violence remains contested (Biddle, Friedman, and Shapiro 2012).

167. Ollivant 2011, 3.

168. Cottam, Huseby, and Baltodano 2016, 3–4.

169. Clayton and Thomson 2014.

170. Bruno 2008.

171. Williams and Adnan 2010.

172. Human Rights Watch 2004, 4.

173. Fearon and Laitin 2003.

174. Edelstein 2004; Enterline and Greig 2008.

175. Bass 2004.

176. Quoted in Best 1980, 49.

177. Walzer 2000, 132. Even some legal skeptics share similar sentiments: "belligerents foresee interaction continuing after the war ends and fear that cheating during the war may invite retaliation after the war" (Goldsmith and Posner 2005, 32).

178. Balcells 2012; Lupu and Peisakhin 2017.

179. Fortna 2004, 21.

180. Stanton 2016, 37–38; Fazal 2018, 50.

181. This is evident in human rights norms concerning governments' treatment of their own citizens, but is also relevant for wartime conduct (Dai 2007, 106; Morrow 2014, 16).

182. Phillips 2006, 7–8.

183. Stork and Abrahams 2004, 94–95.

184. Gordon and Trainor 2006, 484.

185. Cordesman 2008, 48–50. Order No. 2 represented a reneging of sorts on prior US commitments. As the general Anthony Zinni, former chief of US Central Command who oversaw earlier operations in Iraq, remarked "We had spent a decade psyopsing the Iraqi army, telling them we would take care of those who didn't fight. And he [Paul Bremer, CPA Administrator] disbands it" (Ricks 2006, 164).

186. O'Donnell and Schmitter 1986, 37–40.

187. Pirnie and O'Connell 2008, 62.

188. Hashim 2006, 122.

189. Gordon and Trainor 1995, 445.

190. Freedman and Karsh 1993, 424.

191. Though the Hussein regime would later test other aspects of the settlement, including no-fly zones over much of the country and the weapons inspection regime.

192. Carvin 2010, 133.

193. For a study that looks at related questions—albeit, not specifically with regards to international law—in the context of ethnic targeting and the onset and escalation of civil war, see Cederman et al. 2020.

194. Fazal 2018, 70–71.

195. The set of interstate wars is based largely on the Correlates of War (COW) project, along with some modifications and additions (Sarkees and Wayman 2010). Following other researchers, several larger wars, such as the two World Wars, are broken down into separate conflicts (Reiter and Stam 2002, 39).

196. Morrow and Jo 2006, 91.

197. Three further criteria delimit relevant cases of insurgency. First, there must be a minimum of 1,000 battle deaths, with at least one hundred casualties suffered by each side. Second, the non-state actor must have employed a guerrilla warfare strategy, characterized by: 1) reliance on small, mobile units engaging mostly in hit-and-run strikes against incumbent forces, while avoiding direct battles where possible; and 2) aims to obtain the support of at least some segment of the civilian population. Third, insurgencies were only included if they bore some direct relationship to the prior interstate conflict, where the opponent either directly participated, or supported, the insurgents. Episodes of insurgencies are drawn from Lyall and Wilson (2009), and supplemented by several military history compendia (Clodfelter 2008; Phillips and Axelrod 2005).

198. Mahoney and Goertz 2004.

199. Prisoner abuse is a categorical variable distinguishing between low, medium, and high levels across a range of violations, including execution, torture, and harsh living or working conditions, which is based on data from Wallace 2015, 29–31. The treatment of civilians is a dichotomous variable measuring whether a belligerent employed a strategy of civilian victimization where noncombatants are intentionally targeted or force is used indiscriminately, which comes from Downes (2008), as well as other secondary sources. The unit of analysis is the warring-directed-dyad given the quantity of interest is each side's wartime conduct toward their opponent. This implies two possible observations for each pair of belligerents, where each is considered a prospective violator or victim accordingly. Because many small states taking part in wars involving large coalitions frequently do not possess the material or organizational capabilities to target civilians or prisoners independently, the analysis only focuses on the leading belligerents in those conflicts.

200. These include cultural differences, total population of the adversary, and terrain, among others. Details on the variables and additional analyses are included in Supplementary Online Materials.

201. There are 320 total cases when not applying the exclusionary criteria for possible insurgencies.

202. Best 1980, 298–301. Each model is estimated using logistic regression. Predicted probabilities of insurgency onset are then calculated and reported using a kernel-weighted local polynomial smoothing function across levels of prisoner abuse. An earlier version of this analysis was conducted as part of an unpublished manuscript with Jason Lyall (Dartmouth College), "Wartime Prisoner of War (POW) Abuse and the Rise of Postwar Insurgencies," which was prepared for the *Festschrift* honoring Peter J. Katzenstein at Cornell University in October 2011. I thank Jay for allowing me to use and extend some of these data.

203. The pattern is generally similar, though more muted, when including all cases.

204. Weisiger 2014.

205. Jha and Wilkinson 2012; Huff 2024.

206. Results hold when excluding both US-Iraq wars, suggesting these conflicts are not driving the findings.

207. Bush 2006.

208. Yoo 2011.

209. Cheney 2009.

210. Tenet et al. 2014; Baker 2014.

211. Powell 2002, 2.

212. Arsenault 2017, 160–62.

213. Department of the Army 2006, 7-2; McChrystal 2009, E-2.

214. Benard et al. 2011, 73.

215. Executive Order 13491—Ensuring Lawful Interrogations. January 22, 2009.

216. Executive Order 13492—Review and Disposition of Individuals Detained at the Guantánamo Bay Naval Base and Closure of Detention Facilities, January 22, 2009. Though for various bureaucratic and legislative reasons, the facility would remain open throughout Obama's presidency and beyond.

217. Lennard 2011. Though as detailed in chapter 6, the Obama administration would face its own charges of skirting legal obligations, particularly surrounding the use of drones for targeted killings.

218. Eggen 2005.

219. Goldsmith 2012, 131.

220. Ohlin 2015, 155.

5. FROM LAW TO PREFERENCES I

1. However, as will be discussed theoretically and explored empirically, it is exactly the lack of precision in the boundaries of what constitutes torture that can lead to uncertainty (either intentional or unintentional), which in turn can feed abuse.

2. Scarry 1985; Hassner 2022.

3. Quoted in Twining and Twining 1973, 308.

4. Walzer 1973. Though for a critique of torture on utilitarian grounds, see Morgan 2000.

5. Rejali 2007, 22–23.

6. Merolla and Zechmeister 2009, 85–87; Young and Kearns 2020, 19–20.

7. Franck 1990, 35.

8. Ikenberry and Kupchan 1990, 285–86.

9. Coplin 1965, 617.

10. Tyler 1990, 19–27.

11. Morgenthau 1951, 144.

12. Goldsmith and Posner 2005, 3, 42–43.

13. Guzman 2008, 11–17.

14. Posner and Vermeule 2010, 4.

15. Dworkin 1986, 93.

16. Keohane 1988, 382; Reus-Smit 2004, 31.

17. Ohlin 2015, 50.

18. Chayes and Chayes 1993, 178.

19. Finnemore 1996; Goodman and Jinks 2013.

20. Henkin 1979, 64, 74.

21. Finnemore and Sikkink 1998, 891–92.

22. Simmons 2009, 143.

23. Dai 2007, 119–30.

24. Franck 1990, 166–94; Brunnée and Toope 2010, 6–7.

25. Fuller 1969, 41; Tyler 1990, 19–27.

26. Zemans 1983, 697.

27. Andenaes 1966, 950.

28. Kramer 2001, 10–13.

29. Levinson 2011, 4.

30. Goldsmith and Levinson 2009, 1840.

31. Whytock 2005, 181–85; Goldsmith and Levinson 2009, 1829, 1837.

32. Lipson 2003, 81.

33. Ratner 2000, 661.

34. Lipson 1991, 508; Axelrod 1986, 1106–7.

35. Linos and Pegram 2016. The managerial school identifies a lack of precision as one of the main causes of noncompliance, not necessarily because actors want to avoid their commitments but simply because they are not fully aware of their exact obligations (Chayes and Chayes 1993, 188–89).

36. Risse and Sikkink 1999, 11–17.

37. Holsti 2004, 196–231.

38. Drezner 2008.

39. Gelpi, Feaver, and Reifler 2009, 21–22; Kreps 2011, 8–9.

40. As one overview concludes, "Agreements that constrain military operations in the heat of battle present the most significant challenges for international treaties" (Simmons 2010, 281).

41. Merom 2003, 15–19; Wallace 2015, 58–66.

42. Davenport 2007b, 173–74; Downes 2007.

43. Russett 1990, 20.

44. Cardenas 2007, 27–28.

45. Henkin 1979, 135.

46. Goldsmith and Posner 2005, 10. As Krasner describes in the case of torture: "Conventions can but do not necessarily compromise Westphalian sovereignty . . . An international pledge, for instance, to eschew torture might change neither the behavior of rulers nor the attitudes of groups in civil societies. *Whether a convention affects Westphalian sovereignty at all is an empirical question*" (emphasis added; 1999, 106).

47. Danner 2004.

48. Amnesty International 2003.

49. Rodley 2009, 45–46.

50. For example, prohibitions against torture in Article 5 of the African Charter on Human and Peoples' Rights, Article 5(2) of the American Convention on Human Rights, and Article 3 of the European Convention on Human Rights.

51. Even this term carries some baggage. "Shocks the conscience" became the preferred standard in the early years of the Bush administration, where it was interpreted to permit acts that many experts would consider to be torture (Lithwick 2006).

52. The formal title for the annex was Regulations Respecting the Laws and Customs of War on Land.

53. During the First World War, several belligerents negotiated a series of bilateral prisoner-related agreements (Roberts 1994, 124), though most countries eventually saw the value of a multilateral treaty system (Morrow 2002, S54–S55).

54. Torture was also prohibited in the remaining conventions dealing with other categories of protected persons, including the sick and wounded on land (Convention I), at sea (Convention II), and civilians (Convention IV).

55. On the interrelationship between the laws of war and human rights law, which involves areas of complementarity but also tension, see Heintze 2004.

56. Human rights agreements still tend to be quite weak compared to treaties in other issue areas (Hafner-Burton 2005, 603–4).

57. Ratner and Abrams 2001, 161–66. The CAT also established a separate Committee against Torture with several powers, including authority to investigate allegations of systematic torture (Articles 17–24).

58. Rodley 2009, 65–66. Though claims regarding torture's jus cogens status remain contested (Malanczuk 1997, 57–58).

59. Brunnée and Toope 2010, 269.

60. Poe and Tate 1994; Cardenas 2007, 12.

61. For a review of some of the theoretical and empirical challenges to the general study of repression, and in particular the potential role of international agreements, see Davenport 2007a, 16–17.

62. For instance, compare the varying results on the relationship between human rights agreements and repression to be: no effect (Hill Jr. and Jones 2014), constraining (Fariss 2014), or even enabling abuse (Hathaway 2002).

63. Gutierrez 2020.

64. Al Jazeera 2019.

65. Bruck 2016.

66. Politi 2016.

67. Nebehay 2017

68. Huddy et al. 2005.

69. Maoz and McCauley 2008; Conrad et al. 2018. For a discussion of cross-national differences in support for torture, see Miller 2011.

70. Polls identified using the iPOLL Databank from the Roper Center for Public Opinion Research. The period ends in 2016 because polling on support for torture became less common in later years. For US trends covering a shorter timeline, see also Gronke et al. 2010.

71. Values for responses of neutral/undecided, do not know, or refuse are excluded. Full details of the question wording are provided in Supplementary Online Materials.

72. For instance, *Rasul v. Bush* (2004) and *Hamdi v. Rumsfeld* (2004) were decided in the same year the Abu Ghraib revelations broke.

73. For a more in-depth analysis of changes in US attitudes toward torture over time, see Mayer and Armor 2012. Partisan polarization did change during this time with Republicans and independents becoming more supportive, while Democrats remained more opposed (Miller, Gronke, and Rejali 2014, 22, 34). Partisan and ideological differences surrounding torture and international law are examined in greater detail in later sections.

74. Page and Shapiro 1983, 177–78; Gilens 2005, 792.

75. Gronke et al. 2010, 441–42; Mayer and Armor 2012, 443.

76. Blauwkamp, Rowling, and Pettit 2018.

77. Nylen and Carpenter 2019, 151.

78. Shannon 2000, 294.

79. Greenberg 2006, 2; McKeown 2009, 19; Brunnée and Toope 2010, 244.

80. As with several other surveys in this book, the instrument was fielded by Knowledge Networks (presently known as GfK). Support from Time-sharing Experiments for the Social Sciences (TESS), NSF Grant 0094964, Diana C. Mutz and Arthur Lupia, Principal Investigators. From October 24 through November 13, 2008, 4,665 panelists were drawn from the Knowledge Networks panel; 2,817 responded to the invitation, producing a final completion rate of 60.4%.

81. For instance, the second torture survey experiment discussed in greater detail below was run two years later in 2010 and exhibited similar raw levels of support.

82. For a contrast of the two candidates' positions on torture due partly to their respective constituencies, see Hetherington and Weiler 2009, 135–38. However, even here, the authors admit McCain's arguments were not nearly as extreme compared to many other Republican candidates.

83. Springer 2010.

84. The classic ticking time bomb scenario presents a suspect who has knowledge of an imminent terrorist attack, and will disclose said information if they are tortured (Brecher 2007, 1–2).

85. This sort of elite cue (even if not an outright endorsement) presents a particularly tough test for any counter-frame like international law, as a wealth of work suggests elite messaging can significantly shape public attitudes, including in the context of war (Chong and Druckman 2007b, 109). Though see chapter 2 for questions concerning the general power of elite cues theoretically and empirically.

86. On debates over defining torture, see Nowak 2006.

87. Gronke et al. 2010, 437; Nylen and Carpenter 2019, 154. For instance, a common phrasing in surveys from this period asked for opinions "about the use of torture against suspected terrorists in order to gain important information."

88. Rejali 2007, 446–79; Hassner 2022, 6–8.

89. The sequence in which the three treatments were displayed was also randomized to guard against possible order effects.

90. See, in particular, country-level studies of various IHL customary rules in ICRC 2010.

91. For instance, the field of psychology is generally more permissive on using deception, while in experimental economics the general rule is "just don't do it" (Dickson 2011, 65).

92. Carpenter, Montgomery, and Nylen 2021, 3.

93. For other experimental studies on international law making a similar choice of using a null "no mention" control prompt, see Tomz 2008; Chilton 2015; and Chilton and Versteeg 2016. A related study looking at the impact of international law on attitudes toward trade restrictions similarly employs a null control, but also includes a "placebo" offering a generic message with no meaningful content that matches the main treatments in overall length and structure (Chaudoin 2014b). Results showed the placebo yielded similar levels of support to the null control. This provides greater confidence that in the present study any observed differences in support between the international law treatment and the null group can be interpreted as genuine treatment effects.

94. Some of these questions are taken up chapter 6, where I leverage data from a separate conventional survey to examine the effect of individuals' real-world knowledge of international law on their foreign policy attitudes.

95. For a general discussion, see Chilton and Tingley 2013, 225.

96. Valentino, Huth, and Balch-Lindsay 2004; Wallace 2015, 130, 184–88.

97. For a similar approach to the experimental study of the role of democracy on the use of force, see Tomz and Weeks 2013. Admittedly, such a design may not completely achieve information equivalence, and thus fail to eliminate possible confounding of the treatment as respondents update their beliefs about other attributes of the vignette in ways that question the results (Dafoe, Zhang, and Caughey 2018). While these are important issues, this is less of a concern in this study since Enemy Combatant is not the main theoretical trait of interest. Later analyses also show no strong conditional relationship between combatant type and international law on attitudes toward torture.

98. Axelrod 1984, 73–87.

99. Morrow makes a fascinating argument where mutual ratification may actually smooth reciprocity and make retaliation *more* likely by setting common understandings of conduct (2014, 111–17). While intriguing, testing this conjecture experimentally would have required an additional treatment that varied the commitment of the enemy to prevailing international treaties. This would complicate an already intricate design by introducing even more experimental groups, thereby reducing statistical power. Moreover, certain treatment combinations would not be possible since nonstate actors do not have the ability to ratify IHL treaties, though there have been initiatives to create legal-like commitments for rebel groups (Gleditsch et al. 2018).

100. As in chapter 3, comparing various socio-demographic characteristics in this and subsequent surveys to population benchmarks indicates they were fairly representative of the US adult population.

101. Results for this and all subsequent analyses remain substantially the same when estimating regression models on support for torture that include treatment indicators along with common socio-demographic covariates.

102. Tomz 2008; Chaudoin 2014b; Chilton 2014; Chilton 2015; Putnam and Shapiro 2017. For a study finding weaker effects for international law on support for torture, though with some important design differences, see Chilton and Versteeg 2016.

103. For instance, one study finds stronger reciprocity effects when explicitly priming on the presence or absence of abuse by the adversary instead of the more implicit control prompt used here (Chu 2019). However, such design differences do not affect the primary question motivating this chapter regarding the role of international law on public preferences.

104. For instance, respondents exposed to both the international law and reciprocity conditions were slightly less likely to approve of torture in absolute terms compared to those receiving neither the international law nor reciprocity prompts (41% versus 44%), though the difference is not statistically significant.

105. Data collected by TESS, NSF Grant 0818839, Jeremy Freese and Penny Visser, Principal Investigators. A total of 9,213 US adults from Knowledge Networks' panel were initially invited over the period from June 23 to July 5, 2010; 6,101 participated, resulting in a final completion rate of 66.2%.

106. Abbott et al. 2000, 404.

107. For instance, just a trichotomous high, moderate, and low scheme would result in twenty-seven separate experimental groups.

108. Chapter 3 further discusses these choices.

109. Abbott et al. 2000, 406.

110. Rodley 2009, 18–20, 35–36. The full title was the "Declaration on the Protection of All Persons from Being Subjected to Torture and Other Cruel, Inhuman or Degrading Treatment or Punishment, UN General Assembly Resolution 3452 (XXX) of December 9, 1975."

111. Incidentally, the United States signed the ICCPR around the same time in 1977, though it did not officially ratify it until 1994. While not formally obligated, signatories nonetheless are "obliged to refrain from acts which would defeat the object and purpose of a treaty," Article 18 of the 1969 Vienna Convention on the Law of Treaties.

112. A parallel is the translation of texts between different languages, where the primary aim is for consistency in meaning, something rarely achieved through using the exact same words in rote fashion (especially since certain words or concepts do not have direct equivalents in the other language). I thank my mother, a career translator, for highlighting this issue.

113. Kinder and Palfrey 1993, 25. This problem of "multiple meaning" has been described as "one of the most perplexing and pervasive problems in experimentation" (Carlsmith, Ellsworth, and Aronson 1976, 61).

114. On norm institutionalization, see Finnemore and Sikkink 1998, 900. For norm robustness, one of the key dimensions is "concordance," or "how widely accepted the rules are in diplomatic discussions and treaties" (Legro 1997, 34–35).

115. Shaw 2017, 88.

116. Shelton 2006; Shaw 2017, 91–92.

117. Morrow and Jo 2006, 97.

118. Jo and Simmons 2016.

119. Kelley 2007. These deals were also known as Article 98 agreements based on the relevant section of the Rome Statute. The statement for the low delegation prompt was apt at that time. Though in recent years, legal liability for US citizens may have changed, especially with the ICC opening an investigation into alleged crimes in Afghanistan (a party to the Rome Statute), which potentially covers actions by US forces.

120. Bolton 2000b.

121. In the first experiment the average effect for insurgents was a 5% increase in support for torture compared to regular combatants, which closely matches the aggregate difference in approval across the two studies.

122. Ratner 2000, 661.

123. Abbott et al. 2000, 405; Simmons 2010, 277.

124. Shelton 2000b, 17–18; Tingley and Tomz 2020.

125. See Article 38(1) of the Statute of the International Court of Justice (ICJ).

126. Goldsmith and Posner 2005, 39.

127. Norman and Trachtman 2005.

128. Guzman 2008, 193–94. However, notable efforts include observational work by Verdier and Voeten (2015), and a set of laboratory experiments studying the formation of customary rules (Engel 2011).

129. For a similar finding, see Putnam and Shapiro 2017, 252–53.

130. As one of the legal architects of the US detention program during the War on Terror, John Yoo declared that "At this moment in world history, the United States' conduct should bear the most weight in defining customs of war" (2006, 37). Yoo's contention is interesting because the customary status of certain international rules played a pivotal role in the legal justification offered for US practice. In particular, partly through his own capacity in the Office of Legal Counsel (OLC) in the US Department of Justice, "OLC concluded that the Geneva Conventions had not assumed the status of customary international law that bound the United States, nor, for that matter, all nations of the world" (36). The experimental results here regarding US public attitudes toward such "international values" suggest his judgment may have been premature.

131. Lipson 1991, 508; Linos and Pegram 2016, 593.

132. Chayes and Chayes 1993, 188–92. As noted also in chapter 3, managerialists also see a lack of material capacity as another important contributor to noncompliance.

Managerialists thus interpret most instances of noncompliance as honest mistakes (due to ambiguous rules) and/or resource constraints among well-meaning states rather than deliberate violations (Chayes and Chayes 1993, 187–88).

133. On evasive behavior in compliance, see Búzás 2018.

134. Goldsmith and Posner 2005, 168.

135. Greenberg and Dratel 2005.

136. From Jay Bybee, "Standards for Conduct for Interrogation under 18 U.S.C. §§ 2340–2340A" (August 1, 2002). Quoted in Greenberg and Dratel 2005, 176.

137. Brunnée and Toope 2010, 243–44; Hurd 2017, 104–6.

138. Abbott et al. 2000, 405.

139. Beaumont 1996, 278–84.

140. Voeten 2013.

141. Indeed, the US public has been shown to be quite supportive of the ICC, especially when human rights values are emphasized (Zvobgo 2019).

142. The precision treatment effect was not conditional on delegation, meaning first differences for precision held irrespective of whether delegation was high or low.

143. Rathbun 2004, 21–23; Benjamin Jr. 2016.

144. Hetherington and Weiler 2009, 135.

145. Goldstein 2001; McDermott 2015.

146. Brooks and Valentino 2011; Lizotte 2017.

147. Holsti 2001, 41–42; Feaver and Gelpi 2004, 53.

148. Average levels of support for torture in the first experiment across all conditions were as follows: conservatives (53%) versus liberals (29%); Republicans (53%) versus Democrats (33%); men (47%) versus women (39%); and veterans (51%) versus civilians (41%). Similar patterns were also found in the second torture experiment.

149. The less definitive pattern for partisanship may partly be a function of respondents' lower proclivity to self-identify as independents compared to a much greater number considering themselves moderate on the political ideology liberal–conservative scale. When Republican and Democrat "leaners" (those who initially do not indicate a party preference, but only do so when further prompted) are instead coded as independent, patterns in the conditional effects of international law for partisanship more closely resemble those for political ideology.

150. Page and Shapiro 1983, 177–78.

151. Rathbun 2007.

152. Kunda 1987.

153. Taber and Lodge 2006, 757.

154. Braman and Nelson 2007, 943–44.

155. Gerber and Green 1999.

156. Tetlock 1985, 233; Kunda 1990, 481–82.

157. Mercier and Sperber 2011.

158. There is a long pedigree in variants of the democratic peace of mechanisms externalizing domestic norms to foreign policymaking, which also have important legal underpinnings (Russett 1993, 31–32).

159. Eskridge 1990, 623–24; Scalia 1998, 23–25. Textualism is sometimes conflated with originalism, though the two overlap significantly in practice (particularly in terms of adherents; Barnett 1999). Originalism refers to a more specific doctrine concerning the interpretation of the US Constitution, which emphasizes the importance of referring to the document as understood by the people (especially the framers) at the time of its writing (Bork 1971, 1). Neither doctrine is unified with each having variants with sometimes important differences, but a more circumscribed approach to constitutional interpretation runs throughout both.

160. Breyer 2005; Ackerman 2007.

161. Some proponents even offer their own liberal variant of originalism, arguing the framers of the Constitution expressly chose to enunciate a flexible structure of general principles intended to accommodate changing needs and societal expectations (Balkin 2011, 227–29).

162. The Eighth Amendment drew on language from the English Bill of Rights of 1689, itself left open to interpretation.

163. *Trop v. Dulles* 356 U.S. 86 (1958). Other areas where reasoning in line with the Living Constitution has figured prominently include evolving interpretations of equal protection (under the Fifth Amendment) and due process (under the Fourteenth Amendment; Breyer 2005, 18–19).

6. FROM LAW TO PREFERENCES II

1. McDermott 2002, 38–40.

2. Alvarez and Brehm 1995, 1055.

3. Morgenthau 1985, 295; Mearsheimer 1994, 19.

4. Gelpi, Feaver, and Reifler 2009, 21–22; Press, Sagan, and Valentino 2013.

5. Parts of the following sections draw on prior research with Sarah Kreps (Kreps and Wallace 2016), though with important modifications and extensions. I thank Sarah for agreeing to allow me to use some of this work here.

6. I use the terms drones and UAVs interchangeably throughout. For a useful review of different positions on the spread of drones, see Horowitz, Kreps, and Fuhrmann 2016.

7. Fahlstrom and Gleason 2012, 4–7.

8. The mission did not succeed in its primary target, but resulted in the deaths of several other Taliban members (Walsh and Schulzke 2018, 12).

9. Due to the classified nature of the US drone program, which is also spread across several agencies including the Department of Defense and the Central Intelligence Agency (CIA), precise publicly available information is difficult to find. The above figures are drawn from one of the more reputable projects, "Drone Warfare," conducted by the Bureau of Investigative Journalism.

10. Singer 2013.

11. Obama 2013.

12. Johnson 2015.

13. Fuhrmann and Horowitz 2017.

14. Amnesty International 2013; United Nations 2013.

15. For more extensive discussions of the legal implications of drone strikes, see Finkelstein, Ohlin, and Altman 2012.

16. O'Connell 2011.

17. Christopher 2012, 256; Stanford Law School and NYU School of Law 2012, vii.

18. Solis 2010, 251.

19. Shane 2015.

20. Center for Civilians in Conflict 2012, 8–9.

21. Feldstein 2017.

22. Blum and Heymann 2013, 87.

23. Cronin 2013.

24. Pilkington and MacAskill 2015.

25. Obama 2013.

26. Byman 2013; Johnston and Sarbahi 2016.

27. Favole 2013.

28. Hartig 2017.

29. Cronin 2013, 50.

30. Hopkins 2013. While Hayden was referring to leaks regarding US intelligence collection programs, his comments apply equally to the drone program given similar levels of secrecy and controversy.

31. As with attitudes toward torture in chapter 5, polls were identified using iPOLL. Values for responses of neutral/undecided, don't know, or refuse are excluded. Questions asking about the use of drone strikes against US citizens, such as the 2011 killing of al Qaeda member Anwar al-Awlaki, were removed since these polls generally have much lower support and are less comparable to more common questions dealing with foreign militants. Full details of the question wording are provided in Supplementary Online Materials.

32. Kreps 2014; Nylen and Carpenter 2019, 150, 158–59.

33. The survey was fielded by the survey research firm GfK with support from Time-sharing Experiments for the Social Sciences (TESS), NSF Grant SES-0818839, Jeremy Freese and James Druckman, Principal Investigators. From September 6 to 23, 2013, 3,706 panelists were drawn from the GfK panel; 2,394 responded to the invitation, producing a final completion rate of 64.6%. The survey was designed in collaboration with Kreps, and draws on some of the results from Kreps and Wallace 2016.

34. Druckman 2001, 1045.

35. Human Rights Watch 2011b.

36. Gelpi, Feaver, and Reifler 2009, 118.

37. This follows a similar strategy when combining elite voices and competing domestic policy positions, Chong and Druckman 2007a, 642.

38. Treatment groups involve a single issue frame-elite source prompt, meaning we can compare support for each of these issue-actor pairs against each other and the control condition. Allowing a full factorial design for every combination of treatments would result in twenty-seven experimental groups in addition to the baseline control. And enabling the position (pro or con) to also vary by source would have further multiplied the number of treatment conditions. The present design improves statistical power, while still offering a reasonable test of competing frames and voices.

39. Sniderman and Bullock 2004, 337.

40. Though using different operationalizations, see Kreps 2014; Schneider and Macdonald 2016; and Walsh and Schulzke 2018, 144–47.

41. For similar findings regarding asymmetrical effects of violation versus compliance with international legal commitments, see chapter 3 on reputation.

42. Additional analyses do not reveal much in the way of consistent conditional effects between the treatments and various socio-demographic indicators, such as political ideology or partisanship.

43. Gelpi, Feaver, and Reifler 2005; Press, Sagan, and Valentino 2013.

44. The control group was not asked this question because these respondents did not receive any additional prompt involving an elite source.

45. Druckman and Leeper 2012.

46. This is in some ways inevitable for a well-theorized study, since if "research hypotheses have merit, the effects they simulate are likely to have occurred in the real world" (Gaines, Kuklinski, and Quirk 2006, 12).

47. Western 2005, 5.

48. Data were gathered using the Factiva news database, which covers several thousand US newspapers. Full details on the protocol used for identifying relevant news stories and connecting them to specific categories of elite sources are described in Supplementary Online Materials.

49. Broadly similar trends are evident when limited to three national newspapers—the *New York Times, Washington Post,* and *Wall Street Journal*—which had some of the most prominent coverage and often served as a conduit for major voices on the topic. Full discussion available in Supplementary Online Materials.

50. Because a news story could reference two or more elite sources, percentages across the three categories for some months may sum to more than 100%.

51. Walsh and Mehsud 2013.

52. Page, Shapiro, and Dempsey 1987.

53. Chapter 3 further discusses the relative value of the mTurk recruitment platform.

54. Amnesty International 2013; Human Rights Watch 2013.

55. On casualty aversion and support for drone versus conventional strikes, see Walsh and Schulzke 2018, chapter 3. However, their study does not examine the intersection of casualty aversion and international law.

56. For instance, chapter 3 showed how moral considerations also underlay elements in the functioning of reputation as an enforcement device. On the general overlap between normative and instrumental mechanisms, see Simmons 2010, 277.

57. Gaines, Kuklinski, and Quirk 2006, 5–6.

58. ICRC 1999.

59. These are the International Criminal Tribunal for the former Yugoslavia, established in 1993, and the International Criminal Tribunal for Rwanda, begun in 1994.

60. Bellamy 2009, 3–4.

61. Berinsky 2009.

62. Other studies have made use of the ICRC survey to examine related questions (Spini, Elcheroth, and Fasel 2008; Meernik and King 2014).

63. The Security Council members surveyed were France, Russia, and the United Kingdom. The survey was also administered in Switzerland, where the ICRC is headquartered. Conflict countries surveyed were Afghanistan, Bosnia-Herzegovina, Cambodia, El Salvador, Georgia and the breakaway region of Abkhazia, Israel and the Palestinian-occupied territories, Lebanon, Nigeria, the Philippines, Somalia, and South Africa. The ICRC pretested an initial pilot study in Mozambique and Colombia, but the questionnaire differed markedly from the final version employed for the main set of conflict countries subsequently surveyed.

64. Wallace 2019a.

65. For further details on the ICRC's sampling procedures, see ICRC 1999, 87–88.

66. An additional question asked about respondents' support for targeting civilians who provided food and shelter to the enemy. Unfortunately, this item contained a large number of missing values, so was excluded from the analysis. Nevertheless, results do not change substantially when it is included.

67. For some items, respondents were randomly presented with one of two different question wordings that might have more general or specific details (though none having to do with international law). While this led to some differences in responses by question version, they were not always in the same direction. The relative distribution of values across the abuse indices also do not differ markedly based on the version asked. Nevertheless, an indicator for question version is included in subsequent analyses to take into account any possible question wording effects.

68. A Kaiser-Meyer-Olkin measure of sampling adequacy of 0.75 suggests the component variables have enough in common to justify factor analysis, Kaiser 1974. Moreover, following Kaiser's widely used criterion, only this single factor had an eigenvalue greater than one (Kim and Mueller 1978, 43).

69. Morrow 2007.

70. Rescaling the relevant abuse index for each observation "i" was calculated based on the following formula, which employed the minimum (Min Value) and maximum (Max Value) values for the appropriate index observed across the entire set of respondents:

$$(\text{Abuse}_i - \text{Abuse}_{(\text{Min Value})}) \, / \, (\text{Abuse}_{(\text{Max Value})} - \text{Abuse}_{(\text{Min Value})})$$

For a similar approach, see Humphreys and Weinstein 2006.

71. The overall correlation between the civilian and prisoner indices is 0.36, but −0.39 when limited to the lower-end of the scale of values less than 0.1.

72. Morrow and Jo 2006.

73. Best 1994, 136.

74. More specifically, 68% indicated that they had heard of the conventions, but of these only 71% subsequently correctly identified the agreements' purpose. Other work finds lower public understandings of international law (Dill and Schubiger 2021). Similar questions arise domestically regarding the public's knowledge of the US Constitution, though this has been shown to be higher than commonly thought (Gibson and Caldeira 2009).

75. Additional discussion of the merits of this IHL knowledge measure compared to alternatives is provided in Supplementary Online Materials.

76. Holsti 2004, 163–239.

77. For instance, on preferences toward trade or immigration, see Hainmueller and Hiscox 2006, 2007.

78. Krueger and Malečková 2003; Thyne 2006.

79. Knowledge of the Geneva Conventions and education are also only moderately correlated (r = 0.16).

80. These include a variety of model specifications using different estimators and operationalizations for several explanatory and outcome variables, using multiple imputation to deal with missing values, as well as conducting a matching procedure in addition to sensitivity analysis showing that unobserved confounding is unlikely to be driving the main results. The full results are discussed in the Supplementary Online Materials.

81. For prisoners, I considered graver forms of abuse to be items involving the refusal to save a prisoner, torture, killing, and beliefs that prisoners should be allowed to die. More moderate forms of prisoner abuse instead were refusing to allow detainees to contact relatives, or prohibiting visits by outside representatives.

82. Finnemore and Sikkink 1998, 895.

83. Walzer 2000, 151. For different views on the strength of civilian norms, see Sagan and Valentino 2017; and Carpenter and Montgomery 2020.

84. Kinsella 2005; Wallace 2015, 42–45.

85. See also Kahl 2007, 8 n3.

86. Some of the literature on gender, military experience, and the use of force was discussed in chapter 5. On having children and a corresponding decline in support for issues of a military nature, see Smith 2005. To ensure findings from having children were not simply a function of being married, I included an indicator for marital status. Results do not change substantially, while the coefficient for being married never attains statistical significance.

87. More specifically, a series of OLS models was estimated for each abuse outcome index using the same set of explanatory variables as in the full sample, but then limited only to respondents from the relevant subsample (e.g., men versus women). As an alternative, conditional relationships were estimated with a series of models including an interaction term between IHL knowledge and the relevant subsample characteristic (e.g., gender). Results are substantially the same.

88. Feaver and Gelpi 2004, 60; Wallace 2014, 502–3.
89. Predicted probabilities for the first differences were estimated using Stata's "margins" command, while holding all other explanatory variables at their median values. A similar estimation strategy was used in subsequent models for other outcomes.
90. See chapter 3 for further discussion of how instrumental and moral considerations interact in the functioning of reputation.
91. Dai 2005, 366.
92. Simmons 2009, 135.
93. Cardenas 2007, 27–28.
94. Moehler 2008, 29–33.
95. Massoud 2011, 3.
96. This is in some ways consistent with work from domestic legal studies showing greater knowledge of the US Supreme Court is associated with more positive feelings toward the institution and its work (Gibson and Caldeira 2009, 436–37).
97. Taber and Lodge 2006, 756–57.
98. Fortna 2008.
99. Alter 2014.

CONCLUSION: UNDERSTANDING THE PUBLIC AND INTERNATIONAL LAW

1. Journalists are trained to start with a story's most essential details, and avoid the cardinal sin of "burying the lead" (Spark and Harris 2011, 49–50). Some of the most consequential legal documents can be read as "stories" in much the same way.
2. Whytock 2005; Spiro 2006; Goldsmith and Levinson 2009.
3. Ohlin 2015, chapter 2.
4. Tushnet 1999; Kramer 2004b.
5. Hathaway 2002; Simmons and Danner 2010.
6. Lipson 1991; Shelton 2000a.
7. Guzman 2008, 212.
8. Abbott et al. 2000, 405.
9. Carpenter 2008; Human Rights Watch 2020.
10. Leaders are difficult to study directly, while querying elites can be challenging and limited to relatively small samples. Though for some notable studies of elites related to international law, see Tomz 2008; Hafner-Burton et al. 2014; and Bayram 2017.
11. Guzman 2008, 102–9.
12. As one review of interdisciplinary scholarship on international law observes, "for most public international lawyers, customary international law is omnipresent; for most political scientists, it is rarely considered" (Hafner-Burton, Victor, and Lupu 2012, 96). See chapter 5 for additional discussion of existing empirical research on customary law.
13. Meron 2000, 83–85.
14. Shannon 2000; McKeown 2009.
15. Simmons 2010, 275–77.
16. Simmons and Hopkins 2005; von Stein 2005.
17. Koskenniemi 2002; Witt 2013; Hathaway and Shapiro 2017.
18. See Article 38(1)(d) of the Statute of the International Court of Justice (ICJ).
19. Quoted in Hull 2014, 3.
20. Rajagopal 2003; Mantilla 2020.
21. Kramer 2004b.
22. Wallace 2019a.
23. Pew Research Center 2020a.

24. Gibson 2006; Meernik 2015.
25. Jo 2015; Fazal 2018.
26. Kim 2019; Strezhnev, Simmons, and Kim 2019.
27. Cardenas 2007, 27–28.
28. Chapman and Chaudoin 2020.
29. Chaudoin 2016.
30. Lupu and Wallace 2019.
31. Pildes 2012, 1415–16.
32. Risse-Kappen 1991; Weeks 2014, 14–17.
33. Dellmuth et al. 2022a; Kertzer 2022.
34. Cope and Crabtree 2020.
35. Helfer 2002.
36. Lake 2018, 15.
37. Hafner-Burton, Narang, and Rathbun 2019.
38. Voeten 2020.
39. Canovan 1999, 3.
40. Mudde 2004, 543.
41. Canovan 1999, 5.
42. Tribe 2004.
43. Brettschneider 2015, 81–82.
44. Mudde 2004, 544, 561.
45. Parker 2009; Beaumont 2014.
46. McCann 1994; Francis 2014.
47. This is reminiscent of what Cover calls a *nomos* (normative universe), as noted in the epigraph to this chapter (1983, 4–5).
48. Art 2022, 2.
49. Kagan 2018.
50. Goldsmith 2017; Koh 2019, 2.
51. Pew Research Center 2020b.
52. Sparks 2018.
53. Hannah and Gray 2020, 11.
54. Majority support for the ICC has remained fairly stable even among Republicans (LaFranchi 2018).
55. Pew Research Center 2018.
56. Busby and Monten 2018, 53–55.
57. Voeten 2020, 418.
58. Schwarzenberger 1964, 198–99; Hurd 2022. All laws generate both benefits and costs, which are rarely evenly spread. In particular, it is the "costs that are . . . disproportionately distributed: easier to bear for those who have many forms and volumes of capital; a heavier, often disabling burden that reinscribes disadvantage for those with less" (Silbey 2005, 353).
59. Katznelson 2005.
60. Harjo 2014.
61. See Articles I Section 2(3) and IV Section 2(3).
62. Alexander 2012, 189.
63. This represents an animating assumption behind the intellectual movement known as Third World Approaches to International Law (TWAIL; Mutua 2000, 31).
64. Zacher 2001.
65. Roberts 1994, 125.
66. Cover 1986, 1601.
67. Goldstein and Martin 2000.

68. Búzás 2018.

69. Fazal 2018.

70. Bierce 2000, 147.

71. Compare the accounts in Nuñez-Mietz 2016; Arsenault 2017.

72. Franck 1990, 193.

73. Levinson 2011, 4.

74. Kammen 2017, 22.

75. Dworkin 1986, vii.

76. While there are a range of definitions, "Taken most broadly, legal consciousness includes all the ideas about the nature, function and operation of law held by anyone in society at a given time" (Trubek 1984, 592).

77. Silbey 2005.

78. Waldron 1999, 250–52; Brettschneider 2015, 85.

79. From the President's Address on Constitution Day, September 17, 1937. Quoted in Kramer 2004b, 248.

80. Ohlin 2015, 49–50.

81. Simmons and Danner 2010. However, see Chapman and Chaudoin 2013.

82. Moravcsik 2000.

83. Chayes and Chayes 1993, 193–95.

84. Posner 2009, 109–11.

85. Bolton 2000b, 188–89.

86. Rabkin 2005, 263–70.

87. Referenced in Goldsmith 2017.

88. Some critics add a further critique that international laws are inherently antidemocratic. For instance, John Yoo, a legal scholar and former official of the George W. Bush administration, wrote:

> Globalization and its attendant effects, however, place new stresses on our domestic constitutional and political system. Novel forms of international cooperation increasingly call for the transfer of rulemaking authority to international organizations that lack American openness and accountability (2000, 361).

Along similar lines, Rivkin and Casey caution:

> To the extent that international law allows supranational, or extra-national, institutions to determine whether the actions of the United States are lawful, ultimate authority will no longer be vested in the American people, but in these institutions. Thus for all of its humanitarian and democracy-building rhetoric, the new international law is profoundly undemocratic at its core (2000, 38).

89. Yoo 2005; Posner and Vermeule 2010.

90. Goldsmith and Levinson 2009, 1796.

91. Voeten 2020.

92. Boyle 1985, 293–94.

93. Sagan and Valentino 2017.

94. Dill and Schubiger 2021.

95. Chilton and Versteeg 2016; Dellmuth et al. 2022a.

96. Fuller 1960, 1.

97. Tushnet 1999, 194.

References

Abbott, Kenneth W. 2004. "Toward a Richer Institutionalism for International Law and Policy." *Journal of International Law and International Relations* 1 (1–2): 9–34.

Abbott, Kenneth W., Robert O. Keohane, Andrew Moravcsik, Anne-Marie Slaughter, and Duncan Snidal. 2000. "The Concept of Legalization." *International Organization* 54 (3): 401–19.

Abbott, Kenneth W., and Duncan Snidal. 1998. "Why States Act through Formal International Organizations." *Journal of Conflict Resolution* 42 (1): 3–32.

Abbott, Kenneth W., and Duncan Snidal. 2000. "Hard and Soft Law in International Governance." *International Organization* 54 (3): 421–56.

Abreu, Dilip, and Faruk Gul. 2000. "Bargaining and Reputation." *Econometrica* 68 (1): 85–117.

Achen, Christopher H., and Larry M. Bartels. 2016. *Democracy for Realists: Why Elections Do Not Produce Responsive Government.* Princeton, NJ: Princeton University Press.

Acheson, Dean. 1963. "Remarks by the Honorable Dean Acheson." *Proceedings of the Annual Meeting of the American Society of International Law* 57: 13–15.

Ackerman, Bruce. 1991. *We the People: Foundations.* Cambridge, MA: Belknap Press.

Ackerman, Bruce. 2007. "Oliver Wendell Holmes Lectures: The Living Constitution." *Harvard Law Review* 120 (7): 1738–812.

Adler, Emanuel. 1992. "The Emergence of Cooperation: National Epistemic Communities and the International Evolution of the IDEA of Nuclear Arms Control." *International Organization* 46 (1): 101–45.

Adler, Matthew D. 2006. "Popular Constitutionalism and the Rule of Recognition: Whose Practices Ground U.S. Law." *Northwestern University Law Review* 100 (2): 719–805.

Al Jazeera. 2019. "Philippines: Duterte Wants State Auditors 'Kidnapped, Tortured.'" January 8. https://www.aljazeera.com/news/2019/1/8/philippines-duterte-wants-state-auditors-kidnapped-tortured

Aldrich, John H., Christopher Gelpi, Peter Feaver, Jason Reifler, and Kristin Thompson Sharp. 2006. "Foreign Policy and the Electoral Connection." *Annual Review of Political Science* 9: 477–502.

Aldrich, John H., John L. Sullivan, and Eugene Borgida. 1989. "Foreign Affairs and Issue Voting: Do Presidential Candidates 'Waltz Before a Blind Audience?'" *American Political Science Review* 83 (1): 123–41.

Aldrich, Richard J. 2009. "US—European Intelligence Co-Operation on Counter-Terrorism: Low Politics and Compulsion." *British Journal of Politics and International Relations* 11 (1): 122–39.

Alexander, Larry, and Lawrence B. Solum. 2005. "Popular? Constitutionalism?" *Harvard Law Review* 118 (5): 1594–641.

Alexander, Michelle. 2012. *The New Jim Crow: Mass Incarceration in the Age of Colorblindness.* New York: New Press.

Almond, Gabriel A. 1950. *The American People and Foreign Policy.* New York: Harcourt, Brace.

Alter, Karen J. 1998. "Who Are the 'Masters of the Treaty'? European Governments and the European Court of Justice." *International Organization* 52 (1): 121–47.

Alter, Karen J. 2014. *The New Terrain of International Law: Courts, Politics, Rights.* Princeton, NJ: Princeton University Press.

Alvarez, R. Michael, and John Brehm. 1995. "American Ambivalence towards Abortion Policy: Development of a Heteroskedastic Probit Model of Competing Values." *American Journal of Political Science* 39 (4): 1055–82.

Amnesty International. 2003. *Combating Torture: A Manual for Action.* https://www.amnesty.org/en/documents/act40/001/2003/en/

Amnesty International. 2013. *Will I Be Next? US Drone Strikes in Pakistan.* https://www.amnestyusa.org/reports/will-i-be-next-us-drone-strikes-in-pakistan/

Andenaes, Johannes. 1966. "The General Preventive Effects of Punishment." *University of Pennsylvania Law Review* 114 (7): 949–83.

Anderson, John Lee. 2004. *The Fall of Baghdad.* New York: Penguin Books.

Arend, Anthony C. 1996. "Toward an Understanding of International Legal Rules." In *International Rules: Approaches from International Law and International Relations,* edited by Robert J. Beck, Anthony C. Arend, and Robert D. Vander Lugt, 289–310. New York: Oxford University Press.

Arend, Anthony C. 1999. *Legal Rules and International Society.* Oxford, UK: Oxford University Press.

Aron, Raymond. 2003. *Peace and War: A Theory of International Relations.* New Brunswick, NJ: Transaction Publishers.

Arsenault, Elizabeth G. 2017. *How the Gloves Came Off: Lawyers, Policy Makers, and Norms in the Debate on Torture.* New York: Columbia University Press.

Art, David. 2022. "The Myth of Global Populism." *Perspectives on Politics* 20 (3): 999–1011.

Ashworth, Tony. 1980. *Trench Warfare, 1914–1918: The Live and Let Live System.* New York: Holmes and Meier.

Asmus, Ronald D. 2003. "Rebuilding the Atlantic Alliance." *Foreign Affairs* 82 (5): 20–31.

Auerswald, David P. 1999. "Inward Bound: Domestic Institutions and Military Conflicts." *International Organization* 53 (3): 469–504.

Austin, John. 1832. *The Providence of Jurisprudence Determined.* London: John Murray.

Axelrod, Robert. 1984. *The Evolution of Cooperation.* New York: Basic Books.

Axelrod, Robert. 1986. "An Evolutionary Approach to Norms." *American Political Science Review* 80 (4): 1095–111.

Baird, Douglas G., Robert H. Gertner, and Randal C. Picker. 1994. *Game Theory and the Law.* Cambridge, MA: Harvard University Press.

Baker, Peter. 2014. "Dismissing Senate Report, Cheney Defends C.I.A. Interrogations." *New York Times,* December 8. https://www.nytimes.com/2014/12/09/world/dismissing-senate-report-cheney-defends-cia-interrogations.html

Balcells, Laia. 2011. "Continuation of Politics by Two Means: Direct and Indirect Violence in Civil War." *Journal of Conflict Resolution* 55 (3): 397–422.

Balcells, Laia. 2012. "The Consequences of Victimization on Political Identities: Evidence from Spain." *Politics & Society* 40 (3): 311–47.

Balkin, Jack M. 2011. *Constitutional Redemption: Political Faith in an Unjust World.* Cambridge, MA: Harvard University Press.

Barkun, Michael. 1968. *Law without Sanctions: Order in Primitive Societies and the World Community.* New Haven, CT: Yale University Press.

Barnett, Michael. 2002. *Eyewitness to a Genocide: The United Nations and Rwanda.* Ithaca, NY: Cornell University Press.

Barnett, Michael, and Martha Finnemore. 1999. "The Politics, Power, and Pathologies of International Organizations." *International Organization* 53 (4): 699–732.

Barnett, Randy E. 1999. "An Originalism for Nonoriginalists." *Loyola Law Review* 45 (4): 611–54.

Bartels, Larry M. 1991. "Constituency Opinion and Congressional Policy Making: The Reagan Defense Build Up." *American Political Science Review* 85 (2): 457–74.

Bartels, Larry M. 2003. "Democracy with Attitudes." In *Electoral Democracy*, edited by Michael MacKuen, and George Rabinowitz, 48–77. Ann Arbor: University of Michigan Press.

Bartels, Larry M. 2008. *Unequal Democracy: The Political Economy of the New Gilded Age*. Princeton, NJ: Princeton University Press.

Bartov, Omer. 1996. *Murder in Our Midst: The Holocaust, Industrial Killing, and Representation*. New York: Oxford University Press.

Bartov, Omer. 2001. *The Eastern Front, 1941–1945: German Troops and the Barbarisation of Warfare*. Oxford, UK: Palgrave.

Bass, Gary J. 2004. "Jus Post Bellum." *Philosophy & Public Affairs* 32 (4): 384–412.

Baum, Matthew A., and Philip B. K. Potter. 2015. *War and Democratic Constraint: How the Public Influences Foreign Policy*. Princeton, NJ: Princeton University Press.

Baumeister, Roy F., Ellen Bratslavsky, Catrin Finkenauer, and Kathleen D. Vohs. 2001. "Bad Is Stronger Than Good." *Review of General Psychology* 5 (4): 323–70.

Bayram, A. Burcu. 2017. "Due Deference: Cosmopolitan Social Identity and the Psychology of Legal Obligation in International Politics." *International Organization* 71 (S1): S137–63.

Beard, Jack M. 2001. "America's New War on Terror: The Case for Self-Defense under International Law." *Harvard Journal of Law & Public Policy* 25 (2): 559–90.

Beaumont, Elizabeth. 2014. *The Civic Constitution: Civic Visions and Struggles in the Path toward Constitutional Democracy*. New York: Oxford University Press.

Beaumont, Joan. 1996. "Protecting Prisoners of War, 1939–1995." In *Prisoners of War and Their Captors in World War II*, edited by Bob Moore, and Kent Fedorowich, 277–97. Oxford, UK: Berg.

Beck, Robert J., Anthony C. Arend, and Robert D. Vander Lugt, eds. 1996. *International Rules: Approaches from International Law and International Relations*. Oxford, UK: Oxford University Press.

Bederman, David J. 2001. *International Law in Antiquity*. Cambridge, UK: Cambridge University Press.

Beehner, Lionel. 2007. *The "Coalition of the Willing."* New York: Council on Foreign Relations.

Bellamy, Alex J. 2009. *Responsibility to Protect: The Global Effort to End Mass Atrocities*. Cambridge, UK: Polity Press.

Bellamy, Alex J. 2012. *Massacres and Morality: Mass Atrocities in an Age of Civilian Immunity*. Oxford, UK: Oxford University Press.

Bellin, Eva. 2012. "Reconsidering the Robustness of Authoritarianism in the Middle East: Lessons from the Arab Spring." *Comparative Politics* 44 (2): 127–49.

Belz, Dan. 2006. "Is International Humanitarian Law Lapsing into Irrelevance in the War on International Terror?" *Theoretical Inquiries in Law* 7 (1): 97–130.

Benard, Cheryl, Edward O'Connell, Cathryn Quantic Thurston, Andres Villamizar, Elvira N. Loredo, Thomas Sullivan, and Jeremiah Goulka. 2011. *The Battle Behind the Wire: U.S. Prisoner and Detainee Operations from World War II to Iraq*. Santa Monica, CA: RAND Corporation.

Benjamin Jr., Arlin J. 2016. "Right-Wing Authoritarianism and Attitudes toward Torture." *Social Behavior and Personality* 44 (6): 881–87.

Bennett, Andrew, Joseph Lepgold, and Danny Unger. 1994. "Burden-Sharing in the Persian Gulf War." *International Organization* 48 (1): 39–75.

Berinsky, Adam J. 2009. *In Time of War: Understanding American Public Opinion from World War II to Iraq.* Chicago: University of Chicago Press.

Berinsky, Adam J., Gregory A. Huber, and Gabriel S. Lenz. 2012. "Evaluating Online Labor Markets for Experimental Research: Amazon.com's Mechanical Turk." *Political Analysis* 20 (3): 351–68.

Berman, Mitchell N. 2009. "Originalism Is Bunk." *New York University Law Review* 84 (1): 1–96.

Bernstein, Richard. 2003. "Two Years Later: World Opinion; Foreign Views of U.S. Darken after Sept. 11." *New York Times*, September 11. https://www.nytimes.com/2003/09/11/world/two-years-later-world-opinion-foreign-views-of-us-darken-after-sept-11.html

Best, Geoffrey. 1980. *Humanity in Warfare: The Modern History of the International Law of Armed Conflicts.* New York: Columbia University Press.

Best, Geoffrey. 1994. *War and Law since 1945.* Oxford, UK: Clarendon Press.

Beste, Ralf, Dirk Koch, Romain Leick, Gabor Steingart, and Alexander Szandar. 2003. "More Europe." *Der Spiegel*, March 31. https://www.spiegel.de/international/spiegel/cover-story-more-europe-a-242828.html

Biddle, Stephen, Jeffrey A. Friedman, and Jacob N. Shapiro. 2012. "Testing the Surge: Why Did Violence Decline in Iraq in 2007." *International Security* 37 (1): 7–40.

Biden, Joseph R. 2023. "Remarks by President Biden ahead of the One-Year Anniversary of Russia's Brutal and Unprovoked Invasion of Ukraine." *The White House*, February 21. https://www.whitehouse.gov/briefing-room/speeches-remarks/2023/02/21/remarks-by-president-biden-ahead-of-the-one-year-anniversary-of-russias-brutal-and-unprovoked-invasion-of-ukraine/

Bierce, Ambrose. 2000. *The Unabridged Devil's Dictionary.* Athens: University of Georgia Press.

Billias, George A. 2009. *American Constitutionalism Heard Round the World, 1776–1989: A Global Perspective.* New York: New York University Press.

Blauwkamp, Joan M, Charles M Rowling, and William Pettit. 2018. "Are Americans Really Okay with Torture? The Effects of Message Framing on Public Opinion." *Media, War & Conflict* 11 (4): 446–75.

Blum, Gabriella, and Philip B. Heymann. 2013. *Laws, Outlaws, and Terrorists: Lessons from the War on Terrorism.* Cambridge, MA: MIT Press.

Boemeke, Manfred F., Gerald D. Feldman, and Elisabeth Glase, eds. 1998. *The Treaty of Versailles: A Reassessment after 75 Years.* New York: Cambridge University Press.

Bolton, John R. 2000a. "Is There Really 'Law' in International Affairs?" *Transnational Law and Contemporary Problems* 10 (1): 1–48.

Bolton, John R. 2000b. "The Risks and Weaknesses of the International Criminal Court from America's Perspective." *Virginia Journal of International Law* 41 (1): 186–203.

Boot, Max. 2003. "Power Resentment Comes with the Territory." *Washington Post*, March 23. https://www.washingtonpost.com/archive/opinions/2003/03/23/power-resentment-comes-with-the-territory/2807fcf6-8f9b-4253-b309-7804afe6a307/

Bork, Robert H. 1971. "Neutral Principles and Some First Amendment Problems." *Indiana Law Journal* 47 (1): 1–35.

Bowden, Mark. 2004. "Lessons of Abu Ghraib." *Atlantic Monthly* 294 (1): 37–40.

Bowles, Samuel. 1998. "Endogenous Preferences: The Cultural Consequences of Markets and Other Economic Institutions." *Journal of Economic Literature* 36 (1): 75–111.

Boyle, Francis A. 1985. *World Politics and International Law.* Durham, NC: Duke University Press.

Braman, Eileen, and Thomas E. Nelson. 2007. "Mechanism of Motivated Reasoning? Analogical Perception in Discrimination Disputes." *American Journal of Political Science* 51 (4): 940–56.

Brecher, Bob. 2007. *Torture and the Ticking Bomb.* Oxford, UK: Blackwell Publishing.

Brettschneider, Corey. 2015. "Popular Constitutionalism Contra Populism." *Constitutional Commentary* 30 (1): 81–88.

Brewster, Rachel. 2003. "The Domestic Origins of International Agreements." *Virginia Journal of International Law* 44 (2): 501–44.

Brewster, Rachel. 2009a. "The Limits of Reputation on Compliance." *International Theory* 1 (2): 323–33.

Brewster, Rachel. 2009b. "Unpacking the State's Reputation." *Harvard International Law Journal* 50 (2): 231–69.

Breyer, Stephen. 2005. *Active Liberty: Interpreting Our Democratic Constitution.* New York: Knopf.

Brierly, James L. 1928. *Brierly's Law of Nations: An Introduction to the Role of International Law in International Relations.* Oxford, UK: Oxford University Press.

Brinkerhoff, John R., Ted Silva, and John Seitz. 1992. *United States Army Reserve in Operation Desert Storm. Enemy Prisoner of War Operations: The 800th Military Police Brigade.* Washington, DC: Department of the Army.

Brooks, Deborah J., and Benjamin A. Valentino. 2011. "A War of One's Own: Understanding the Gender Gap in Support for War." *Public Opinion Quarterly* 75 (2): 270–86.

Brown, Rebecca L. 1998. "Accountability, Liberty, and the Constitution." *Columbia Law Review* 98 (3): 531–79.

Brownlie, Ian. 2008. *Principles of Public International Law.* New York: Oxford University Press.

Bruck, Connie. 2016. "Why Obama Has Failed to Close Guantánamo." *New Yorker,* July 25. https://www.newyorker.com/magazine/2016/08/01/why-obama-has-failed-to-close-guantanamo

Brunnée, Jutta, and Stephen J. Toope. 2010. *Legitimacy and Legality in International Law: An Interactional Account.* Cambridge, UK: Cambridge University Press.

Bruno, Greg. 2008. "Finding a Place for the 'Sons of Iraq.'" *Council on Foreign Relations.* https://www.cfr.org/backgrounder/finding-place-sons-iraq

Brutger, Ryan, and Joshua D. Kertzer. 2018. "A Dispositional Theory of Reputation Costs." *International Organization* 72 (3): 693–724.

Brutger, Ryan, Joshua D. Kertzer, Jonathan Renshon, Dustin Tingley, and Chagai M. Weiss. 2023. "Abstraction and Detail in Experimental Design." *American Journal of Political Science* 67 (4): 979–95.

Bryce, James. 1909. *The American Commonwealth.* Vol. 2, *The Party System, Public Opinion.* New York: Macmillan.

Budiansky, Stephen. 1993. "A New World's Signs of Confusion." *U.S. News & World Report* 115 (1): 8.

Bull, Hedley. 1977. *The Anarchical Society: A Study of Order in World Politics.* New York: Columbia University Press.

Burke, Edmund. [1796] 1999. *Edmund Burke, the Select Works of Edmund Burke.* Vol. 3, *Letters on a Regicide Peace.* Indianapolis: Liberty Fund.

Burkholder, Richard. 2004. "Gallup Poll of Iraq: Liberated, Occupied, or in Limbo?" *Gallup*, April 28. https://news.gallup.com/poll/11527/gallup-poll-iraq-liberated-occupied-limbo.aspx

Burley, Anne-Marie, and Walter Mattli. 1993. "Europe before the Court: A Political Theory of Legal Integration." *International Organization* 47 (1): 41–76.

Busby, Joshua, and Jonathan Monten. 2018. "Has Liberal Internationalism Been Trumped?" In *Chaos in the Liberal Order: The Trump Presidency and International Politics in the Twenty-First Century*, edited by Robert Jervis, Francis Gavin, Joshua Rovner, and Diane Labrosse, 49–60. New York: Columbia University Press.

Bush, George W. 2001. "Remarks by the President to Employees at the Pentagon." *The White House*, September 21. https://georgewbush-whitehouse.archives.gov/news/releases/2001/09/20010917-3.html

Bush, George W. 2002. *The National Security Strategy of the United States of America*. Washington, DC: U.S. Government Printing Office.

Bush, George W. 2003. *National Strategy for Combating Terrorism*. Washington, DC: U.S. Government Printing Office.

Bush, George W. 2006. "President Bush's Speech on Terrorism." *New York Times*, September 6. https://www.nytimes.com/2006/09/06/washington/06bush_transcript.html

Búzás, Zoltán I. 2018. "Is the Good News about Law Compliance Good News about Norm Compliance? The Case of Racial Equality." *International Organization* 72 (2): 351–85.

Byers, Michael. 1999. *Custom, Power and the Power of Rules: International Relations and Customary International Law*. Cambridge, UK: Cambridge University Press.

Byman, Daniel. 2013. "Why Drones Work: The Case for Washington's Weapon of Choice." *Foreign Affairs* 92 (4): 32–43.

Campbell, Angus, Philip E. Converse, Warren E. Miller, and Donald E. Stokes. 1960. *The American Voter*. Chicago: University of Chicago Press.

Canes-Wrone, Brandice. 2006. *Who Leads Whom?: Presidents, Policy, and the Public*. Chicago: University of Chicago Press.

Canes-Wrone, Brandice. 2015. "From Mass Preferences to Policy." *Annual Review of Political Science* 18: 147–65.

Canovan, Margaret. 1999. "Trust the People! Populism and the Two Faces of Democracy." *Political Studies* 47 (1): 2–16.

Cardenas, Sonia. 2007. *Conflict and Compliance: State Responses to International Human Rights Pressure*. Philadelphia: University of Pennsylvania Press.

Carlsmith, J. Merrill, Phoebe C. Ellsworth, and Elhot Aronson. 1976. *Methods of Research in Social Psychology*. Reading, MA: Addison-Wesley.

Carpenter, Charli. 2008. "Geneva 2.0." *National Interest* 96: 60–67.

Carpenter, Charli, and Alexander H. Montgomery. 2020. "The Stopping Power of Norms: Saturation Bombing, Civilian Immunity and U.S. Attitudes toward the Laws of War." *International Security* 45 (2): 140–69.

Carpenter, Charli, Alexander H. Montgomery, and Alexandria Nylen. 2021. "Breaking Bad? How Survey Experiments Prime Americans for War Crimes." *Perspectives on Politics* 19 (3): 912–24.

Carr, Edward H. 1939. *The Twenty Years Crisis, 1919–1939: An Introduction to the Study of International Relations*. London: MacMillan.

Carrubba, Clifford J. 2009. "A Model of the Endogenous Development of Judicial Institutions in Federal and International Systems." *Journal of Politics* 71 (1): 55–69.

Carvin, Stephanie. 2010. *Prisoners of America's Wars: From the Early Republic to Guantanamo*. New York: Columbia University Press.

Caspary, William R. 1970. "The 'Mood Theory': A Study of Public Opinion and Foreign Policy." *American Political Science Review* 64 (2): 536–47.

Cass, Deborah Z. 2001. "The 'Constitutionalization' of International Trade Law: Judicial Norm-Generation as the Engine of Constitutional Development in International Trade." *European Journal of International Law* 12 (1): 39–75.

Cassese, Antonio. 1986. *International Law in a Divided World*. Oxford, UK: Clarendon Press.

Cederman, Lars-Erik, Simon Hug, Livia I. Schubiger, and Francisco Villamil. 2020. "Civilian Victimization and Ethnic Civil War." *Journal of Conflict Resolution* 64 (7–8): 1199–225.

Center for Civilians in Conflict. 2012. *The Civilian Impact of Drones: Unexamined Costs, Unanswered Questions*. https://civiliansinconflict.org/publications/research/civilian-impact-drones-unexamined-costs-unanswered-questions/

Chakravarty, Anuradha. 2012. "Political Science and the 'Micro-Politics' Research Agenda." *Journal of Political Sciences & Public Affairs* 1 (1): e103.

Chapman, Terrence L. 2011. *Securing Approval: Domestic Politics and Multilateral Authorization for War*. Chicago: University of Chicago Press.

Chapman, Terrence L., and Stephen Chaudoin. 2013. "Ratification Patterns and the International Criminal Court." *International Studies Quarterly* 57 (2): 400–409.

Chapman, Terrence L., and Stephen Chaudoin. 2020. "Public Reactions to International Legal Institutions: The ICC in a Developing Democracy." *Journal of Politics* 82 (4): 1305–20.

Charlesworth, Hilary, Christine Chinkin, and Shelley Wright. 1991. "Feminist Approaches to International Law." *American Journal of International Law* 85 (4): 613–45.

Chaudoin, Stephen. 2014a. "Audience Features and the Strategic Timing of Trade Disputes." *International Organization* 68 (4): 877–911.

Chaudoin, Stephen. 2014b. "Promises or Policies? An Experimental Analysis of International Agreements and Audience Reactions." *International Organization* 68 (1): 235–56.

Chaudoin, Stephen. 2016. "How Contestation Moderates the Effects of International Institutions: The International Criminal Court and Kenya." *Journal of Politics* 78 (2): 557–71.

Chaudoin, Stephen, Helen V. Milner, and Xun Pang. 2015. "International Systems and Domestic Politics: Linking Complex Interactions with Empirical Models in International Relations." *International Organization* 69 (2): 275–309.

Chaudoin, Stephen, Helen V. Milner, and Dustin H. Tingley. 2010. "The Center Still Holds: Liberal Internationalism Survives." *International Security* 35 (1): 75–94.

Chayes, Abram, and Antonia H. Chayes. 1993. "On Compliance." *International Organization* 47 (2): 175–205.

Chayes, Abram, and Antonia H. Chayes. 1995. *The New Sovereignty: Compliance with International Regulatory Agreements*. Cambridge, MA: Harvard University Press.

Chayes, Abram, Thomas Ehrlich, and Andreas F. Lowenfeld. 1968. *International Legal Process; Materials for an Introductory Course*. Boston: Little, Brown.

Chayes, Antonia. 2008. "How American Treaty Behavior Threatens National Security." *International Security* 33 (1): 45–81.

Checkel, Jeffrey T. 2001. "Why Comply? Social Learning and European Identity Change." *International Organization* 55 (3): 553–88.

Chemerinsky, Erwin. 2004. "In Defense of Judicial Review: A Reply to Professor Kramer." *California Law Review* 92 (4): 1013–26.

Chen, Frederick R., Jon C. W. Pevehouse, and Ryan M. Powers. 2023. "Great Expectations: The Democratic Advantage in Trade Attitudes." *World Politics* 75 (2) 316–52.

Cheney, Richard B. 2001. "Remarks at the 56th Annual Alfred E. Smith Memorial Foundation Dinner." *The White House*, October 18. https://georgewbush-whitehouse. archives.gov/vicepresident/news-speeches/speeches/vp20011018.html

Cheney, Richard B. 2009. "Remarks by Richard B. Cheney." *American Enterprise Institute*, May 21. https://www.aei.org/research-products/speech/ remarks-by-richard-b-cheney/

Chilton, Adam S. 2014. "The Influence of International Human Rights Agreements on Public Opinion: An Experimental Study." *Chicago Journal of International Law* 15 (1): 110–37.

Chilton, Adam S. 2015. "The Laws of War and Public Opinion: An Experimental Study." *Journal of Institutional and Theoretical Economics* 171 (1): 181–201.

Chilton, Adam S., and Katerina Linos. 2021. "Preferences and Compliance with International Law." *Theoretical Inquiries in Law* 22 (2): 247–98.

Chilton, Adam S., and Dustin H. Tingley. 2013. "Why the Study of International Law Needs Experiments." *Columbia Journal of Transnational Law* 52 (1): 173–238.

Chilton, Adam S., and Mila Versteeg. 2015. "The Failure of Constitutional Torture Prohibitions." *Journal of Legal Studies* 44 (2): 417–52.

Chilton, Adam S., and Mila Versteeg. 2016. "International Law, Constitutional Law, and Public Support for Torture." *Research & Politics* 3 (1): 1–9.

Chiu, Yvonne. 2019. *Conspiring with the Enemy: The Ethic of Cooperation in Warfare.* New York: Columbia University Press.

Chong, Dennis, and James N. Druckman. 2007a. "Framing Public Opinion in Competitive Democracies." *American Political Science Review* 10 (4): 637–55.

Chong, Dennis, and James N. Druckman. 2007b. "Framing Theory." *Annual Review of Political Science* 10 103–26.

Christopher, Russell. 2012. "Imminence in Justified Targeted Killing." In *Targeted Killings: Law and Morality in an Asymmetrical World*, edited by Claire Finkelstein, Jens D. Ohlin, and Andrew Altman, 253–84. Oxford, UK: Oxford University Press.

Chu, Jonathan A. 2019. "A Clash of Norms? How Reciprocity and International Humanitarian Law Affect American Opinion on the Treatment of POWs." *Journal of Conflict Resolution* 63 (5): 1140–64.

Chu, Jonathan Art, and Stefano Recchia. 2022. "Does Public Opinion Affect the Preferences of Foreign Policy Leaders? Experimental Evidence from the UK Parliament." *Journal of Politics* 84 (3): 1874–77.

Clancy, Tom, and Chuck Horner. 1999. *Every Man a Tiger: The Gulf War Air Campaign.* Rev. ed. New York: Berkley.

Clark, Grenville, and Louis B. Sohn. 1958. *World Peace through World Law.* Cambridge, MA: Harvard University Press.

Clayton, Govinda, and Andrew Thomson. 2014. "The Enemy of My Enemy is My Friend . . . the Dynamics of Self-Defense Forces in Irregular War: The Case of the Sons of Iraq." *Studies in Conflict & Terrorism* 37 (11): 920–35.

Clodfelter, Michael. 2008. *Warfare and Armed Conflicts: A Statistical Reference to Casualty and Other Figures, 1494–2007.* Jefferson, NC: McFarland.

Cody, Edward. 1991. "Friendly Persuasion-Stick, Then Carrot." *Washington Post*, February 7. https://www.washingtonpost.com/archive/politics/1991/02/07/ friendly-persuasion_stick-then-carrot/4e1996b4-293d-4f20-ab45-db9e4ce6d1fe/

Coggins, Bridget. 2014. *Power Politics and State Formation in the Twentieth Century: The Dynamics of Recognition.* Cambridge, UK: Cambridge University Press.

Coleman, Jules. 1982. "Negative and Positive Positivism." *Journal of Legal Studies* 11 (1): 139–64.

Conetta, Carl. 2002. *Strange Victory: A Critical Appraisal of Operation Enduring Freedom and the Afghanistan War.* Cambridge, MA: Project on Defense Alternatives.

Conover, Pamela Johnston, and Stanley Feldman. 1984. "How People Organize the Political World: A Schematic Model." *American Journal of Political Science* 28 (1): 95–126.

Conrad, Courtenay R., Sarah E. Croco, Brad T. Gomez, and Will H. Moore. 2018. "Threat Perception and American Support for Torture." *Political Behavior* 40 (4): 989–1009.

Converse, Philip E. 1964. "The Nature of Belief Systems in Mass Publics." In *Ideology and Discontent*, edited by David Apter, 206–61. New York: Free Press of Glencoe.

Converse, Philip E. 1970. "Attitudes and Non-Attitudes: Continuation of a Dialogue." In *The Quantitative Analysis of Social Problems*, edited by Edward R. Tufte, 168–90. Reading, MA: Addison-Wesley.

Cope, Kevin L., and Charles Crabtree. 2020. "A Nationalist Backlash to International Refugee Law: Evidence from a Survey Experiment in Turkey." *Journal of Empirical Legal Studies* 17 (4): 752–88.

Coplin, William D. 1965. "International Law and Assumptions About the State System." *World Politics* 17 (4): 615–34.

Cordell, Rebecca. 2021. "The Political Costs of Abusing Human Rights: International Cooperation in Extraordinary Rendition." *Journal of Conflict Resolution* 65 (2–3): 255–82.

Cordesman, Anthony H. 2008. *Iraq's Insurgency and the Road to Civil Conflict.* Westport, CT: Praeger Security International.

Cortell, Andrew P., and James W. Davis. 1996. "How Do International Institutions Matter? The Domestic Impact of International Rules and Norms." *International Studies Quarterly* 40 (4): 451–78.

Cortright, David, and George A. Lopez. 1999. "Are Sanctions Just? The Problematic Case of Iraq." *Journal of International Affairs* 52 (2): 735–55.

Cottam, Martha L., Joe W. Huseby, and Bruno Baltodano. 2016. *Confronting Al Qaeda: The Sunni Awakening and American Strategy in Al Anbar.* Lanham, MD: Rowman & Littlefield.

Cover, Robert M. 1983. "The Supreme Court, 1982 Term—Foreword: *Nomos* and Narrative." *Harvard Law Review* 97 (1): 4–68.

Cover, Robert M. 1986. "Violence and the Word." *Yale Law Journal* 95 (8): 1601–29.

Crandall, Samuel B. 1904. *Treaties, Their Making and Enforcement.* New York: Columbia University Press.

Crawford, Neta C. 1993. "Decolonization as an International Norm: The Evolution of Practices, Arguments, and Beliefs." In *Emerging Norms of Justified Intervention: A Collection of Essays from a Project of the American Academy of Arts and Sciences*, edited by L. W. Reed, and C. Kaysen, 37–61. Cambridge, MA: Committee on International Security Studies, American Academy of Arts and Sciences.

Crescenzi, Mark J. C., Jacob D. Kathman, Katja B. Kleinberg, and Reed M. Wood. 2012. "Reliability, Reputation, and Alliance Formation." *International Studies Quarterly* 56 (2): 259–74.

Cronin, Audrey Kurth. 2013. "Why Drones Fail: When Tactics Drive Strategy." *Foreign Affairs* 92 (4): 44–54.

Croson, Rachel. 2009. "Experimental Law and Economics." *Annual Review of Law and Social Science* 5: 25–44.

Cross, Frank B. 1999. "The Relevance of Law in Human Rights Protection." *International Review of Law and Economics* 19 (1): 87–98.

D'Amato, Anthony. 1984. "Is International Law Really 'Law'?" *Northwestern University Law Review* 79 (5 & 6): 1293–314.

D'Amato, Anthony A. 1987. *International Law: Process and Prospect.* Dobbs Ferry, NY: Transnational Publishers.

Daalder, Ivo H. 2003. "The Coalition That Isn't." *Brookings Daily War Report*, March 24. https://www.brookings.edu/articles/the-coalition-that-isnt/

Dafoe, Allan, Jonathan Renshon, and Paul Huth. 2014. "Reputation and Status as Motives for War." *Annual Review of Political Science* 17: 371–93.

Dafoe, Allan, Baobao Zhang, and Devin Caughey. 2018. "Information Equivalence in Survey Experiments." *Political Analysis* 26 (4): 399–416.

Dahl, Robert. 1989. *Democracy and Its Critics.* New Haven, CT: Yale University Press.

Dai, Xinyuan. 2005. "Why Comply? The Domestic Constituency Mechanism." *International Organization* 53 (2): 363–98.

Dai, Xinyuan. 2007. *International Institutions and National Policies.* Cambridge, UK: Cambridge University Press.

Dancy, Geoff, and Christopher J. Fariss. 2017. "Rescuing Human Rights Law from International Legalism and Its Critics." *Human Rights Quarterly* 39 (1): 1–36.

Dancy, Geoffrey T. 2021. "The Hidden Impacts of the ICC: An Innovative Assessment Using Google Data." *Leiden Journal of International Law* 34 (3): 729–47.

Danner, Mark. 2004. *Torture and Truth: America, Abu Ghraib, and the War on Terror.* New York: New York Review of Books.

Davenport, Christian. 2007a. "State Repression and Political Order." *Annual Review of Political Science* 10: 1–23.

Davenport, Christian. 2007b. *State Repression and the Domestic Democratic Peace.* Cambridge, UK: Cambridge University Press.

Davenport, Christian A. 1996. "'Constitutional Promises' and Repressive Reality: A Cross-National Time-Series Investigation of Why Political and Civil Liberties Are Suppressed." *Journal of Politics* 58 (3): 627–54.

de Sola Pool, Ithiel. 1973. "Communication in Totalitarian Societies." In *Handbook of Political Communication*, edited by Ithiel de Sola Pool and Wilbur Schramm, 462–511. Chicago: Rand McNally College Publishing.

de Tocqueville, Alexis. 1945. *Democracy in America.* New York: Alfred A. Knopf.

Delahunty, Robert J., and John Yoo. 2006. "Executive Power v. International Law." *Harvard Journal of Law & Public Policy* 73 (1): 73–113.

Delli Carpini, Michael X., and Scott Keeter. 1996. *What Americans Know about Politics and Why it Matters.* Princeton, NJ: Princeton University Press.

Dellmuth, Lisa, Jan Aart Scholte, Jonas Tallberg, and Soetkin Verhaegen. 2022a. *Citizens, Elites, and the Legitimacy of Global Governance.* Oxford, UK: Oxford University Press.

Dellmuth, Lisa, Jan Aart Scholte, Jonas Tallberg, and Soetkin Verhaegen. 2022b. "The Elite–Citizen Gap in International Organization Legitimacy." *American Political Science Review* 116 (1): 283–300.

Dellmuth, Lisa M., and Jonas Tallberg. 2021. "Elite Communication and the Popular Legitimacy of International Organizations." *British Journal of Political Science* 51 (3): 1292–313.

Dempsey, Judy. 2004. "Hungary Joins Others in Pulling Troops from Iraq." *New York Times*, November 4. https://www.nytimes.com/2004/11/04/world/europe/hungary-joins-others-in-pulling-troops-from-iraq.html

Department of the Army. 1992. *FM 34–52: Intelligence Interrogation*. Washington, DC: U.S. Government Printing Office.

Department of the Army. 2006. *FM 3–24: Counterinsurgency*. Washington, DC: U.S. Government Printing Office.

Dickson, Eric. 2011. "Economics versus Psychology Experiments: Stylization, Incentives, and Deception." In *Cambridge Handbook of Experimental Political Science*, edited by James N. Druckman, Donald P. Green, James H. Kuklinski, and Arthur Lupia, 58–69. Cambridge, UK: Cambridge University Press.

Dill, Janina, and Livia I. Schubiger. 2021. "Attitudes towards the Use of Force: Instrumental Imperatives, Moral Principles and International Law." *American Journal of Political Science* 65 (3): 612–33.

DiMaggio, Paul J., and Walter L. Powell. 1991. "Introduction." In *The New Institutionalism in Organizational Analysis*, edited by Walter L. Powell, and Paul J. DiMaggio, 1–38. Chicago: University of Chicago Press.

Donnelly, Tom. 2012. "Making Popular Constitutionalism Work." *Wisconsin Law Review* 2012 (1): 159–94.

Dowdle, Michael. 2012. "Popular Constitutionalism and the Constitutional Meaning of Charter 08." In *Liu Xiaobo, Charter 08, and the Challenges of Political Reform in China*, edited by Jean-Philippe Beja, and Hualing Fu, 205–28. Hong Kong: University of Hong Kong Press.

Downes, Alexander B. 2007. "Restraint or Propellant? Democracy and Civilian Fatalities in Interstate Wars." *Journal of Conflict Resolution* 51 (6): 872–904.

Downes, Alexander B. 2008. *Targeting Civilians in War*. Ithaca, NY: Cornell University Press.

Downs, George W., and Michael A. Jones. 2002. "Reputation, Compliance, and International Law." *Journal of Legal Studies* 31 (1): S95–S114.

Downs, George W., David M. Rocke, and Peter N. Barsoom. 1996. "Is the Good News about Compliance Good News about Cooperation?" *International Organization* 50 (3): 379–406.

Doyle, Robert C. 2010. *The Enemy in Our Hands: America's Treatment of Prisoners of War from the Revolution to the War on Terror*. Lexington: University Press of Kentucky.

Drezner, Daniel W. 2008. "The Realist Tradition in American Public Opinion." *Perspectives on Politics* 6 (1): 51–70.

Druckman, James N. 2001. "On the Limits of Framing Effects: Who Can Frame?" *Journal of Politics* 63 (4): 1041–66.

Druckman, James N. 2022. *Experimental Thinking: A Primer on Social Science Experiments*. Cambridge, UK: Cambridge University Press.

Druckman, James N., Donald P. Green, James H. Kuklinski, and Arthur Lupia. 2006. "The Growth and Development of Experimental Research in Political Science." *American Political Science Review* 100 (4): 1–9.

Druckman, James N., and Lawrence R. Jacobs. 2015. *Who Governs?: Presidents, Public Opinion, and Manipulation*. Chicago: University of Chicago Press.

Druckman, James N., and Thomas J. Leeper. 2012. "Learning More from Political Communication Experiments: Pretreatment and Its Effects." *American Journal of Political Science* 56 (4): 875–96.

Duffy, Helen. 2005. *The "War on Terror" and the Framework of International Law*. Cambridge, UK: Cambridge University Press.

Dunlap, Charles J., Jr. 2001. "Law and Military Interventions: Preserving Humanitarian Values in 21st Century Conflicts." Paper presented at the Humanitarian Challenges in Military Intervention Conference, Carr Center for Human Rights Policy, Kennedy School of Government, November 29.

Dunning, Thad. 2012. *Natural Experiments in the Social Sciences: A Design-Based Approach*. Cambridge, UK: Cambridge University Press.

Dunoff, Jeffrey L., and Joel P. Trachtman. 1999. "Economic Analysis of International Law." *Yale Journal of International Law* 24 (1): 1–60.

Dworkin, Ronald. 1986. *Law's Empire*. Cambridge, MA: Harvard University Press.

Economist. 2001. "Soft Words, Uneasy Thoughts." October 13, 23. https://www.economist.com/special-report/2001/10/11/soft-words-uneasy-thoughts

Edelstein, David M. 2004. "Occupational Hazards: Why Military Occupations Succeed or Fail." *International Security* 29 (1): 49–91.

Edwards, George C. 1997. "Aligning Tests with Theory: Presidential Approval as a Source of Influence in Congress." *Congress & the Presidency* 24 (2): 113–30.

Edwards, George C. 2006. *On Deaf Ears: The Limits of the Bully Pulpit*. New Have, CT: Yale University Press.

Edwards, Janis L. 1997. *Political Cartoons in the 1988 Presidential Campaign: Image, Metaphor, and Narrative*. New York: Garland Publishing.

Eggen, Dan. 2005. "Gonzales Nomination Draws Military Criticism." *Washington Post*, January 4. https://www.washingtonpost.com/archive/politics/2005/01/04/gonzales-nomination-draws-military-criticism/71e5a456-123d-4531-a935-cf9945002b44/

Elkins, Zachary, Tom Ginsburg, and James Melton. 2009. *The Endurance of National Constitutions*. Cambridge, UK: Cambridge University Press.

Elkins, Zachary, Tom Ginsburg, and Beth Simmons. 2013. "Getting to Rights: Treaty Ratification, Constitutional Convergence, and Human Rights Practice." *Harvard International Law Journal* 54 (1): 61–95.

Engel, Christoph. 2011. "The Emergence of a New Rule of Customary Law: An Experimental Contribution." *Review of Law & Economics* 7 (3): 767–89.

Enloe, Cynthia H. 2014. *Bananas, Beaches and Bases: Making Feminist Sense of International Politics*. Berkeley: University of California Press.

Enterline, Andrew J., and J. Michael Greig. 2008. "Perfect Storms?: Political Instability in Imposed Polities and the Futures of Iraq and Afghanistan." *Journal of Conflict Resolution* 52 (6): 880–915.

Eskridge, William N. 1990. "The New Textualism." *UCLA Law Review* 37 (4): 621–91.

Evangelista, Matthew. 1997. "Domestic Structure and International Change." In *New Thinking in International Relations Research*, edited by Michael W. Doyle, and G. John Ikenberry, 202–28. Boulder: Westview Press.

Fagan, Moira, and Christine Huang. 2019. "United Nations Gets Mostly Positive Marks from People around the World." *Pew Research Center*, September 23. https://www.pewresearch.org/short-reads/2019/09/23/united-nations-gets-mostly-positive-marks-from-people-around-the-world/

Fagen, Richard R. 1960. "Some Assessments and Uses of Public Opinion in Diplomacy." *Public Opinion Quarterly* 24 (3): 448–57.

Fahlstrom, Paul G., and Thomas J. Gleason. 2012. *Introduction to UAV Systems*. Chichester, UK: Wiley.

Falk, Richard A. 1964. "Janus Tormented: The International Law of Internal War." In *International Aspects of Civil Strife*, edited by James N. Rosenau, 185–248. Princeton, NJ: Princeton University Press.

Farber, Daniel A. 1989. "Statutory Interpretation and Legislative Supremacy." *Georgetown Law Journal* 78 (2): 281–318.

Fariss, Christopher J. 2014. "Respect for Human Rights Has Improved over Time: Modeling the Changing Standard of Accountability." *American Political Science Review* 108 (2): 297–318.

Fassbender, Bardo. 1998. "The United Nations Charter as Constitution of the International Community." *Columbia Journal of Transnational Law* 36 (3): 529–619.

Favole, Jared A. 2013. "White House Defends Drone Operations." *Wall Street Journal*, October 22. https://www.wsj.com/articles/BL-WB-41303

Fazal, Tanisha M. 2018. *Wars of Law: Unintended Consequences in the Regulation of Armed Conflict*. Ithaca, NY: Cornell University Press.

Fearon, James, and Alexander Wendt. 2002. "Rationalism v. Constructivism: A Skeptical View." In *Handbook of International Relations*, edited by Walter Carlsnaes, Thomas Risse, and Beth A. Simmons, 52–72. Thousand Oaks, CA: SAGE Publications.

Fearon, James D. 1997. "Signaling Foreign Policy Interests: Tying Hands versus Sinking Costs." *Journal of Conflict Resolution* 41 (1): 68–90.

Fearon, James D., and David D. Laitin. 2003. "Ethnicity, Insurgency, and Civil War." *American Political Science Review* 97 (1): 75–90.

Feaver, Peter, and Edmund Malesky. 2000. "A Compassionate Foreign Policy?" *Washington Examiner*, September 25. https://www.washingtonexaminer.com/weekly-standard/a-compassionate-foreign-policy

Feaver, Peter D., and Christopher Gelpi. 2004. *Choosing Your Battles: American Civil-Military Relations and the Use of Force*. Princeton, NJ: Princeton University Press.

Feldstein, Steven. 2017. "Under Trump, US Airstrikes Are Killing More Civilians." *Salon*, October 10. https://www.salon.com/2017/10/20/under-trump-presidency-us-airstrikes-kill-more-civilians_partner-2/

Ferguson, Niall. 2004. "Prisoner Taking and Prisoner Killing in the Age of Total War: Towards a Political Economy of Military Defeat." *War in History* 11 (2): 148–92.

Fiedler, Klaus, Malte Schott, and Thorsten Meiser. 2011. "What Mediation Analysis Can (Not) Do." *Journal of Experimental Social Psychology* 47 (6): 1231–36.

Filkins, Dexter. 2014. "Khalid Sheikh Mohammed and the C.I.A." *New Yorker*, December 31. https://www.newyorker.com/news/news-desk/khalid-sheikh-mohammed-cia

Finkelstein, Claire, Jens D. Ohlin, and Andrew Altman, eds. 2012. *Targeted Killings: Law and Morality in an Asymmetrical World*. Oxford, UK: Oxford University Press.

Finnemore, Martha. 1996. *National Interests in International Society*. Ithaca, NY: Cornell University Press.

Finnemore, Martha. 2000. "Are Legal Norms Distinctive?" *New York University Journal of International Law and Politics* 32 (3): 699–705.

Finnemore, Martha, and Kathryn Sikkink. 1998. "International Norm Dynamics and Political Change." *International Organization* 52 (4): 887–917.

Fisher, Roger. 1961. "Bringing Law to Bear on Governments." *Harvard Law Review* 74 (6): 1130–40.

Fogarty, Gerald P. 2005. *Guantanamo Bay—Undermining the Global War on Terror*. Carlisle, PA: U.S. Army War College.

Fortna, Virginia Page. 2003. "Scraps of Paper? Agreements and the Durability of Peace." *International Organization* 57 (2): 337–72.

Fortna, Virginia Page. 2004. *Peace Time: Cease-Fire Agreements and the Durability of Peace*. Princeton, NJ: Princeton University Press.

Fortna, Virginia Page. 2008. *Does Peacekeeping Work? Shaping Belligerent's Choices after Civil War*. Princeton, NJ: Princeton University Press.

Francis, Megan M. 2014. *Civil Rights and the Making of the Modern American State*. Cambridge, UK: Cambridge University Press.

Franck, Thomas M. 1990. *The Power of Legitimacy among Nations*. New York: Oxford University Press.

Freedman, Lawrence, and Efraim Karsh. 1993. *The Gulf Conflict 1990–1991: Diplomacy and War in the New World Order*. Princeton, NJ: Princeton University Press.

Frieden, Jeffry, and Ronald Rogowski. 1996. "The Impact of the International Economy on National Policies: An Analytical Overview." In *Internationalization and Domestic Politics*, edited by Robert O. Keohane, and Helen V. Milner, 25–47. Cambridge, UK: Cambridge University Press.

Friedman, Barry. 2003. "Mediated Popular Constitutionalism." *Michigan Law Review* 101 (8): 2596–636.

Friedman, Barry. 2009. *The Will of the People: How Public Opinion Has Influenced the Supreme Court and Shaped the Meaning of the Constitution*. New York: Farrar, Straus and Giroux.

Friedmann, Wolfgang. 1964. *The Changing Structure of International Law*. New York: Columbia University Press.

Fuhrmann, Matthew, and Michael C. Horowitz. 2017. "Droning on: Explaining the Proliferation of Unmanned Aerial Vehicles." *International Organization* 71 (2): 397–418.

Fuller, Lon L. 1960. "Adjudication and the Rule of Law." *Proceedings of the American Society of International Law at Its Annual Meeting* 54: 1–8.

Fuller, Lon L. 1969. *The Morality of Law*. New Haven, CT: Yale University Press.

Gaines, Brian J., James H. Kuklinski, and Paul J. Quirk. 2006. "The Logic of the Survey Experiment Reexamined." *Political Analysis* 15 (1): 1–20.

Gallup, George. 1938. "Testing Public Opinion." *Public Opinion Quarterly* 2 (1): 8–14.

Gambetta, Diego. 1993. *The Sicilian Mafia: The Business of Private Protection*. Cambridge, MA: Harvard University Press.

Garrett, Geoffrey. 1995. "The Politics of Legal Integration in the European Union." *International Organization* 49 (1): 171–81.

Gartzke, Erik, and Kristian S. Gleditsch. 2004. "Why Democracies May Actually Be Less Reliable Allies." *American Journal of Political Science* 48 (4): 775–95.

Gaubatz, Kurt T. 1996. "Democratic States and Commitment in International Relations." *International Organization* 50 (1): 109–39.

Gelpi, Christopher, Peter Feaver, and Jason Reifler. 2005. "Success Matters: Casualty Sensitivity and the War in Iraq." *International Security* 30 (3): 7–46.

Gelpi, Christopher, Peter D. Feaver, and Jason Reifler. 2009. *Paying the Human Costs of War: American Public Opinion and Casualties in Military Conflicts*. Princeton, NJ: Princeton University Press.

Gerber, Alan, and Donald Green. 1999. "Misperceptions about Perceptual Bias." *Annual Review of Political Science* 2: 189–210.

Gibler, Douglas M. 2008. "The Costs of Reneging: Reputation and Alliance Formation." *Journal of Conflict Resolution* 52 (3): 426–54.

Gibson, James L. 2006. *Overcoming Apartheid: Can Truth Reconcile a Divided Nation?* New York: Russell Sage Foundation.

Gibson, James L., and Gregory A. Caldeira. 2009. "Knowing the Supreme Court? A Reconsideration of Public Ignorance of the High Court." *Journal of Politics* 71 (2): 429–41.

Gibson, James L., Gregory A. Caldeira, and Vanessa A. Baird. 1998. "On the Legitimacy of National High Courts." *American Political Science Review* 92 (2): 343–58.

Gibson, Josh. 2017. "The Chartists and the Constitution: Revisiting British Popular Constitutionalism." *Journal of British Studies* 56 (1): 70–90.

Gigerenzer, G, and W. Gaissmaier. 2011. "Heuristic Decision Making." *Annual Review of Psychology* 62: 451–82.

Gilens, Martin. 2005. "Inequality and Democratic Responsiveness." *Public Opinion Quarterly* 69 (5): 778–96.

Ginsburg, Tom, Svitlana Chernykh, and Zachary Elkins. 2008. "Commitment and Diffusion: How and Why National Constitutions Incorporate International Law." *University of Illinois Law Review* 2008 (1): 201–38.

Gleditsch, Kristian S., Simon Hug, Livia I. Schubiger, and Julian Wucherpfennig. 2018. "International Conventions and Non-State Actors: Selection, Signaling, and Reputation Effects." *Journal of Conflict Resolution* 62 (2): 346–80.

Glennon, Michael J. 2001. *Limits of Law, Prerogatives of Power: Interventionism After Kosovo*. New York: Palgrave Macmillan.

Goldsmith, Jack. 2017. "The Trump Onslaught on International Law and Institutions." *Lawfare*, March 17. https://www.lawfaremedia.org/article/trump-onslaught-international-law-and-institutions

Goldsmith, Jack L. 2012. *Power and Constraint: The Accountable Presidency After 9/11*. New York: W. W. Norton.

Goldsmith, Jack L., and Daryl Levinson. 2009. "Law for States: International Law, Constitutional Law, Public Law." *Harvard Law Review* 122 (7): 1791–868.

Goldsmith, Jack L., and Eric A. Posner. 2005. *The Limits of International Law*. Oxford, UK: Oxford University Press.

Goldstein, Joshua S. 2001. *War and Gender: How Gender Shapes the War System and Vice Versa*. Cambridge, UK: Cambridge University Press.

Goldstein, Judith, and Robert O. Keohane. 1993. "Ideas and Foreign Policy: An Analytical Framework." In *Ideas and Foreign Policy: Beliefs, Institutions, and Political Change*, edited by Judith Goldstein, and Robert O. Keohane, 3–30. Ithaca, NY: Cornell University Press.

Goldstein, Judith L., and Lisa Martin. 2000. "Legalization, Trade Liberalization, and Domestic Politics: A Cautionary Note." *International Organization* 54 (3): 603–32.

Gonzales, Alberto R. 2002. "Memorandum for the President. Decision Re Application of the Geneva Convention on Prisoners of War to the Conflict with Al Qaeda and the Taliban." *National Security Archive, George Washington University*. January 25. http://www.gwu.edu/~nsarchiv/NSAEBB/NSAEBB127/02.01.25.pdf

Goodman, Ryan, and Derek Jinks. 2013. *Socializing States: Promoting Human Rights through International Law*. Oxford, UK: Oxford University Press.

Gopnik, Alison, Andrew N. Meltzoff, and Patricia K. Kuhl. 1999. *The Scientist in the Crib: Minds, Brains, and How Children Learn*. New York: William Morrow.

Gordon, Michael R., and Bernard E. Trainor. 1995. *The Generals' War: The Inside Story of the Conflict in the Gulf*. Boston: Little, Brown.

Gordon, Michael R., and Bernard E. Trainor. 2006. *Cobra II: The Inside Story of the Invasion and Occupation of Iraq*. New York: Pantheon Books.

Gourevitch, Peter. 1978. "The Second Image Reversed: The International Sources of Domestic Politics." *International Organization* 32 (4): 881–912.

Gowa, Joanne. 1994. *Allies, Adversaries, and International Trade*. Princeton, NJ: Princeton University Press.

Gowa, Joanne. 1998. "Politics at the Water's Edge: Parties, Voters, and the Use of Force Abroad." *International Organization* 52 (2): 307–24.

Graber, Doris A. 1968. *Public Opinion, the President, and Foreign Policy: Four Case Studies from the Formative Years.* New York: Holt, Rinehart and Winston.

Graber, Mark A. 2013. *A New Introduction to American Constitutionalism.* Oxford, UK: Oxford University Press.

Graham, Euan. 2016. "The Hague Tribunal's South China Sea Ruling: Empty Provocation or Slow-Burning Influence?" *Council of Councils,* August 18. https://www.cfr. org/councilofcouncils/global-memos/hague-tribunals-south-china-sea-ruling-empty-provocation-or-slow-burning-influence

Grauer, Ryan. 2014. "Why Do Soldiers Give Up? A Self-Preservation Theory of Surrender." *Security Studies* 23 (3): 622–55.

Great Britain War Office. 1958. *The Law of War on Land: Being Part III of the Manual of Military Law.* London: H. M. Stationary.

Greenberg, David. 2016. *Republic of Spin: An Inside History of the American Presidency.* New York: W. W. Norton.

Greenberg, Karen J. 2006. "The Rule of Law Finds Its Golem: Judicial Torture Then and Now." In *The Torture Debate in America,* edited by Karen J. Greenberg, 1–9. New York: Cambridge University Press.

Greenberg, Karen J., and Joshua L. Dratel, eds. 2005. *The Torture Papers: The Road to Abu Ghraib.* New York: Cambridge University Press.

Gronke, Paul, Darius Rejali, Dustin Drenguisa, James Hicksa, Peter Millera, and Bryan Nakayama. 2010. "U.S. Public Opinion on Torture, 2001–2009." *PS: Political Science & Politics* 43 (3): 437–44.

Gruber, Lloyd. 2000. *Ruling the World: Power Politics and the Rise of Supranational Institutions.* Princeton, NJ: Princeton University Press.

Guisinger, Alexandra. 2017. *American Opinion on Trade: Preferences without Politics.* Oxford, UK: Oxford University Press.

Gutierrez, Jason. 2020. "Court Finds Evidence of Crimes against Humanity in the Philippines." *New York Times,* December 15. https://www.nytimes.com/2020/12/15/world/asia/philippines-duterte-drugs-icc.html

Guzman, Andrew T. 2008. *How International Law Works: A Rational Choice Theory.* Oxford, UK: Oxford University Press.

Guzman, Andrew T., and Timothy L. Meyer. 2010. "International Soft Law." *Journal of Legal Analysis* 2 (1): 171–225.

Haas, Peter M. 1989. "Do Regimes Matter? Epistemic Communities and Mediterranean Pollution Control." *International Organization* 43 (3): 377–403.

Hafner-Burton, Emilie M. 2005. "Trading Human Rights: How Preferential Trade Agreements Influence Government Repression." *International Organization* 59 (3): 593–629.

Hafner-Burton, Emilie M., Brad L. LeVeck, David G. Victor, and James H. Fowler. 2014. "Decision Maker Preferences for International Legal Cooperation." *International Organization* 68 (4): 845–76.

Hafner-Burton, Emilie M., Neil Narang, and Brian C. Rathbun. 2019. "Introduction: What Is Populist Nationalism and Why Does It Matter?" *Journal of Politics* 81 (2): 707–11.

Hafner-Burton, Emilie M., and Jacob N. Shapiro. 2010. "Tortured Relations: Human Rights Abuses and Counterterrorism Cooperation." *PS: Political Science & Politics* 43 (3): 415–19.

Hafner-Burton, Emilie M., David G. Victor, and Yonatan Lupu. 2012. "Political Science Research on International Law: The State of the Field." *American Journal of International Law* 106 (1): 47–97.

Haggard, Stephan, and Beth A. Simmons. 1987. "Theories of International Regimes." *International Organization* 41 (3): 491–517.

Hainmueller, Jens, and Michael J. Hiscox. 2006. "Learning to Love Globalization: Education and Individual Attitudes toward International Trade." *International Organization* 60 (2): 469–98.

Hainmueller, Jens, and Michael J. Hiscox. 2007. "Educated Preferences: Explaining Attitudes toward Immigration in Europe." *International Organization* 61 (2): 399–442.

Hakimi, Monica. 2007. "The Council of Europe Addresses CIA Rendition and Detention Program." *American Journal of International Law* 101 (1): 442–52.

Halloran, Richard. 1984. "U.S. Will Not Drift into a Latin War, Weinberger Says." *New York Times*, November 29, A5.

Hamilton, Daniel W. 2006. "A Symposium on *The People Themselves: Popular Constitutionalism and Judicial Review*; Introduction." *Chicago-Kent Law Review* 81 (3): 809–12.

Hand, Keith J. 2006. "Using Law for a Righteous Purpose: The Sun Zhigang Incident and Evolving Forms of Citizen Action in the People's Republic of China." *Columbia Journal of Transnational Law* 45 (1): 114–47.

Hannah, Mark, and Caroline Gray. 2020. *Diplomacy & Restraint: The Worldview of American Voters*. New York: Eurasia Group Foundation.

Harjo, Susan S., ed. 2014. *Nation to Nation: Treaties between the United States & American Indian Nations*. Washington, DC: Smithsonian Books.

Harrison, Glenn W., and John A. List. 2004. "Field Experiments." *Journal of Economic Literature* 42 (4): 1009–55.

Hart, H. L. A. 1958. "Positivism and the Separation of Law and Morals." *Harvard Law Review* 71 (4): 593–629.

Hart, H.L.A. 2012. *The Concept of Law*. Oxford, UK: Oxford University Press.

Hartig, Luke. 2017. "Trump's New Drone Strike Policy: What's Any Different? Why It Matters." *Just Security*, September 22. https://www.justsecurity.org/45227/trumps-drone-strike-policy-different-matters/

Hasenclever, Andreas, Peter Mayer, and Volker Rittberger. 1997. *Theories of International Regimes*. Cambridge, UK: Cambridge University Press.

Hashim, Ahmed S. 2006. *Insurgency and Counter-Insurgency in Iraq*. Ithaca, NY: Cornell University Press.

Hassner, Ron E. 2022. *Anatomy of Torture*. Ithaca, NY: Cornell University Press.

Hathaway, Oona, and Scott J. Shapiro. 2011. "Outcasting: Enforcement in Domestic and International Law." *Yale Law Journal* 121 (2): 252–349.

Hathaway, Oona, and Scott J. Shapiro. 2017. *The Internationalists: How a Radical Plan to Outlaw War Remade the World*. New York: Simon & Schuster.

Hathaway, Oona A. 2002. "Do Human Rights Treaties Make a Difference?" *Yale Law Journal* 111 (8): 1935–2042.

Hathaway, Oona A. 2005. "Between Power and Principle: An Integrated Theory of International Law." *University of Chicago Law Review* 72 (2): 469–536.

Hathaway, Oona A. 2022. "A Crime in Search of a Court: How to Hold Russia Accountable." *Foreign Affairs*, May 19. https://www.foreignaffairs.com/articles/ukraine/2022-05-19/crime-search-court

Hawkins, Darren G., David A. Lake, Daniel L. Nielson, and Michael J. Tierney. 2006. "Delegation Under Anarchy: States, International Organizations, and Principal-Agent Theory." In *Delegation and Agency in International Organizations*, edited by Darren G. Hawkins, David A. Lake, Daniel L. Nielson, and Michael J. Tierney, 3–38. Cambridge, UK: Cambridge University Press.

Heintze, Hans-Joachim. 2004. "On the Relationship between Human Rights Law Protection and International Humanitarian Law." *International Review of the Red Cross* 86 (856): 789–814.

Helfer, Laurence R. 2002. "Overlegalizing Human Rights: International Relations Theory and the Commonwealth Caribbean Backlash against Human Rights Regimes." *Columbia Law Review* 102 (7): 1832–911.

Henkin, Louis. 1979. *How Nations Behave: Law and Foreign Policy*. New York: Columbia University Press.

Henkin, Louis. 1996. *Foreign Affairs and the United States Constitution*. New York: Oxford University Press.

Hersh, Seymour M. 2005. *Chain of Command: The Road From 9/11 to Abu Ghraib*. New York: Harper Collins.

Hess, Stephen. 1968. *The Ungentlemanly Art: A History of American Political Cartoons*. New York: Macmillan.

Hetherington, Marc J., and Jonathan D. Weiler. 2009. *Authoritarianism and Polarization in American Politics*. Cambridge, UK: Cambridge University Press.

Hill, Daniel W., Jr., and Zachary M. Jones. 2014. "An Empirical Evaluation of Explanations for State Repression." *American Political Science Review* 108 (3): 661–87.

Hillebrand, Claudia. 2012. *Counter-Terrorism Networks in the European Union: Maintaining Democratic Legitimacy after 9/11*. Oxford, UK: Oxford University Press.

Hinsley, F.H. 1986. *Sovereignty*. Cambridge, UK: Cambridge University Press.

Ho, Daniel E., and Donald B. Rubin. 2011. "Credible Causal Inference for Empirical Legal Studies." *Annual Review of Law and Social Science* 7: 17–40.

Hobbes, Thomas. [1651] 1904. *Leviathan: Or, the Matter, Forme & Power of a Commonwealth, Ecclesiasticall and Civill*. Cambridge, UK: Cambridge University Press.

Hoffmann, Stanley. 1968. "International Law and the Control of Force." In *The Relevance of International Law: Essays in Honor of Leo Gross*, edited by Karl W. Deutsch, and Stanley Hoffmann, 21–46. Cambridge, UK: Schenkman Publishing.

Holmes, Richard. 1985. *Acts of War: The Behavior of Men in Battle*. New York: Free Press.

Holquist, Peter. 2004. "The Russian Empire as a 'Civilized State': International Law as Principle and Practice in Imperial Russia, 1874–1878." National Council for Eurasian and East European Research, Washington, DC. https://www.ucis.pitt.edu/nceeer/2004_818-06g_Holquist.pdf

Holsti, Ole R. 1992. "Public Opinion and Foreign Policy: Challenges to the Almond-Lippmann Consensus." *International Studies Quarterly* 36 (4): 439–66.

Holsti, Ole R. 2001. "Of Chasms and Convergences: Attitudes and Beliefs of Civilians and Military Elites at the Start of a New Millenium." In *Soldiers and Civilians: The Civil-Military Gap and American National Security*, edited by Peter D. Feaver, and Richard H. Kohn, 15–99. Cambridge, MA: MIT Press.

Holsti, Ole R. 2004. *Public Opinion and American Foreign Policy*. Ann Arbor: University of Michigan Press.

Hopkins, Nick. 2013. "Former NSA Chief: Western Intelligence Agencies Must Be More Transparent." *Guardian*, September 30. https://www.theguardian.com/world/2013/sep/30/nsa-director-intelligence-public-support

Horowitz, Michael C., Sarah E. Kreps, and Matthew Fuhrmann. 2016. "Separating Fact from Fiction in the Debate over Drone Proliferation." *International Security* 41 (2): 7–42.

Huddy, Leonie, Stanley Feldman, Charles Taber, and Gallya Lahav. 2005. "Threat, Anxiety, and Support of Antiterrorism Policies." *American Journal of Political Science* 49 (3): 593–608.

Huff, Connor. 2024. "Counterinsurgency Tactics, Rebel Grievances, and Who Keeps Fighting." *American Political Science Review* 118 (1): 475–80.

Hull, Isabel V. 2014. *A Scrap of Paper: Breaking and Making International Law During the Great War*. Ithaca, NY: Cornell University Press.

Hulsebosch, Daniel J. 2005. "Bringing the People Back in." *New York University Law Review* 80 (2): 653–93.

Human Rights Watch. 2003. "Hearts and Minds: Post-War Civilian Casualties in Baghdad by U.S. Forces." https://www.hrw.org/report/2003/10/20/hearts-and-minds/post-war-civilian-casualties-baghdad-us-forces

Human Rights Watch. 2004. "The Road to Abu Ghraib." https://www.hrw.org/report/2004/06/09/road-abu-ghraib

Human Rights Watch. 2011a. "Getting Away with Torture: The Bush Administration and Mistreatment of Detainees." https://www.hrw.org/report/2011/07/12/getting-away-torture/bush-administration-and-mistreatment-detainees

Human Rights Watch. 2011b. "Q&A: US Targeted Killings and International Law." https://www.hrw.org/news/2011/12/19/q-us-targeted-killings-and-international-law

Human Rights Watch. 2013. "'Between a Drone and Al-Qaeda': The Civilian Cost of US Targeted Killings in Yemen." https://www.hrw.org/report/2013/10/22/between-drone-and-al-qaeda/civilian-cost-us-targeted-killings-yemen

Human Rights Watch. 2020. "New Weapons, Proven Precedent: Elements of and Models for a Treaty on Killer Robots." https://www.hrw.org/report/2020/10/20/new-weapons-proven-precedent/elements-and-models-treaty-killer-robots

Hume, David. [1741] 1993. "Of the First Principles of Government." In *Hume: Political Essays*, edited by Knud Haakonssen, 16–19. Cambridge, UK: Cambridge University Press.

Humphreys, Macartan, and Jeremy M. Weinstein. 2006. "Handling and Manhandling Civilians in Civil War." *American Political Science Review* 100 (3): 429–47.

Hurd, Ian. 2007. *After Anarchy: Legitimacy and Power in the United Nations Security Council*. Princeton, NJ: Princeton University Press.

Hurd, Ian. 2015. "The International Rule of Law and the Domestic Analogy." *Global Constitutionalism* 4 (3): 365–95.

Hurd, Ian. 2017. *How to Do Things with International Law*. Princeton, NJ: Princeton University Press.

Hurd, Ian. 2022. "The Case against International Cooperation." *International Theory* 14 (2): 263–84.

Hurwitz, Jon, and Mark Peffley. 1987. "How Are Foreign Policy Attitudes Structured? A Hierarchical Model." *American Political Science Review* 81 (4): 1099–120.

Huth, Paul K. 1996. *Standing Your Ground: Territorial Disputes and International Conflict*. Ann Arbor: University of Michigan Press.

Huth, Paul K. 1997. "Reputations and Deterrence: A Theoretical and Empirical Assessment." *Security Studies* 7 (1): 72–99.

Hyde, Susan D. 2015. "Experiments in International Relations: Lab, Survey, and Field." *Annual Review of Political Science* 18 (1): 403–24.

Hyde, Susan D., and Elizabeth N. Saunders. 2020. "Recapturing Regime Type in International Relations: Leaders, Institutions, and Agency Space." *International Organization* 74 (2): 363–95.

Ignatieff, Michael. 2003. "The American Empire: The Burden." *New York Times Magazine*, January 5. https://www.nytimes.com/2003/01/05/magazine/the-american-empire-the-burden.html

Ikenberry, G. John. 1998. "Institutions, Strategic Restraint, and the Persistence of American Postwar Order." *International Security* 23 (3): 43–78.

Ikenberry, G. John. 2001. *After Victory: Institutions, Strategic Restraint, and the Rebuilding of Order after Major Wars*. Princeton, NJ: Princeton University Press.

Ikenberry, G. John, and Charles A. Kupchan. 1990. "Socialization and Hegemonic Power." *International Organization* 44 (3): 283–315.

Imai, Kosuke, Luke Keele, Dustin Tingley, and Teppei Yamamoto. 2011. "Unpacking the Black Box of Causality: Learning about Causal Mechanisms from Experimental and Observational Studies." *American Political Science Review* 105 (4): 765–89.

International Committee of the Red Cross. 1999. "The People on War Report: ICRC Worldwide Consultation on the Rules of War." https://www.icrc.org/en/doc/resources/documents/article/other/57jqht.htm

International Committee of the Red Cross. 2004. "Report of the International Committee of the Red Cross (ICRC) on the Treatment by the Coalition Forces of Prisoners of War and Other Protected Persons by the Geneva Conventions in Iraq During Arrest, Internment and Interrogation." https://www.icrc.org/en/doc/resources/documents/news-release/2009-and-earlier/5yrl67.htm

International Committee of the Red Cross. 2010. "Customary International Humanitarian Law Database." https://ihl-databases.icrc.org/en/customary-ihl

Jacobs, Lawrence R., and Robert Y. Shapiro. 2000. *Politicians Don't Pander: Political Manipulation and the Loss of Democratic Responsiveness*. Chicago: University of Chicago Press.

Janis, Mark W. 1999. *An Introduction to International Law*. Gaithersburg, MD: Aspen Law & Business.

Janis, Mark W. 2010. *America and the Law of Nations 1776–1939*. Oxford, UK: Oxford University Press.

Jentleson, Bruce W. 1992. "The Pretty Prudent Public: Post Post-Vietnam American Opinion on the Use of Military Force." *International Studies Quarterly* 36 (1): 49–73.

Jervis, Robert. 1976. *Perception and Misperception in International Politics*. Princeton, NJ: Princeton University Press.

Jervis, Robert. 1982. "Deterrence and Perception." *International Security* 7 (3): 3–30.

Jervis, Robert, Keren Yarhi-Milo, and Don Casler. 2021. "Redefining the Debate Over Reputation and Credibility in International Security." *World Politics* 73 (1): 167–203.

Jha, Saumitra, and Steven I. Wilkinson. 2012. "Does Combat Experience Foster Organizational Skill? Evidence from Ethnic Cleansing During the Partition of South Asia." *American Political Science Review* 106 (4): 883–907.

Jo, Hyeran. 2015. *Compliant Rebels: Rebel Groups and International Law in World Politics*. Cambridge, UK: Cambridge University Press.

Jo, Hyeran, and Beth A. Simmons. 2016. "Can the International Criminal Court Deter Atrocity?" *International Organization* 70 (3): 443–75.

Johnson, Jenna. 2015. "Donald Trump Promises to 'Bomb the Hell Out of ISIS' in New Radio Ad." *Washington Post*, November 18. https://www.washingtonpost.com/news/post-politics/wp/2015/11/18/donald-trump-promises-to-bomb-the-hell-out-of-isis-in-new-radio-ad/

Johnson, Tana. 2013. "Institutional Design and Bureaucrats' Impact on Political Control." *Journal of Politics* 75 (1): 183–97.

Johnston, Patrick, and Anoop K. Sarbahi. 2016. "The Impact of US Drone Strikes on Terrorism in Pakistan." *International Studies Quarterly* 60 (2): 203–19.

Jones, Jeffrey B., and Jack N. Summe. 1997. *Psychological Operations in Desert Shield, Desert Storm and Urban Freedom*. Landpower Essay Series No. 97–3. Institute of Land Warfare, Association of the United States Army.

Kagan, Kimberly. 2009. *The Surge: A Military History*. New York: Encounter Books.

Kagan, Robert. 2002. "Power and Weakness." *Policy Review* (113): 3–28.

Kagan, Robert. 2018. "'America First' Has Won." *New York Times*, September 23. https://www.nytimes.com/2018/09/23/opinion/trump-foreign-policy-america-first.html

Kagan, Robert, and William Kristol. 2000. "The Present Danger." *The National Interest* 59 (1): 57–69.

Kahl, Colin H. 2007. "In the Crossfire or the Crosshairs? Norms, Civilian Casualties, and U.S. Conduct in Iraq." *International Security* 32 (1): 7–46.

Kaiser, Henry F. 1974. "An Index of Factorial Simplicity." *Psychometrika* 39 (1): 31–36.

Kalyvas, Stathis N. 2006. *The Logic of Violence in Civil War*. Cambridge, UK: Cambridge University Press.

Kalyvas, Stathis N., and Matthew A. Kocher. 2009. "The Dynamics of Violence in Vietnam: An Analysis of the Hamlet Evaluation System (HES)." *Journal of Peace Research* 46 (3): 335–55.

Kammen, Michael. 2017. *A Machine That Would Go of Itself: The Constitution in American Culture*. New York: Routledge.

Kang, Shin-Goo, and G. Bingham Powell. 2010. "Representation and Policy Responsiveness: The Median Voter, Election Rules, and Redistributive Welfare Spending." *Journal of Politics* 72 (4): 1014–28.

Karon, Tony. 2004. "How the Prison Scandal Sabotages the U.S. in Iraq." *Time*, May 4. https://content.time.com/time/world/article/0,8599,632967,00.html

Katzenstein, Peter J., ed. 1996. *The Culture of National Security: Norms and Identity in World Politics*. New York: Columbia University Press.

Katzenstein, Peter J., and Robert O. Keohane. 2007. "Varieties of Anti-Americanism: A Framework for Analysis." In *Anti-Americanisms in World Politics*, edited by Peter J. Katzenstein, and Robert O. Keohane, 9–38. Ithaca, NY: Cornell University Press.

Katznelson, Ira. 2005. *When Affirmative Action Was White: An Untold History of Racial Inequality in Twentieth-Century America*. New York: W. W. Norton.

Keane, John. 2003. *Global Civil Society?* Cambridge, UK: Cambridge University Press.

Keck, Margaret E., and Kathryn Sikkink. 1998. *Activists beyond Borders: Advocacy Networks in International Politics*. Ithaca, NY: Cornell University Press.

Keegan, John. 1976. *The Face of Battle*. New York: Viking Press.

Keegan, John. 2005. *The Iraq War: The Military Offensive, from Victory in 21 Days to the Insurgent Aftermath*. New York: Vintage Books.

Keith, Linda Camp, C. Neal Tate, and Steven C. Poe. 2009. "Is the Law a Mere Parchment Barrier to Human Rights Abuse." *Journal of Politics* 71 (2): 644–60.

Kelley, Judith. 2007. "Who Keeps International Commitments and Why? The International Criminal Court and Bilateral Nonsurrender Agreements." *American Political Science Review* 101 (03): 573–89.

Kelsen, Hans. 1948. *Law and Peace in International Relations: The Oliver Wendell Holmes Lectures, 1940–41*. Cambridge, MA: Harvard University Press.

Kennan, George F. 1979. *The Decline of Bismarck's European Order: Franco-Russian Relations 1875–1890*. Princeton, NJ: Princeton University Press.

Kennedy-Pipe, Caroline, and Rhiannon Vickers. 2007. "'Blowback' for Britain?: Blair, Bush, and the War in Iraq." *Review of International Studies* 33 (2): 205–21.

Kennedy, David. 1980. "Theses about International Law Discourse." *German Yearbook of International Law* 23: 353–91.

Keohane, Robert O. 1984. *After Hegemony: Cooperation and Discord in the World Political Economy*. Princeton, NJ: Princeton University Press.

Keohane, Robert O. 1988. "International Institutions: Two Approaches." *International Studies Quarterly* 32 (4): 379–96.

Keohane, Robert O. 1997. "International Relations and International Law: Two Optics." *Harvard International Law Journal* 38 (2): 487–502.

Keohane, Robert O., and David G. Victor. 2011. "The Regime Complex for Climate Change." *Perspectives on Politics* 9 (1): 7–23.

Kertzer, Joshua D. 2016. *Resolve in International Politics*. Princeton, NJ: Princeton University Press.

Kertzer, Joshua D. 2017. "Microfoundations in International Relations." *Conflict Management and Peace Science* 34 (1): 81–97.

Kertzer, Joshua D. 2022. "Re-Assessing Elite-Public Gaps in Political Behavior." *American Journal of Political Science* 66 (3): 539–53.

Kertzer, Joshua D., and Kathleen M. McGraw. 2012. "Folk Realism: Testing the Microfoundations of Realism in Ordinary Citizens." *International Studies Quarterly* 56 (2): 245–58.

Kertzer, Joshua D., and Dustin Tingley. 2018. "Political Psychology in International Relations: Beyond the Paradigms." *Annual Review of Political Science* 21 319–39.

Kertzer, Joshua D., and Thomas Zeitzoff. 2017. "A Bottom-Up Theory of Public Opinion about Foreign Policy." *American Journal of Political Science* 61 (3): 543–58.

Key, V. O. 1961. *Public Opinion and American Democracy*. New York: Knopf.

Keynes, John Maynard. 1920. *The Economic Consequences of the Peace*. New York: Harcourt, Brace and Howe.

Kilcullen, David. 2006. "Twenty-Eight Articles: Fundamentals of Company-Level Counterinsurgency." *Military Review* 86 (3): 134–39.

Kim, Jae-On, and Charles W. Mueller. 1978. *Factor Analysis: Statistical Methods and Practical Issues*. Beverly Hills, CA: SAGE Publications.

Kim, Matthew D. 2019. "Reputation and Compliance with International Human Rights Law: Experimental Evidence from the US and South Korea." *Journal of East Asian Studies* 19 (2): 215–38.

Kinder, Donald R., and Thomas R. Palfrey. 1993. "On Behalf of an Experimental Political Science." In *Experimental Foundations of Political Science*, edited by Donald R. Kinder, and Thomas R. Palfrey, 1–39. Ann Arbor: University of Michigan Press.

King, Gary, Jennifer Pan, and Margaret E. Roberts. 2013. "How Censorship in China Allows Government Criticism but Silences Collective Expression." *American Political Science Review* 107 (2): 326–43.

Kinsella, Helen M. 2005. "Discourses of Difference: Civilians, Combatants, and Compliance with the Laws of War." *Review of International Studies* 31 (Supplement S1): 163–85.

Kirshner, Jonathan. 1995. *Currency and Coercion: The Political Economy of International Monetary Power*. Princeton, NJ: Princeton University Press.

Kissinger, Henry. 1994. *Diplomacy*. New York: Simon & Schuster.

Knowles, Helen J. 2016. "Remember, It Is the Supreme Court That Is Expounding: The Least Dangerous Branch and Popular Constitutionalism." *University of Dayton Law Review* 41 (1): 33–43.

Knowles, Helen J., and Julianne A. Toia. 2014. "Defining 'Popular Constitutionalism': The Kramer versus Kramer Debate." *Southern University Law Review* 42 (1): 31–59.

Kocher, Matthew A., Stathis N. Kalyvas, and Thomas B. Pepinsky. 2011. "Aerial Bombing and Counterinsurgency in the Vietnam War." *American Journal of Political Science* 55 (2): 201–18.

Kocs, Stephen A. 1994. "Explaining the Strategic Behavior of States: International Law as System Structure." *International Studies Quarterly* 38 (4): 535–56.

Koh, Harold H. 1996. "Why Do Nations Obey International Law?" *Yale Law Journal* 106 (8): 2599–660.

Koh, Harold H. 2019. *The Trump Administration and International Law*. Oxford, UK: Oxford University Press.

Koremenos, Barbara, Charles Lipson, and Duncan Snidal. 2001. "The Rational Design of International Institutions." *International Organization* 55 (4): 761–800.

Koskenniemi, Martti. 2002. *The Gentle Civilizer of Nations: The Rise and Fall of International Law 1870–1960*. Cambridge, UK: Cambridge University Press.

Kramer, Larry D. 2001. "The Supreme Court 2000 Term: Foreword: We the Court." *Harvard Law Review* 115 (1): 4–169.

Kramer, Larry D. 2004a. "Popular Constitutionalism, Circa 2004." *California Law Review* 92 (4): 959–1011.

Kramer, Larry D. 2004b. *The People Themselves: Popular Constitutionalism and Judicial Review*. Oxford, UK: Oxford University Press.

Kramer, Larry D. 2006. "'The Interest of the Man': James Madison, Popular Constitutionalism, and the Theory of Deliberative Democracy." *Valparaiso University Law Review* 41 (2): 697–754.

Krasner, Stephen. 1982. "Structural Causes and Regime Consequences: Regimes as Intervening Variables." *International Organization* 36 (2): 185–205.

Krasner, Stephen D. 1999. *Sovereignty: Organized Hypocrisy*. Princeton, NJ: Princeton University Press.

Kratochwil, Friedrich, and John Gerard Ruggie. 1986. "International Organization: A State of the Art on an Art of the State." *International Organization* 40 (4): 753–75.

Kreps, David, and Robert Wilson. 1982. "Reputation and Imperfect Information." *Journal of Economic Theory* 27 (2): 253–79.

Kreps, Sarah. 2014. "Flying under the Radar: A Study of Public Attitudes towards Unmanned Aerial Vehicles." *Research & Politics* 1: 1–7.

Kreps, Sarah, and Stephen Roblin. 2019. "Treatment Format and External Validity in International Relations Experiments." *International Interactions* 45 (3): 576–94.

Kreps, Sarah E. 2011. *Coalitions of Convenience: United States Military Interventions after the Cold War*. Oxford, UK: Oxford University Press.

Kreps, Sarah E., and Geoffrey P. R. Wallace. 2016. "International Law, Military Effectiveness, and Public Support for Drone Strikes." *Journal of Peace Research* 53 (6): 830–44.

Kris, David S. 2011. "Law Enforcement as a Counterterrorism Tool." *Journal of National Security Law and Policy* 5 (1): 1–104.

Kronstadt, Alan. 2003. *Pakistan-U.S. Anti-Terrorism Cooperation*. Washington, DC: Congressional Research Service.

Krueger, Alan B, and Jitka Malečková. 2003. "Education, Poverty and Terrorism: Is There a Causal Connection?" *Journal of Economic Perspectives* 17 (4): 119–44.

Kull, Steven, Clay Ramsay, Stephen Weber, Evan Lewis, and Ebrahim Mohseni. 2009. "Public Opinion in the Islamic World on Terrorism, Al Qaeda, and US Policies." *WorldPublicOpinion.org*, February 25. http://worldpublicopinion.net/wp-content/uploads/2017/12/STARTII_Feb09_rpt.pdf

Kunda, Ziva. 1987. "Motivated Inference: Self-Serving Generation and Evaluation of Evidence." *Journal of Personality and Social Psychology* 53 (4): 636–47.

Kunda, Ziva. 1990. "The Case for Motivated Reasoning." *Psychological Bulletin* 108 (3): 480–98.

Kupchan, Charles A. 2020. *Isolationism: A History of America's Efforts to Shield Itself from the World.* Oxford, UK: Oxford University Press.

LaFranchi, Howard. 2018. "Challenge to US Sovereignty? In Polls Public Accepts Constraints on Power." *Christian Science Monitor,* September 11. https://www.csmonitor.com/USA/Foreign-Policy/2018/0911/Challenge-to-US-sovereignty-In-polls-public-accepts-constraints-on-power

LaFraniere, Sharon. 2001. "Vatican Says Use of Force by U.S. Can be Justified." *Washington Post,* September 25, A14.

Lahno, Bernd. 1995. "Trust, Reputation, and Exit in Exchange Relationships." *Journal of Conflict Resolution* 39 (3): 495–510.

Lake, David A. 2009. "Open Economy Politics: A Critical Review." *Review of International Organizations* 4 (3): 219–44.

Lake, David A. 2018. "International Legitimacy Lost? Rule and Resistance When America Is First." *Perspectives on Politics* 16 (1): 6–21.

Landemore, Hélène, and Jon Elster, eds. 2012. *Collective Wisdom: Principles and Mechanisms.* Cambridge, UK: Cambridge University Press.

Law, Davis S., and Mila Versteeg. 2020. "Is the Influence of the U.S. Constitution Declining?" In *Modern Constitutions,* edited by Rogers M. Smith, and Richard R. Beeman, 17–63. Philadelphia: University of Pennsylvania Press.

Lazarsfeld, Paul F., Bernard Berelson, and Hazel Gaudet. 1948. *The People's Choice: How the Voter Makes Up His Mind in a Presidential Campaign.* New York: Columbia University Press.

Lee, Wayne E. 2011. *Barbarians and Brothers: Anglo-American Warfare, 1500–1865.* Oxford, UK: Oxford University Press.

Leeds, Brett A. 2003. "Alliance Reliability in Times of War: Explaining State Decisions to Violate Treaties." *International Organization* 57 (4): 801–27.

Leeds, Brett Ashley, Andrew G. Long, and Sara M. Mitchell. 2000. "Reevaluating Alliance Reliability: Specific Threats, Specific Promises." *Journal of Conflict Resolution* 44 (5): 686–99.

Legro, Jeffrey W. 1997. "Which Norms Matter? Revisiting the 'Failure' of Internationalism." *International Organization* 51 (1): 31–64.

Lennard, Natasha. 2011. "The Obama/Gitmo Timeline." *Salon,* April 25. https://www.salon.com/2011/04/25/obama_guantanamo_rhetoric/

Levi, Margaret. 1997. *Consent, Dissent, and Patriotism.* Cambridge, UK: Cambridge University Press.

Levinson, Sanford. 2011. *Constitutional Faith.* Princeton, NJ: Princeton University Press.

Levitsky, Steven, and Lucan Way. 2002. "The Rise of Competitive Authoritarianism." *Journal of Democracy* 13 (2): 51–65.

Levy, Jack S., Michael K. McKoy, Paul Poast, and Geoffrey P. R. Wallace. 2015. "Backing Out or Backing in? Commitment and Consistency in Audience Costs Theory." *American Journal of Political Science* 59 (4): 988–1001.

Liddell Hart, B. H. 1946. *The Revolution in Warfare.* London: Faber and Faber.

Lindsay, James M., and Randall B. Ripley. 1992. "Foreign and Defense Policy in Congress: A Research Agenda for the 1990s." *Legislative Studies Quarterly* 17 (3): 417–49.

Linos, Katerina. 2013. *The Democratic Foundations of Policy Diffusion: How Health, Family, and Employment Laws Spread across Countries.* Oxford, UK: Oxford University Press.

Linos, Katerina, and Tom Pegram. 2016. "The Language of Compromise in International Agreements." *International Organization* 70 (3): 587–621.

Lippmann, Walter. 1955. *Essays in the Public Philosophy.* Boston: Little, Brown.

Lipson, Charles. 1991. "Why Are Some International Agreements Informal?" *International Organization* 45 (4): 495–538.

Lipson, Charles. 1993. "International Cooperation in Economic and Security Affairs." *World Politics* 37 (1): 1–23.

Lipson, Charles. 2003. *Reliable Partners: How Democracies Have Made a Separate Peace.* Princeton, NJ: Princeton University Press.

Lithwick, Dahlia. 2006. "Stream of Conscience: Why It Matters What Definition of Torture We Use." *Slate*, September 13. https://slate.com/news-and-politics/2006/09/does-it-really-matter-what-definition-of-torture-we-use.html

Lizotte, Mary-Kate. 2017. "Gender Differences in Support for Torture." *Journal of Conflict Resolution* 61 (4): 772–87.

Lüdtke, Alf, ed. 1995. *The History of Everyday Life: Reconstructing Historical Experiences and Ways of Life.* Princeton, NJ: Princeton University Press.

Lupia, Arthur, and Mathew D. McCubbins. 1998. *The Democratic Dilemma: Can Citizens Learn What They Need to Know?* Cambridge, UK: Cambridge University Press.

Lupu, Noam, and Leonid Peisakhin. 2017. "The Legacy of Political Violence across Generations." *American Journal of Political Science* 61 (4): 836–51.

Lupu, Yonatan. 2015. "Legislative Veto Players and the Effects of International Human Rights Agreements." *American Journal of Political Science* 59 (3): 578–94.

Lupu, Yonatan, and Geoffrey P. R. Wallace. 2019. "Violence, Non-Violence, and the Effects of International Human Rights Law." *American Journal of Political Science* 63 (2): 411–26.

Lyall, Jason, and Isaiah Wilson. 2009. "Rage against the Machines: Explaining the Outcomes in Counterinsurgency Wars." *International Organization* 63 (1): 67–106.

Lynch, Marc. 2003. "Beyond the Arab Street: Iraq and the Arab Public Sphere." *Politics & Society* 31 (1): 55–91.

MacAskill, Ewen, and Julian Borger. 2004. "Iraq War Was Illegal and Breached UN Charter, Says Annan." *Guardian*, September 15. https://www.theguardian.com/world/2004/sep/16/iraq.iraq

Machiavelli, Niccolo. [1532] 1998. *The Prince.* Chicago: University of Chicago Press.

Macmillan, Margaret. 2001. *Paris 1919: Six Months That Changed the World.* New York: Random House.

Madison, James. 1791. "Public Opinion." *National Gazette*, December 19, 14.

Mahoney, James, and Gary Goertz. 2004. "The Possibility Principle: Choosing Negative Cases in Comparative Research." *American Political Science Review* 98 (4): 653–69.

Malanczuk, Peter. 1997. *Akehurst's Modern Introduction to International Law.* New York: Routledge.

Malhotra, Neil, Yotam Margalit, and Cecilia H. Mo. 2013. "Economic Explanations for Opposition to Immigration: Distinguishing between Prevalence and Conditional Impact." *American Journal of Political Science* 57 (2): 391–410.

Mallet, Elizabeth E. 1997. "Propaganda and Psychological Operations as Tools of Warfare during the Persian Gulf Conflict, 1990–91." *Cambridge Review of International Affairs* 10 (2): 280–97.

Manner, George. 1952. "The Object Theory of the Individual in International Law." *American Journal of International Law* 46 (3): 428–49.

Manning, James A., ed. 1848. *Political Aphorisms, Moral and Philosophical Thoughts of Emperor Napoleon.* London: T. C. Newby.

Mantilla, Giovanni. 2020. *Lawmaking under Pressure: International Humanitarian Law and Internal Armed Conflict.* Ithaca, NY: Cornell University Press.

Maoz, Ifat, and Clark McCauley. 2008. "Threat, Dehumanization, and Support for Retaliatory Aggressive Policies in Asymmetric Conflict." *Journal of Conflict Resolution* 52 (1): 93–116.

Marmor, Andrei. 1998. "Legal Conventionalism." *Legal Theory* 4 (4): 509–31.

Marshall, Thomas R. 1989. *Public Opinion and the Supreme Court*. Winchester, MA: Unwin Hyman.

Martin, Lisa L. 2000. *Democratic Commitments: Legislatures and International Cooperation*. Princeton, NJ: Princeton University Press.

Martin, Lisa L., and Beth A. Simmons. 1998. "Theories and Empirical Studies of International Institutions." *International Organization* 52 (4): 729–58.

Massoud, Mark F. 2011. "Do Victims of War Need International Law? Human Rights Education Programs in Authoritarian Sudan." *Law & Society Review* 45 (1): 1–32.

Masters, Roger D. 1964. "World Politics as a Primitive Political System." *World Politics* 16 (4): 595–619.

Mattes, Michaela. 2012. "Reputation, Symmetry, and Alliance Design." *International Organization* 66 (4): 679–707.

Mattes, Michaela, and Mariana Rodríguez. 2014. "Autocracies and International Cooperation." *International Studies Quarterly* 58 (3): 527–38.

Mayer, Jane. 2005. "Outsourcing Torture: The Secret History of America's 'Extraordinary Rendition' Program." *New Yorker*, February 14. https://www.newyorker.com/magazine/2005/02/14/outsourcing-torture

Mayer, Jeremy D., and David J. Armor. 2012. "Support for Torture Over Time: Interrogating the American Public about Coercive Tactics." *The Social Science Journal* 49 (4): 439–46.

McCann, Michael W. 1994. *Rights at Work: Pay Equity Reform and the Politics of Legal Mobilization*. Chicago: University of Chicago Press.

McCartney, Robert J. 2003. "Opponents of War Decry U.S. Stance; Many Nations Assail End of Diplomacy." *Washington Post*, March 19, A17.

McChrystal, Stanley. 2009. *Initial United States Forces—Afghanistan (USFOR-A) Assessment*. Headquarters, International Security Assistance Force (ISAF). https://casebook.icrc.org/case-study/afghanistan-assessment-isaf-strategy

McDermott, Rose. 2002. "Experimental Methods in Political Science." *Annual Review of Political Science* 5: 31–61.

McDermott, Rose. 2011. "New Directions for Experimental Work in International Relations." *International Studies Quarterly* 55 (2): 503–20.

McDermott, Rose. 2015. "Sex and Death: Gender Differences in Aggression and Motivations for Violence." *International Organization* 69 (3): 753–75.

McDougal, Myres S., and Harold D. Lasswell. 1959. "The Identification and Appraisal of Diverse Systems of Public Order." *American Journal of International Law* 53 (1): 1–29.

McGillivray, Fiona, and Alastair Smith. 2000. "Trust and Cooperation through Agent-Specific Punishments." *International Organization* 54 (4): 809–24.

McGinty, Brian. 2008. *Lincoln and the Court*. Cambridge, MA: Harvard University Press.

McKeown, Ryder. 2009. "Norm Regress: US Revisionism and the Slow Death of the Torture Norm." *International Relations* 23 (1): 5–25.

Mearsheimer, John J. 1994. "The False Promise of International Institutions." *International Security* 19 (3): 5–49.

Mearsheimer, John J. 2001. *The Tragedy of Great Power Politics*. New York: W. W. Norton.

Meernik, James. 2015. "Explaining Public Opinion on International Criminal Justice." *European Political Science Review* 7 (4): 567–91.

Meernik, James, and Kimi King. 2014. "A Psychological Jurisprudence Model of Public Opinion and International Prosecution." *International Area Studies Review* 17 (1): 3–20.

Meet the Press. 2001. "Interview with Dick Cheney." September 16. https://georgewbush-whitehouse.archives.gov/vicepresident/news-speeches/speeches/vp20010916.html

Mendelsohn, Barak. 2009. *Combating Jihadism: American Hegemony and Interstate Cooperation in the War on Terrorism.* Chicago: University of Chicago Press.

Mercer, Jonathan. 1996. *Reputation and International Politics.* Ithaca, NY: Cornell University Press.

Mercer, Jonathan. 2005. "Rationality and Psychology in International Politics." *International Organization* 59 (1): 77–106.

Mercier, Hugo, and Dan Sperber. 2011. "Why Do Humans Reason? Arguments for an Argumentative Theory." *Behavioral and Brain Sciences* 34 (2): 57–111.

Merolla, Jennifer L., and Elizabeth J. Zechmeister. 2009. *Democracy at Risk: How Terrorist Threats Affect the Public.* Chicago: Chicago University Press.

Merom, Gil. 2003. *How Democracies Lose Small Wars: State, Society, and the Failures of France in Algeria, Israel in Lebanon, and the United States in Vietnam.* Cambridge, UK: Cambridge University Press.

Meron, Theodor. 2000. "The Martens Clause, Principles of Humanity, and Dictates of Public Conscience." *American Journal of International Law* 94 (1): 78–89.

Milbank, Dana. 2003. "Many Willing, But Only a Few Are Able." *Washington Post,* March 25. https://www.washingtonpost.com/archive/politics/2003/03/25/many-willing-but-only-a-few-are-able/1160e73c-12fe-416d-9b37-77dcee4e4358/

Miles, Edwin A. 1973. "After John Marshall's Decision: Worcester v. Georgia and the Nullification Crisis." *Journal of Southern History* 39 (4): 519–44.

Miller, Greg, and Adam Goldman. 2014. "Rise and Fall of CIA's Overseas Prisons Traced in Senate Report on Interrogations." *Washington Post,* December 11. https://www.washingtonpost.com/world/national-security/rise-and-fall-of-cias-overseas-prisons-traced-in-senate-report-on-interrogations/2014/12/11/067232b4-8143-11e4-9f38-95a187e4c1f7_story.html

Miller, Gregory D. 2012. *The Shadow of the Past: Reputation and Military Alliances before the First World War.* Ithaca, NY: Cornell University Press.

Miller, Peter. 2011. "Torture Approval in Comparative Perspective." *Human Rights Review* 12 (4): 441–63.

Miller, Peter, Paul Gronke, and Darius Rejali. 2014. "Torture and Public Opinion: The Partisan Dimension." In *Examining Torture: Empirical Studies of State Repression,* edited by Tracy Lightcap, and James P. Pfiffner, 11–42. New York: Palgrave Macmillan.

Milner, Helen. 1992. "International Theories of Cooperation among Nations: Strengths and Weaknesses." *World Politics* 44 (3): 466–96.

Milner, Helen V. 1991. "The Assumption of Anarchy in International Relations Theory: A Critique." *Review of International Studies* 17 (1): 67–85.

Milner, Helen V. 1997. *Interests, Institutions, and Information: Domestic Politics and International Relations.* Princeton, NJ: Princeton University Press.

Milner, Helen V., and Dustin Tingley. 2015. *Sailing the Water's Edge: The Domestic Politics of American Foreign Policy.* Princeton, NJ: Princeton University Press.

Mitchell, Sara M., and Emilia J. Powell. 2011. *Domestic Law Goes Global: Legal Traditions and International Courts.* Cambridge, UK: Cambridge University Press.

Moehler, Devra C. 2008. *Distrusting Democrats: Outcomes of Participatory Constitution Making.* Ann Arbor: University of Michigan Press.

Moravcsik, Andrew. 1997. "Taking Preferences Seriously: A Liberal Theory of International Politics." *International Organization* 51 (4): 513–53.

Moravcsik, Andrew. 2000. "The Origins of Human Rights Regimes: Democratic Delegation in Postwar Europe." *International Organization* 54 (2): 217–52.

Moravcsik, Andrew. 2017. "Liberal Theories of International Law." In *Interdisciplinary Perspectives on International Law and International Relations: The State of the Art*, edited by Jeffrey L. Dunoff, and Mark A. Pollack, 83–118. Cambridge, UK: Cambridge University Press.

Morgan, Rod. 2000. "The Utilitarian Justification of Torture: Denial, Desert, and Disinformation." *Punishment and Society* 2 (2): 181–96.

Morgenthau, Hans J. 1951. *In Defense of the National Interest: A Critical Examination of American Foreign Policy*. New York: Knopf.

Morgenthau, Hans J. 1985. *Politics among Nations: The Struggle for Power and Peace*. New York: McGraw-Hill.

Morrow, James D. 2002. "The Laws of War, Common Conjectures, and Legal Systems in International Relations." *Journal of Legal Studies* 41 (S1): S41–S60.

Morrow, James D. 2007. "When Do States Follow the Laws of War?" *American Political Science Review* 101 (3): 559–72.

Morrow, James D. 2014. *Order within Anarchy: The Laws of War as an International Institution*. New York: Cambridge University Press.

Morrow, James D., and Hyeran Jo. 2006. "Compliance with the Laws of War: Dataset and Coding Rules." *Conflict Management and Peace Science* 23 (1): 91–113.

Morse, Julia C., and Tyler Pratt. 2022. "Strategies of Contestation: International Law, Domestic Audiences, and Image Management." *Journal of Politics* 84 (4): 2080–93.

Morton, Rebecca B., and Kenneth C. Williams. 2010. *Experimental Political Science and the Study of Causality: From Nature to the Lab*. Cambridge, UK: Cambridge University Press.

Moustafa, Tamir, and Tom Ginsburg. 2008. "Introduction: The Functions of Courts in Authoritarian Politics." In *Rule by Law: The Politics of Courts in Authoritarian Regimes*, edited by Tom Ginsburg, and Tamir Moustafa, 1–22. Cambridge, UK: Cambridge University Press.

Mudde, Cas. 2004. "The Populist Zeitgeist." *Government and Opposition* 39 (4): 541–63.

Mutua, Makau. 2000. "What is TWAIL?" *Proceedings of the Annual Meeting (American Society of International Law)* 94: 31–40.

Mutz, Diana C. 2011. *Population-Based Survey Experiments*. Princeton, NJ: Princeton University Press.

Nasr, Octavia. 2009. "Abu Ghraib Photos Provoked Shock, Then Anger, for Arabs." *CNN*, May 21. https://www.cnn.com/2009/WORLD/meast/05/21/iraq.abu.ghraib.impact/index.html

Navasky, Victor S. 2013. *The Art of Controversy: Political Cartoons and Their Enduring Power*. New York: Alfred A. Knopf.

Nebehay, Stephanie. 2017. "Trump Breaking Torture Taboo, Global Laws Threatened: U.N. Rights Boss." *Reuters*, June 27. https://www.reuters.com/article/us-un-rights/trump-breaking-torture-taboo-global-laws-threatened-u-n-rights-boss-idUSKBN19I0T8

Nelson, Stephen C. 2010. "Does Compliance Matter? Assessing the Relationship between Sovereign Risk and Compliance with International Monetary Law." *Review of International Organizations* 5 (2): 107–39.

Nettl, J. P. 1968. "The State as a Conceptual Variable." *World Politics* 20 (4): 559–92.

Neustadt, Richard E. 1990. *Presidential Power and the Modern Presidents: The Politics of Leadership from Roosevelt to Reagan*. New York: Free Press.

Norman, George, and Joel P. Trachtman. 2005. "The Customary International Law Game." *American Journal of International Law* 99 (3): 541–80.

Nowak, Manfred. 2006. "What Practices Constitute Torture? US and UN Standards." *Human Rights Quarterly* 28 (4): 809–41.

Nuñez-Mietz, Fernando G. 2016. "Lawyering Compliance with International Law: Legal Advisers in the 'War on Terror.'" *European Journal of International Security* 1 (2): 215–38.

Nye, Joseph S. 1990. *Bound to Lead: The Changing Nature of American Power*. New York: Basic Books.

Nye, Joseph S. 2004. "Soft Power and American Foreign Policy." *Political Science Quarterly* 119 (2): 255–70.

Nylen, Alexandria, and Charli Carpenter. 2019. "Questions of Life and Death: (De)constructing Human Rights Norms through US Public Opinion Surveys." *European Journal of International Security* 4 (2): 142–62.

O'Donnell, Guillermo, and Philippe C. Schmitter. 1986. *Transitions from Authoritarian Rule: Prospects for Democracy*. Baltimore: Johns Hopkins University Press.

O'Connell, Daniel P. 1965. *International Law*. London: Stevens.

O'Connell, Mary E. 2011. "Remarks: The Resort to Drones under International Law." *Denver Journal of International Law & Policy* 39 (4): 585–600.

O'Hanlon, Michael E., and Adriana Lins de Albuquerque. 2004. "Iraq Index Tracking: Variables of Reconstruction & Security in Post-Saddam Iraq." *Brookings Institution*. https://www.brookings.edu/wp-content/uploads/2020/08/fp_20200825_iraq_index.pdf

Obama, Barack. 2013. "Obama's Speech on Drone Policy." *New York Times*, May 23. https://www.nytimes.com/2013/05/24/us/politics/transcript-of-obamas-speech-on-drone-policy.html

Obama, Barack. 2014. "Full Transcript: President Obama Gives Speech Addressing Europe, Russia on March 26." *Washington Post*, March 26. https://www.washingtonpost.com/world/transcript-president-obama-gives-speech-addressing-europe-russia-on-march-26/2014/03/26/07ae80ae-b503-11e3-b899-20667de76985_story.html

Ohlin, Jens D. 2015. *The Assault on International Law*. Oxford, UK: Oxford University Press.

Ollivant, Douglas A. 2011. "Countering the New Orthodoxy: Reinterpreting Counterinsurgency in Iraq." New America Foundation, National Security Studies Program Policy Paper. https://static.newamerica.org/attachments/4344-countering-the-new-orthodoxy/Ollivant_Reinterpreting_Counterinsurgency.5d769bb8f672493a9fd1086919de9f51.pdf

Olson, Mancur. 1993. "Dictatorship, Democracy, and Development." *American Political Science Review* 87 (3): 567–76.

Oppenheim, Lassa. 1908. "The Science of International Law: Its Task and Method." *American Journal of International Law* 2 (2): 313–56.

Page, Benjamin I., and Robert Y. Shapiro. 1982. "Changes in Americans' Policy Preferences, 1935–1979." *Public Opinion Quarterly* 46 (1): 24–42.

Page, Benjamin I., and Robert Y. Shapiro. 1983. "Effects of Public Opinion on Policy." *American Political Science Review* 77 (1): 175–90.

Page, Benjamin I., Robert Y. Shapiro, and Glenn R. Dempsey. 1987. "What Moves Public Opinion?" *American Political Science Review* 81 (1): 23–44.

Paine, Thomas. 1894. *The Writings of Thomas Paine*. New York: G. P. Putnam's Sons.

Pape, Robert A. 2005. "Soft Balancing Against the United States." *International Security* 30 (1): 72–108.

Parent, Joseph M. 2011. *Uniting States: Voluntary Union in World Politics.* Oxford, UK: Oxford University Press.

Parker, Christopher S. 2009. *Fighting for Democracy: Black Veterans and the Struggle against White Supremacy in the Postwar South.* Princeton, NJ: Princeton University Press.

Pastor, Peter. 1983. "Introduction." In *Essays on World War I: Origins and Prisoners of War,* edited by Samuel R. Williamson, and Peter Pastor, 113–17. New York: Columbia University Press.

Pataki, Jessica. 2020. "The United States Interferes with the Rule of Law Once Again?" *Cambridge Global Affair,* July 10. https://www.thecambridgeglobalaffair.co.uk/our-articles/the-united-states-interferes-with-the-rule-of-law-once-again

Paulsen, Michael S. 1994. "The Most Dangerous Branch: Executive Power to Say What the Law is." *Georgetown Law Journal* 83 (2): 217–346.

Pauly, Robert J., and Tom Lansford. 2005. *Strategic Preemption: U.S. Foreign Policy and the Second Iraq War.* Burlington, VT: Ashgate.

Paust, Jordan J. 2002. "Use of Armed Force against Terrorists in Afghanistan, Iraq, and Beyond." *Cornell Journal of International Law* 35 (3): 533–57.

Peer, Eyal, Gabriele Paolacci, Jesse Chandler, and Pam Mueller. 2012. "Screening Participants from Previous Studies on Amazon Mechanical Turk and Qualtrics." *Experimental Turk.* https://experimentalturk.files.wordpress.com/2012/02/screening-amt-workers-on-qualtrics-5-2.pdf

Pelc, Krzysztof J. 2013. "Googling the WTO: What Search-Engine Data Tell US about the Political Economy of Institutions." *International Organization* 67 (3): 629–55.

Persily, Nathaniel, Jack Citrin, and Patrick J. Egan, eds. 2008. *Public Opinion and Constitutional Controversy.* Oxford, UK: Oxford University Press.

Pew Research Center. 2001. "Bush Unpopular in Europe, Seen as Unilateralist." August 15. https://www.pewresearch.org/global/2001/08/15/bush-unpopular-in-europe-seen-as-unilateralist/

Pew Research Center. 2003. "America's Image Further Erodes, Europeans Want Weaker Ties." March 18. https://www.pewresearch.org/global/2003/03/18/americas-image-further-erodes-europeans-want-weaker-ties/

Pew Research Center. 2018. "Americans are Generally Positive about Free Trade Agreements, More Critical of Tariff Increases." May 10. https://www.pewresearch.org/short-reads/2018/05/10/americans-are-generally-positive-about-free-trade-agreements-more-critical-of-tariff-increases/

Pew Research Center. 2020a. "Trump Ratings Remain Low around Globe, While Views of U.S. Stay Mostly Favorable." January 8. https://www.pewresearch.org/global/2020/01/08/trump-ratings-remain-low-around-globe-while-views-of-u-s-stay-mostly-favorable/

Pew Research Center. 2020b. "International Cooperation Welcomed across 14 Advanced Economies." September 21. https://www.pewresearch.org/global/2020/09/21/international-cooperation-welcomed-across-14-advanced-economies/

Pfundstein Chamberlain, Dianne. 2016. *Cheap Threats: Why the United States Struggles to Coerce Weak States.* Washington, DC: Georgetown University Press.

Phillips, Charles, and Alan Axelrod, eds. 2005. *Encyclopedia of Wars.* New York: Facts on File.

Phillips, David L. 2006. *Losing Iraq: Inside the Postwar Reconstruction Fiasco.* New York: Basic Books.

Pildes, Richard A. 2012. "Law and the President." *Harvard Law Review* 125 (6): 1381–424.

Pilkington, Ed, and Ewen MacAskill. 2015. "Obama's Drone War a 'Recruitment Tool' for ISIS, Say US Air Force Whistleblowers." *Guardian*, November 18. https://www.theguardian.com/world/2015/nov/18/obama-drone-war-isis-recruitment-tool-air-force-whistleblowers

Pirnie, Bruce R., and Edward O'Connell. 2008. *Counterinsurgency in Iraq (2003–2006)*. Santa Monica, CA: RAND Corporation.

Poe, Steven C., and C. Neal Tate. 1994. "Repression of Human Rights to Personal Integrity in the 1980s: A Global Analysis." *American Political Science Review* 88 (4): 853–72.

Politi, Daniel. 2016. "Donald Trump Vows to Legalize Torture." *Slate*, March 6. https://slate.com/news-and-politics/2016/03/donald-trump-vows-to-legalize-torture.html

Popkin, Samuel L. 1994. *The Reasoning Voter: Communication and Persuasion in Presidential Campaigns*. Chicago: University of Chicago Press.

Posner, Eric A. 2003. "A Theory of the Laws of War." *University of Chicago Law Review* 70 (1): 297–317.

Posner, Eric A. 2009. *The Perils of Global Legalism*. Chicago: University of Chicago Press.

Posner, Eric A., and Alan O. Sykes. 2013. *Economic Foundations of International Law*. Cambridge, MA: Belknap Press.

Posner, Eric A., and Adrian Vermeule. 2007. *Terror in the Balance: Security, Liberty, and the Courts*. Oxford, UK: Oxford University Press.

Posner, Eric A., and Adrian Vermeule. 2010. *The Executive Unbound: After the Madisonian Republic*. Oxford, UK: Oxford University Press.

Posner, Eric A., and John Yoo. 2005. "Judicial Independence in International Tribunals." *California Law Review* 93 (1): 1–74.

Post, Robert, and Reva Siegel. 2004. "Popular Constitutionalism, Departmentalism, and Judicial Supremacy." *California Law Review* 92 (4): 1027–43.

Powe, L.A. 2005. "Are 'the People' Missing in Action (and Should Anyone Care)?" *Texas Law Review* 83 (3): 855–96.

Powell, Colin L. 2002. "Draft Decision Memorandum for the President on the Applicability of the Geneva Convention to the Conflict in Afghanistan." January 26. *NSA Archive, George Washington University*. https://nsarchive2.gwu.edu/NSAEBB/NSAEBB127/02.01.26.pdf

Powell, Colin L. 2003. *My American Journey*. New York: Ballantine Books.

Powell, Emilia Justyna, and Jeffrey K. Staton. 2009. "Domestic Judicial Institutions and Human Rights Treaty Violation." *International Studies Quarterly* 53 (1): 149–74.

Powell, G. Bingham. 2004. "The Chain of Responsiveness." *Journal of Democracy* 15 (4): 91–105.

Press, Daryl G. 2005. *Calculating Credibility: How Leaders Assess Military Threats*. Ithaca, NY: Cornell University Press.

Press, Daryl G., Scott D. Sagan, and Benjamin A. Valentino. 2013. "Atomic Aversion: Experimental Evidence on Taboos, Traditions, and the Non-Use of Nuclear Weapons." *American Political Science Review* 107 (1): 188–206.

Price, Richard. 1998. "Reversing the Gun Sights: Transnational Civil Society Targets Land Mines." *International Organization* 52 (3): 613–44.

Priest, Dana. 2005a. "CIA Holds Terror Suspects in Secret Prisons." *Washington Post*, November 2. https://www.washingtonpost.com/archive/politics/2005/11/02/cia-holds-terror-suspects-in-secret-prisons/767f0160-cde4-41f2-a691-ba989990039c/

Priest, Dana. 2005b. "Foreign Network at Front of CIA's Terror Fight." *Washington Post*, November 18. https://www.washingtonpost.com/archive/politics/2005/11/18/foreign-network-at-front-of-cias-terror-fight/b15b27dd-8de2-441e-9eb5-8509770a1d53/

Puleo, Stephen. 2016. *American Treasures: The Secret Efforts to Save the Declaration of Independence, the Constitution, and the Gettysburg Address*. New York: St. Martin's Press.

Putnam, Robert. 1988. "Diplomacy and Domestic Politics: The Logic of Two-Level Games." *International Organization* 42 (3): 427–60.

Putnam, Tonya L., and Jacob N. Shapiro. 2017. "International Law and Voter Preferences: The Case of Foreign Human Rights Violations." *Human Rights Review* 18 (3): 243–62.

Pyszczynski, Tom, Sheldon Solomon, and Jeff Greenberg. 2003. *In the Wake of 9/11: The Psychology of Terror*. Washington, DC: American Psychological Association.

Rabkin, Jeremy A. 2005. *Law without Nations? Why Constitutional Government Requires Sovereign States*. Princeton, NJ: Princeton University Press.

Rachamimov, Alon. 2002. *POWs and the Great War: Captivity on the Eastern Front*. Oxford, UK: Berg.

Rajagopal, Balakrishna. 2003. *International Law from Below: Development, Social Movements and Third World Resistance*. Cambridge, UK: Cambridge University Press.

Rasmussen, Anne, Stefanie Reher, and Dimiter Toshkov. 2019. "The Opinion-Policy Nexus in Europe and the Role of Political Institutions." *European Journal of Political Research* 58 (2): 412–34.

Rathbun, Brian C. 2004. *Partisan Interventions: European Party Politics and Peace Enforcement in the Balkans*. Ithaca, NY: Cornell University Press.

Rathbun, Brian C. 2007. "Hierarchy and Community at Home and Abroad: Evidence of a Common Structure of Domestic and Foreign Policy Beliefs in American Elites." *Journal of Conflict Resolution* 51 (3): 379–407.

Rathbun, Brian C. 2012. *Trust in International Cooperation: International Security Institutions, Domestic Politics and American Multilateralism*. Cambridge, UK: Cambridge University Press.

Ratner, Steven R. 2000. "Does International Law Matter in Preventing Ethnic Conflict?" *New York University Journal of International Law and Politics* 32 (3): 591–698.

Ratner, Steven R., and Jason S. Abrams. 2001. *Accountability for Human Rights Atrocities in International Law: Beyond the Nuremberg Legacy*. Oxford, UK: Oxford University Press.

Raub, Werner, and Jeroen Weesie. 1990. "Reputation and Efficiency in Social Interactions: An Example of Network Effects." *American Journal of Sociology* 96 (3): 626–54.

Raustiala, Kal, and Anne-Marie Slaughter. 2002. "International Law, International Relations and Compliance." In *Handbook of International Relations*, edited by Walter Carlsnaes, Thomas Risse, and Beth A. Simmons, 538–58. Thousand Oaks, CA: SAGE Publications.

Rawls, John. 1999. *The Law of Peoples*. Cambridge, MA: Harvard University Press.

Reid, John P. 1991. *Constitutional History of the American Revolution: Authority to Legislate*. Madison: University of Wisconsin Press.

Reisman, W. Michael. 1981. "International Lawmaking: A Process of Communication." *Proceedings of the Annual Meeting of the American Society of International Law* 75: 101–20.

Reiter, Dan, and Allan C. Stam. 2002. *Democracies at War*. Princeton, NJ: Princeton University Press.

Rejali, Darius. 2007. *Torture and Democracy*. Princeton, NJ: Princeton University Press.

Renshon, Jonathan. 2017. *Fighting for Status: Hierarchy and Conflict in World Politics*. Princeton, NJ: Princeton University Press.

Renshon, Jonathan, Allan Dafoe, and Paul Huth. 2018. "To Whom Do Reputations Adhere? Experimental Evidence on Influence-Specific Reputations." *American Journal of Political Science* 62 (2): 325–39.

Reus-Smit, Christian. 2004. "The Politics of International Law." In *The Politics of International Law*, edited by Christian Reus-Smit, 14–44. Cambridge, UK: Cambridge University Press.

Reuters. 2020. "EU Executive Very Concerned about British Bill Plans, Would Undermine Trust." September 9. https://www.reuters.com/article/uk-britain-eu-commission-bill/eu-executive-very-concerned-about-british-bill-plans-would-undermine-trust-idINKBN2601VY

Ricks, Thomas E. 2006. *Fiasco: The American Military Adventure in Iraq.* New York: Penguin Press.

Ricks, Thomas E. 2010. *The Gamble: General David Petraeus and the American Military Adventure in Iraq, 2006–2008.* New York: Penguin Books.

Risse-Kappen, Thomas. 1991. "Public Opinion, Domestic Structure, and Foreign Policy in Liberal Democracies." *World Politics* 43 (4): 479–512.

Risse, Thomas, and Kathryn Sikkink. 1999. "The Socialization of International Human Rights Norms into Domestic Practices: Introduction." In *The Power of Human Rights: International Norms and Domestic Change*, edited by Thomas Risse, Stephen C. Ropp, and Kathryn Sikkink, 1–38. New York: Cambridge University Press.

Rivers, Douglas, and Nancy L. Rose. 1985. "Passing the President's Program: Public Opinion and Presidential Influence in Congress." *American Journal of Political Science* 29 (2): 183–96.

Rivkin, David B., and Lee A. Casey. 2000. "The Rocky Shoals of International Law." *The National Interest* 62: 35–45.

Rivkin, David B., and Lee A. Casey. 2003. "Leashing the Dogs of War." *National Interest* 73 57–69.

Roberts, Adam. 1993. "The Laws of War in the 1990–91 Gulf Conflict." *International Security* 18 (3): 134–81.

Roberts, Adam. 1994. "Land Warfare: From Hague to Nuremberg." In *The Laws of War: Constraints on Warfare in the Western World*, edited by Michael Howard, George J. Andreopoulos, and Mark R. Shulman, 116–39. New Haven, CT: Yale University Press.

Rochester, J. Martin. 2011. *Between Peril and Promise: The Politics of International Law.* Thousand Oaks, CA: SAGE Publications.

Rodley, Nigel S. 2009. *The Treatment of Prisoners under International Law.* Oxford, UK: Oxford University Press.

Rose, Gideon. 1998. "Neoclassical Realism and Theories of Foreign Policy." *World Politics* 51 (1): 144–72.

Rosenbaum, David E. 1993. "Washington Memo; Clinton's Plan for Economy May Hinge on His Popularity." *New York Times*, April 29, A1.

Rowe, Peter. 1993. "Prisoners of War in the Gulf Area." In *The Gulf War 1990–91 in International and English Law*, edited by Peter Rowe, 188–204. London, UK: Routledge.

Ruggie, John G. 1982. "International Regimes, Transactions, and Change: Embedded Liberalism in the Postwar Economic Order." *International Organization* 36 (2): 379–415.

Russett, Bruce. 1993. *Grasping the Democratic Peace.* Princeton, NJ: Princeton University Press.

Russett, Bruce M. 1990. *Controlling the Sword: The Democratic Governance of National Security*. Cambridge, MA: Harvard University Press.

Sagan, Scott D., and Benjamin A. Valentino. 2017. "Revisiting Hiroshima in Iran: What Americans Really Think about Using Nuclear Weapons and Killing Noncombatants." *International Security* 42 (1): 41–79.

Sandholtz, Wayne. 2007. *Prohibiting Plunder: How Norms Change*. New York: Oxford University Press.

Sands, Philippe. 2006. *Lawless World: Making and Breaking Global Rules*. New York: Penguin Books.

Sarkees, Meredith, and Frank W. Wayman. 2010. *Resort to War: 1816–2007*. Washington, DC: CQ Press.

Sartori, Anne E. 2005. *Deterrence by Diplomacy*. Princeton, NJ: Princeton University Press.

Saunders, Elizabeth N. 2017. "No Substitute for Experience: Presidents, Advisers, and Information in Group Decision Making." *International Organization* 71 (S1): S219–S247.

Scalia, Antonin. 1998. *A Matter of Interpretation: Federal Courts and the Law*. Princeton, NJ: Princeton University Press.

Scarry, Elaine. 1985. *The Body in Pain: The Making and Unmaking of the World*. New York: Oxford University Press.

Schabas, William A. 2011. *An Introduction to the International Criminal Court*. Cambridge, UK: Cambridge University Press.

Schachter, Oscar. 1977. "The Twilight Existence of Nonbinding International Agreements." *American Journal of International Law* 71 (2): 296–304.

Schachter, Oscar. 1991. *International Law in Theory and Practice*. Boston: Martinus Nijhoff Publishers.

Schattschneider, E. E. 1960. *The Semisovereign People: A Realist's View of Democracy in America*. New York: Holt, Rinehart and Winston.

Schelling, Thomas C. 1966. *Arms and Influence*. New Haven, CT: Yale University Press.

Schenker, Nathaniel, and Jane F. Gentleman. 2001. "On Judging the Significance of Differences by Examining the Overlap between Confidence Intervals." *American Statistician* 55 (3): 182–86.

Schimmelfennig, Frank. 2005. "Strategic Calculation and International Socialization: Membership Incentives, Party Constellations, and Sustained Compliance in Central and Eastern Europe." *International Organization* 59 (4): 827–60.

Schneider, Jacquelyn, and Julia Macdonald. 2016. *U.S. Public Support for Drone Strikes: When Do Americans Prefer Unmanned over Manned Platforms?* Washington, DC: Center for a New American Century.

Schultz, Kenneth A. 2001. "Looking for Audience Costs." *Journal of Conflict Resolution* 45 (1): 32–60.

Schutte, Sebastian. 2017. "Violence and Civilian Loyalties: Evidence from Afghanistan." *Journal of Conflict Resolution* 61 (8): 1595–625.

Schwartz, Herman. 2000. *The Struggle for Constitutional Justice in Post-Communist Europe*. Chicago: University of Chicago Press.

Schwarzenberger, Georg. 1964. *Power Politics*. New York: Praeger.

Scott, Robert E., and Paul B. Stephan. 2006. *The Limits of Leviathan: Contract Theory and the Enforcement of International Law*. Cambridge, UK: Cambridge University Press.

Searles, Kathleen, Martha Humphries Ginn, and Jonathan Nickens. 2016. "For Whom the Poll Airs: Comparing Poll Results to Television Poll Coverage." *Public Opinion Quarterly* 80 (4): 943–63.

Segal, Abraham M., ed. 1961. *Conversations with Lincoln*. New York: Putnam.

Sen, Amartya. 1997. *Choice, Welfare and Measurement*. Cambridge, MA: Harvard University Press.

Senate Select Committee on Intelligence. 2014. *Committee Study of the Central Intelligence Agency's Detention and Interrogation Program*. https://www.intelligence.senate.gov/sites/default/files/publications/CRPT-113srpt288.pdf

Shadish, William R., Thomas D. Cook, and Donald T. Campbell. 2002. *Experimental and Quasi-Experimental Designs for Generalized Causal Inference*. Boston: Houghton Mifflin.

Shaffer, Gregory, and Tom Ginsburg. 2012. "The Empirical Turn in International Legal Scholarship." *American Journal of International Law* 106 (1): 1–46.

Shane, Scott. 2015. "Drone Strikes Reveal Uncomfortable Truth: US is Often Uncertain Who Will Die." *New York Times*, April 23. https://www.nytimes.com/2015/04/24/world/asia/drone-strikes-reveal-uncomfortable-truth-us-is-often-unsure-about-who-will-die.html

Shannon, Vaughn P. 2000. "Norms Are What States Make of Them: The Political Psychology of Norm Violation." *International Studies Quarterly* 44 (2): 293–316.

Shapiro, Jacob N. 2005. *The Terrorist's Dilemma: Managing Violent Covert Organizations*. Princeton, NJ: Princeton University Press.

Shapiro, Robert Y., and Benjamin I. Page. 1988. "Foreign Policy and the Rational Public." *The Journal of Conflict Resolution* 32 (2): 211–47.

Shapiro, Scott J. 2002. "Law, Plans, and Practical Reason." *Legal Theory* 8 (4): 387–441.

Shaw, Malcolm N. 2017. *International Law*. Cambridge, UK: Cambridge University Press.

Shelton, Dinah, ed. 2000a. *Commitment and Compliance: The Role of Non-Binding Norms in the International Legal System*. Oxford, UK: Oxford University Press.

Shelton, Dinah. 2000b. "Introduction: Law, Non-Law, and the Problem of 'Soft Law.'" In *Commitment and Compliance: The Role of Non-Binding Norms in the International Legal System*, edited by Dinah Shelton, 1–18. Oxford, UK: Oxford University Press.

Shelton, Dinah. 2006. "Normative Hierarchy in International Law." *American Journal of International Law* 100 (2): 291–323.

Shklar, Judith N. 1986. *Legalism: Law, Morals, and Political Trials*. Cambridge, MA: Harvard University Press.

Shue, Henry, and David Rodin, eds. 2007. *Preemption: Military Action and Moral Justification*. Oxford, UK: Oxford University Press.

Siegel, Jonathan R. 2009. "The Inexorable Radicalization of Textualism." *University of Pennsylvania Law Review* 158 (1): 117–78.

Silbey, Susan S. 2005. "After Legal Consciousness." *Annual Review of Law and Social Science* 1: 323–68.

Simmons, Beth A. 1998. "Compliance with International Agreements." *Annual Review of Political Science* 1 (1): 75–93.

Simmons, Beth A. 2000. "International Law and State Behavior: Commitment and Compliance in International Monetary Affairs." *American Political Science Review* 94 (4): 819–35.

Simmons, Beth A. 2009. *Mobilizing for Human Rights: International Law in Domestic Politics*. Cambridge, UK: Cambridge University Press.

Simmons, Beth A. 2010. "Treaty Compliance and Violation." *Annual Review of Political Science* 13: 272–96.

Simmons, Beth A., and Allison Danner. 2010. "Credible Commitments and the International Criminal Court." *International Organization* 64 (2): 225–56.

Simmons, Beth A., and Daniel J. Hopkins. 2005. "The Constraining Power of International Treaties: Theory and Methods." *American Political Science Review* 99 (4): 623–31.

Singer, J. David. 1961. "The Level-of-Analysis Problem in International Relations." *World Politics* 14 (1): 77–92.

Singer, Peter W. 2013. "Finally, Obama Breaks His Silence on Drones." *Los Angeles Times,* May 23. https://www.latimes.com/opinion/la-xpm-2013-may-23-la-oe-0523-singer-obama-national-security-20130523-story.html

Slaughter Burley, Anne-Marie. 1993. "International Law and International Relations Theory: A Dual Agenda." *American Journal of International Law* 87 (2): 205–39.

Slaughter, Anne-Marie. 1995. "International Law in a World of Liberal States." *European Journal of International Law* 6 (1): 505–38.

Slaughter, Anne-Marie. 2000. "A Liberal Theory of International Law." *Proceedings of the Annual Meeting (American Society of International Law)* 94: 240–53.

Slaughter, Anne-Marie, and William Burke-White. 2006. "The Future of International Law Is Domestic (or, the European Way of Law)." *Harvard International Law Journal* 47 (2): 327–52.

Smith, Hugh. 2005. "What Costs Will Democracies Bear? A Review of Popular Theories of Casualty Aversion." *Armed Forces & Society* 31 (4): 487–512.

Sniderman, Paul M., and John Bullock. 2004. "A Consistency Theory of Public Opinion and Political Choice: The Hypothesis of Menu Dependence." In *Studies in Public Opinion: Attitudes, Nonattitudes, Measurement Error, and Change*, edited by Willem E. Saris, and Paul M. Sniderman, 337–57. Princeton, NJ: Princeton University Press.

Solis, Gary D. 2010. *The Law of Armed Conflict: International Humanitarian Law in War.* Cambridge, UK: Cambridge University Press.

Solomon, Ty, and Brent J. Steele. 2017. "Micro-Moves in International Relations Theory." *European Journal of International Relations* 23 (2): 267–91.

Son, Bui, and Pip Nicholson. 2017. "Activism and Popular Constitutionalism in Contemporary Vietnam." *Law & Social Inquiry* 42 (3): 677–710.

Spark, David, and Geoffrey Harris. 2011. *Practical Newspaper Reporting.* Thousand Oaks, CA: SAGE Publications.

Sparks, Grace. 2018. "Majority Say US Should Not Withdraw from Iran Nuclear Agreement." *CNN*, May 9. https://www.cnn.com/2018/05/08/politics/poll-iran-agreement/index.html

Spini, Dario, Guy Elcheroth, and Rachel Fasel. 2008. "The Impact of Group Norms and Generalization of Risks across Groups on Judgments of War Behavior." *Political Psychology* 29 (6): 919–41.

Spinoza, Benedict de. [1677] 1854. *A Treatise on Politics.* London: Holyoake.

Spiro, Peter J. 2000. "The New Sovereigntists: American Exceptionalism and Its False Prophets." *Foreign Affairs* 79 (6): 9–15.

Spiro, Peter J. 2006. "A Negative Proof of International Law." *Georgia Journal of International and Comparative Law* 34 (2): 445–62.

Springer, Paul J. 2010. *America's Captives: Treatment of POWs From the Revolutionary War to the War on Terror.* Lawrence: University of Kansas Press.

Stanford Law School and NYU School of Law. 2012. "Living under Drones: Death, Injury, and Trauma to Civilians from US Drone Practices in Pakistan." https://law.stanford.edu/international-human-rights-and-conflict-resolution-clinic/projects/living-under-drones/

Stanton, Jessica A. 2016. *Violence and Restraint in Civil War: Civilian Targeting in the Shadow of International Law.* Cambridge, UK: Cambridge University Press.

Staton, Jeffrey K. 2010. *Judicial Power and Strategic Communication in Mexico*. Cambridge, UK: Cambridge University Press.

Staton, Jeffrey K., and Will H. Moore. 2011. "Judicial Power in Domestic and International Politics." *International Organization* 65 (3): 553–87.

Stein, Arthur A. 1982. "Coordination and Collaboration: Regimes in an Anarchic World." *International Organization* 36 (2): 299–324.

Stein, Rachel M. 2019. *Vengeful Citizens, Violent States: A Theory of War and Revenge*. Cambridge, UK: Cambridge University Press.

Steinberg, Richard H. 2002. "In the Shadow of Law or Power? Consensus-Based Bargaining and Outcomes in the GATT/WTO." *International Organization* 56 (2): 339–74.

Steinberg, Richard H. 2013. "Wanted—Dead or Alive: Realism in International Law." In *Interdisciplinary Perspectives on International Law and International Relations: The State of the Art*, edited by Jeffrey L. Dunoff, and Mark A. Pollack, 146–72. Cambridge, UK: Cambridge University Press.

Steinberg, Richard H., and Jonathan M. Zasloff. 2006. "Power and International Law." *The American Journal of International Law* 100 (1): 64–87.

Steyn, John. 2004. "Guantanamo Bay: The Legal Black Hole." *International and Comparative Law Quarterly* 53 (1): 1–15.

Stibbe, Matthew, ed. 2013. *Captivity, Forced Labour and Forced Migration in Europe during the First World War*. New York: Routledge.

Stone, Alec. 1994. "What Is a Supranational Constitution? An Essay in International Relations Theory." *The Review of Politics* 56 (3): 441–74.

Stork, Joe, and Fred Abrahams. 2004. "Sidelined: Human Rights in Postwar Iraq." In *World Report 2004: Human Rights and Armed Conflict*, edited by Human Rights Watch, 93–119. New York: Human Rights Watch.

Strange, Susan. 1982. "*Cave! Hic Dragones*: A Critique of Regime Analysis." *International Organization* 36 (2): 479–96.

Strezhnev, Anton, Beth A. Simmons, and Matthew D. Kim. 2019. "Rulers or Rules? International Law, Elite Cues and Public Opinion." *European Journal of International Law* 30 (4): 1281–302.

Surowiecki, James. 2005. *The Wisdom of the Crowds*. New York: Anchor Books.

Swaine, Edward T. 2002. "Rational Custom." *Duke Law Journal* 52 (3): 559–627.

Swanson, Ana. 2019. "Trump Cripples W.T.O. as Trade War Rages." *New York Times*, December 8. https://www.nytimes.com/2019/12/08/business/trump-trade-war-wto.html

Szasz, Paul C. 1997. "General Law-Making Processes." In *The United Nations and International Law*, edited by Christopher C. Joyner, 27–64. Cambridge, UK: Cambridge University Press.

Taber, Charles S., and Milton Lodge. 2006. "Motivated Skepticism in the Evaluation of Political Beliefs." *American Journal of Political Science* 50 (3): 755–69.

Tannenwald, Nina. 2007. *The Nuclear Taboo: The United States and the Non-Use of Nuclear Weapons since 1945*. Cambridge, UK: Cambridge University Press.

Tenet, George J., Porter J. Goss, Michael V. Hayden, John E. McLaughlin, Albert M. Calland, and Stephen R. Kappes. 2014. "Ex-CIA Directors: Interrogations Saved Lives." *Wall Street Journal*, December 10. https://www.wsj.com/articles/cia-interrogations-saved-lives-1418142644

Tetlock, Philip E. 1985. "Accountability: A Social Check on the Fundamental Attribution Error." *Social Psychology Quarterly* 48 (3): 227–36.

Thomas, Daniel C. 2002. *The Helsinki Effect: International Norms, Human Rights, and the Demise of Communism*. Princeton, NJ: Princeton University Press.

Thomas, Ward. 2001. *The Ethics of Destruction: Norms and Force in International Relations.* Ithaca, NY: Cornell University Press.

Thompson, Alexander. 2006. "Coercion Through IOs: The Security Council and the Logic of Information Transmission." *International Organization* 60 (1): 1–34.

Thompson, Alexander. 2009. *Channels of Power: The UN Security Council and U.S. Statecraft in Iraq.* Ithaca, NY: Cornell University Press.

Thompson, Alexander. 2013. "Coercive Enforcement of International Law." In *Interdisciplinary Perspectives on International Law and International Relations: The State of the Art,* edited by Jeffrey L. Dunoff, and Mark A. Pollack, 502–23. Cambridge, UK: Cambridge University Press.

Thompson, E.P. 1966. "History from Below." *Times Literary Supplement,* April 7, 279–80.

Thucydides. 1996. *The Landmark Thucydides: A Comprehensive Guide to the Peloponnesian War.* New York: Free Press.

Thyne, Clayton L. 2006. "ABC's, 123's, and the Golden Rule: The Pacifying Effect of Education on Civil War, 1980–1999." *International Studies Quarterly* 50 (4): 733–54.

Tingley, Dustin, and Michael Tomz. 2020. "International Commitments and Domestic Opinion: The Effect of the Paris Agreement on Public Support for Policies to Address Climate Change." *Environmental Politics* 29 (7): 1135–56.

Tomz, Michael. 2007. *Reputation and International Cooperation: Sovereign Debt across Three Centuries.* Princeton, NJ: Princeton University Press.

Tomz, Michael. 2008. "Reputation and the Effect of International Law on Preferences and Beliefs." Unpublished manuscript.

Tomz, Michael, and Jessica L. Weeks. 2013. "Public Opinion and the Democratic Peace." *American Political Science Review* 107 (3): 849–65.

Tomz, Michael, Jessica L. P. Weeks, and Keren Yarhi-Milo. 2020. "Public Opinion and Decisions about Military Force in Democracies." *International Organization* 74 (1): 119–43.

Trachtenberg, Marc. 2005. "The Iraq Crisis and the Future of the Western Alliance." In *The Atlantic Alliance under Stress,* edited by David M. Andrews, 201–31. Cambridge, UK: Cambridge University Press.

Trachtman, Joel P. 2010. "International Law and Domestic Political Coalitions: The Grand Theory of Compliance with International Law." *Chicago Journal of International Law* 11 (1): 127–58.

Tribe, Laurence H. 2004. "'The People Themselves': Judicial Populism." *New York Times,* October 4. https://www.nytimes.com/2004/10/24/books/review/the-people-themselves-judicial-populism.html

Trimble, Phillip R. 1990. "International Law, World Order and Critical Legal Studies." *Stanford Law Review* 42 (3): 811–45.

Trubek, David M. 1984. "Where the Action Is: Critical Legal Studies and Empiricism." *Stanford Law Review* 36 (1/2): 575–622.

Tuchman, Barbara. 1990. *The Guns of August.* New York: Ballantine Books.

Tufte, Edward R. 1978. *Political Control of the Economy.* Princeton, NJ: Princeton University Press.

Tushnet, Mark. 1999. *Taking the Constitution Away from the Courts.* Princeton, NJ: Princeton University Press.

Tushnet, Mark. 2003. *The New Constitutional Order.* Princeton, NJ: Princeton University Press.

Tushnet, Mark. 2006. "Popular Constitutionalism as Political Law." *Chicago-Kent Law Review* 81 (3): 991–1006.

Twining, W. L., and P. E. Twining. 1973. "Bentham on Torture." *Northern Ireland Legal Quarterly* 24 (3): 305–56.

Tyler, Tom R. 1990. *Why People Obey the Law*. New Haven, CT: Yale University Press.

U.S. Department of Defense. 1992. *Final Report to Congress on the Conduct of the Persian Gulf War*. Washington, DC: Government Printing Office.

Underwood, Rodman L. 2008. *Waters of Discord: The Union Blockade of Texas during the Civil War*. Jefferson, NC: McFarland.

United Nations. 2013. "UN Rights Experts Call for Transparency in the Use of Armed Drones, Citing Risks of Illegal Use." https://news.un.org/en/story/2013/10/453832

United States Department of State. 1965. *Foreign Relations of the United States, 1964–1968*. Volume 3, *Vietnam, June–December 1965*. Washington, DC: Government Printing Office.

Valentino, Benjamin A., Paul K. Huth, and Dylan Balch-Lindsay. 2004. "'Draining the Sea': Mass Killing and Guerrilla Warfare." *International Organization* 58 (2): 375–407.

Vanberg, Georg. 2005. *The Politics of Constitutional Review in Germany*. Cambridge, UK: Cambridge University Press.

Vance, Jonathan F. 2006. *Encyclopedia of Prisoners of War and Internment*. Millerton, NY: Grey House.

Verba, Sidney, and Norman H. Nie. 1972. *Participation in America: Political Democracy and Social Equality*. Chicago: University of Chicago Press.

Verdier, Pierre-Hugues, and Mila Versteeg. 2015. "International Law in National Legal Systems: An Empirical Investigation." *American Journal of International Law* 109 (3): 514–33.

Verdier, Pierre-Hugues, and Erik Voeten. 2015. "How Does Customary International Law Change? The Case of State Immunity." *International Studies Quarterly* 59 (2): 209–22.

Voeten, Erik. 2005. "The Political Origins of the UN Security Council's Ability to Legitimize the Use of Force." *International Organization* 59 (3): 527–57.

Voeten, Erik. 2013. "Public Opinion and the Legitimacy of International Courts." *Theoretical Inquiries in Law* 14 (2): 411–36.

Voeten, Erik. 2020. "Populism and Backlashes Against International Courts." *Perspectives on Politics* 18 (2): 407–22.

von Bogdandy, Armin. 2004. "Globalization and Europe: How to Square Democracy, Globalization, and International Law." *European Journal of International Law* 15 (5): 885–906.

von Bogdandy, Armin, Matthias Goldmann, and Ingo Venzke. 2017. "From Public International to International Public Law: Translating World Public Opinion into International Public Authority." *European Journal of International Law* 28 (1): 115–45.

von Stein, Jana. 2005. "Do Treaties Constrain or Screen? Selection Bias and Treaty Compliance." *American Political Science Review* 99 (4): 611–22.

Waldron, Jeremy. 1999. *Law and Disagreement*. New York: Oxford University Press.

Wallace, Geoffrey P. R. 2014. "Martial Law? Military Experience, International Law, and Support for Torture." *International Studies Quarterly* 58 (3): 501–14.

Wallace, Geoffrey P. R. 2015. *Life and Death in Captivity: The Abuse of Prisoners During War*. Ithaca, NY: Cornell University Press.

Wallace, Geoffrey P. R. 2019a. "Condemning or Condoning the Perpetrators? International Humanitarian Law and Attitudes Toward Wartime Violence." *Law & Social Inquiry* 44 (1): 192–226.

Wallace, Geoffrey P. R. 2019b. "Supplying Protection: The United Nations and Public Support for Humanitarian Intervention." *Conflict Management and Peace Science* 36 (3): 248–69.

Wallace, William, and Tim Oliver. 2005. "A Bridge Too Far: The United Kingdom and the Transatlantic Relationship." In *The Atlantic Alliance Under Stress*, edited by David M. Andrews, 152–76. Cambridge, UK: Cambridge University Press.

Walsh, Declan, and Ihsanullah Tipu Mehsud. 2013. "Civilian Deaths in Drone Strikes Cited in Report." *New York Times*, October 22. https://www.nytimes.com/2013/10/22/world/asia/civilian-deaths-in-drone-strikes-cited-in-report.html

Walsh, James I., and Marcus Schulzke. 2018. *Drones and Support for the Use of Force*. Ann Arbor: University of Michigan Press.

Walt, Stephen M. 2005. *Taming American Power: The Global Response to U.S. Primacy*. New York: W. W. Norton.

Walter, Barbara F. 2009. *Reputation and Civil War*. Cambridge, UK: Cambridge University Press.

Waltz, Kenneth N. 1959. *Man, the State, and War: A Theoretical Analysis*. New York: Columbia University Press.

Waltz, Kenneth N. 1979. *Theory of International Politics*. Reading, MA: Addison-Wesley.

Walzer, Michael. 1973. "Political Action: The Problem of Dirty Hands." *Philosophy and Public Affairs* 2 (2): 160–80.

Walzer, Michael. 2000. *Just and Unjust Wars*. New York: Basic Books.

Washington, George. 1796. "Washington's Farewell Address." *Avalon Project, Yale University*. https://avalon.law.yale.edu/18th_century/washing.asp

Waters, Tony. 2015. *Weber's Rationalism and Modern Society: New Translations on Politics, Bureaucracy, and Social Stratification*. New York: Palgrave Macmillan.

Weeks, Jessica L. 2008. "Autocratic Audience Costs: Regime Type and Signaling Resolve." *International Organization* 62 (1): 35–64.

Weeks, Jessica L. 2014. *Dictators at War and Peace*. Ithaca, NY: Cornell University Press.

Weeramantry, C. G. 2004. *Universalising International Law*. Boston: M. Nijhoff Publishers.

Weil, Prosper. 1983. "Towards Relative Normativity in International Law." *American Journal of International Law* 77 (3): 413–42.

Weisiger, Alex. 2014. "Victory without Peace: Conquest, Insurgency, and War Termination." *Conflict Management and Peace Science* 31 (4): 357–82.

Weiss, Jessica Chen. 2014. *Powerful Patriots: Nationalist Protest in China's Foreign Relations*. New York: Oxford University Press.

Weiss, Jessica Chen, and Allan Dafoe. 2019. "Authoritarian Audiences, Rhetoric, and Propaganda in International Crises: Evidence from China." *International Studies Quarterly* 63 (4): 963–73.

Wendt, Alexander. 1999. *Social Theory of International Politics*. Cambridge, UK: Cambridge University Press.

Wendt, Alexander. 2003. "Why a World State Is Inevitable." *European Journal of International Relations* 9 (4): 491–542.

Western, Jon. 2005. *Selling Intervention and War: The Presidency, the Media, and the American Public*. Baltimore: John Hopkins University Press.

Wheatley, Steven. 2010. *The Democratic Legitimacy of International Law*. Oxford, UK: Hart Publishing.

White House. 2002. "Humane Treatment of al Qaeda and Taliban Detainees." February 7. https://www.washingtonpost.com/wp-srv/nation/documents/020702bush.pdf

Whytock, Christopher A. 2005. "Thinking beyond the Domestic-International Divide: Toward a Unified Concept of Public Law." *Georgetown Journal of International Law* 36 (1): 155–93.

Whytock, Christopher A. 2018. "From International Law and International Relations to Law and World Politics." In *Oxford Research Encyclopedia of Politics*, edited by William R. Thompson, 1–46. New York: Oxford University Press.

Wildhaber, Luzius, and Stephan Breitenmoser. 1980. "The Relationship between Customary International Law and Municipal Law in Western European Countries." In *International Law: Cases and Materials*, edited by Louis Henkin, Richard Pugh, Oscar Schachter, and Hans Smit, 163–207. St. Paul: West Publishing.

Williams, Timothy, and Duraid Adnan. 2010. "Sunnis in Iraq Allied with U.S. Rejoin Rebels." *New York Times*, October 16. https://www.nytimes.com/2010/10/17/world/middleeast/17awakening.html

Witt, John F. 2013. *Lincoln's Code: The Laws of War in American History*. New York: Free Press.

Wittkopf, Eugene R. 1990. *Faces of Internationalism: Public Opinion and American Foreign Policy*. Durham, NC: Duke University Press.

Wolford, Scott. 2015. *The Politics of Military Coalitions*. New York: Cambridge University Press.

Woodward, Bob. 2001. "CIA Told to Do 'Whatever Necessary' to Kill Bin Laden." *Washington Post*, October 21. https://www.washingtonpost.com/archive/politics/2001/10/21/cia-told-to-do-whatever-necessary-to-kill-bin-laden/19d0e8f1-dbe5-4b07-9c47-44c5b4328f1f/

Yarbrough, Beth V., and Robert M. Yarbrough. 1997. "Dispute Settlement in International Trade: Regionalism and Procedural Coordination." In *The Political Economy of Regionalism*, edited by Edward D. Mansfield, and Helen V. Milner, 134–63. New York: Columbia University Press.

Yoo, John. 2003. "International Law and the War in Iraq." *American Journal of International Law* 97 (3): 563–76.

Yoo, John. 2005. *The Powers of War and Peace: The Constitution and Foreign Affairs after 9/11*. Chicago: University of Chicago Press.

Yoo, John. 2006. *War by Other Means: An Insider's Account of the War on Terror*. New York: Atlantic Monthly Press.

Yoo, John. 2011. "From Guantanamo to Abbottabad." *Wall Street Journal*, May 4, A17.

Yoo, John C. 1999. "Globalism and the Constitution: Treaties, Non-Self-execution, and the Original Understanding." *Columbia Law Review* 99 (8): 1955–2094.

Yoo, John C. 2000. "UN Wars, US War Powers." *Chicago Journal of International Law* 1 (2): 355–73.

Young, Joseph K., and Erin M. Kearns. 2020. *Tortured Logic: Why Some Americans Support the Use of Torture in Counterterrorism*. New York: Columbia University Press.

Young, Oran R. 1980. "International Regimes: Problems of Concept Formation." *World Politics* 32 (3): 331–56.

Zacher, Mark W. 2001. "The Territorial Integrity Norm: International Boundaries and the Use of Force." *International Organization* 55 (2): 215–50.

Zacher, Mark W., and Richard A. Matthew. 1995. "Liberal International Theory: Common Threads, Divergent Strands." In *Controversies in International Relations Theory: Realism and the Neo-Liberal Challenge*, edited by Charles W. Kegley, 107–50. Basingstoke, UK: Macmillan.

Zaller, John. 1992. *The Nature and Origins of Mass Opinion*. Cambridge, UK: Cambridge University Press.

Zelikow, Philip. 1996. "The Masque of Institutions." *Survival* 38 (1): 6–18.

Zemans, Frances K. 1983. "Legal Mobilization: The Neglected Role of the Law in the Political System." *American Political Science Review* 77 (3): 690–703.

Zvobgo, Kelebogile. 2019. "Human Rights versus National Interests: Shifting US Public Attitudes on the International Criminal Court." *International Studies Quarterly* 63 (4): 1065–78.

Index

Abu Ghraib prison, 136, 140–41, 143, 148, 152–53, 174, 295n72
Acheson, Dean, 16, 39, 267n121
actors
  internationalized actors, 33
  rights and responsibilities, 32–33
Afghanistan and Afghan War, 129–33, 141–43, 150, 160, 176, 201, 298n119, 300n8
African Charter on Human Peoples' Rights, 294n50
Afrobarometer, 218
Agassi, Andre, 123
Almond, Gabriel, 70–71, 275n182
Almond-Lippmann consensus, 70, 72
al Qaeda, 126–27, 130–31, 141–42, 147–48, 152–53, 202–3, 301n31
Amazon's Mechanical Turk (MTurk) service, 113, 213, 285n141
American Convention on Human Rights, 294n50
Amnesty International, 202
Annan, Kofi, 130
Anti-Ballistic Missile (ABM) Treaty, 128
Arend, Anthony C., 264n4, 265n60
Aristotle, 71
Aron, Raymond, 43, 48, 268n141
Aung San Suu Kyi, 247
Austin, John, 38–39, 41, 75, 80
authoritarian states, 48, 69–70, 80, 250, 269n200
al-Awlaki, Anwar, 301n31
Axelrod, Robert, 93

Bartov, Omer, 86
Bentham, Jeremy, 163
Bethmann Hollweg, Theobold von, 33, 36
Biden, Joe, 64, 191, 201, 252
Bierce, Ambrose, 254
bin Laden, Osama, 126, 129, 159
Blair, Tony, 138
Bolton, John, 22, 34, 268n148
Boyle, Francis, 258
Brewster, Rachel, 96, 280n36
Budiansky, Stephen, 37, 267n110
Bull, Hedley, 26, 28, 57, 64, 265n60, 266n66

Burke, Edmund, 27
Bush, George H. W., 67, 128, 138–40
Bush, George W. and Bush administration
  "coalition of the willing," 130, 135, 137, 139, 148
  counterterrorism strategy, 126, 240
  drone strikes and, 201–2
  end to Iraq war and casualties, 149
  Europeans' opinion of, 135
  Geneva Conventions and, 61
  Guantanamo Bay detention facility and, 144
  harsh interrogation techniques, 142, 160
  intelligence cooperation failure, 143–44
  international courts vilified, 191
  international law disregard for or rejection of, 11, 128–29, 140–41, 159–60, 174
  Iraq War and, 128, 140
  media investigation of detention policies, 143
  military cooperation and Iraq war, 138
  Security Council and, 130
  "shocks the conscience," 295n51
  Taliban and al Qaeda treatment, 131
  terrorists condemnation, 127
  "Torture Memos," 190
  treatment of prisoners, 147–48
  world opinion and, 136
  See also War on Terror
Bush Doctrine, 130, 288n23
Bybee, Jay, 190

Carney, Jay, 203
Carr, Edward Hallett (E. H.), 40, 48, 62, 269n196
Casey, Lee A., 306n88
Central Intelligence Agency (CIA), 128, 131, 136, 141–45, 159–60, 290n101, 300n9
Cheney, Richard, 125, 127, 133, 159
Chirac, Jacques, 138, 144
Cicero, 126
City of Boerne v. Flores (1997), 278n260
Claude, Inis, 38, 40, 57, 267n114
climate change, 254n15, 268n153
Clinton, Bill and Clinton administration, 69, 128, 135